THE JEWISH LISTS

Physicists and Generals, Actors and Writers, and Hundreds of Other Lists of Accomplished Jews

Martin H. Greenberg

SCHOCKEN BOOKS • NEW YORK

First published by Schocken Books 1979
10 9 8 7 6 5 4 3 2   80 81 82 83 84

Library of Congress Cataloging in Publication Data

Greenberg, Martin Harry.
    The Jewish lists.

    Includes indexes.
    1. Jews—Biography.   I. Title.
DS115.G67   920′.0092′924   79-14349

Manufactured in the United States of America.

Contents

PART IX:
Prize Winners

ACKNOWLEDGMENTS AND SOURCES

I should like to thank my typists, Mary Tushie and Judy Le Mense, for their very considerable efforts. Errors are, of course, my responsibility.

This book would have been immeasurably more difficult to compile without the magnificent *Encyclopaedia Judaica* and its Yearbooks. This work has been a major source of information in almost all the categories treated and is highly recommended. Other general works that proved indispensable were *The World Almanac and Book of Facts* (numerous editions), *Who Won What Where*, a very handy compilation of award winners in many walks of life; *Contemporary Authors*, which, in addition to supplying information on authors, contains valuable information on people in all areas who have written books; the monthly journal *Current Biography*; *Pseudonyms: The Names Behind The Names* by Joseph F. Clarke, which was very helpful in determining real names; and *Who's Who in World Jewry* (various editions). I also benefited from consulting a wide variety of *Who's Who*-type publications of all kinds. Also used were a multitude of magazines, including some of particularly Jewish interest like *Moment*, all the way to *Time* and *Newsweek*, as well as newspapers.

More specifically, the following were helpful, and in a few cases crucial, in particular categories:

For Music: *The Encyclopedia of Pop, Rock and Soul* by Irwin Stambler and *Rock On: The Illustrated Encyclopedia of Rock n' Roll* by Norm N. Nite.

For Motion Pictures, the Theater, and Television: *The Filmgoer's Companion* by Leslie Halliwell (several editions); *The International Motion Picture Almanac* (several editions); *TV Movies* by Leonard Maltin; *Who's Who in Hollywood* by David Ragan; *The Complete Encyclopedia of Television Programs 1947–1976* by Vincent Terrace; and *Reel Facts: The Movie Book of Records* by Cobbett Steinberg.

For Politics broadly defined: *Jews and American Politics* by Stephen D. Isaacs, *The Almanac of American Politics* (various editions), and the *Biographical Directory of the American Congress 1774–1971*.

For Sports: the wonderful *Encyclopedia of Jews in Sports* by Bernard Postal, Jesse Silver, and Roy Silver; the late and lamented *Jewish Sports Review*; the bulletins of the U.S. Committee, Sports for Israel; and specialist journals such as *Track and Field News*.

For Science Fiction: *The Encyclopedia of Science Fiction and Fantasy* by Donald Tuck.

For Spies and Counterspies: *The Encyclopedia of Espionage* by Ronald Seth.

For Chess: *The Encyclopedia of Chess* by Anne Sunnucks.

INTRODUCTION

The "giftedness"—so to speak—of a certain part at least of the Jewish people is a historical problem, a problem of the first order for the historians. I can risk a speculative explanation: we are the only people, the only European people, who have survived from antiquity pretty much intact. That means we kept our identity, and it means we are the only people who have never known analphabetism. We were always literate because you cannot be a Jew without being literate. The women were less literate than the men but even they were much more literate than their counterparts elsewhere. Not only the elite knew how to read but every Jew had to read—the whole people, in all its classes and on all levels of giftedness and intelligence.

—Hannah Arendt

The prominence and "success" of Jews and persons of Jewish origin have been noted by a wide variety of observers. Among Nobel Prize winners, noted scientists, political leaders, performers, artists—indeed, in almost every area of human endeavor, the percentage of those of Jewish origin is far above this group's share of the general population. The current estimate of 15 million for the world Jewish population means that this group constitutes no more than *one-third of one percent* of the current world population, and 2.7 percent of the United States population.

The reasons for this success are, as Hannah Arendt indicates, a mystery. Explanations ranging from genetic structure to "marginality" have been put forward, although none has been widely accepted (with the exception of "culture," which does not really explain the phenomenon). I cannot contribute to this discourse, but I have tried in this book to record some of the noteworthy persons and accomplishments of this unique group, including such dubious "achievements" as those of gangsters, political assassins, and the like.

The task has been a monumental one for several reasons. First is the problem of who is a Jew. This issue has generated much heat, a little light, and no agreement. The question obviously has cultural, genetic, and religious dimensions, and I am not going to engage it. I have included some people of Jewish origin who formally converted to Christianity, even sometimes people who do not consider themselves Jews, and people whose ancestors were Jews, especially if they descend from a well-known Jewish family, and I have tried to indicate this in the short annotations that accompany the listings. I *have* included individuals who have converted *to* Judaism.

Second is the problem of choosing whom to include. This is a personal book in many respects, and the relative completeness or lack thereof in individual lists reflects my interest in particular subjects—for example, chess. I have omitted many outstanding people whose major contributions are in Jewish affairs, so there are few religious figures, Zionists, Israeli leaders, or "professional Jews" in the book.

Third is the problem of numbers. I estimate that there are at least 20,000 individuals who deserve mention in a book like this, but to include them all is clearly impossible. I hope that the omissions will be listed and discussed in future volumes.

Fourth, there are undoubtedly many worthy individuals who I don't know are Jewish or whom I don't know about.

So this is a very partial, selective listing, one that may well contain many errors of omission and, it is hoped, only a few errors of commission. Establishing the "Jewishness" of a person is not always easy, and I have tried not to rely upon names—which are often useless for determining religion or cultural heritage—except in those cases where I was able to locate the names at birth of listed individuals or where I had other corroboration. Even so, of course, I can only hope that the identification of Jews is correct, and any error is, naturally, unintentional. The great bulk of the listings derives from information contained in the sources listed in the Acknowledgments. In addition, I have tried to keep my annotations as brief as possible in order to make room for more names, and I have also deliberately kept my notes on the very famous—Einstein, Freud, Marx, et al.—quite short, since these people's accomplishments are so well known.

This book is not primarily an exercise in putting together yet another reference book. Rather, it is a celebration of the Jewish presence (often against great odds in some places and at some times) in many fields that should be of interest to the trivia buff, the browser, and the celebrity watcher. It was written for readers of all types, but I hope that it will be read by, and give inspiration to, the younger generation as an aid in their search for their "roots."

In the vast majority of entries the adjectives and nouns used to describe people simply reflect widely held opinion—words like *foremost*, *world-famous*, *leading*, *expert*, and *authority* derive from expert opinion other than my own. I have, however, used my own expertise (and expressed my own preferences) in several areas, and these are usually noted.

Each entry contains the person's name, followed by date of birth and date of death and his or her birthplace, and I have included real names wherever applicable and possible. I have not been able to uncover these facts for everyone in this book, and there may certainly be some entries that are incomplete. Death notices are especially difficult to find for those who have died in the last few years. For this reason, I have listed only the birthdate (for example: b. 1896, Los Angeles) for persons born before 1900 for whom I could find no date of death. (For those still living at the time of publication, the date takes the form, for example: 1913– .)

Birthplaces, of course, do not refer to the places where people were raised or lived later, if those were different from their places of birth. The geographic index contains a number of things that were surprising to me, including the astonishing concentrations of talented people who were born in some places. I will leave to others the opportunity to draw generalizations about the patterns that can be found in this index and in the book as a whole.

Part I
Public Life

PART I

GOVERNMENT OFFICIALS

(*See also* Political Figures; Men and Women of the Left;
Revolutionaries; Mayors.)

AMERICANS

WALTER N. ANNENBERG (1908- , Milwaukee)—Appointed by President Nixon as U.S. Ambassador to the United Kingdom in 1969, he controls Triangle Publications, publishers of the *Philadelphia Inquirer*, *TV Guide*, and *Seventeen*. He was also the publisher of *The Daily Racing Form* and one of Nixon's largest campaign contributors.

HERMAN BARUCH (1872-1953)—Served as American Ambassador to Portugal, 1945-1947, and as Ambassador to the Netherlands, 1947-1949.

JUDAH P. BENJAMIN (1811-1884, St. Thomas, V.I.)—The famous Secretary of State of the Confederacy, he also served as Secretary of War, as Attorney General, and as U.S. Senator. He escaped capture by the Union forces and became a well-known lawyer in Great Britain.

RONALD BERMAN (1930- , New York)—The author of *America in the Sixties*, he became Chairman of the National Endowment for the Humanities in 1971.

HERMAN BERNSTEIN (1876-1935, Lithuania)—American Envoy to Albania, 1931-1933.

W. MICHAEL BLUMENTHAL (1926- , Oranienburg, Germany)—Formerly President of International Operations of the Bendix Corporation, he was selected by President Carter to be Secretary of the Treasury.

HAROLD BROWN (1927- , New York)—Secretary of Defense in the Carter administration, he had earlier served as Secretary of the Air Force in the Johnson administration and as President of the California Institute of Technology.

ARTHUR F. BURNS (1904- , Stanislau, Austria)—Became Chairman of the Board of Governors of the U.S. Federal Reserve System in 1969 and was one of the strongest and most controversial persons ever to hold that post.

MORRIS E. CHAFETZ (1924- , Worcester, Mass.)—Became Director of HEW's National Institute on Alcohol Abuse and Alcoholism in 1971.

EDWIN S. COHEN (1914- , Richmond, Va.)—Assistant Secretary of the Treasury in the 1970s, specializing in tax reform.

WILBUR J. COHEN (1913- , Milwaukee)—Undersecretary of HEW, and then Secretary beginning in 1968.

EDWIN DE LEON (1828-1891)—American Consul General in Egypt for almost a decade.

MATTHEW DROSDOFF (1908- , Chicago)—Served as Chief of the Agricultural Division of the U.S. Agency for International Development in Vietnam in the early 1960s.

STUART E. EIZENSTAT (1943- , Chicago)—Assistant to the President for Domestic Affairs and Policy in the Carter administration.

ABRAM I. ELKUS (1867-1947, New York City)—U.S. Ambassador to Turkey, 1916-1919, crucial years which saw the break-up of the Ottoman Empire.

RUTH FARKAS (1906- , New York City)—Born Ruth Lewis. Became U.S. Ambassador to Luxembourg in 1973.

ABRAHAM H. FELLER (1905-1952, New York City)—General Counsel to the UN and legal adviser to the Secretary General beginning in 1946. He committed suicide.

LEONARD GARMENT (1924- , Brooklyn)—Became Special Counsel to

President Nixon after the firing of John Dean. A long-time Democrat, he was untouched by the Watergate scandal.

ARTHUR J. GOLDBERG (1908- , Chicago)—The distinguished public servant who was a noted labor lawyer, Secretary of Labor, and American Ambassador to the UN. He was also a Justice of the Supreme Court, and his resignation from that body was one of the great personal and national mistakes in U.S. governmental history.

ALAN GREENSPAN (1926- , New York City)—Became Chairman of President Nixon's Council of Economic Advisers in 1974.

HARRY F. GUGGENHEIM (1890-1971)—Founder and President of *Newsday*, he was also an American Ambassador to Cuba.

NORMAN HACKERMAN (1912- , Baltimore)—Chairman of the National Science Foundation, he was the President of Rice University in the late sixties.

ALFRED E. KAHN (1917- , Paterson, N.J.)—An economist, he was Robert Julius Thorne Professor of Economics at Cornell U. before becoming Director of the Civil Aeronautics Board, where he led the fight to deregulate the airline industry. He is now the government's "chief inflation fighter."

JULIUS L. KATZ (1925- , New York City)—Assistant Secretary of State for Economic Affairs.

LEON H. KEYSERLING (1908- , Charleston, S.C.)—Served as Chairman of the Council of Economic Advisers in the Truman administration and is the author of *Progress and Poverty* (1964).

HENRY A. KISSINGER (1923- , Fürth, Germany)—The famous Secretary of State who was a refugee from Nazi Germany. He was also Director of the National Security Agency and the recipient of the Nobel Peace Prize. See Nobel Prize Winners.

PHILLIP M. KLUTZNICK (1907-)—Federal Housing Commissioner, 1944–1946, and later U.S. Ambassador to the UN Economic and Social Council.

EDWARD H. LEVI (1911- , Chicago)—A distinguished legal scholar, he was President of the U. of Chicago before becoming Attorney General of the U.S. in the Nixon administration.

DAVID E. LILIENTHAL (1899- , Morton, Ill.)—The famous Chairman of the Tennessee Valley Authority, later Chairman of the Atomic Energy Commission.

ROBERT J. LIPSHUTZ (1921- , Atlanta)—Counsel to President Carter.

FREDERICK R. MANN (1903- , Gomel, Russia)—First American Ambassador to Barbados after that island country became independent in 1966.

HENRY MORGENTHAU (1856-1946, Mannheim, Germany)—U.S. Ambassador to Turkey, 1913–1916.

HENRY MORGENTHAU, JR. (1891-1967, New York City)—An expert on American agriculture, he directed the Federal Farm Board and the Farm Credit Administration before becoming a noted Secretary of the Treasury in 1934.

IRA N. MORRIS (1875-1942, Chicago)—U.S. Minister to Sweden, 1914–1923.

ROBERT MOSES (1888- , New Haven, Conn.)—As the most famous administrator in the history of New York, he built most of the major highways around that city as well as the Triborough Bridge. He served as President of the 1964 World's Fair.

ARNOLD H. PACKER (1935- , Brooklyn)—Assistant Secretary for Policy, Evaluation and Research in the Department of Labor.

BENJAMIN F. PEIXOTTO (1834-1890, New York City)—The first American Consul in Bucharest, Rumania, and later Consul in Lyons, France.

FRANK PRESS (1924- , Brooklyn)—Considered the outstanding seismologist in the U.S. while at Cal Tech and M.I.T., he became Chief Scientific Adviser to President Carter.

GERALD RAFSHOON (1934-)—An Assistant to the President in the Carter administration, he was assigned the task of improving the President's image. He has been associated with Carter since 1966.

ABRAHAM RATSHESKY (1864-1943, Boston)—A banker, he was U.S. Minister to Czechoslovakia, 1930–1933.

ANNA M. ROSENBERG (1902- , Budapest)—Born Anna Lederer. Assistant Secretary of Defense after World War II, the highest position yet attained by a woman in the defense bureaucracy. She played a key role in the racial integration of the American armed forces and was awarded both the Medal of Freedom and Medal for Merit.

EUGENE ROSTOW (1913- , New York City)—Undersecretary of State in the Johnson years, he was formerly Dean of the Yale Law School.

WALT W! ROSTOW (1916- , New York City)—Served Democratic presidents all through the 1960s and was a key architect of Vietnam policy as Special Assistant for National Security Affairs to President Johnson. A world-famous economist, he wrote *Stages of Economic Growth* (1952), considered a landmark work.

LEO S. ROWE (1871-1946)—One of the first professors of political science in the U.S. and an expert on Latin America, he was Assistant Secretary of the Treasury and then director of the Latin American division of the State Department. He also served as President of the American Academy of Political and Social Sciences for almost 30 years.

CHARLES I. SCHOTTLAND (1906- , Chicago)—Served twice as President of the National Conference of Social Welfare and once as Commissioner of Social Security in HEW.

L. WILLIAM SEIDMAN (1921- , Grand Rapids, Mich.)—A long-time associate of President Ford, he served as his Chief Economic Adviser.

LAURENCE H. SILBERMAN (1935- , York, Pa.)—Deputy Attorney General of the U.S. from 1974.

SIMON E. SOBELOFF (1894-)—Solicitor General of the U.S. under Eisenhower, he helped design the position taken by the U.S. government in the famous desegregation case of *Brown* v. *the Board of Education.*

MORRIS J. SOLOMON (1919- , New York City)—Chief of Operations Research, U.S. Bureau of the Census.

HELMUT SONNENFELDT (1926-)—An important adviser to Kissinger and a member of the staff of the National Security Council, he had previously been Director of Soviet Research in the State Department. One of the most influential and least appreciated forces in the U.S. government during the Nixon years.

HERBERT STEIN (1916- , Detroit)—Chairman of the President's Council of Economic Advisers, 1972–1974, under Nixon.

LAURENCE A. STEINHARDT (1892-1950, New York City)—A career diplomat who held many posts, including those of Minister to Sweden and Ambassador to Peru, the Soviet Union (during the crucial years 1939–1941), and Canada, where he died in an air accident.

NATHAN STRAUS, JR. (1889-1961)—Headed the U.S. Housing Authority, 1937–1942.

OSCAR S. STRAUS (1850-1926)—Most famous as Teddy Roosevelt's Secretary of Commerce and Labor, he also served as Minister and then Ambassador to Turkey and was a member of the International Court of Arbitration.

LEWIS L. STRAUSS (1896- , Charleston, W.Va.)—A Rear Admiral, he served on and later Chaired the Atomic Energy Commission. He failed to become Secretary of Commerce only because of Senate opposition.

ROBERT S. STRAUSS (1918- , Lockhart, Tex.)—One of the most powerful individuals in the Democratic party (he was both National Chairman and Treasurer), he was a former FBI agent. He served President Carter as his Special Counselor on Inflation.

LEONARD UNGER (1917- , San Diego, Ca.)—U.S. Ambassador to Taiwan.

DAVID W. WAINHOUSE (1900- , Vilna, Lithuania)—Deputy Assistant Secretary of State, 1953–1956.

PAUL M. WARBURG (1868-1932, Hamburg, Germany)—The famous banker and philanthropist who was a Vice-Governor of the Federal Reserve Board and one of the principal figures in the creation of the Federal Reserve System.

JEROME B. WIESNER (1915- , Detroit)—JFK's Special Assistant for Science and Technology and the Director of the Office of Science and Technology. He later became President of M.I.T.

MARVIN WEISSMAN (1927- , Cleveland)—U.S. Ambassador to Costa Rica.

JILL WINE-VOLNER (1943- , Chicago)—General Counsel for the Department of the Army, she was a leading government lawyer in the Watergate affair.

ARGENTINES

DAVID BLEJER (1913-)—Served as Ambassador to Mexico, Undersecretary of the Interior, and Undersecretary of Labor and Social Security.

JOSÉ BER GELBARD (1917- , Poland)—An important and controversial Minister of Economics during the 1970s. A considerable amount of anti-Semitism was directed at him.

AUSTRALIANS

MOSES H. CASS (1927- , Corrigin)—Became Minister of Environment and Conservation in 1972, and, later, Minister for the Media, in Australia.

SIR ISAAC A. ISAACS (1855-1948, Melbourne)—The famous Governor-General and Chief Justice of Australia, he was one of that country's outstanding public officials.

ABRAM LANDA (1902- , Belfast, N. Ireland)—Minister for Labor and Industry, Minister for Housing, and Minister for Housing and Cooperative Societies in the Government of New South Wales during the 1950s and early 1960s.

SIR DANIEL LEVY (1873-1937, London)—A noted lawyer and Speaker of the House in New South Wales, he also served as Minister of Justice.

AUSTRIANS

EMIN (PASHA) (1840-1892, Silesia)—Governor of the Equatorial Province of Egypt. A noted explorer, he was killed by Arab slave traders. His real name was Eduard Schnitzer. He had been baptized in childhood.

JULIUS A. GLASER (1831-1885, Postelberg, Bohemia)—Minister of Justice of Austria and then Attorney General in the 1870s. He became a Christian.

LUDO M. HARTMANN (1865-1924)—Austrian Ambassador to Germany, 1918–1921, he was a leading member of the Social Democratic party.

BRUNO KREISKY (1911- , Vienna)—Chancellor of Austria since 1970, he had earlier been Foreign Minister. He has had some unkind things to say about both Israel and the Jewish people.

EMIL STEINBACH (1846-1907, Vienna)—Austrian Minister of Finance, 1891, he later served as President of the Austrian Supreme Court. He was baptized to further his career.

JOSEF UNGER (1828-1913)—A convert to Christianity, Unger was a Minister without Portfolio in the Austrian government and later President of the Supreme Court.

BRITISH

SIR ANDREW COHEN (1909-1968)—Occupied a series of important positions at a time when the Empire was being dismantled. He was Undersecretary of State at the Colonial Office, Governor of Uganda, 1952–1957, and the first Secretary of the Ministry of Overseas Development.

SIR EDGAR COHEN (1908-1973, Manchester)—Great Britain's Delegate to GATT (General Agreement on Tariffs and Trade) and to the Council of the European Free Trade Association.

JOHN DIAMOND (1907- , Leeds)—A baron and a long-time MP, he served as the Chief Secretary to the. British Treasury in the second half of the 1960s.

BENJAMIN DISRAELI (1804-1881)—The famous Chancellor of the Exchequer and Prime Minister of Great Britain. He had been baptized.

SIR DEREK EZRA (1919-)—Chairman of the National Coal Board in the 1970s.

SIR MARK HENIG (1911-)—Served as Chairman of the British Tourist Board.

SIR KEITH JOSEPH (1918-)—One of the most important political figures in England, he has been Minister of State at the Board of Trade, Minister for Welsh Affairs, Minister of Housing and Local Government, and Minister of Health and Social Services.

GERALD KAUFMAN (1930- , Leeds)—A Labor MP, he was Undersecretary of State in the Department of Environment before becoming Minister of State for Industry.

CECIL KISCH (1884-1961)—Assistant Undersecretary of State for India, and Deputy Undersecretary for India in the 1930s and early '40s.

HERMANN M. KISCH (1850-1942)—Was a Director General of the Indian Post Office.

ARTHUR M. S. MANCROFT (1872-1942)—A baron, he was Lord Mayor of Norwich, a Conservative MP, Minister for the Department of Overseas Trade, and Financial Secretary to the British Treasury.

STORMONT MANCROFT (1914-)—A baron, he served as Parliamentary Secretary to the Ministry of Defense, Undersecretary to the Home Office, and Minister without Portfolio in British governments in the 1950s and '60s.

ALFRED M. MOND (1868-1930)—A baron and a titan of the British chemical industry, he was a Liberal MP and Minister of Health in the early 1920s.

JULIAN E. A. MOND (1925-)—Chairman of the British Steel Industry from 1967.

EDWIN S. MONTAGU (1879-1924)—Served as Financial Secretary to the Treasury, Minister of Munitions, and Secretary of State for India.

HARRY L. NATHAN (1889-1963, London)—A baron and former Chairman of the Royal Geographical Society, he was Minister of Civil Aviation, 1946–1958.

SIR MATTHEW NATHAN (1862-1939)—An important colonial official, he was Governor of the Gold Coast (not Miami Beach), Governor of Hong Kong, and Governor of Natal, all 1900–1910.

GERALD R. READING (1889-1960)—Undersecretary of State for Foreign Affairs, he later became Minister of State for Foreign Affairs.

RUFUS D. I. READING (1860-1935, London)—Became Lord Reading, Lord Chief Justice of England. He served as Viceroy of India, 1920–1926, and then briefly as Foreign Secretary. Many feel that he was the finest lawyer in modern English history.

SIR PHILIP SASSOON (1888-1939)—Undersecretary of State for Aviation through most of the 1920s and '30s.

SIR FRANK SCHON (1912- , Vienna)—Chairman of the British National Research Development Corporation in the 1970s.

ANDREW A. SHONFIELD (1917-)—Director of the prestigious Royal Institute of International Affairs in the 1970s.

JOHN E. SILKIN (1923-)—Minister of Building in the late 1960s and Minister for Planning and Local Government in the 1970s.

LORD LEWIS SILKIN (1889-1972, London)—Minister of Town and Country Planning, 1945-1950.

GEORGE R. STRAUSS (1901-)—Minister of Supply in the late 1940s, he was given the important task of implementing the policy of nationalization of British steel.

HENRY DE WORMS (1840-1903)—A baron, he was Undersecretary of State for the Colonies in the late 1880s and early 1890s.

LORD SOLLY ZUCKERMAN (1904- , Cape Town, South Africa)—Served as Chief Scientific Adviser to the Government of Great Britain in the second half of the 1960s, after serving as Chairman of the Defense Research Policy Committee. He was one of the leading experts in the world on primate behavior, and wrote one of the most famous books on the subject, *The Social Life of Monkeys and Apes.*

CANADIANS

DAVID BARRETT (1930-)—One of the leading figures in the New Democratic party, he was elected Premier of the Province of British Columbia.

CHARLES GAVSIE (1906-1967, New York City)—Was President of the St. Lawrence Seaway Authority.

MARVIN GELBER (1912- , Toronto)—An MP representing the Liberal party, he was a member of the Canadian delegation to the UN and served as his country's chief delegate to its Economic and Social Council.

VICTOR GOLDBLOOM (1923-)—Minister for Municipal Affairs and Minister without Portfolio in the 1970s.

H. CARL GOLDENBERG (1907- , Montreal)—A Special Adviser to Prime Minister Trudeau on legal matters, he was one of the most famous labor mediators in Canadian history.

ALLAN GOTIER (1928- , Winnipeg)—Assistant Undersecretary of State for External Affairs, beginning in 1967.

HERBERT GRAY (1931- , Windsor)—Became Minister of National Revenue in the Canadian government in 1970.

ALLAN GROSSMAN (1910-)—Minister of Correctional Services in the 1970s.

LIONEL MORRIS (1907- , Toronto)—Was a Special Assistant to Prime Minister Diefenbaker and became a well-known writer on international politics.

SYDNEY D. PIERCE (1901-)—A long-time and distinguished member of the Canadian foreign service, he was Ambassador to Mexico, Associate Deputy Minister of Trade and Commerce, Ambassador to Brazil, Ambassador to Belgium, and Ambassador to the European Common Market.

LOUIS RASMINSKY (1908- , Montreal)—A famous economist who helped to design the International Monetary Fund, he became Governor of the Bank of Canada in 1961.

SYDNEY SPIVAK (1928-)—Served as Minister of Trade and Commerce in the Provincial government of Manitoba.

CHILEANS

DANIEL SCHWEITZER (1896- , Buenos Aires)—Led the Chilean delegation to the UN, 1959-1964.

MIGUEL SCHWEITZER (1908- , Antofagasta)—Chilean Minister of Labor in the 1960s.

ENRIQUE TESTA (1916-)—President of the Chilean State Defense Council and an influential figure in the early 1970s.

CZECHS

LUDWIG CZECH (1870-1942, Lemberg)—An important figure as the Chairman of the Social Democratic party, he served as Minister of Social Welfare and later as Minister of Works.

EUGEN LOEBL (1907- , Holic)—A leading Czech economist who was First Deputy of the Ministry of Foreign Trade. One of the leaders of the movement known as "communism with a human face" he eventually had to flee the country.

JAROSLAV STRANSKY (1884-1973)—Served as Minister of Education, Minister of Justice, and Deputy Prime Minister after World War II.

LEV WINTER (1876-1935, Hroby)—Became Minister of Social Welfare shortly after Czechoslovakia was established.

DANES

CARL E. BRANDES (1847-1931)—Born Cohen. Finance Minister of Denmark, 1909–1910 and 1913–1920.

HENRY GRUENBAUM (1911-)—Editor of the Danish Labor party newspaper, he served as Minister of Economics and Nordic Affairs, and as Finance Minister, 1965–1968.

DUTCH

MICHAEL H. GODEFROI (1813-1883)—Minister of Justice of the Netherlands in the 1860s.

SALOMON RODRIGUES DE MIRANDA (1878-1941)—Minister of Housing and Public Works before World War II. He died in a Nazi concentration camp.

CAREL H. F. POLAK (1909-)—One of the leading legal scholars in Holland, he was Minister of Justice, 1967–1971.

WILLEM POLAK (1924- , Amsterdam)—Became Undersecretary of the Interior in 1973.

IVO SAMKALDEN (1912-)—Twice Minister of Justice of the Netherlands, he was elected Mayor of Amsterdam in 1967.

EDUARD E. VAN RAALTE (1841-1921, Rotterdam)—Served as Minister of Justice beginning in 1905.

FRENCH

LÉON BLUM (1872-1950, Paris)—One of the most famous political figures in French history, he was the first socialist to lead that country. He became Premier in 1936 in a government that lasted for less than a year and was Premier again for a short time in 1938. After his liberation from a Nazi concentration camp in 1945, he headed another short-lived government and was Vice-Premier in 1948. He was without doubt one of the great socialist leaders of all time.

MAURICE BOKANOWSKI (1879-1928)—French Minister of the Navy, 1924, and Minister of Commerce and Industry, 1926–1927. He died in an air crash.

ISAAC A. CREMIEUX (1796-1880, Nîmes)—Minister of Justice in the provisional government during the 1848 Revolution and again after the end of the Second Republic.

ACHILLE FOULD (1800-1897)—Minister of Finance under Louis Napoleon.

MICHEL GOUDCHAUX (1797-1862, Nancy)—Minister of Finance in the Second French Republic, he was also Vice-President of the National Assembly.

GILBERT GRANDVAL (1904- , Paris)—Born Hirsch-Ollendorf. French Resident General in Morocco, Secretary of State for Foreign Trade, and Minister of Labor.

LOUIS-LUCIEN KLOTZ (1868-1930, Paris)—French Minister of Finance six times and Minister of the Interior on one occasion in the first quarter of this century. A Radical Socialist Deputy for over 30 years, he was a signer of the Versailles Treaty.

GEORGES MANDEL (1885-1944, Chatou)—Born Jeroboam Rothchild. Minister of the Interior of the French government just before the surrender to Germany. He was executed by German collaborators before the liberation of France.

DANIEL MAYER (1909-　, Paris)—In the bedlam that was the French government in 1945-1949, he was Minister of Veterans' Affairs, Minister of Public Health, and Minister of Labor, not necessarily in that order.

RENE MAYER (1895-1972, Paris)—An outstanding French politician of the postwar era, he served as Minister of Finance, Minister of Justice, and finally as Prime Minister in 1953.

PIERRE MENDES-FRANCE (1907-　, Paris)—The famous Prime Minister who took France out of the Indochina War, he later served as Minister without Portfolio.

LEON MEYER (1868-1957, Le Havre)—A Mayor of Le Havre, Undersecretary of State (twice), and, in 1932, Minister for the Mercantile Marine.

JULES S. MOCH (1893-　, Paris)—One of the most important politicians in French socialist circles, he served in a variety of posts: Undersecretary of State, Minister of Public Works (at least twice), Minister of the Interior, Minister of Defense, and Vice-Premier.

DAVID RAYNAL (1841-1903, Paris)—Minister of Public Works twice during the 1880s and briefly Minister of the Interior at the end of that decade.

JACQUES STERN (1881-1949, Paris)—Minister for the Merchant Marine and then a very important Minister for the Colonies in several French governments of the 1930s. He committed suicide.

OLIVER B. WORMSER (1913-　, Paris)—Ambassador to the Soviet Union and then Governor of the Bank of France in the 1960s.

JEAN ZAY (1904-1944, Orléans)—French Undersecretary of State and Minister of National Education in 1936, he was murdered by the Nazis.

GERMANS

LUDWIG BAMBERGER (1823-1899, Mainz)—An important economic adviser to Bismarck, he was a leading German banker.

KURT EISNER (1867-1919)—The most important individual in the short-lived Bavarian Republic and its Prime Minister. One of the leading socialists in Germany, he was assassinated in Feb. 1919 by Count Aro-Valley, himself of Jewish descent.

MORITZ ELLSTAETTER (1827-1905, Karlsruhe)—Minister of Finance for the state of Baden.

HANS GOSLAR (1889-1945)—Director of the Press Section of the Prussian State Government of the Weimar Republic.

LUDWIG HAAS (1875-1930, Freiburg)—Minister of the Interior in the Baden government for a brief time.

OTTO LANDSBURG (1869-1957, Rybnik)—Minister of Justice in Germany and later Ambassador to Belgium. He fought against the Versailles Peace Treaty, resigning his post rather than be associated with it.

HUGO PREUSS (1860-1925, Berlin)—Architect of the Weimar Constitution, he served as Minister of the Interior of Germany after World War I.

WALTHER RATHENAU (1867-1922)—The famous Foreign Minister of the Weimar Republic who was assassinated. He had earlier been Minister of Reconstruction.

FRIEDRICH WOLF (1888-1953)—Winner of East Germany's National Prize for literature on two occasions, he was that country's Ambassador to Poland, 1949–1951.

HUNGARIANS

ERNO GERO (1898- , Budapest)—A leading member of the Hungarian Communist party (he was its First Secretary), he fought against the Hungarian uprising in 1956. He was also Minister of Transport. Gero was kicked out of the party in the early 1960s.

OSZKAR JASZI (1875-1957, Nagykaroly)—Minister of National Minorities of the revolutionary regime in 1918. Converted to Christianity.

BELA KUN (1886-1939, Szilagycseh)—An important member of the Executive of the Communist International and the head of the revolutionary Hungarian government after World War I. He was killed during the purges.

MATYAS RAKOSI (1892-1971, Ada)—The infamous dictator of Hungary in the late 1940s and '50s, he escaped death on several occasions. Rakosi was not proud of his Jewish origin.

BELA SOMOGYI (1868-1920, Halasto)—Director of the Ministry of Education after the Hungarian Revolution, he was murdered by his fellow revolutionaries.

PAL SZENDE (1879-1935, Nyirbator)—Minister of Finance in the revolutionary government.

LIPOT VADASZ (1861-1924, Kisvarda)—Became Undersecretary of State of the Ministry of Justice just before World War I.

PETER VALYI (1919-1973, Szombathely)—An important member of the Hungarian Communist party, he became Minister of Finance and then Deputy Prime Minister.

VILMOS VAZSONYI (1868-1926)—Minister of Justice in World War I.

ITALIANS

ISAAC ARTOM (1829-1900)—Undersecretary of State for Foreign Affairs of Italy in the 1870s.

LUIGI LUZZATI (1841-1927, Venice)—Prime Minister of Italy in 1910, Minister of the Treasury several times, and Minister of Agriculture once.

GIACOMO MALVANO (1841-1922, Turin)—A distinguished diplomat, he was the Secretary General of the Italian Foreign Ministry for more than 20 years and also served as President of the Italian Council of State.

LODOVISO MORTARA (1855-1937)—Minister of Justice after World War I.

MAURIZIO RAVA (b. 1878, Milan)—Governor of Italian Somaliland in the mid-1930s, in spite of his Jewish origin.

CARLO SCHANZER (b. 1865, Vienna)—Foreign Minister of Italy in 1922. He had previously served as Minister of Finance.

EMILIO SERENI (1907-)—Minister of Public Works and Minister of Social Welfare immediately after World War II.

SIDNEY SONNINO (1847-1922, Pisa)—Sonnino was a Protestant, although his father was Jewish. He was Prime Minister of Italy twice in the decade 1900–1910, and was Foreign Minister during World War I. After the war he represented Italy at the Versailles Peace Conference.

LEONE WOLLEMBORG (1859-1932, Padua)—Served as Minister of Finance at the turn of the century.

JAMAICANS

SIR NEVILLE N. ASHENHEIM (1900- , Kingston)—Minister without Portfolio, 1962; Ambassador to the U.S., 1962–1967 (the first person to hold this post); and Minister of State for Finance, beginning in 1967.

ELI MATALON (1924- , Kingston)—A onetime Mayor of Kingston, he served as Minister of Education and then as a very powerful and controversial Minister of Public Security.

POLES

SIMON ASKENAZY (1867-1937)—Polish Delegate to the League of Nations after independence, he was one of the most famous historians in Polish history.

LEON CHAJN (1910-)—Deputy Chairman of the Democratic (Communist) party, he was Deputy Minister of Justice after World War II.

JULIUSZ KATZ-SUCHY (1912-1971, Warsaw)—Long-time Polish Ambassador to the UN, he was also Ambassador to India and Director of the Polish Institute for International Affairs.

HILARY MINC (1905- , Kazimierz Dolny)—An important figure in the Polish Communist party, he was Minister for Industry and Commerce, Chairman of the State Planning Commission, and Vice-Premier of Poland in the post–World War II period.

EUGENIUS SZYR (1915- , Warsaw)—A member of the Central Committee of the Polish United Workers' party, he was Chairman of the State Planning Commission and a Vice-Premier.

ROMAN ZUMBROWSKI (1909-)—Minister for State Control, he had earlier been Secretary of the Polish United Workers' party Central Committee and one of the most influential men in the country. Like many Jewish officials, he was stripped of his posts during the anti-Semitic purges of the mid-1960s.

RUMANIANS

GHEORGHE GASTON-MARIN (1919- , Petrosani)—Born Grossman. Served as Minister of Electrical Energy, First Vice-Chairman of the State Planning Commission, and Deputy Premier of Rumania.

ANA PAUKER (1890-1960, Bucharest)—One of the most powerful figures in the Rumanian Communist party, she was Secretary of the party's Central Committee, Minister of Foreign Affairs (one of the few women in the world to hold this post), and First Deputy Prime Minister.

RUSSIANS AND CLOSE RELATIVES

See also Men and Women of the Left.

ADOLPH A. JOFFE (1883-1927, Simferopol)—An important Soviet diplomat, he was in charge of the Brest-Litovsk peace talks with the Germans in World War I until he was removed for his hard-line position. He served as Soviet Ambassador to Germany, China, Austria, and Japan before he took his own life in 1927. At one time his articles appeared frequently in *Pravda*.

LAZAR M. KAGANOVICH (1893-)—One of the few early Bolsheviks to outlast the purges, he was an important figure in Soviet domestic affairs, serving as Minister for Communications and, most importantly, Minister for Heavy Industry. He was a contender for leadership after the death of Stalin and was a member of the Politburo.

MAXIM M. LITVINOV (1867-1951, Bialystok)—Born Meir Wallach. One of the most famous Soviet Foreign Ministers, he opened up relationships with the U.S. before World War II. His removal was a sure sign that an agreement was going to be worked out between the Russians and the Germans. He served as Ambassador to the U.S. in the early to mid-1940s.

ARNOLD MARGOLIN (1877-1956, Kiev)—A lawyer, he was Deputy Foreign Minister of the short-lived Ukrainian regime of 1918.

PAUL MINTZ (b. 1870, Dvinsk)—State Controller of Latvia and a famous lawyer who perished in a Russian prison.

SOUTH AFRICANS

HENRY GLUCKMAN (1893-   )—A Member of Parliament, he became Minister of Health and Housing in 1945.

LEOPOLD LOVELL (1905-   )—Minister of Finance, Commerce, and Industry for Swaziland.

YUGOSLAVIANS

LEON GERSKOVIC (1910-   , Buje)—A member of the Yugoslavian National Assembly during the 1950s, he had earlier been Minister of the Interior of Croatia.

MOSES PIJADE (1890-1957, Belgrade)—A leading member of the Yugoslav Communist party (he was on its Central Committee) and a close associate of Marshal Tito, he served as Chairman of the National Assembly and as President of the Serbian Republic.

OTHERS

ALBERT BESSIS (b. 1883, Tunis)—Minister of Housing and Town Planning and later Minister of Public Works in Tunisia during the 1950s.

JULIUS BLUM (1843-1919, Budapest)—A noted banker who was Undersecretary of Finance in Austria-Hungary, 1877–1890.

JOSEPH A. CATTAUI (1861-1942)—Minister of Finance and Minister of Communications of Egypt in the 1920s.

MAX DELVALLE (1911-   , Panama City)—Minister of Public Works and then Vice-President of Panama, he was Acting President of that country for a short time in the 1960s.

RENE DESOLA (1919-   , Caracas)—Minister of Justice in Venezuela in the 1970s.

SIR JOSHUA HASSAN (1915-   , Gibraltar)—Chief Minister of Gibraltar, 1965--1969, and earlier the Mayor of the city of Gibraltar on two occasions.

PAUL HYMANS (1865-1941, Brussels)—One of the most distinguished public figures in Belgium, he served as President of the Assembly of the League of Nations, Ambassador to Great Britain during World War I, and Foreign Minister of Belgium on four occasions.

EDWARD E. ISBEY (b. England)—Became Undersecretary of the New Zealand Ministry of Labor in 1973.

MAX JAKOBSON (1923-   , Viborg)—Formerly the Chief of the Press Department of the Foreign Ministry of Finland, he became that country's Representative to the UN in the mid-1960s. It is widely assumed that he would have been UN Secretary General if he had not been Jewish.

HORACIO LAFER (1893-1965, São Paulo)—Onetime Governor of the World Bank and a long-time member of the Brazilian Chamber of Deputies as well as Minister of Finance and later Foreign Minister of Brazil.

DAVID S. MARSHALL (1908-   )—Onetime Chief Minister and Commerce Minister of Singapore and leader of that country's United Labor Front party.

SIR ARTHUR M. MYERS (1867-1926)—New Zealand's Minister of Finance, Defense, and Railways, and Minister of Customs, Munitions, and Supplies during World War I. He was also Mayor of Auckland, 1905–1909.

CHARLES PHILIPSON (1928-   , Oslo)—Ombudsman for Consumers in the Norwegian government, beginning in 1973.

SIR EZEKIEL SASSON (1860-1932, Baghdad)—Iraqi Minister of Finance five times during the 1920s.

SIR JULIUS VOGEL (1835-1899, London)—Prime Minister of New Zealand in 1873.

SIR ROY WELENSKY (1907-   )—The first Prime Minister of the Rhodesian Federation.

JUDGES

(*See also* Lawyers; Legal Scholars.)

SIR SIDNEY ABRAHAMS (1885-1957, Birmingham, England)—Chief Justice of Uganda, 1933–1934; Chief Justice of Tanganyika, 1934–1936; and Chief Justice of Ceylon, 1936–1939.

NORMAN C. ADDLESON (1902-   , Queenstown, South Africa)—A Judge of the South African Supreme Court.

JENNIE L. BARON (1891-1969, Boston)—Associate Justice of the State Superior Court of Massachusetts.

DAVID L. BAZELON (1909-   , Superior, Wis.)—Chief Judge of the U.S. Court of Appeals for the District of Columbia and a leading jurist.

NATHAN BIJUR (1862-1930)—A distinguished member of the New York State Supreme Court for many years.

HYMAN M. BLOCH (1905-1963, South Africa)—A Judge of the South African Supreme Court.

LOUIS D. BRANDEIS (1856-1941, Louisville)—The very distinguished Justice of the U.S. Supreme Court and one of the most famous Jews in the U.S. during his lifetime.

BENJAMIN N. CARDOZO (1870-1938, New York City)—Not only a great Justice of the U.S. Supreme Court but a leading legal scholar whose *Nature of the Judicial Process* was a major work.

GEORGE COLMAN (1908-   , Johannesburg)—A Judge of the South African Supreme Court.

LOUIS DUBINSKY (1910-   )—A member of the Supreme Court of Nova Scotia.

SIR ISADORE V. ELYAN (1909-   , Dublin)—Served as Chief Justice of Swaziland.

PHILIP FORMAN (1895-   , New York)—Judge for the U.S. Court of Appeals for the Third District, and a leading jurist.

ABE FORTAS (1910-   , Memphis, Tenn.)—LBJ's lawyer for many years, he was appointed Justice of the Supreme Court in 1965 but resigned in 1969 amid charges of financial irregularities.

JEROME FRANK (1889-1957, New York City)—Former Chairman of the Securities and Exchange Commission, he later served as Judge for the Second District of the U.S. Court of Appeals.

FELIX FRANKFURTER (1882-1965, Vienna)—The great Justice of the U.S. Supreme Court and the recipient of the Medal of Freedom.

JOSEPH J. FRIEDMAN (1908-   , Kimberley, South Africa)—A Judge of the South African Supreme Court since 1964.

HUGO M. FRIEND (1882-1966, Prague)—A leading American Appellate Court Judge from the First District of Illinois, he was a member of the U.S. Track and Field Team at the Olympic Games of 1906.

STANLEY H. FULD (1903-   )—One of the leading jurists in the U.S. and Chief Judge of the New York Court of Appeals.

OSCAR GALGUT (1906-   , Pretoria)—A Judge of the South African Supreme Court since 1958.

BENNIE GOLDIN (1918- , Cape Town)—A Justice of the High Court of Rhodesia.

ALLAN GOODMAN (1920-)—A Justice of the Supreme Court of Ontario.

PAUL GUGGENHEIM (1899- , Zurich)—A leading figure at the International Arbitration Court at The Hague.

ROSE HEILBRON (1914- , Liverpool)—The first woman ever to become a major criminal judge (called a Recorder) in England.

HARRY A. HOLLZER (1880-1946, New York City)—A prominent Judge of the U.S. District Court.

SIR GEORGE JESSEL (1824-1883, London)—Widely considered one of the greatest jurists in British history, he was Solicitor General of England.

SIMON M. KUPER (1906-1963)—A Judge of the South African Supreme Court, he was murdered by parties unknown.

MANFRED LACHS—Became President of the International Court of Justice (The Hague) in 1973.

BORA LASKIN (1912- , Fort William, Canada)—Chief Justice of the Canadian Supreme Court.

SIR HERSCH LAUTERPACHT (1897-1960, Zolkiew, Galicia)—A Judge of the International Court of Justice, he was one of the leading figures in international law and a Professor at Cambridge.

ABRAHAM LEFF (1903-)—A Justice of the Ontario Supreme Court.

RAYMOND N. LEON (1925- , Johannesburg)—Yet another Judge of the South African Supreme Court.

MAYER LERNER—A Justice of the Ontario Supreme Court.

THEODORE LEVIN (1897-1971, Chicago)—Chief Federal Judge of the Eastern District of Michigan.

JAN J. LITAUER (1873-1949)—A Judge of Poland's Supreme Court and one of the leading jurists in the country.

PHILIP MILLIN (1888-1952)—Yes, another Judge of the South African Supreme Court.

SIR MICHAEL MYERS (1873-1950, Motueka, New Zealand)—Chief Justice of New Zealand, 1929–1946, and one of the most distinguished jurists in the country's history.

SIR NATHANIEL NATHAN (1843-1916)—A Justice of the Supreme Court of Trinidad.

SIR CYRIL B. SALMON (1903- , London)—Lord Justice of Appeal of Great Britain.

HENRY TORRES (1891-1966)—Onetime President of the French Broadcasting Authority, he was Vice-President of the French High Court of Justice.

LODEWIJK E. VISSER (1871-1942, Amersfoort, the Netherlands)—One of the leading jurists in Holland, he served as President of the Dutch Supreme Court at the beginning of World War II.

CHARLES E. WYZANSKI, JR. (1906- , Boston)—Federal District Judge for the District of Massachusetts, he was mentioned several times as a candidate for the U.S. Supreme Court.

U.S. SENATORS

JUDAH P. BENJAMIN—Louisiana, 1853–1861. *See* Government Officials: Americans.

RUDY BOSCHWITZ (1933- , Berlin)—R., Minnesota, 1978–.

ERNEST H. GRUENING (1887-1974, New York City)—Alaska, 1959–1969. One of the very few senators to hold a medical degree, he was an important journalist (Editor of the *Nation*, 1920–1923) before becoming Territorial Governor of Alaska in 1939. He led the struggle for Alaskan statehood and was one of the state's first two senators. He was a Democrat.

SIMON GUGGENHEIM (1867-1941, Philadelphia)—Colorado, 1907–1913. A member of the great family of bankers, miners, and industrialists, he is best remembered as the founder of the Guggenheim Foundation, whose grants have benefited scholars and the nation for more than 50 years. He was a Republican.

JACOB K. JAVITS (1904- , New York City)—R., New York, 1957- . A leader of the liberal wing of the Republican party for more than 20 years, he served in the House of Representatives, 1946–1954, then was elected Attorney General of New York State. According to a Ralph Nader study, Javits was rated as the brightest man in the Senate as well as the second most influential, his power deriving in no small measure from his senior position on the Foreign Relations Committee.

BENJAMIN FRANKLIN JONAS (1834-1911, Williamsport, Ky.)—Louisiana, 1879–1885. A Confederate veteran of the Civil War, Jonas was defeated in a reelection bid in 1884. He was an open and practicing Jew and a Democrat.

HERBERT H. LEHMAN (1878-1963, New York City)—D., New York, 1949–1957. A member of the great banking family, Lehman was an outstanding Governor of New York, 1933–1942, having won the election by an enormous margin. Never defeated as Governor, he chose to accept the leadership of the UN Relief and Rehabilitation Administration, in which capacity he worked to help wartime refugees. Lehman defeated John Foster Dulles in 1949 to attain his Senate seat, and was an effective and courageous opponent of Joe McCarthy.

CARL LEVIN (1934-)—D., Michigan, 1978–.

HOWARD METZENBAUM (1917- , Cleveland)—Ohio, 1973–1974, 1976- . A long-time veteran of Ohio politics, Metzenbaum served in both the State House and Senate, masterminded and managed Stephen Young's Senate campaigns, and lost the 1970 Senate race before finally becoming a winner in 1976. He had earlier served in the Senate as an appointee. He is a Democrat.

RICHARD L. NEUBERGER (1912-1960, Portland, Ore.)—D., Oregon, 1955–1960. Covered the Pacific Northwest for the *New York Times*, 1939–1954, and served in the Oregon House and Senate before being elected as the first Democrat in almost 40 years to represent that state in the U.S. Senate. He died while in office and was succeeded by his non-Jewish wife, Maurine.

ISIDOR RAYNER (1850-1912, Baltimore)—D., Maryland, 1905–1912. One of the most powerful men in Maryland politics for 30 years, Rayner served in the state legislature, in the U.S. House of Representatives (*see* Congressmen and Congresswomen), and as Attorney General of Maryland. He overcame the opposition of the very corrupt Democratic party in Maryland to win his Senate seat, and he championed black civil rights in his home state.

ABRAHAM A. RIBICOFF (1910- , New Britain, Conn.)—D., Connecticut, 1963- . When a list of the great political speeches in American history is compiled, it will have to include the "American dream" appeal of Abe Ribicoff as he successfully overcame anti-Semitism in his struggle to capture the governorship of Connecticut (*see* Governors of American States). As a leading member of the Senate, he will always be remembered as the leader of the fight to bring medical insurance to all Americans.

JOSEPH SIMON (1851-1935, Bechtheim, Germany)—Oregon, 1898–1903. Elected to the Senate in 1898 in a special election to fill a vacancy, he did not seek reelection. He was one of a number of Jews to serve as Mayor of Portland, Ore.

RICHARD STONE (1928- , New York City)—D., Florida, 1974- . Served in the Florida Senate and as Secretary of State before becoming the first Jew since David Levy Yulee to be elected to the U.S. Senate from Florida. He has been an effective spokesman for American support for Israel.

DAVID LEVY YULEE (1810-1866, St. Thomas, V.I.)—Florida, 1845-1851, 1855-1861. Was instrumental in attaining statehood for Florida and became that state's first senator. Like his better-known coreligionist Uriah Phillips Levy (no relation), he fought against the practice of flogging in the U.S. Navy. A champion of secession and of the institution of slavery, Levy (who changed his name to Yulee in 1846) later served in the Confederate Congress.

EDWARD ZORINSKY (1928-   , Omaha)—D., Nebraska, 1977-   . Republican Mayor of Omaha, 1973-1977. He switched over to the Democrats in 1975 and won the 1976 senatorial election in something of an upset.

U.S. CONGRESSMEN AND CONGRESSWOMEN

BELLA ABZUG (1920-   , New York City)—D., New York. An outspoken legislator, she served in the House, 1971-1977.

MARTIN C. ANSORGE (1882-1967, Corning, N.Y.)—R., New York, 1921-1923.

ISAAC BACHARACH (1870-1956, Philadelphia)—R., New Jersey, 1915-1937.

ANTHONY C. BEILENSON (1932-   , New Rochelle, N.Y.)—D., California, 1977-

VICTOR L. BERGER (1860-1929, Nieder Rebbach, Austria-Hungary)—One of the founders of the American Socialist party, he served as a Socialist from Wisconsin, 1911-1913 and 1923-1929.

SOL BLOOM (1870-1949, Pekin, Ill.)—D., New York, 1923-1949. He was Chairman of the powerful Foreign Affairs Committee for a number of years.

JACOB A. CANTOR (1854-1921, New York City)—D., New York, 1913-1915.

EMANUEL CELLER (1888-   , Brooklyn)—D., New York, 1923-1973. He was one of the first to speak out against the tactics and philosophy of Joe McCarthy.

EARL CHUDOFF (1907-   , Philadelphia)—D., Pennsylvania, 1949-1958.

WILLIAM M. CITRON (1896-   , New Haven)—D., Connecticut, 1935-1939.

WILLIAM W. COHEN (1874-1940, Brooklyn)—D., New York, 1927-1929.

IRWIN D. DAVIDSON (1906-   , New York City)—Democrat-Liberal from New York, 1955-1956.

SAMUEL DICKSTEIN (1885-1954, Vilna, Lithuania)—D., New York, 1923-1945.

ISIDORE DOLLINGER (1903-   , New York City)—D., New York, 1949-1959.

MORRIS M. EDELSTEIN (1888-1941, Meseritz, Poland)—D., New York, 1940-1941. He died in the House chambers.

JOSHUA EILBERG (1921-   , Philadelphia)—D., Pennsylvania, 1967-

EDWIN EINSTEIN (1842-1905, Cincinnati)—R., New York, 1879-1881.

HENRY ELLENBOGEN (1900-   , Vienna)—D., Pennsylvania, 1933-1938.

DANIEL ELLISON (1886-1960, Russia)—R., Maryland, 1943-1945.

MARTIN EMERICH (1846-1922, Baltimore)—D., Illinois, 1903-1905.

LEONARD FARBSTEIN (1902-   , New York City)—D., New York, 1957-1971.

SIDNEY A. FINE (1903-, New York City)—D., New York, 1951-1956.

ISRAEL F. FISCHER (1858-1940, New York City)—R., New York, 1895-1899.

NATHAN FRANK (1852-1931, Peoria, Ill.)—Republican-Union Laborist from Missouri, 1889-1891. He was the founder and owner of the St. Louis Star.

SAMUEL N. FRIEDEL (b. 1898, Washington, D.C.)—D., from Maryland, 1953-1971.

MARTIN FROST—D., Texas, 1978-   .

JACOB H. GILBERT (1920-   , New York City)—D., New York, 1960-1971.

BENJAMIN A. GILMAN (1922- , Poughkeepsie, N.Y.)—R., New York, 1973- .

DAN GLICKMAN (1944- , Wichita, Kans.)—D., Kansas, 1977–.

BENJAMIN M. GOLDER (1891-1946, Alliance, N.J.)—R., Pennsylvania, 1925–1933.

HENRY M. GOLDFOGLE (1856-1929, New York City)—D., New York, 1901–1915 and 1919–1921.

JULIUS GOLDZIER (1854-1925, Vienna)—D., Illinois, 1893–1895.

WILLIS GRADISON, JR. (1928- , Cincinnati)—R., Ohio, 1975–.

MICHAEL HAHN (see Governors)—As a Unionist from Louisiana, 1862–1863; as a Republican, 1885–1886.

SEYMOUR HALPERN (1913- , New York City)—R., New York, 1959–1973.

EMANUEL B. HART (1809-1897, New York City)—D., New York, 1841–1853.

LOUIS B. HELLER (1905- , New York City)—D., New York, 1949–1954.

ELIZABETH HOLTZMAN (1941- , Brooklyn)—D., New York, since 1973.

LESTER HOLTZMAN (1913- , New York City)—D., New York, 1953–1961.

JULIUS HOUSEMAN (1832-1891, Zeckendorf, Germany)—D., Michigan, 1883-1885. He was Mayor of Grand Rapids, 1873–1875.

LEO ISACSON (1910- , New York City)—American Labor party representative from New York, 1948–1949.

MEYER JACOBSTEIN (1880-1963, New York City)—D., New York, 1923–1929. A noted economist, he was on the staff of the Brookings Institution, 1939–1946.

JACOB K. JAVITS—R., New York, 1947–1954. See U.S. Senators.

CHARLES S. JOELSON (1916- , Paterson, N.J.)—D., New Jersey, 1961–1969.

FLORENCE PRAG KAHN (1868-1948, Salt Lake City)—R., California, 1925–1937.

JULIUS KAHN (1861-1924, Kuppenheim, Germany)—R., California, 1899–1903 and 1905–1924. He was a noted actor (not the political kind).

DAVID S. KAUFMAN (1813-1851, Boiling Springs, Pa.)—D., Texas, 1846–1851. He was Chargé d'Affaires of Texas to the U.S. in 1845.

ARTHUR G. KLEIN (1904-1968, New York City)—D., New York, 1941–1945 and 1946–1956.

EDWARD I. KOCH (1924- , New York City)—D., New York, 1969–1977. See also Mayors.

HERMAN P. KOPPLEMANN (1880-1957, Odessa, Russia)—D., Connecticut, 1933–1939; 1941–1943; and 1945–1947.

KEN KRAMER—R., Colorado, 1978- .

MILTON KRAUS (1866-1942, Kokomo, Ind.)—R., Indiana, 1917–1923.

JOHN KREBS (1926- , Berlin)—D., California, 1975–1979.

FIORELLO H. LA GUARDIA (1882-1947, New York City)—A Fusion Representative from New York, 1917–1919 and 1923–1933. He was one of New York City's most famous and effective mayors, 1934–1945. His mother was Jewish.

WILLIAM LEHMAN (1913- , Selma, Ala.)—D., Florida, 1973- .

MONTAGUE LESSLER (1869-1938, New York City)—R., New York, 1902–1903.

LEWIS C. LEVIN (1808-1860, Charleston, S.C.)—American party Representative from Pennsylvania, 1845–1851. He was cofounder of the American party in 1842 and editor of the Philadelphia Daily Sun.

ELLIOTT H. LEVITAS (1930- , Atlanta)—D., Georgia, 1975- .

JEFFERSON M. LEVY (1852-1924, New York City)—D., New York, 1899–1901, and 1911–1915. At one time he owned Monticello, the home of Thomas Jefferson.

LUCIUS N. LITTAUER (1859-1944, Gloversville, N.Y.)—R.,New York, 1897–1907.

MEYER LONDON (1871-1926, Kalvaria, Russia)—Socialist from New York, 1915-1919 and 1921-1923. He was killed in an automobile wreck.

ALLARD K. LOWENSTEIN (1929- , Newark)—Democrat-Liberal from New York, 1969-1971. He was a leading opponent of the Vietnam War.

MARC L. MARKS (1927- , Farrell, Pa.)—R., Pennsylvania, 1977–

SAMUEL MARX—Elected Representative from New York in 1922, he died before he could take his seat.

MITCHELL MAY (1870-1961, Brooklyn)—D., New York, 1899-1901.

ADOLPH MEYER (1842-1908, Natchez, Miss.)—D., Louisiana, 1891-1908. He was a brigadier general.

EDWARD MEZVINSKY—D., Iowa, 1973-1975.

ABNER J. MIKVA (1926- , Milwaukee)—D., Illinois, 1969-1973 and 1975–

LEOPOLD MORSE (1831-1892, Wachenhiem, Bavaria)—D., Massachusetts, 1877-1885 and 1887-1889.

ABRAHAM J. MULTER (1900- , New York City)—D., New York, 1947-1967.

RICHARD L. OTTINGER (1929- , New York City)—D., New York, 1965-1971 and 1975- . He was a founder of the Peace Corps.

NATHAN D. PERLMAN (1887-1952, Poland)—R., New York, 1920-1927.

THEODORE A. PEYSER (1873-1937, Charleston, W.Va.)—D., New York, 1933-1937.

HENRY M. PHILLIPS (1811-1884, Philadelphia)—D., from Pennsylvania, 1857-1859.

PHILIP PHILLIPS (1807-1884, Charleston, S.C.)—D., Alabama, 1853-1855.

BERTRAM L. PODELL (1925- , Brooklyn)—D., New York, 1968-1975.

BENJAMIN J. RABIN (1896-1969, Rochester, N.Y.)—D., New York, 1945-1947.

LEO F. RAYFIEL (b. 1888, New York)—D., New York, 1945-1947.

ISIDOR RAYNER—D., Maryland, 1887-1889 and 1891-1895. *See also* U.S. Senators.

JOSEPH Y. RESNICK (1924-1969, Ellenville, N.Y.)—D., New York, 1965-1969.

ABRAHAM A. RIBICOFF (*see* Senators)—D., Connecticut, 1949-1953.

FREDERICK W. RICHMOND (1923- , Mattapan, Mass.)—D., New York, 1975- .

BENJAMIN L. ROSENBLOOM (1880-1965, Braddock, Pa.)—R., West Virginia, 1921-1925.

BENJAMIN S. ROSENTHAL (1923- , New York City)—Democrat-Liberal from New York, 1962- .

ALBERT B. ROSSDALE (1878-1946, New York City)—R., New York, 1921-1923.

ADOLPH J. SABATH (1866-1952, Zabori, Czechoslovakia)—D., Illinois, 1907-1952. He was a powerful figure in the Democratic party.

LEON SACKS (1902- , Philadelphia)—D., Pennsylvania, 1937-1943.

JAMES H. SCHEUER (1920- , New York City)—Democrat-Liberal from New York, 1965-1973 and 1975- .

ISAAC SIEGEL (1880-1947, New York City)—R., New York, 1915-1923.

WILLIAM I. SIROVICH (1882-1939, York, Pa.)—D., New York, 1927-1939.

STEPHEN J. SOLARZ (1940- , New York City)—D., New York, 1975- .

GLADYS NOON SPELLMAN (1918- , New York City)—D., Maryland, 1975- .

SAM STEIGER (1929- , New York City)—R., Arizona, 1967-1977.

ISIDOR STRAUS (1845-1912, Ottenberg, Germany)—D., New York, 1894-1895. He died in the *Titanic* disaster.

MYER STROUSE (1825-1878, Oberstraw, Bavaria)—D., Pennsylvania, 1863-1867. He was the lawyer who defended the "Molly Maguires" in the coal fields of Pennsylvania.

LUDWIG TELLER (1911- , New York City)—D., New York, 1957–1961. He was also a professor of law at NYU.

HERBERT TENZER (1905- , New York City)—D., New York, 1965–1969.

HERMAN TOLL (1907–1967, Kiev, Russia)—D., Pennsylvania, 1959–1967.

LESTER D. VOLK (1884–1962, Brooklyn)—R., New York, 1920–1923.

HENRY A. WAXMAN (1939- , Los Angeles)—D., California, 1975- .

SAMUEL A. WEISS (1902- , Warsaw, Poland)—D., Pennsylvania, 1941–1946. He was also a leading referee in the National Football League.

THEODORE S. WEISS (1927- , Gava, Hungary)—D., New York, 1977- .

HARRY B. WOLF (1880–1944, Baltimore)—D., Maryland, 1907–1909.

LESTER L. WOLFF (1919- , New York City)—D., New York, 1965- .

HOWARD WOLPE—D., Michigan, 1978- .

SIDNEY R. YATES (1909- , Chicago)—D., Illinois, 1949–1963 and 1965- .

HERBERT ZELENKO (1906- , New York City)—D., New York, 1955–1963.

GOVERNORS OF AMERICAN STATES

MOSES ALEXANDER (1853–1932, Obrigheim, Germany)—Idaho, 1915–1919. The first elected Jewish Governor in American history. He was a former Mayor of Boise before his election to statewide office, and the community of Alexander, Idaho, is named in his honor.

SIMON BAMBERGER (1846–1926, Germany)—Utah, 1917–1921. A proud and practicing Jew, he was a pioneer railroad builder in Utah before being elected to the State Senate in 1903. He was the first non-Mormon governor of Utah.

MICHAEL HAHN (1830–1886, Bavaria)—Louisiana, 1864–1865. He also served in the House of Representatives in the 1860s and 1880s.

HENRY HORNER (1878–1940, Chicago)—Illinois, 1933–1940. He is famous in Illinois history because he was one of the few political figures to defy the corrupt Democratic machine in Chicago and still win nomination and election. A close friend of Carl Sandburg's and a collector of Lincoln memorabilia, he will always be remembered for his honesty and integrity.

HERBERT H. LEHMAN—New York, 1933–1942. See U.S. Senators.

FRANK LICHT (1916- , Providence)—Rhode Island, 1969–1973. A Harvard Law School graduate, Licht served in the Rhode Island Senate, 1949–1956, and as an Associate Justice of the State Supreme Court before winning the Governorship in a heavily Catholic state.

MARVIN MANDEL (1920- , Baltimore)—Maryland, 1969–1977. One of the most tragic figures in modern American political history, Marvin Mandel was a powerful and popular force in Maryland before his conviction for bribery, later reversed. Before his election to the Governorship by the General Assembly, he was an effective Speaker of the Maryland House, 1963–1969.

JULIUS MEIER (1874–1937, Portland, Oreg.)—Oregon, 1931–1935. Active in the Jewish community, he was the upset winner in the 1930 governor's race in Oregon. Campaigning as an independent, he defeated both the Republican and Democratic candidates.

ABRAHAM A. RIBICOFF—Connecticut, 1955–1961. See Senators.

SAMUEL H. SHAPIRO (1907- , Kankakee, Ill.)—Became nonelected Governor of Illinois in 1968 after having served as Lieutenant Governor. He lost the 1968 race for the governorship.

MILTON SHAPP (1912- , Cleveland)—Pennsylvania, 1971- . Shapp wanted to be a politician in Pennsylvania for a long time—in fact, he failed in an attempt for the U.S. Senate nomination in 1964 and lost the 1966 gubernatorial race as the Democratic candidate. A businessman with no previous political experience, he was a controversial governor with open presidential ambitions.

MAYORS

HARRY BACHARACH (1873-1947, Atlantic City, N.J.)—Three-time Mayor of Atlantic City, he was Chairman of the New Jersey Public Utilities Commission.

NATHAN BARNERT (1838-1927, Santomischel, Prussia)—Mayor of Paterson, N.J., 1883–1885, 1889–1891.

E. BASCH—Mayor of Bulawayo, Rhodesia, 1907–1911.

ABRAHAM D. BEAME (1906- , London)—Mayor of New York City, 1973–1978.

MARTIN BEHRMAN (1864-1926, New York City)—President of the League of American Municipalities and Mayor of New Orleans, 1904–1920.

ABE BLOOMBERG—Mayor of Cape Town, South Africa, 1945–1947.

ROBERT BRISCOE (1894-1969)—The famous Jewish Lord Mayor of Dublin, Ireland, in the 1950s and '60s, he also served in the Irish parliament, the Dail, for almost 40 years.

SIR BERNARD W. COHEN (1914-)—Lord Mayor of London, 1960–1961.

DAVID A. CROLL (1900- , Mogilev, Russia)—A noted lawyer, he became Mayor of Windsor, Ontario, in 1929.

MORRIS A. DZIALYNSKI (1841-1907)—Mayor of Jacksonville, Fla.

MEYER C. ELLENSTEIN (1886-1967, New York City)—Mayor of Newark, N.J., in the 1930s.

MATTHEW FELDMAN (1920-)—Mayor of Teaneck, N.J., 1959–1966.

JULIUS FLEISCHMANN (1872-1925, Cincinnati)—The famous yeast maven, he was elected Mayor of Cincinnati in 1900 and 1902.

ISAAC S. FOX (1896-1971)—Mayor of Chester, England, 1932–1933.

LUMLEY FRANKLIN (1812-1873)—Became Mayor of Victoria, British Columbia, in 1865.

PHILIP S. GIVENS (1922- , Toronto)—A Member of the Canadian Parliament, he served as Mayor of Toronto, 1963–1966.

LOUIS GLASS—Mayor of Birmingham, England, 1963–1964.

HERMAN GLOGOWSKI—Mayor of Tampa, Fla., 1886–1894.

GERALD Y. GOLDBERG—Lord Mayor of Cork, Ireland, in the 1970s.

GERALD GOLDMAN (1934- , Brooklyn)—Mayor of Passaic, N.J., from 1971.

J. GOLDWASSER—Mayor of Bulawayo, Rhodesia, 1968–1973.

EUGENE GORDON (1931-)—Elected Mayor of Bulawayo, Rhodesia, in 1973.

LOUIS GRADNER—Mayor of Cape Town, South Africa, 1933–1935.

SIR HARRY GRAUMANN (1868-1938)—Onetime Mayor of Johannesburg, South Africa.

RALPH S. HARRIS (1928- , Bulawayo, Rhodesia)—Became Mayor of—guess where—Bulawayo in 1972.

FELIX C. HOLLANDER (1876-1955)—A long-time legislator in South Africa, he was also Mayor of Durban, 1910–1913.

JULIUS HOUSEMAN—A Mayor of Grand Rapids, Mich. See U.S. Congressmen and Congresswomen.

SIR ROLAND E. JACOBS (1891-)—Lord Mayor of Adelaide, Australia.

NATHAN JAFFA—A Mayor of Roswell and Santa Fe, N.M. See also Political Figures.

ALEC JAFFE (1918-   )—Mayor of Johannesburg, South Africa, in the mid 1950s.

HENRY N. JAFFE (1846-1901)—The first Mayor of Albuquerque, N.M.

SIR OTTO JAFFE (1846-1929, Hamburg, Germany)—A titan of the linen industry, he served as Lord Mayor and High Sheriff of Belfast.

LIONEL JAWNO—Mayor of Kimberley, South Africa, 1959-1961.

SIR SAMUEL G. JOSEPH (1888-1944, London)—At one time the Sheriff of London, he was the Lord Mayor of that great city for two years during World War II.

WILLIAM KARUS—Mayor of Toledo, Ohio, 1869 and 1870.

ISAAC H. KEMPNER—Mayor of Galveston, Tex., 1917-1919.

JACOB KLEIN—Mayor of Bridgeport, Conn., 1886-1889.

EDWARD I. KOCH (1924-   , New York City)—Elected Mayor of New York in 1977. See also U.S. Congressmen and Congresswomen.

MORITZ LEVISEUR—Mayor of Bloemfontein, South Africa, in the early 1900s.

HYMAN LIBERMAN—Mayor of Cape Town, South Africa, in the early 1900s.

HENRY LUPIN—Mayor of Butte, Mont., in the 1880s.

MICHAEL MANDELL—Became the Mayor of Albuquerque, N.M., in 1880.

GUIDO MARX—Mayor of Toledo, Ohio, in the 1880s.

SAM MASSELL, JR. (1927-   , Atlanta)—When he became Mayor of Atlanta, Ga., in 1969, he was the youngest man (age 42) ever to hold that post. He was not reelected.

HYMAN MILLER (1907-   , Pennsylvania)—Mayor of Johannesburg, South Africa, in the early 1950s.

OSIP S. MINOR (1861-1932, Minsk)—A major figure in the Russian Social Revolutionary party, he served as Mayor of Moscow between the two revolutions in 1917.

SAMUEL MOSS (1922-   , Johannesburg)—Mayor of Johannesburg in the early 1950s.

SIR ARTHUR MYERS—Mayor of Auckland, New Zealand, 1905-1908.

HERMAN MYERS (1847-1909)—Mayor of Savannah, Ga., 1895-1897 and 1899-1907.

MORDECAI MYERS (1776-1871)—Mayor of Schenectady, N.Y., 1851-1854.

DAVID NAAR—Mayor of Elizabeth, N.J., 1850-1852.

ERNESTO NATHAN (1845-1921, England)—Mayor of Rome, Italy, 1907-1913.

DAVID OPPENHEIMER—Became Mayor of Vancouver, British Columbia, in 1888.

SIR ERNEST OPPENHEIMER—Mayor of Kimberley, South Africa, 1913-1915.

NATHAN PHILLIPS (1892-   , Brockville, Ontario)—Mayor of Toronto, 1954-1962.

PHILIP A. PHILIPS—Mayor of Auckland, New Zealand, 1869-1874.

LAWRENCE ROOS (1918-   , St. Louis)—Served as Supervisor of St. Louis County, the local equivalent of "Super Mayor," 1966-1972.

WILLIAM SAGAR—Another of the large number of Jews to serve as Mayor of Kimberley, South Africa; 1906-1908.

HYMAN H. SALOMON—Mayor of Port Elizabeth, South Africa, in the mid-1870s.

SIR DAVID SALOMONS (1797-1873)—Lord Mayor of London beginning in 1855.

CORNELL SCHREIBER—Mayor of Toledo, Ohio, 1916-1918.

MURRAY SEASONGOOD—Mayor of Cincinnati, Ohio, 1926-1930.

HENRY SEELIGSON—Mayor of Galveston, Tex., beginning in 1855.

DAVID D. SOLIS-COHEN—Mayor of Portland, Ore., 1896–1898.

JUDAH M. SOLOMON (1818-1880)—Mayor of Adelaide, Australia, beginning in 1869.

VABIAN L. SOLOMON (1853-1908, Adelaide)—Mayor of Darwin, Australia.

ISRAEL SOMEN (1903- , London)—Mayor of Nairobi, Kenya, 1955–1957.

FREDERICK SPIEGEL— Mayor of Cincinnati, Ohio, 1914–1916.

PHILIP C. STERN (1847-1933)—Mayor of Kingston, Jamaica, on several occasions.

ADOLPH SUTRO (1830-1898, Aachen, Prussia)—One of the outstanding mining engineers in the U.S., he was Mayor of San Francisco in the 1890s.

ISAAC TAUSSIG—Mayor of Jersey City, 1881–1883.

MAURITS TROOSTWIJK (1914- , Leeuwarden)—Mayor of Amersfoort, Netherlands, from 1972.

GUSTAVE WETZLAR—Mayor of East London, South Africa, in 1899.

ALFRED B. WIDMAN (1921- , Cape Town)—Mayor of Johannesburg, South Africa, in the early 1970s.

HARRY ZIMMAN—Mayor of Omaha, Nebr., in the early 1900s.

POLITICAL FIGURES

AMERICANS

SAMUEL ALSCHULER (1859-1939)—A judge and one of the leading lawyers in Illinois, he lost the 1900 election for Governor of that state on the Democratic ticket.

JACOB M. ARVEY (1893- , Chicago)—One of the most powerful figures in the Democratic party in Chicago and nationally, he was a strong supporter of Adlai Stevenson.

BERNARD BARUCH (1870-1965, Camden, S.C.)—The legendary adviser to many American Presidents, he served as American representative to the UN Atomic Energy Commission and was the powerful Chairman of the War Industries Board in World War I.

AUGUST BELMONT (1816-1890, Alzev, Germany)—The powerful Chairman of the Democratic National Committee for more than ten years, he also was American Minister at The Hague. A racetrack in New York bears his name.

BERL I. BERNHARD (1929- , New York City)—Campaign Manager for Senator Edmund Muskie's unsuccessful try for the Democratic presidential nomination in 1972.

SOLOMON BLATT (1896- , Blackville, S.C.)—The long-time Speaker of the House in South Carolina, still going strong in the 1970s.

MURRAY CHOTINER (1910-1974)—A political adviser to Richard M. Nixon for 25 years.

BENJAMIN V. COHEN (1894- , Muncie, Ind.)—A member of FDR's "Brain Trust," he was a major architect of some of the most important legislation in American history, including the Fair Labor Standards Act and the Securities Exchange Act. He may also have been one of the drafters of the Charter of the UN, but this has never been clearly established.

SAMUEL DASH (1925- , Camden, N.J.)—Famous as the Senate's Chief Counsel during the Watergate trial, he had earlier been Director of the International League for the Rights of Man.

M. JEROME DIAMOND (1942- , Chicago)—Attorney General of Vermont.

DANIEL ELLSBERG (1931- , Chicago)—Became famous when he supplied the "Pentagon Papers" to the *New York Times* in 1971.

MAX M. FISHER (1908-   )—A long-time force in the Republican party and on the National Committee, he was one of the leading Republican fund raisers and served as a Special Adviser to President Nixon.

LOUIS HARRIS (1921-   , New Haven, Conn.)—One of the most famous pollsters in the world, he is Director of the Time–Harris Poll.

BRUCE HERSCHENSON (1932-   , Milwaukee)—Special Assistant to President Nixon, 1972–1974.

SOLOMON HIRSCH (1839-1902, Württemberg, Germany)—A leading merchant in the state of Oregon, he was President of the Oregon Senate and lost an election for the U.S. Senate by one vote in the closest senatorial battle in American history.

NATHAN JAFFA—Lieutenant Governor of New Mexico Territory in the late 1800s. He was also Mayor of Roswell and Sante Fe.

LOUIS J. LEFKOWITZ (1904-   , New York City)—The long-time Attorney General of New York.

ARTHUR LEVITT (1900-   , Brooklyn)—Comptroller of the state of New York.

JOSEPH I. LIEBERMAN (1942-   , Stamford, Conn.)—Became Majority Leader of the Connecticut State Senate in 1975.

SAMUEL LUBELL (1911-   , Poland)—A leading public opinion expert and commentator and the author of *The Future of American Politics*.

JULIUS C. MICHAELSON (1922-   , Salem, Mass.)—Attorney General of Rhode Island.

CHARLES MICHELSON (1869-1948, Virginia City, Nev.)—Was Publicity Director of the Democratic National Committee and made major innovations in the way political campaigns were run and the use of media in them. He had earlier been the Washington Bureau Chief of the *New York World*.

MORTIZ PINNER (1828-1909, Prussia)—A leading abolitionist and one of the founders of the Republican party.

JOSEPH M. PROSKAUER (1877-1971, Mobile, Ala.)—A leading American lawyer, he was Alfred E. Smith's most intimate political adviser.

MAXWELL M. RABB (1910-   , Boston)—One of President Eisenhower's lawyers and Secretary of the Cabinet in the 1950s.

ALEX ROSE (1898-1976, Warsaw)—Born Olesh Royz. The leading force in the Liberal party.

FRED ROSENBLATT (1914-   , New York City)—Press Secretary for Senator Estes Kefauver, 1952–1956.

SAMUEL I. ROSENMAN (1896-   , San Antonio, Tex.)—A close adviser to President Roosevelt, he wrote many of his most famous speeches. The term *New Deal* was his idea.

JACK RUBY (1911-1967)—Born Jacob Rubenstein. He killed Lee Harvey Oswald in Dallas in 1963.

GLORIA SCHAFFER (1930-   , New London, Conn.)—Secretary of State of Connecticut. She lost a bid for the U.S. Senate in 1978.

ROBERT L. SHEVIN (1934-   , Miami)—Attorney General of Florida. He lost an election for the Democratic nomination as Governor.

THEODORE C. SORENSEN (1928-   , Lincoln, Nebr.)—Special Counsel to JFK and LBJ. His mother was Jewish.

HENRY D. SPALDING (1915-   , New York City)—Editor of *Hollywood Talent News*. He originated the slogan "I Like Ike," which Eisenhower used with great success in his two presidential campaigns.

ADAM WALINSKY (1937-   , New York City)—A close associate of Robert Kennedy, he wrote most of the senator's speeches.

BEN J. WATTENBERG (1933- , New York City)—A major speechwriter for LBJ and a leading expert on American politics, he wrote *The Real Majority*.

AUSTRIANS

RUDOLF GOLDSCHEID (1870-1932, Vienna)—One of the world's leading pacifists, he was a noted sociologist who helped to establish the German Sociological Society.

JOSEPH REDLICH (1869-1936, Göding, Moravia)—Twice Minister of Finance in Austria. He became a Christian.

BRITISH

EDMUND DELL (1921-)—Minister of State, Board of Trade, 1968-1969; Minister of State, Department of Employment and Productivity, 1969-1970.

SIR LOUIS H. GLUCKSTEIN (1897-)—A long-time MP from the Conservative party.

SIR FRANCIS H. GOLDSMID (1808-1878)—Served as MP in the House of Lords, as did his sons.

PHILIP GOODHART (1925-)—An MP and an important figure in the Conservative party.

SIR PERCY HARRIS (1876-1952, London)—Served as Deputy Leader of the Liberal party in Parliament.

LORD LESLIE HORE-BELISHA (1898-1957)—Served as Minister of Transport and then Secretary of State for War in the 1930s.

LORD BARNETT JANNER (1892- , Barry, Wales)—Served in Parliament representing both the Liberals and the Labor party (but not at the same time).

GRENVILLE E. JANNER (1928-)—Entered Parliament when his father, Lord Barnett Janner, stepped down.

NORMAN H. LEVER (1914- , Manchester)—A Labor MP who made important contributions as an adviser on fiscal matters.

LORD EMANUEL SHINWELL (b. 1884- , London)—A leading Labor politician, he served as Minister of Mines, Minister of Fuel and Power, Minister for War, and Minister of Defense.

SAMUEL S. SILVERMAN (1895-1968)—Led a long and finally successful struggle to end the death sentence in England.

CANADIANS

I. H. ASPER (1932- , Minnedosa, Manitoba)—Head of Manitoba's Liberal party in the 1970s.

MORRIS A. GRAY (1889-1966)—A leading figure in the development of the New Democratic party in Manitoba and nationally.

BENJAMIN GUSS (1905- , Dorbian, Lithuania)—A noted lawyer, he was National Chairman of the Canadian Young Conservatives.

DUTCH

ANNA GOUDSMIT (1933-)—Helped found the Democrats 66 party in Holland and served in the Dutch Parliament.

ASSER B. KLEEREKOPER (1880-1943)—A leading Dutch socialist politician and a long-time member of Parliament.

JOSEPH LIMBURG (1866-1940)—Helped establish the Dutch Liberal Democratic party. He died by suicide.

CAREL H. F. POLAK (1909- , Rotterdam)—A Liberal party senator, he had served as Dutch Minister of Justice.

EDUARD VAN THIJN (1934-)—A leader of the Dutch Labor party.

FRENCH

ABRAHAM SCHRAMECK (1867-1948, St. Etienne)—Minister of the Interior of France on two occasions, Minister of Justice of France, and Governor-General of Madagascar.

MAURICE SCHUMANN (1911- , Paris)—Foreign Minister (twice), Minister of Social Affairs, and Minister of State for Scientific Research. He became a Christian.

PIERRE VILLON (1901- , Soultz)—Born Pierre Gintzburger. Served in the National Assembly and was a leading member of the French Communist party.

GERMANS

WOLF FRANKENBURGER (1827-1889, Obbach)—A prominent member of the Reichstag in the 1870s.

LEVIN GOLDSCHMIDT (1829-1897)—A leader of the National Liberal party and a noted jurist.

PAUL HIRSCH (1868-1938)—Prime Minister of Prussia in the short-lived revolutionary government at the end of World War I.

BRUNO A. KAFKA (1881-1931, Prague)—One of the founders of the German Democratic party. He became a Christian.

OTTO LANDSBERG (1869-1957, Rybnik)—The famous Weimar Republic Minister of Justice of Germany before the rise of Hitler.

EDUARD LASKER (1829-1884, Posen, Poland)—Founder of the Liberal Union which opposed authoritarianism in Germany. He earlier was founder and leader of the German National Liberal party.

HERBERT WEICHMANN (1896-)—As President of Bundestag in the 1960s, he was Acting President of Germany whenever the President was out of the country.

IRISH

ELLEN BISCHOFFSHEIM (1857-1933)—The first woman to become a Senator after Irish independence.

BENJAMIN BRISCOE (1934-)—A member of Dail (Irish Parliament), he is the son of the famous former Lord Mayor of Dublin.

ITALIANS

JOSEPH FINZI (1815-1886, Mantua)—A leader in the struggle for a unified Italy and a leader of the Italian Senate.

GUIDO JUNG—Italian Minister of Finance, 1932–1935—a Jew in the fascist government.

LEONE ROMANIN JACUR (1847-1928)—Italian Undersecretary for the Interior and Undersecretary of State for Public Works around the turn of the century.

RUSSIANS

NAPHTALI FRIEDMAN (1863-1921)—Represented the Russian Constitutional Democratic party in the Duma.

VICTOR MANDELBERG (1870-1944)—A doctor, he served in the Second Duma in 1907.

SOLOMON SCHWARZ (1883- , Vilna)—One of the leading Mensheviks, he spent time in prison after the 1917 revolution.

MARK VISHNIAK—Secretary of the Constituent Assembly selected after the abdication of the Czar in 1917.

SOUTH AFRICANS AND RHODESIANS

ELLY BROOMBERG (1915-   , Johannesburg)—A member of the Rhodesian Parliament from 1969.

MORRIS KENTRIDGE (1881-1964, Lithuania)—A member of the South African Parliament for 38 years.

JOEL PINCUS (1907-   , Ladybrand, South Africa)—A member of the Rhodesian Senate from 1970.

HELEN SUZMAN (1917-   , Germiston, South Africa)—The most famous anti-apartheid politician, she founded the Progressive party in that country to fight for equal rights for black Africans.

OTHERS

RAFAEL SERFATY BENAZAR (1919-   , Los Teques, Venezuela)—A Senator in Venezuela from the early 1960s.

JO BENKO (1925-   , Oslo)—Served in the Parliament of Norway.

DAVID Z. FARBSTEIN (1868-1953, Warsaw)—Served in the Parliament of Switzerland for more than 20 years.

JACOBO GUELMAN (1900-   , Argentina)—First a Deputy and then a Senator representing the Liberal party in Uruguay.

DANIEL HART (1800-1852)—A leading lawyer in Jamaica, he served in the island's House of Assembly.

ANGEL FAIVOVICH HITZCOVICH (1900-   , Argentina)—President of the Radical party in Chile and Vice-President of the Chilean Senate.

SANTIAGO I. NUDELMAN (1904-   , Medanos, Argentina)—A Deputy in the Argentine Federal Chamber for almost ten years.

JACOBO SCHAULSON NUMHAUSER (1917-   , Santiago, Chile)—President of the Chilean Chamber of Deputies in the early 1960s.

DAVID SCHAPIRA (1901-   , Carlos Casares, Argentina)—A Senator and Deputy in Argentina.

AARAO STEINBRUCH (1915-   , Pôrto Alegre, Brazil)—President of the Brazilian Labor party, he served in both the Chamber and the Senate.

MILITARY FIGURES

AMERICANS

JULIUS O. ADLER (1892-1955, Chattanooga, Tenn.)—A Major General in the U.S. Army, he was Commanding Officer of the 77th Infantry Division in World War II.

WILLIAM S. BELLER (1919-   , Cleveland)—A Senior Editor from 1960 of *Missiles and Rockets*, one of the leading military journals in the U.S.

JACOB BESER—A Lieutenant in the U.S. Air Force, he was Radar Officer on the *Enola Gay*, the B-29 that dropped the atomic bomb on Hiroshima.

CLAUDE BLOCH (1878-1967, Woodbury, Ky.)—A full Admiral in the U.S. Navy, Bloch commanded the battleship *California* and became Commander in Chief of the U.S. Fleet in 1938.

JOSEPH BLOOMFIELD—A U.S. Brigadier General in the War of 1812.

LEOPOLD BLUMENBERG (1827-1876, Brandenburg, Prussia)—A Brevet Brigadier General of Volunteers in the Union Army, he commanded a Maryland Volunteer Regiment. He was badly wounded in combat at Antietam.

BERNARD BRODIE (1910- , Chicago)—A Professor of Political Science at UCLA, he is one of the world's leading naval strategists, best known for his *Guide to Naval Strategy* (1942, 1964) and *War and Politics* (1973).

ABRAHAM COHN—Won the Congressional Medal of Honor in the Civil War.

ABEL DAVIS (1878-1937, Lithuania)—A Brigadier General in the U.S. Army.

DAVID C. DE LEON (1816-1872, Camden, S.C.)—Surgeon General of the Confederate Army in the Civil War.

MAX EINSTEIN—A Brigadier General commanding the 59th New York Volunteer Regiment in the Civil War.

EDWARD ELLSBERG (1891- , New Haven)—A Rear Admiral in the U.S. Navy, he was the world's leading expert in the field of recovering sunken submarines. He won the Distinguished Service Medal.

IMMANUEL ESTERMANN (1900- , Berlin)—A leading physicist involved with the Manhattan Project, he was the Scientific Director of the Office of Naval Research in London.

HERMAN FELDMAN (1889- , New York)—A Major General and Quartermaster of the U.S. Army in the late 1940s and early 1950s.

MILTON J. FOREMAN (1862-1935)—A Lieutenant General in the U.S. Army, he was one of the founders of the American Legion (and later its National Commander).

DAVID S. FRANKS (1743?-1793)—Lieutenant Colonel in the Continental army in the revolutionary war.

ISAAC GANS—Won the Congressional Medal of Honor in the Civil War.

SYDNEY G. GUMPERTZ (1879-1953)—Was awarded the Congressional Medal of Honor.

EDWARD S. GREENBAUM (1890-1970, New York City)—A Brigadier General who received the Distinguished Service Medal.

LEVI M. HARBY—A Captain of the U.S. Navy and a gunboat Commander during the attack on Galveston during the Civil War.

HENRY HELLER—Won the Congressional Medal of Honor during the Civil War.

REUBEN E. HERSHFIELD—A Lieutenant Colonel, he commanded Fort Leavenworth, Kans., during frontier days.

CHARLES W. HOFFMAN—Awarded the Congressional Medal of Honor in World War I.

ROBERT S. HOROWITZ (1924- , Baltimore)—Associate Editor of the *Army Times* since 1951.

PHILLIP J. JOACHIMSON (1818-1890)—A Brigadier General in the Union Army in the Civil War.

LOUIS M. JOSEPHTAL (1869-1929, New Rochelle, N.Y.)—A Rear Admiral in the U.S. Navy.

NICHOLAS KALDOR (1908- , Budapest)—A British subject, Kaldor served as Chief of the Economic Planning Staff of the U.S. Strategic Bombing Survey of World War II, the results of which had a profound effect on the nation's postwar defense posture.

LEOPOLD KARPELES—Fought for the Union during the Civil War and won the Congressional Medal of Honor.

PHILIP C. KATZ—Won the Congressional Medal of Honor in World War I.

BENJAMIN KAUFMAN (b. 1894)—Won the Congressional Medal of Honor.

JULIUS KLEIN (1901- , Chicago)—A Major General in the U.S. Army, he was later an active figure in national Democratic party politics.

FREDERICK KNEFLER—A resident of Indianapolis, he was a Major General in the Union Army during the Civil War.

MELVIN L. KRULEWITCH (1895-1978, New York City)—A Major General in the U.S. Marine Corps, he had a distinguished career as a public servant in New York State.

CHARLES LAUCHEIMER (1859-1920)—A General in the U.S. Army at the turn of the century.

SAMUEL T. LAWTON (1894-   , Peoria, Ill.)—A Major General, he commanded the 33rd Division early in World War II.

BENJAMIN LEVY—Won the Congressional Medal of Honor during the Civil War.

CHARLES LEVY—A Lieutenant in the U.S. Air Force, he was the bombardier on the B-29 that dropped the atomic bomb on Nagasaki.

JONAS P. LEVY (1807-1883, Philadelphia)—A Commander in the U.S. Navy during the war with Mexico, he was the Commanding Officer in Veracruz during the American occupation of that city.

URIAH PHILLIPS LEVY (1792-1862, Philadelphia)—A famous figure in U.S. naval history, he was Commodore of the U.S. Fleet in the Mediterranean. He is most famous for his struggle to eliminate corporal punishment in the Navy.

RAYMOND LUSSMAN—Won the Congressional Medal of Honor in World War II.

EDWARD N. LUTTWAK (1942-   , Arad, Rumania)—A leading U.S. military strategist and the author of many books, including *Coup d'État–A Practical Handbook* (1968).

ADOLPH MARIX—A Rear Admiral, he was the first Jew to achieve this rank in the U.S. Navy. He was Commander of the battleship *Maine*, but not when it exploded in Havana Harbor.

MAURICE MATLOFF (1915-   , New York City)—Chief Historian of the Department of the Army.

ALFRED MORDECAI (1804-1887, Warrenton, N.C.)—Graduated first in his class at West Point and went on to a distinguished career that saw him command the Frankford and Watervliet military arsenals. He was the author of the standard Ordnance Manual used by the U.S. Army in the 1800s.

ABRAHAM C. MYERS—A South Carolinian and a Colonel in the U.S. Army, he commanded Fort Myers, Florida. That city is named for him.

DAVID OBRANSKI—Won the Congressional Medal of Honor fighting for the Union in the Civil War.

JOHN ORDRAONAUX (1778-1841)—A naval Captain, he was responsible for the capture of ten British vessels, including a frigate, in the War of 1812.

IRVING J. PHILLIPSON (b. 1882)—A Major General, he was Chief of Staff of the U.S. Second Corps during World War II.

NORMAN POLMAR (1938-   , Washington, D.C.)—A leading naval strategist and the author of *Soviet Naval Power* (1972).

HYMAN RICKOVER (1900-   , Russia)—The legendary figure who is considered the father of the atomic submarine. He was promoted to full Admiral in 1973.

MAURICE ROSE (1899-1945, Middletown, Conn.)—A Major General and Chief of Staff of the Second Armored Division, he commanded units in North Africa and in Germany, where he died in combat shortly before the end of the war. He was awarded the Congressional Medal of Honor, one of the highest-ranking soldiers ever to receive this award.

EDWARD S. SALOMON (1836-1913)—A fighting officer in the Union Army, he became Governor of Washington Territory after the Civil War.

SAMUEL SAMPLER—Won the Congressional Medal of Honor in World War I.

WILLIAM SAWELSON—Won the Congressional Medal of Honor in World War I.

HERBERT Y. SCHANDLER (1928- , Asheville, N.C.)—One of the most heavily decorated soldiers in the Vietnam war, he won four Legions of Merit, thirteen Air Medals, three Bronze Stars, and three Vietnam Crosses of Gallantry. He was a battalion commander in that conflict and wrote the Tet Offensive parts of the Pentagon Papers. He became a Specialist in National Defense for the Congressional Research Service of the Library of Congress.

BENJAMIN STERNBERG (1914-)—A Major General with U.S. forces in Vietnam.

JOSEPH STRAUSS (1861-1920)—A Rear Admiral and Commander of the battleship *Nevada*. A destroyer in the U.S. Navy was named after him.

LEWIS STRAUSS—The distinguished American who was a Rear Admiral in World War II.

MAXIMILLIAN TOCH (1864-1946, New York City)—A chemist, he developed the Toch system, one of the most widely used methods of camouflage.

AUSTRALIANS

LEONARD KEYSOR—A Private in the Australian army, he won the Victoria Cross for bravery during fighting at Gallipoli in World War I.

SAMUEL LANDAU (1915- , Melbourne)—Became Secretary of the Australian Navy Department in the mid-1960s.

SIR JOHN MONASH (1865-1931, Melbourne)—An active member of the Jewish community, he became one of the most famous generals in Australian history as the Commander of all Australian forces in Europe in World War I.

SIR CHARLES ROSENTHAL—A Major General commanding all Australian and New Zealand artillery in World War I.

AUSTRIANS, HUNGARIANS, AND AUSTRO-HUNGARIANS

VILMOS BOHN (1880-1947)—Commander in Chief of the Hungarian army during the brief Marxist regime in Hungary in 1919.

ALEXANDER VON EIS (1832-1921, Piesling)—A Major General in the Hapsburg army, he received the Order of the Iron Crown and the Order of the Maria Theresa, two of the highest military awards in the empire. He was also a crack shot who killed several men in duels.

MORITZ VON FUNK (1831-1905)—A Commander in the Hapsburg navy.

SAMU HAZAI (1851-1942, Rimazombat)—Director of the Officer's School of the Hungarian army. He was a Field Marshal-Lieutenant and Hungarian Minister of Defense in 1910.

ADOLPH KORNHABER (1856-1925)—Field Marshal-Lieutenant in the Hungarian army at the turn of the century.

TOBIAS VON OESTERREICHER (1831-1893)—Rose to Rear Admiral in the Hapsburg navy.

SIEGFRIED POPPER (1848-1933)—A Rear Admiral in the Ottoman navy and in charge of all naval construction.

EDUARD VON SCHWEITZER (1844-1920)—A Field Marshal-Lieutenant in the Austro-Hungarian army. He would have gone further in his career, but he refused to convert from Judaism.

JOSEPH SINGER (1797-1871, Lemberg)—Chief of Staff of the Austrian army in Italy, he became a Field Marshal Lieutenant.

EMIL VON SOMMER (1868-1946, Bukovina)—A Major General, he led the Austrian forces that captured Burgenland.

SIMON VOGEL (1850-1917, Karczag)—A Major General in the Hungarian army, he became Governor of Sarajevo in the early 1900s.

BRITISH

SIR EDWARD BEDDINGTON (1884-1966)—A Brigadier in the British army, he served as the Deputy Director of Military Intelligence in World War II.

WILLIAM BEDDINGTON (b. 1893)—A Major General in the British army, he was on the Staff of the Joint Supreme Headquarters of the Allied Expeditionary Forces in Europe in World War II.

HERMAN BONDI (1919- , Vienna)—A mathematician of international repute, he was Chief Scientific Adviser to the British Ministry of Defense in 1970. He had earlier been Director-General of the European Space Research Organization and had done pioneering research on radar during and after World War II.

ABRAHAM BRISCOE (b. 1892, Ireland)—An Air Commodore in the RAF.

PAUL A. CULLEN (1909- , Newcastle)—Rose to the rank of Major General in the British army.

JAMES A. D'AVIGDOR-GOLDSMID (1912-)—A Major General, he commanded the British territorial army.

ALBERT E. W. GOLDSMID (1846-1904, Poona, India)—A Colonel in the British army, he was one of the outstanding soldiers in the Boer War.

SIR FREDERICK J. GOLDSMID (1818-1908)—A Major General in the British army. The first telegraph lines in Persia (now Iran) were built under his supervision.

BARNARD GOLDSTONE (b. 1896)—A Brigadier in the British army.

T. GOULD—A Lieutenant in World War II, he won the Victoria Cross.

ROBERT D. Q. HENRIQUES (1905-1967)—A Colonel on the Staff of Field Marshall Bernard Montgomery and a member of the British Commandos, he won the Silver Star, awarded by the U.S. Army.

DAVID HIRSCH—A Captain in World War II, he won the Victoria Cross.

FREDERICK H. KISCH (1888-1943, Darjeeling, India)—Headed the British Military Intelligence Section at the Paris Peace Conference after World War I. Kisch was an expert in mine warfare and was a Brigadier and Chief Engineer of the British Eighth Army in World War II. He was killed by a German mine.

STEPHEN LAKEMAN (1812-1897)—An Englishman, he was a General in the Ottoman army and was known as "Mazar Pasha."

SIR BEN LOCKSPEISER (b. 1891, London)—Directed the British Air Defense Department before World War II. During the war he directed research at the Air Ministry and became Director General of the Ministry of Aircraft Production. After the war he served as Chief Scientist at the Ministry of Supply.

EDMUND MEYERS (1906-)—Was Chief Engineer of the British troops in the Suez Canal Zone.

FREDERICK MORRIS (1888-1941)—A Brigadier in the British army.

BERNARD SCHLESINGER (1896-1945)—A Brigadier in the British army.

HERBERT SELIGMAN (1872-1951, London)—Commander of Artillery in the British Seventh Division in World War I, he later commanded the Artillery Branch of the Cavalry Corps.

SOLOMON J. SOLOMON (1860-1927, London)—Once President of the British Royal Society of Artists, he was a leading authority on camouflage and the author of the standard *Strategic Camouflage*.

SIR DAVID XIMENES (1776-1848, London)—A Lieutenant General in the British army, he fought in campaigns all over Europe.

CANADIANS

ISADORE C. CORNBLATT (1914- , Ontario)—An Air Vice Marshall in the RCAF, he was Assistant Chief of Staff of the NATO Air Forces.

MAURICE LIPTON (1916- , Sydney Harbour, Nova Scotia)—Director of all RCAF training during World War II, he became Chief of Operations of the RCAF in 1959.

ROBERT P. ROTHSCHILD (1914-)—A Major General and Quartermaster General of the Canadian army.

FRENCH

BERNARD ABRAHAM (1824-1900)—A Brigadier General in the French army.

RENÉ ALEXANDER (1864-1931)—Rose to the rank of Brigadier General before World War I.

RENÉ BLOCH (1923- , Frankfort)—A Captain in the French navy and a well-known aeronautical engineer, he was Technical Director of Aviation for that service in the 1950s and later served in the Ministry of Defense.

PIERRE BORIS—A Major General in the French army between the world wars.

GABRIEL G. BRISAC (1817-1890)—A Brigadier General in the French army in the last half of the 1800s.

MARTIN CERFBEER—A Colonel in the French army during the 1800s, he won the Legion of Honor Medal.

AMRAM DARMON (1815-1878, Algiers)—A Chevalier of the Legion of Honor and an outstanding French soldier.

DARIUS P. DASSAULT (b. 1882, Paris)—Born Bloch, a member of the famed French military family, he became a General d'Armée, commanded the Fifth Army Corps in World War II, and later served as Governor of Paris and Inspector General of Artillery.

MARCEL DASSAULT (1892- , Paris)—Born Bloch. Head of one of the most famous aircraft design firms in the world, he became a Catholic and changed his name to Dassault after his liberation from a Nazi concentration camp. His company produced the Mystère and Mirage aircraft, both of which became famous in the hands of Israeli pilots. Dassault had a warm relationship with Israel and Israeli officials.

JUSTIN DENNERY (1847-1928)—A Major General in the French army.

GEDEON GEISMAR (1863-1931)—A Brigadier General before World War I.

PAUL E. GRUMBACH (1861-1931)—Another Brigadier General in the French army.

JULES HEYMANN (1850-1928)—A Major General commanding important French units at the turn of the century.

ADOLPHE HINSTEIN (1820-1890)—A Brigadier General who fought in the Franco-Prussian War.

LOUIS KAHN (1895-1967, Versailles)—One of the most important French naval engineers, his pioneering designs of aircraft carriers and cruisers were widely imitated. He was French Minister of Defense in the early 1950s.

AIMÉ LAMBERT (1825-1896, Nancy)—A Lieutenant General, he was Commander of the French Occupation Army in Tunisia in the 1870s.

CAMILLE BARUCH LEVI (1860-1933)—A Major General, he was one of the highest-ranking Jewish officers in the French army at the turn of the century.

LUCIEN LEVI (1859-1932)—A Brigadier General in the French army.

ABRAHAM E. LEVY (1826-1917)—A Brigadier General in the late 1800s.

ALEXANDRE MARCQUEFOY—A Captain in the army of Napoleon, who personally made him a Chevalier of the Legion of Honor.

LEOPOLD SEE (1822-1904, Bergheim)—A Lieutenant General, a veteran of the Crimean War, and a Chevalier of the Legion of Honor.

ADRIENNE WEIL (1903- , Paris)—An outstanding naval engineer, she did much important work for the French navy.

ANDRÉ WEILLER (1865-1940)—A Brigadier General in the French army.

EDGAR WOLFFE (1840-1901)—A Brigadier General in the French army.

MARC-JEAN-JEROME WOLFFE (1776-1848)—A Brigadier General and the Commander of the First Cavalry Brigade of Napoleon's army.

GERMANS

ELLIS DUNITZ (1888-1913)—Directed the training operations of the German Naval Air Service and was a pioneer aviator in Germany.

LOUISE MANUEL GRAFEMUS (1785-1852)—In one of the strangest incidents in military history, she disguised herself as a man and enlisted in the Prussian army. Her motive was to locate her missing husband, and in the course of her search she was wounded in combat, became a Sergeant Major, and won the Iron Cross.

LUDWIG LOEWE (1839-1886, Heiligenstadt, Germany) and ISIDOR LOEWE (1848-1910)—Ludwig developed one of the largest plants producing rifles in Germany. Later his son, Isidor, merged their factory with the famous Mauser company and it became the largest plant in the world.

WALTER VON MOSSNER (1846-1932, Berlin)—Baptized so he could advance through the ranks of the German military, he became a Major General, commanded the famous Third Cavalry Division, and was a member of the German General Staff.

INDIANS

The Jewish community of India has produced a surprisingly high number of notable military figures considering its tiny percentage in the general population.

JACK F. R. JACOB (1923- , Calcutta)—A Major General and the Chief of Staff of the Indian Eastern Command in the war against Pakistan in 1971, which saw the emergence of Bangladesh as an independent state.

JOSEPH E. JHIRAD—A distinguished Indian combat soldier who attained the rank of Colonel before he was killed in action in the 1965 war with Pakistan.

BENJAMIN A. SAMSON (1916- , Poona)—The youngest man ever to achieve the rank of Rear Admiral in the history of the Indian navy. One of the most famous naval officers in the country's history, he was made Commander of the Indian Fleet in the 1965 war with Pakistan.

JONATHAN R. SAMSON—A Major General in the Indian Army, he directed the Armoured Vehicle Factory in that country in the 1970s.

ITALIANS

GIACOMO ALAGIA (1876-1947)—A Major General in the Italian army.

CARLO ARCHIVOLTI (1873-1944)—A Major General in the Italian army.

ALDO ASCOLI (1882-1956)—A distinguished Rear Admiral of the Italian navy. He became Commander of the Fleet in the Aegean Sea in the early 1930s.

ETTORE ASCOLI (1873-1943)—A General of Artillery and an Army Corps Commander in the Italian army, he was killed in action fighting the Germans at the age of 70.

ARMANDO BACHI (1883-1943, Verona)—An outstanding artillery and motorized corps Commander, he was a Lieutenant General. He was killed in a Nazi concentration camp.

AGUSTO CAPON (1872-1944)—An Admiral in the Italian navy and its Chief of Intelligence in the early 1930s. He was killed in a Nazi concentration camp.

ACHILLE COEN (1851-1925)—A Lieutenant General in the Italian army.

RAIMONDO FOA (1877-1940, Casale Monferrato)—A Lieutenant General in the Italian army who fought in World War I.

ENRICO GUASTALLA (1828-1903, Guastalla)—A Major in the army of Garibaldi, who was fighting to unify Italy. He became a member of the Italian Parliament.

GIORGIO LIUZZI (b. 1896)—Chief of Staff of the Italian army in the late 1950s.

GUIDO LIUZZI (1866-1942, Reggio Emilia)—A Lieutenant General and army corps Commander during and after World War I, he was Director of the Italian Military Academy.

PAOLO MARANI (1884-1950)—A Vice-Admiral in the Italian navy.

ANGELO MODENA (b. 1867, Reggio Emilia)—A Major General and army corps Commander.

FRANCO NUNES (1868-1943)—An Admiral in the Italian navy.

ADOLFO OLIVETTI (1878-1944)—A member of a famous Italian family, he was a Major General in the army.

GIUSEPPE OTTOLENGHI (1838-1904, Sabionetta)—A Lieutenant General in the Italian army, he became Minister of War in 1902.

EMANUELE PUGLIESE (b. 1874)—An army corps Commander and the Military Commander of Sardinia in the early 1930s.

UMBERTO PUGLIESE (1880-1961, Alessandria)—A world-renowned naval architect who designed many famous Italian battleships, he was General Inspector of the Naval Corps of Engineers. His Pugliese Water-Line was employed to salvage major ships.

GUIDO SEGRE (1871-1942)—An Admiral in the Italian navy.

ROBERTO SEGRE (1872-1936)—Chief of Staff of the Italian Fifth Army Corps in World War I, he rose to the rank of Lieutenant General.

PAOLO SUPINO (b. 1893, Paris)—A full General and the Commanding Officer of the elite Centauro Armored Division in the late 1950s, he had earlier served as Commander of the Italian War College.

RUBINO VENTURA (1792-1858, Finalenell, Emilia)—Commanded an Indian army against Afghanistan forces in northwestern India. He was married to an Indian ranee.

POLES

BEREK JOSELEWICZ (1770-1809, Kretinga)—A Colonel in the Polish Legion of Napoleon, he won the Cross of the Legion of Honor. He was killed in combat.

BERNHARD S. MOND (1887-1944, Stanislav)—A Major General in the Polish army, he was commanding officer of an entire army corps in World War II.

RUSSIANS

I. S. BESKIN—A Lieutenant General, he commanded large units at the Battle of Stalingrad in World War II.

IVAN D. CHERNYAKHOVSKI (1906-1945, Uman)—A full General in the Red Army, he retook the cities of Vilna, Grodno, Minsk, and Kiev from the Germans. He was Commander of the Third Belorussian Army. At the time of his death in combat late in the war, he was the youngest Russian commander in history. He was made a Hero of the Soviet Union and a town was renamed in his honor.

CHAIM DISKIN (1923-   )—A Major General in the Soviet Medical Corps and a Hero of the Soviet Union.

LEV DOVATOR—A Major General, he died in combat resisting the German onslaught in 1941.

DAVID A. DRAGUNSKI(Y) (1910-   )—A Lieutenant General and two-time Hero of the Soviet Union, he was frequently paraded before the press to tell how wonderful life is for Jews in the U.S.S.R.

ISRAEL FISANOVICH—A submarine commander in the Soviet navy in World War II and a Hero of the Soviet Union.

YEFIM M. FOMIN—Carried out a heroic defense of the Brest-Litovsk sector at the time of the Nazi invasion in 1941. He was captured and killed by the Germans, and was posthumously declared a Hero of the Soviet Union.

YAN B. GAMARNIK (1894-1938)—One of the most powerful figures in the Red Army for 20 years as its chief political officer, he also edited its journal. He was a victim of purges of the late 1930s—he "committed suicide."

POLINA GELMAN—A pilot in World War II, she became a Hero of the Soviet Union.

J. B. GOLDBERG (1884-1946)—Fought side-by-side with Lenin in the civil war following the revolution and later became Deputy Commander of the Red Air Force.

ILYA B. KATUNIN (1908-1944)—An air force pilot who became a Hero of the Soviet Union.

JACOB KREISER (1905-1969)—A General of the Soviet army, and a Hero of the Soviet Union, Kreiser commanded several armies in World War II, and in the 1960s was the Commanding Officer of the sensitive Far East region opposite China.

SEMION KRIVOSHEIN—A Lieutenant General whose troops were among the first to enter Berlin in World War II.

LAZAR LICHTMACHER (b. 1880)—Was awarded the St. George Cross, one of the highest decorations in the czarist army, for his bravery under fire in the Russo-Japanese War in 1905.

LILA LITVAK—Yet another woman pilot made a Hero of the Soviet Union in World War II.

LEV Z. MEKHLIS (1889-1953, Odessa)—Was in charge of the powerful political arm of the Soviet army in the late 1930s. A Lieutenant General in the war, he won four Lenin Medals and later became Minister for State Control in the Soviet government.

HIRSH PLASKOV—A Lieutenant General, he was Artillery Commander of the Second Guards Army during its drive on Berlin in World War II.

MICHAEL PLOTKIN—A Hero of the Soviet Union, he participated in the first Soviet air raid on Berlin in World War II.

ISAAK M. RABINOVICH (b. 1886)—A Major General in the Soviet Army in charge of the Engineering Corps.

YAACOV SHMUSHEKEVICH (1902-1941, Rokiskis, Lithuania)—Twice a Hero of the Soviet Union, he became a Colonel General in control of all the Soviet Air Forces in 1941, but was mysteriously executed for treason within weeks of assuming his post.

GRIGORI STERN (d. 1940)—One of the most outstanding military figures in this book, Stern was a General in command of all Soviet armies in the Far East, where he conquered Mongolia for the Soviet Union. He later died in combat in Finland. Earlier he had served as Chief Adviser to the Spanish Republican Army in the mid-1930s.

HARVEY WEINRUB—A Lieutenant General who commanded forces at the Battle of Stalingrad.

YONAH YAKIR—A famous General of the Red Army during the Russian civil war, he later pioneered the use of armored vehicles in the Soviet military. He was serving as Military Commander of the Ukraine and was on the Supreme Military Staff when he fell victim to the purges and was killed.

SOUTH AFRICANS

SIR DAVID HARRIS (1852-1942)—A Lieutenant Colonel who commanded troops defending Kimberley during the famous siege of that city in the Boer War. He was one of the owners of the great De Beers Consolidated Mines.

OTHERS

SIDNEY J. VAN DEN BERGH (b. 1898, Rotterdam)—Became the Dutch Minister of Defense in 1959.

LOUIS BERNHEIM (1861-1931, Saint-Josse-ten-Noode, Belgium)—A Lieutenant General in the Belgian army, he commanded three divisions during World War I and was heavily decorated.

SAM DREBEN (1878-1925)—An American mercenary, he fought for and against countries all over the world, including Mexico, Nicaragua, and China.

MORRIS A. "TWO-GUN" COHEN (1887-1970, London)—The legendary soldier of fortune and a friend of Sun-Yat-sen (for whom he trained and developed the Kuomintang army) who was actually the *de facto* Secretary of Defense of China. Captured by the Japanese in World War II, he later lived in Canada.

JOSE B. SCHER—A Brigadier General and air force Commander in Chile in the 1970s.

ERNEST E. WIENER (1882-1973, Brussels)—Commander of the Belgian Military Academy, 1929-1936, he became a Major General in the Belgian army.

LABOR LEADERS

DAVID DUBINSKY (b. 1892, Brest-Litovsk)—The great leader of the International Ladies Garment Workers Union and a major figure in the labor movement in the United States.

MORRIS FEINSTONE (1878-1945, Warsaw)—Helped found the Labor party in Great Britain and was also active in labor affairs in the U.S.

NATHANIEL GOLDFINGER (1917-1976)—Was Chief Economist of the AFL-CIO for many years.

SAMUEL GOMPERS (1850-1924, London)—The father of the labor movement in the U.S. and its leading advocate for a generation.

SIDNEY HILLMAN (1887-1946, Zagare, Lithuania)—A founder of the CIO and a close adviser to FDR, he was a political activist and President of the Amalgamated Clothing Workers of America.

DAVID A. MORSE (1907- , New York City)—A former Assistant Secretary of Labor and Director General of the ILO, he was a leading labor lawyer and the General Counsel of the National Labor Relations Board.

JOSEPH A. PADWAY (1891-1947, Leeds, England)—Served as General Counsel of the AFL when that organization was formed.

SELIG PERLMAN (1888-1959, Bialystok, Poland)—A leading American labor historian and economist, he wrote *A Theory of the Labor Movement*.

JACOB S. POTOFSKY (1894- , Russia)—A leading figure in the American labor movement, he was Vice-President of the AFL-CIO.

JOSEPH L. RAUH (1911- , Cincinnati)—General Counsel of the UAW (United Automobile Workers) and the lawyer representing Joseph Yablonski in the United Mineworkers power struggle, he was one of the leading labor lawyers in the U.S. and helped to found the Americans for Democratic Action, of which he served as National Chairman.

LUDWIG ROSENBERG (1903- , Berlin)—Chairman of the Federation of Trade Unions in Germany in the 1960s.

FRANK ROSENBLUM (1887-1973, New York City)—The long-time Vice-President of the CIO.

ROSE SCHNEIDERMAN (1882-1972, Saven, Poland)—The long-time President of the Women's Trade Union League, she was one of the founders of the International Ladies Garment Workers, and the leading woman unionist in the U.S.

ALBERT SHANKER (1928-   , New York City)—The powerful President of the United Federation of Teachers.

CIVIL RIGHTS LEADERS

AUGUST BONDI (?-1907, Vienna)—One of the early abolitionists and followers of John Brown in Kansas.

ALFRED M. COHEN (1859-1949, Cincinnati)—One of the foremost members of the Urban League and a leading lawyer.

OSMOND FRAENKEL (b. 1888-)—A leading American lawyer and activist with the ACLU, he helped the defense in the Scottsboro trial.

ELMER GERTZ (1906-   , Chicago)—The noted Special Counsel for the NAACP and one of the leading civil rights lawyers in the U.S.

MAYER C. GOLDMAN (1874-1939, New Orleans)—One of the great pioneer champions of the concept of the public defender.

JACK GREENBERG (1924-   )—The famous Chief Legal Counsel of the NAACP for decades.

ARTHUR GARFIELD HAYS (1881-1954, Rochester, N.Y.)—The greatest civil rights lawyer of his generation, he worked in the Scottsboro trial and the Sacco and Vanzetti trial, with Darrow in the Scopes "monkey" trial, and as General Counsel of the ACLU.

KIVIE KAPLAN (1904-1975)—President of the NAACP, 1966–1975.

WILLIAM KUNSTLER (1919-   , New York City)—The celebrated lawyer who specializes in "political" cases, he was defense counsel in the trial of the Chicago Seven and a bulwark of the National Lawyer's Guild.

SAMUEL S. LEIBOWITZ (1893-1978, Jassy, Rumania)—One of the most famous criminal and civil rights lawyers in the U.S. Al Capone was one of his clients, Leibowitz was chief defense counsel in the famous Scottsboro trial.

MORRIS MILGRAM (1916-   , New York City)—A leader in the struggle for open housing in the U.S.

ARYEH NEIER (1937-   , Berlin)—One of the leading figures in the ACLU, he was formerly Executive Director of the New York Civil Liberties Union.

EDWARD A. NORMAN (1900-1955)—Long concerned with the civil rights of minorities, he was Chairman of the Finance Commission of the Association of American Indian Affairs and also served as Treasurer of the Urban League for more than ten years.

WALTER H. POLLAK (1887-1940, New Jersey)—A leading American civil rights lawyer, he participated in some of the most famous cases in American history, including those of Scopes, Scottsboro, and Gitlow.

ALBERT L. SACHS (1935-   , Johannesburg)—An attorney arrested for anti-apartheid activities, he is now in self-simposed exile in Great Britain.

ARTHUR B. SPINGARN (1878-1971)—President of the NAACP, 1940–1965.

JOEL E. SPINGARN (1875-1939, New York City)—Cofounder, Chairman (1913–1919) and President (1939) of the NAACP.

FEMINISTS

BETSY BAKKER-NORT (1874-1946, Netherlands)—A pioneer lawyer and a leading advocate of women's rights in the Netherlands.

SHULAMITH FIRESTONE (1945- , Ottawa)—A leading American feminist and author of *The Dialectic of Sex.*

BETTY FRIEDAN (1921- , Peoria, Ill.)—Author of *The Feminine Mystique,* considered one of the most important books in the history of the women's movement.

ALETTA JACOBS (1854-1929)—Reputed to be the first or one of the first women admitted to a university in the Netherlands and one of the very first women physicians in that country, she was the leading figure in the holding of the 1915 Hague International Peace Congress.

LUCY KOMISAR (1942- , New York City)—An important American feminist and social critic.

FANNY LEWALD (1811-1899, Königsberg)—A leading German novelist, she was an important figure in the feminist movement.

LINA MORGENSTERN (1830-1909, Breslau)—Born Baver. A noted German feminist and a sponsor of the International Women's Congress of 1896.

ANITA POLLITZER (1895-1975)—She was the famous leader of the U.S. National Women's Party.

ERNESTINE ROSE (1810-1892, Piotrkow, Poland)—Cofounder of the Women's Suffrage Society, she played an important role in the holding of the National Women's Rights Convention. Her maiden name was Potovsky.

ALICE SALOMON (1872-1948, Berlin)—An important figure in the history of social work in Germany, she was Vice-President of the International League of Women. She became a Christian.

LYNDA SCHOR (1938- , Brooklyn)—Born Nyfield. An important feminist writer.

ROSIKA SCHWIMMER (1877-1948, Budapest)—Cofounder of the Women's Peace party. She served as President of the International Campaign for World Government and as Vice-President of the International League for Peace and Freedom.

LILY SOLOMON (1863-1940)—One of the first women to pilot a plane, drive an automobile, and ride a motorcycle.

GLORIA STEINEM (1936-)—One of the most prominent feminists in the U.S..

MEN AND WOMEN OF THE LEFT

AMERICANS

ISRAEL AMPTER (1881-1954, Denver)—Cofounder and an important member of the National Committee of the Communist party of the U.S.

MAX BEDACHT (b. 1885, Munich, Germany)—At one time a leading American Communist who served on the National Executive Committee of the party, he was expelled in 1946.

ALEXANDER BERKMAN (1870-1936, Russia)—A fascinating personality, he was one of America's leading anarchists. He served more than a decade in prison for shooting a man, went to the Soviet Union, didn't like what he saw, and ultimately took his own life. He was the author of *The Bolshevik Myth* and other books.

ALEXANDER BITTELMAN (b. 1890, Odessa, Russia)—A major figure in the American Communist party, he served on its National Committee and then served a prison term for violations of the Smith Act.

DANIEL DE LEON (1852-1914, Curaçao, Netherlands Antilles)—The famous Editor of *The People*, the newspaper of the Socialist Labor party, in which he played a prominent role. He was one of the founders of the Industrial Workers of the World.

BENJAMIN GITLOW (1891-1965, New Jersey)—A founder of the American Communist Labor party, he served on the Presidium of the Communist International and was General Secretary of the American Communist party. Expelled in 1929, he later cofounded the Workers Communist League, which later became the Socialist party of the U.S.

BENJAMIN GOLD (1898- , Bessarabia)—A leading American Communist who eventually left the party.

GIL GREEN (1906- , Chicago)—National President of the Young Communist League, 1932–1939 (Communists stay young a long time) and a member of the party's Central Committee. He served eight years in prison under the Smith Act.

MORRIS HILLQUIT (1869-1933, Riga, Latvia)—A leading American socialist, he was a major force in the Socialist party of the U.S. after leaving the Socialist Labor party.

JAY LOVESTONE (1898- , Lithuania)—Born Jacov Liebstein. One of the founders of the American Communist party, he turned against Stalinism and became a vigorous anti-Communist, leading the American Federation of Labor's struggle against infiltration and becoming one of the leading advocates of an interventionist U.S. foreign policy.

ABRAHAM SHIPLACOFF (1877-1934, Chernigov, Russia)—Was a leading member of the National Executive of the Socialist party.

JACOB STACHEL (1900-1966, Galicia)—A life-long Communist, he was Executive Secretary of the American Communist party's Executive Committee. He was imprisoned in the 1950s.

ROSE PASTOR STOKES (1879-1933, Augustow, Poland)—Born Wieslander. One of the most famous lecturers on socialism in the U.S. and a founder of the American Communist party.

AUSTRIANS

FRIEDRICH ADLER (1879-1960, Vienna)—Was Secretary of the Socialist International and the assassin of Count Sturgkh, the Prime Minister of Austria.

MAX ADLER (1873-1937, Vienna)—A leading revisionist socialist, he was a deputy representing the Austrian Social Democratic party for two decades.

VICTOR ADLER (1852-1918, Prague)—A great early leader of the Social Democratic party in Austria, he served as Foreign Minister of that country for a brief period in 1918. He became a Christian.

OTTO BAUER (1881-1938)—A leading socialist, he opposed Communism and served as Austrian Foreign Minister in 1918 and 1919.

JULIUS BRAUNTHAL (1891-1972)—Was Secretary of the Socialist International in the post–World War II period and had earlier edited the important journal *Der Kamp* and (from England) the *International Socialist Forum*.

WILHELM ELLENBOGEN (1863-1951, Breclav, Moravia)—A prominent Austrian politician representing the Social Democrats.

RUTH FISCHER (1895-1961)—Served on the Presidium of the Communist party of Germany and played a major role in its affairs.

EGON E. KISCH (1885-1948, Prague)—The leader of the Red Guard Communist movement in Austria, he was driven into exile.

BRITISH

HAROLD J. LASKI (1893-1950, Manchester, England)—Chairman of the Labor party at the end of World War II, and a noted Fabian socialist, he was one of the most important political theorists in England and a professor at the London School of Economics.

FRENCH

DANIEL COHN-BENDIT—The famous "Danny the Red," one of the leaders of the 1968 "uprising" among students and workers in France.

SALOMON GRUMBACH (1884-1952)—Served in the Chamber of Deputies and on the Central Committee of the French Socialist party.

MAURICE KRIEGEL-VALRIMONT (1914- , Strasbourg)—After serving on the Central Committee of the French Communist party, he was expelled for deviating from the party line.

CHARLES RAPPOPORT (1865-1941, Doukshty, Lithuania)—Before coming to France, he was involved with an attempt on the life of Czar Alexander II. He later was Editor of *Humanité*, the official paper of the French Communist party, which he later left.

GERMANS

EDUARD BERNSTEIN (1850-1932)—One of the most important socialist thinkers of his generation, he was considered a revisionist by most Marxists.

ADOLF BRAUN (1862-1929)—An important figure in the German Social Democratic party, on whose Executive Committee he served.

HEINRICH BRAUN (1854-1927)—Cofounder of *Neue Zeit*, an important journal of the German Social Democratic party. He was also a member of the Reichstag.

LUDWIG FRANKL (1810-1894, Chrast, Bohemia)—Became famous as author of the song "Die Universität," sung by young revolutionaries during the 1848 uprisings, in which he played a part.

HUGO HAASE (1863-1919, Allenstein, Germany)—A major figure in the provisional revolutionary government formed in 1918 and a founder of the German Independent Social Democratic party. He was murdered.

MOSES HESS (1812-1875, Bonn)—A great pioneer theorist of socialism and a bitter intellectual enemy of Karl Marx.

RUDOLF HILFERDING (1877-1941, Vienna)—A leading Austrian socialist theoretician and author of *Das Finanzkapital*, he was also a major figure in the German Social Democratic party. He was Minister of Finance of Germany on two occasions. He was probably murdered by the SS.

KURT HILLER (b. 1885, Berlin)—Advocated a socialist world ruled by writers and artists–a notion that was somewhat popular among writers and artists, but few others.

PAUL HIRSCH (1868-1938)—Was a socialist Prime Minister of Prussia.

JOHANN JACOBY (1806-1877, Königsberg)—An important theorist and advocate of democracy in Germany.

SIEGFRIED LANDSHUT (1897-1968, Strasbourg)—A leading German authority on Marx and editor of some of his writings.

FERDINAND LASSALLE (1825-1864, Breslau)—Born Lassal. One of the great early figures in socialism, both as a theorist and as an activist. The political party he founded is considered the predecessor of the Social Democrats in Germany. He was killed in a duel.

PAUL LEVI (1883-1930)—A founder and major figure in the Spartacus League, which became the Communist party of Germany.

ROSA LUXEMBURG (1871-1919, Zamosc, Poland)—The legendary leftist and revolutionary who founded the Spartacus League and was a major force in the Socialist International. Her murder by elements of the German officer corps is one of the most famous political killings in modern history.

KARL MARX (1818-1883)—The baptized Jew who is considered the father of Communism and one of the most influential men in the history of the world.

ERICH MUEHSAM (1878-1934, Berlin)—A major figure in German anarchism and an active revolutionary who spent years in prison. After his release, he was the Editor of *Fanal*, one of the leading anarchist journals in the world. He was killed by followers of Hitler.

ARTHUR ROSENBERG (1889-1943, Berlin)—One of the few Communists to be active in Jewish affairs (he had earlier become a Christian), he served on the Central Committee of the Communist party of Germany before the rise of Hitler. His return to Judaism took place after he denounced Communism.

PAUL SINGER (1844-1911, Berlin)—Chairman of the Executive Committee of the German Social Democrats in the late 1800s.

ERNST TOLLER (1893-1939, Samotschin, Germany)—An active leader of the Red Guard and a famous revolutionary playwright (*Masses and Man*), he took his own life after fleeing Hitler.

HUNGARIANS

LEO FRANKEL (1844-1896)—A leader of the Paris Commune, he was an assistant to Friedrich Engels and served on the Council of the Socialist International.

ZSIGMOND KUNFI (1879-1929, Nagykanizsa, Hungary)—Born Kohn. A prominent figure in the 1918 revolution in Hungary, he served as Minister of Social Welfare, Minister of Education, and later as Commissar of Education under Kun. He took his own life after becoming disillusioned with Communism.

JOZSEF LENGYEL (1896-   )—Helped to organize the Communist party of Hungary.

GEORG LUKACS (1885-1971, Budapest)—One of the most brilliant and innovative Marxist philosophers, he was President of the Hungarian Academy of Sciences after World War II and wrote a standard biography of Lenin.

RODION MARKOVITS (1888-1948)—A leading Hungarian literary figure who fought with the International Brigade in the Russian civil war, he is most famous for his book *Garrison* (1929).

ITALIANS

VITTORIO E. MODIGLIANI (1872-1947, Leghorn)—Served as Chairman of the Italian Socialist party after World War II.

UMBERTO TERRANINI (1895-   )—A leading member of the Italian Communist party, he was their presidential candidate in the mid-1960s. He spent more than ten years in prison during the fascist period.

POLES

JACOB BERMAN (1901- , Warsaw)—A leading member of the Polish Communist party, he served as Deputy Premier, 1952–1956, then was dismissed from the party and branded a Stalinist.

HERMAN DIAMOND (1860-1930, Lvov)—Helped to organize the Social Democrat party of Poland and was one of its leading figures.

SZYMON DICKSTEIN (1858-1884, Warsaw)—A leading socialist theorist who introduced Marxism to Polish-speaking audiences.

BOLESLAW DROBNER (1883-1968, Cracow)—A leading figure in the socialist movement in Poland, he helped found the Polish Independent Socialist party.

HENRYK DRZEWIECKI (1902-1937)—Born Hercel Rosenbaum. A leading left-wing novelist famous for his *Kwasniacy*, he fled the Polish authorities and went to the Soviet Union, where he was killed in the purges of the 1930s.

FELIKS KON (1864-1941, Warsaw)—An important figure in revolutionary circles in Poland, he became one of the best-known political writers in the Soviet Union.

HERMAN LIEBERMAN (1870-1914, Drogobycz)—Served on the Central Committee of the Socialist party of Poland and was later Minister of Justice in exile. He helped to write the 1921 Polish Constitution.

ADAM SCHAFF (1913- , Lvov)—The leading Marxist philosopher in Poland, he was on the Central Committee of the party and was the author of *Marxism and the Human Individual.*

ADOLF WARSKI-WARSZAWSKI (1868-1937, Cracow)—Served on the Central Committee of the Communist party of Poland, which he helped found. After going to the U.S.S.R., he was killed during the purges.

HENRYK WOHL (1842-1907, Warsaw)—A leading revolutionary in Poland and a participant in the uprisings of the 1860s, he spent 20 years in a Siberian labor camp.

RUMANIANS

LUDWIG L. GELERTER (1873-1945, Rumania)—Founder of Rumania's Socialist Workers' party.

CONSTANTIN GHEREA-DOBROGEANU (1855-1920, Slavianka, Russia)—Born Solomon Katz. One of the foremost socialist philosophers in Rumania. He became a Christian.

MAX WECHSLER (1870-1917)—One of the foremost figures in socialist circles in Rumania and active in the Jewish community, he was executed by the government.

RUSSIANS

RAPHAEL ABRAMOWITZ (1880-1963, Dvinsk, Latvia)—A prominent Menshevik, he served on the Executive Council of the Socialist International and on the Central Committee of the Social Democratic party.

FYODOR I. DAN (1871-1947, St. Petersburg)—Born Gurvich. A leading Menshevik who served on the Presidium of the Petrograd Soviet and later worked for the Menshevik cause outside of Russia.

ABRAM M. DEBORIN (1881-1963)—Born Abram Joffe. A very important Marxist philosopher in the Soviet Union. He barely escaped execution during the purges and later was a member of the Soviet Academy of Sciences.

GRIGORI GOLDENBERG (1855-1880)—Assassin of the Governor General of Kharkov, he took his own life while in police custody.

LEV B. KAMENEV (1883-1936, Moscow)—Born Lev Rosenfeld. A close associate of Lenin's and a prominent Bolshevik leader. He served on the Politburo, as Chairman of the Moscow Soviet, as Deputy Chairman of the Council of People's Commissars, and as Editor of *Pravda.* He was killed during the purges.

YURI LARIN (1882-1932, Simferopol)—Born Mikhail Lurye. Became a leading Bolshevik after leaving the Mensheviks, and was an important economist.

SOLOMON A. LOZOVSKI (1878-1952, Danilovka)—Born Solomon Dridzo. Served on the Central Committee of the Soviet Communist party after having previously been Deputy Commissar of Foreign Affairs and Director of the Trade Union International. He was murdered during the 1952 purge.

JULIUS MARTOV (b. 1873, Constantinople)—Born Iulii O. Tsederbaum. A cofounder of *Iskra* and a leading opponent of Lenin's conception of the Communist party.

MARK B. MITIN (1901- , Zhitomir)—Holder of the Order of Lenin and the Stalin Prize, he served on the Central Committee of the party and was one of the chief ideologists of Soviet Communism.

MARC NATANSON (1849-1920, Grodno)—A leading figure of the terroristic Narodnava Volya, he founded the Land of Liberty movement in Russia.

KARL RADEK (1885-?, Lemberg)—Born Karl Sobelsohn. A major figure in the Communist International, a writer for *Pravda*, and a close associate of Lenin. Imprisoned after one of the most famous trials of the purges, he disappeared in the late 1930s.

ISAAC N. STEINBERG (1888-1957, Dvinsk)—Minister of Justice in the Provisional Government in 1917 and a prominent member of the Social Revolutionary party.

YAKOV M. SVERDLOV (1885-1919, Nizhni-Novgorod)—A leading Bolshevik, he was on the Central Committee of the party and later served as Chairman of the All-Russian Central Executive Committee. The city of Sverdlovsk is named after him.

LEON TROTSKY (1879-1940, Ivanovka)—Born Lev D. Bronstein. One of the key figures in the success of the Russian Revolution. He served as Commissar for Foreign Affairs, was a member of the Bolshevik Central Committee, and was the brilliant architect of the Red Army as its Commissar for Military Affairs. Driven into exile and hunted constantly, he was finally killed in Mexico. His name became part of the lexicon of the left, and he is one of its most legendary figures.

YEMELYAN YAROSLAVSKY (1878-1943, Chita)—Born Gubelman. A Deputy of the Supreme Soviet, a member of the Central Committee of the party, and a close associate of Stalin.

GRIGORI ZINOVIEV (1883-1936, Yelizavetgrad)—Lost a key power struggle to Stalin and had to leave the party. Before that, he was one of the most powerful figures in the party Politburo and a committed revolutionary. He lost his life during the purges.

OTHERS

AVRAHAM BEN-AROYA (b. 1887)—A major figure in the Socialist party and later of the Social Democratic party of Greece, he later left that country for Israel.

HENRI CURIEL (1914- , Egypt)—Cofounder of the Egyptian Communist party.

DAVID FRANKFURTER (1909- , Daruvar, Croatia)—Assassinated the Swiss Nazi Wilhelm Gustoff in 1936. He eventually emigrated to Israel after his release from prison.

HERSCHEL GRYNSZPAN (b. 1921, Hanover, Germany)—The famous assassin of the Nazi Ernst vom Rath in Paris. He disappeared.

DAVID LEWIS (1909- , Svisloch, Belorussia)—Helped to found what became the New Democratic party in Canada and became its leader.

GEORGE LICHTEIM (1912- , Berlin)—A world authority on Marxism and socialism.

ARTUR LONDON (1915- , Ostrava, Czechoslovakia)—Deputy Minister of Foreign Affairs of Czechoslovakia, he served on the Central Committee of the Czech Communist party. He fell from grace during the Slansky purges.

ERNEST MANDEL (1923-)—One of the world's leading Marxist scholars.

SHALOM SCHWARZBARD (1886-1938, Izmail, Bessarabia)—The famous assassin of Simon Petlyura, the Cossack leader who led vicious pogroms against the Jews of the Ukraine.

RUDOLF SLANSKY (b. 1901)—The Secretary General of the Communist party of Czechoslovakia who was the object of a massive purge after World War II. He was sentenced to death after a show trial and executed in the late 1940s.

VOLODIA TEITELBAUM (1916-   , Chile)—A prominent member of the Chilean Communist party, she served as both a Deputy and a Senator.

DAVID WIJNKOOP (1876-1941, Amsterdam)—Chairman of the Communist party of the Netherlands, which he helped found (the party, not the Netherlands).

REVOLUTIONARIES

PAVEL AXELROD (1850-1928, Russia)—The leader of the Liberation of Labor faction, the predecessor to the Social Democratic party of Russia, and the famous Editor of *Iskra*. A high-ranking member of the International Bureau of the Socialist International, Axelrod was an uncompromising enemy of the Bolsheviks and a major figure among the Mensheviks.

DMITRI BOGROV (1888-1911)—Bogrov worked for the secret police while he was a feared terrorist, although whether or not he was a double agent has never been completely established. He was killed by the Russian authorities after putting several bullets into Prime Minister Stolypin.

SIMON DEUTSCH (1822-1877, Nikolsburg, Austria)—An important member of the Directory Committee of the Communist International, he was a veteran of the Paris Commune.

SIMON DIAMANSTEIN (1886-1937, Russia)—Served as Commissar for Nationality Affairs in the Soviet Union and was a close associate of Stalin, who rewarded him by having him killed in the purges.

ADOLF FISCHHOFF (1816-1893, Austria)—An important figure during the 1848 revolution.

GRIGORI A. GERSHUNI (1870-1908, Tavrova, Russia)—One of the most feared terrorists in czarist Russia, he planned many assassinations, and was the daring director of the Socialist-Revolutionary party, which he founded.

LAZAR GOLDENBERG (1846-1916, Russia)—Forced to flee Russia, he came to the U.S. where he continued the struggle against the Czar. He later went to England.

BERNARD GOLDMAN (1841-1901, Warsaw)—A leading Polish revolutionary who fought to free his country from Russian rule, he was one of the relatively few men to ever successfully escape from Siberia.

EMMA GOLDMAN (1869-1940, Kovno, Lithuania)—One of the most important figures in the history of anarchism, she was a pioneer champion of birth control practices and Editor of *Mother Earth*, an influential anarchist journal.

MORITZ HARTMANN (1821-1872, Dusniky)—A participant in the 1848 revolution and a member of the Young Bohemia circle of revolutionary intellectuals in Germany.

HESSIA M. HELFMAN (1855-1882, Mazir, Russia)—A terrorist for the Narodnaya Volya party, she may have had a role in the death of Czar Alexander II. She was killed by the czarist police after having been allowed to deliver her baby in prison.

HERMANN JELLINEK (1822-1848)—A leading enemy and critic of the Hapsburg Empire, he was killed for his criticism.

MARK NATANSON (1849-1919, Svenziany, Russia)—One of the most fearless of the Czar's opponents. He planned the escape of Peter Kropotkin, a close associate of Lenin, and was the major leader of the Chaikovski Circle of revolutionary students.

AARON ZUNDELEVITCH (1852-1923, Vilna)—A leader of the Narodnaya Volya revolutionaries and an important champion of the use of terror. He became disillusioned with the Bolsheviks after they seized power.

SPIES AND COUNTERSPIES

EUGENE AZEFF (1869-1918 or 1919, Lyskovo, Russia)—One of the most famous double agents of all time, he became a leading revolutionary opposed to the Czar while working for the Russian Secret Police. He designed several assassinations and was incredibly daring. He died in a German prison after fleeing Russia.

MOSES J. BIRNBOIM (1789-1831)—A leading czarist agent of the era, he spied on suspected revolutionaries inside and outside of Russia. He was particularly harsh on his fellow Jews and was eventually killed by them.

GEORGE BLAKE (1922- , Rotterdam)—Born Behar; he was part Jewish. Blake worked for British intelligence (MI6) during World War II and was rumored to have been brainwashed by the Chinese during the Korean War. In any event he became a double agent for the Soviets in Berlin, and was eventually caught by the British and sentenced to a long prison term. His escape from the maximum security prison at Wormwood Scrubs is widely considered to be one of the greatest escapes of all time. He was smuggled out of England by the KGB and made his way to Moscow.

PIERRE BLOCH (1905- , Paris)—Director of Free French counterespionage during World War II. After the war he was an important personality in French Socialist circles.

CHESTER L. COOPER (1917- , Boston)—Director of the International Division of the Institute for Defense Analysis, he was Chief of the Estimates Staff of the Office of National Estimates of the CIA.

SAMUEL FRANKEL (1905- , Cincinnati)—A Rear Admiral in the U.S. Navy, Frankel was Director of the Naval Intelligence School, Assistant Head of Naval Intelligence for the Pacific, Deputy Director of Naval Intelligence, and Chief of Staff of the Defense Intelligence Agency.

HARRY GOLD (b. Berne, Switzerland)—Born Golodnotzky. Part of the Soviet spy ring in the U.S. which transferred atomic secrets to the U.S.S.R.

OTTO KATZ (1900-1952)—An agent for SMERSH, he was active in both Czechoslovakia and the U.S. He developed a number of Communist cells in the Hollywood film community and was a key participant in the conspiracy to kill Foreign Minister Masaryk. He was executed during the Slansky purges.

EWEN E. MONTAGU (1901-)—A veteran of British Naval Intelligence during World War II, he wrote one of the best and most famous spy novels ever to appear—*The Man Who Never Was* (1953).

MULLA I. NATHAN (1816-1868, Meshed, Persia)—One of the leading British agents in the Near East, he did important work for the British in Afghanistan.

IGNACE REISS (b. 1899)—A leading Soviet agent, he was Resident Director of all Soviet spy networks in France between World Wars I and II. He quit the spy business but was murdered by the Soviets.

THE ROSENBERGS: ETHEL (1920-1953) **and JULIUS** (1918-1953)—They were at the center of the most famous spy case in modern American history. Executed for spying for the Soviet Union, their case remains controversial and somewhat ambiguous. They were the first nonmilitary persons in the history of the U.S. to be executed for spying.

SIGMUND G. ROSENBLUM (b. 1874, Odessa)—As "Sidney Reilly" he was a legendary British secret agent, possibly the greatest in the distinguished history of British Intelligence. He spied on the Germans during World War I, dropping behind the front lines and posing (and on some occasions actually enlisting) as a German soldier. His most famous exploit was when he became a driver for a colonel on the German General Staff, then murdered the man and impersonated him at important meetings. He disappeared in 1925 and it is believed that he was murdered by Soviet agents.

MORTON SOBELL (1918-)—An associate of the Rosenbergs, he was convicted of spying and served more than 17 years in prison.

IGNATIUS TREBITSCH-LINCOLN (1879-1943, Hungary)—A Member of Parliament, he was a Presbyterian, an Anglican, and then a Quaker. He was imprisoned for spying for the Germans during World War I and then went to China and became a Buddhist monk, although in reality he worked for Japanese Intelligence. Certainly one of strangest figures in the history of espionage.

LEOPOLD TREPPER (1904- , Nowy Targ, Poland)—Also known as Leiba Domb, he was the famous "conductor" of the "Red Orchestra," the Soviet intelligence network in Belgium and France during World War II, which acquired significant information on the German army. He left the Soviet Union for Israel in the late 1970s.

COPS AND ROBBERS (including CRIMINOLOGISTS)

DAVID ABRAHAMSEN (1903- , Trondheim, Norway)—A prominent American criminologist, he was Director of Science Research at Sing Sing for four years. One of his outstanding books is *The Psychology of Crime* (1960).

FREDA ADLER (1934- , Philadelphia)—Author of *Sisters in Crime* (1975), one of the best books on criminality among women.

DAVID ALMOG—A resident of Tel Aviv, he is President of the World Association of Detectives.

GUSTAV ASCHAFFENBURG (1866-1944, Zweibrücken, Germany)—A leading criminologist of the early 1900s, he championed the prevention of crime as well as the rehabilitation of criminals.

MORITZ BENEDIKT (1835-1920, Eisenstadt, Hungary)—A famous neurologist who was among the first to study the link beteen brain pathology and criminal behavior. He published the results of his research in 1891 as *Anatomical Studies upon Brains of Criminals.*

LOUIS BUCHALTER (1897-1944)—Known as "Lepke," Buchalter was reputed to be the head of "Murder, Inc." He was finally convicted of murder and executed.

EDWARD DAVIS (1816-1841, England)—Known as "Teddy the Jewboy," he was sent to Australia when it was a penal colony, escaped from prison, and led a group of ex-convicts on a rampage through the Outback. He was eventually executed for murder.

SIMON DINITZ (1926- , New York City)—A Professor of Sociology at Ohio State U., and President of the American Society of Criminology, 1970–1971.

JOSEPH FINK (1915-)—Deputy Inspector of Police of N.Y.C., from 1967–1971.

KATE FRIEDLANDER (1902-1949, Innsbruck, Austria)—A leading expert on juvenile delinquency, she is best known for her book *The Psychoanalytical Approach to Juvenile Delinquency* (1947).

SHELDON GLUECK (1896- , Warsaw) and **ELEANOR GLUECK**—Husband and wife, they were two of the leading authorities on juvenile delinquency in the

U.S. for many decades. Most of their theories were summarized in *Unraveling Juvenile Delinquency* (1950).

ALEXANDER S. GOLDENWEISER (1855-1915, Yekaterinoslav, Russia)—A leading Russian criminologist and the author of the important *Crime as Punishment and Punishment as Crime.*

MAX GRUENHUT (1893-1964, Magdeburg, Germany)—Author of *Penal Reform*, considered one of the landmark works on the subject. He became a Christian.

MANFRED GUTTMACHER (1898-1966, Baltimore)—An expert on the psychopathic criminal and the author of *Mind of the Murderer* (1960).

JACOB HAYS—High Constable of N.Y.C., 1802–1849, and one of the first to use modern detective methods.

STEPHAN HURWITZ (1901- , Copenhagen)—Author of *Criminology*, for years a standard textbook all over the world.

SOLOMON KOBRIN (1910- , Chicago)—A leading expert on juvenile delinquency.

CESARE LOMBROSO (1835-1909, Verona)—One of the most controversial students of the criminal, Lombroso argued that criminals were born and not made. His theories are given little credence today.

HERMANN MANNHEIM (b. 1889, Russia)—A pioneer criminologist in England, he was one of the founders and editors of the *British Journal of Criminology.*

HUGO PAM (1870-1930, Chicago)—A noted judge, he also served as President of the American Institute of Criminal Law and Criminology.

SIR LEON RADZINOWICZ (1906- , Poland)—One of the leading British criminologists, he founded and directed the Institute of Criminology. He was author of *In Search of Criminology* and President of the British Academy of Forensic Sciences. He became a Christian.

SOPHIA ROBISON (1888-1969, New York City)—A leading authority on juvenile delinquency and the author of the famous *Juvenile Delinquency: Its Nature and Control.*

ARNOLD ROTHSTEIN (1882-1928, New York City)—One of the leading hoods in American history, he was murdered by an irate creditor.

STEPHEN SCHAFER (1911- , Hungary)—One of the leading authorities in the world on restitution for the victims of crimes.

BUGSY SIEGEL (1905-1947, New York City)—Benjamin Siegel was reported to be head of the rackets in Los Angeles. He was killed in a gangland-style slaying.

JACKSON TOBY (1925-)—A leading urban criminologist and the author of *Contemporary Society: Social Process and Social Structure in Urban Industrial Societies.*

Part II
The Professions

PART II
JOURNALISTS

See also Pulitzer Prize Winners.

ELIE ABEL (1920- , Montreal)—The famous NBC reporter who had earlier written for the *New York Times*, he became Dean of Columbia University's Graduate School of Journalism in 1969.

FRANKLIN PIERCE ADAMS (1881-1960, Chicago)—The famous "F.P.A." of the *New York Tribune*, his column "The Conning Tower" had a wide and devoted following. He later became a radio personality on "Information Please."

LAURENCE I. BARRETT (1935- , New York City)—N.Y. Bureau Chief and political reporter for *Time* magazine.

MEYER BERGER (1898-1959, New York City)—The famous and long-time reporter for the *New York Times* and a Pulitzer Prize winner.

CARL BERNSTEIN (1944- , Washington, D.C.)—The journalist of the *Washington Post* who, with Woodward, exposed the Watergate affair and changed American political history.

THEODORE M. BERNSTEIN (1904- , New York City)—Had a long career on the *New York Times*, serving as Assistant Managing Editor and Foreign Editor. He has published several books on English usage.

HENRI DE BLOWITZ (1825-1903, Bohemia)—Born Adolf Opper. One of the great early investigative reporters. He was Paris correspondent of the *London Times* and had contacts all over the Continent, especially in Germany.

BILL BOYARSKY (1936- , Berkeley, Calif.)—National Reporter for the *Los Angeles Times*.

ANITA BRENNER (1905- , Aguascalientes, Mexico)—Free-lanced for the North American Newspaper Alliance for almost 30 years and had many scoops, including an exclusive *New York Times* interview with Leon Trotsky when he was in hiding.

LESTER BROMBERG (1909- , New York City)—A sportswriter and columnist specializing in boxing, he worked on the *new York Post*, 1920–1930 and 1966–1978, and the *New York World Telegram & Sun*, 1930–1966. *Webster's Unabridged Dictionary*, Third Edition, quotes him to illustrate the term *welter*.

ART BUCHWALD (1925- , Mt. Vernon, N.Y.)—One of the funniest men in America, and one of the most perceptive. His hilarious columns appear in the *Washington Post* and are nationally syndicated.

ALEXANDER CHAKOVSKI (1913-)—Chief Editor of *Literaturnaya gazeta*, the most influential literary journal in the Soviet Union, he is also Secretary of the Soviet Writer's Union.

MORTON A. EDELSTEIN (1925- , Chicago)—Author of "Mort's Column" in the *Chicago Daily News*, he was formerly a reporter for the *Chicago American* and won an Emmy Award and the Edward R. Murrow Award for Investigative Reporting.

GERALD ESKENAZI (1936- , New York City)—A sportswriter for the *New York Times* since 1959 and one of the best in the business.

HAROLD FABER (1919- , New York City)—National News Editor of the *New York Times* since 1952.

ERNST FEDER (1881-1964, Berlin)—A leading contributor to and Home Politics Editor of the *Berliner Tageblatt*, a major German newspaper between World Wars I and II.

ARTHUR FEILER (1879-1942, Breslau)—A Senior Editor of the German *Frankfurter Zeitung*, 1910–1930, and a noted economist.

LEO FISCHER (b. 1897, Chicago)—A great baseball writer and Sports Editor of the *Chicago American*.

BENJAMIN W. FLEISHER (1870-1946)—The leading American journalist in Japan for almost half a century.

ROSE N. FRANZBLAU (1905-   , Vienna)—Had a very popular column on psychology in the *New York Post* for many years and also a regular radio show.

BEN W. GILBERT (1918-   , New York City)—Born Goldberg. City Editor of the *Washington Post*, 1945–1964, and Associate Editor, 1969–1970.

MARCUS D. GLEISSER (1923-   , Buenos Aires)—Writer and reporter for the *Cleveland Plain Dealer*.

MICHAEL GOLD (1893-1967, New York City)—Born Irwin Granich. A prominent columnist for the *Daily Worker* and Editor of *The Liberator* and *New Masses*. He was also the author of *Jews without Money*.

WILLIAM E. GOLD (1912-   , Brooklyn)—Wrote "The District Line," a political column in *the Washington Post*, for many years.

MITCHELL GORDON (1925-   , Los Angeles)—A leading correspondent with the *Wall Street Journal* since 1957.

PAUL GREENBERG (1937-   , Shreveport, La.)—Editorial Page Editor of the *Pine Bluff Arkansas Commercial*. He won the Pulitzer Prize in 1969.

JAMES L. GREENFIELD (1924-   , Cleveland)—Foreign Editor of the *New York Times* since 1969, he was Assistant Secretary of State for Public Affairs, 1964–1966.

JOHN GROSS (1935-   , London)—Editor of the influential London *Times Literary Supplement*, and former Literary Editor of the *New Statesman*.

ED GUTHMAN (1919-   , Seattle)—A former aide to Robert Kennedy, he is National Editor of the *Los Angeles Times*.

DAVID HALBERSTAM (1934-   , New York City)—Pulitzer Prize–winning former *New York Times* investigative reporter who wrote *The Best and the Brightest* (1974).

FRED M. HECHINGER (1920-   , Nuremberg, Germany)—The influential Education Editor of the *New York Times*.

MARK HELLINGER (1903-1947)—A leading Broadway reporter for the New York *Daily News* and then the *New York Daily Mirror*, he became a well-known movie producer.

SEYMOUR HERSH (1937-   , Chicago)—Perhaps the outstanding investigative reporter in the U.S., he was Press Secretary to Eugene McCarthy during the senator's presidential campaign. In addition to many other awards, he won the Pulitzer Prize for his expose of the My Lai atrocities and the George Polk Award for his exposure of domestic spying by the CIA. He works for the *New York Times*.

THEODOR HERTZKA (1845-1924, Budapest)—Editor in Chief of *Magyar hirlap*, one of the leading newspapers in Hungary, he wrote *Freeland: A Social Anticipation* (1891), which advocated a utopian state in Africa.

STAN ISAACS (1929-   , Brooklyn)—A sports columnist for *Newsday*.

SYDNEY JACOBSON (1908-   , South Africa)—Political Editor of the *London Daily Mirror*, he later became Editor of the *Daily Herald* (later known as the *Sun*). He was an influential figure in British Labor party affairs.

HERBERT KAMM (1917-   , Long Branch, N.J.)—Editor of the Editorial Page of the *Cleveland Press*.

RONALD KESSLER (1943-   , New York City)—The investigative reporter for the *Washington Post* who exposed FBI wiretapping activities.

ALBERT KINROSS (1870-1929, Russia)—A noted foreign correspondent for the *Boston Evening Transcript*.

ROBERT KLEIMAN (1918-   , New York City)—A member of the Editorial Board of the *New York Times*.

EDWARD KLEIN (1936-   , Yonkers, N.Y.)—A former editor with *Newsweek*, he is Editor of the *New York Times Magazine.*

SAUL KOHLER (1928-   , New York City)—The White House correspondent for Newhouse Newspapers, he writes the column "The Presidency."

LEONARD KOPPETT (1923-   , Moscow)—Born Kopeliovitch. The noted *New York Times* sportswriter.

JOSEPH KRAFT (1929-   , South Orange, N.J.)—The well-known nationally syndicated columnist, he was previously Washington correspondent for *Harper's.*

DAVID KRASLOW (1926-   , New York City)—Washington Bureau Chief of the *Los Angeles Times* since 1963.

ARTHUR KROCK (1886-1974, Glasgow, Ky.)—Formerly Editor in Chief of the *Louisville Times*, he became one of America's leading political commentators with a career lasting more than 35 years at the *New York Times*. He won the Pulitzer Prize three times.

DAN KURZMAN (1927-   , San Francisco)—A long-time reporter for NBC, the *Washington Star*, and the *Washington Post*, he wrote *The Race for Rome* (1975).

JONATHAN KWITNY (1941-   , Indianapolis)—A national reporter for the *Wall Street Journal.*

ANN LANDERS (1918-   , Sioux City, Iowa)—Born Esther Friedman. The popular advice columnist. She is the twin of Abigail Van Buren.

WILLIAM L. LAURENCE (b. 1888, Lithuania)—One of the greatest science reporters of all time, he worked for the *New York Times*. Winner of the Pulitzer Prize. Perhaps his most famous exclusive stories were his coverage of the atomic bomb test in New Mexico (delayed in the paper, of course), and his coverage of the Nagasaki nuclear attack.

PIERRE LAZAREFF (1907-1972)—Editor of *Paris-Soir* before World War II, he operated *France-Soir* after 1945. He also directed the Voice of America radio operation.

IRVING LEIBOWITZ (1922-   , New York City)—Managing Editor of the *Indianapolis Times* since 1960.

MAX LERNER (1902-   , Minsk, Russia)—One of the most famous liberal columnists in America. His column for the *New York Post* was nationally syndicated.

RICHARD E. LERNER (1941-   , New York City)—Congressional and White House correspondent for UPI since 1968.

ISAAC DON LEVINE (b. 1892, Mozyr, Russia)—Was a foreign correspondent for several papers, including the *Chicago Daily News*, and an outspoken critic of Stalin and the Soviet Union.

JOSEPH L. LEVY (1870-1945, Liverpool)—The noted Editor of the *Johannesburg Sunday Times*, South Africa's largest paper.

LILLIAN LEVY (1918-   , Chicago)—A Senior Science Writer for NASA, she was the only woman to report on a manned space flight and also has the distinction of being the first correspondent to take a commercial airplane flight after the Iron Curtain went up.

ANTHONY LEWIS (1927-   , New York City)—The nationally syndicated columnist of the *New York Times.*

FLORA LEWIS—European Diplomatic Correspondent and Chief of the Paris Bureau of the *New York Times.*

GRACE LICHTENSTEIN (1941-   , New York City)—A *New York Times* reporter since 1970, she wrote *A Long Way Baby* (1974), a very interesting account of the world of professional women's tennis.

DAVID LIDMAN (1905-   , Norfolk, Va.)—The long-time News Editor of the *New York Times* who retired in 1973.

DAVID LIPMAN (1931-   , Springfield, Mo.)—A sportswriter and Assistant Managing Editor of the *St. Louis Post Dispatch.*

WALTER LIPPMANN (1889-1975, New York City)—Perhaps the outstanding American journalist of his era and very influential, his column for the *New York Herald Tribune* was carried by hundreds of newspapers all over the world. He won several Pulitzer Prizes, founded the *New Republic*, and wrote the very important *Public Opinion*.

PETER I. LISAGOR (1915-1976)—Chief of the Washington Bureau of the *Chicago Daily News* from 1959 until his untimely death.

DAVID LOSHAK (1933- , London)—Foreign correspondent for the *London Daily Telegraph* and the *Sunday Telegraph*.

J. ANTHONY LUKAS (1933- , New York City)—Now a free-lance writer, he was an outstanding reporter for the *New York Times* and the author of *Nightmare: The Underside of the Nixon Years*.

LEONARD LYONS (1906-1976, New York City)—The famous nationally syndicated Broadway columnist ("The Lyons Den") of the *New York Post*.

LESTER MARKEL (1894-1977, New York City)—Associate Editor of the *New York Times*, he had earlier served as Sunday Editor for the paper and developed most of the popular features of that edition. His "News of the Week in Review" section won a Pulitzer Prize.

STANLEY MEISLER (1931- , New York City)—International correspondent of the *Los Angeles Times*.

LAWRENCE R. MEYER (1941- , Chicago)—A noted *Washington Post* reporter.

MORTON A. MINTZ (1922- , Ann Arbor, Mich.)—The award-winning reporter of the *Washington Post*.

HERBERT MITGANG (1920- , New York City)—Worked at the *New York Times* in various capacities, as reviewer, correspondent, and member of the editorial board.

IVOR MONTAGU (1904- , London)—A noted left-wing journalist and critic, he was Foreign Correspondent of the *Daily Worker* from 1936 to 1937 and was awarded the Lenin Peace Prize in 1960.

ESTHER MOYAL (1873-1948, Beirut)—Wrote for *Al-Ahram*, the most important paper in the Arab world.

CASPAR H. NANNES (1906- , Fall River, Mass.)—Long-time (since 1943) reporter for the *Washington Star*.

JOHN B. OAKES (1913- , Elkins Park, Pa.)—Editor of the Editorial Page of the *New York Times* since 1961.

MURRAY OLDERMAN (1922- , New York City)—A leading sportswriter, he was President of the Football Writers of America.

MIRIAM OTTENBERG (1914- , Washington, D.C.)—A leading investigative reporter, at the *Washington Star* since 1937, she won a Pulitzer Prize for local reporting in 1960.

JAMES J. PACKMAN (1907-)—Managing Editor of the *Milwaukee Sentinel*, 1943-1952. He had previously worked for many years on the *Los Angeles Examiner*.

IRVING P. PFLAUM (1906- , Chicago)—Foreign Editor of the *Chicago Sun-Times*, 1939-1963.

OSCAR PULVERMACHER (1883-1958, London)—Became Editor of the *London Daily Mail* in 1927 and helped build it into one of the world's largest papers.

SELWYN RAAB (1934- , New York City)—A leading *New York Times* reporter since 1974, he won the Heywood Broun Award of the Newspaper Guild.

KENNETH REICH (1938- , Los Angeles)—Political correspondent of the *Los Angeles Times*.

PAUL J. REUTER (1816-1899, Kassel, Germany)—Born Israel Josaphat. Started the world-famous Reuter's News Agency. He became a Christian.

MILTON RICHMAN (1922- , New York City)—Sports Editor of UPI.

MORTON ROSENBLUM (1943- , Milwaukee)—Paris Bureau Chief of the Associated Press from 1977.

HARRY M. ROSENFELD (1929- , Berlin)—Has served as Metropolitan Editor and Foreign Editor of the *Washington Post*.

A. M. ROSENTHAL (1922- , Sault Ste. Marie, Ontario)—The Pulitzer Prize–winning journalist and Editor of the *New York Times*.

MERRYLE S. RUKEYSER (1897- , Chicago)—One of the leading financial reporters in the U.S., noted for her column "Everybody's Money." She was Financial Editor of the *New York Tribune* and later the *New York Evening Journal*.

WILLIAM SAFIRE (1929-)—Special Assistant to President Nixon from 1968 to 1973, he became an important columnist for the *New York Times* and wrote *Before the Fall* (1975). He won a Pulitzer Prize for Commentary in 1978.

PAUL SANN (1914- , New York City)—Executive Editor of the *New York Post*.

SYDNEY H. SCHANBERG (1934- , Clinton, Mass.)—The noted reporter of the *New York Times*.

DAVID SCHNEIDERMAN (1927-)—Editor in Chief of the *Village Voice* since 1978, he formerly was Editor of the Op Ed page of the *New York Times*.

GEORGE SELDES (b. 1890)—Author of the famous *Lords of the Press*, a scathing attack on American journalism, he had been Chief of the Berlin Bureau (and also of the Rome Bureau) for the *Chicago Tribune*.

LOUIS B. SELTZER (1897- , Cleveland)—A member of the committee that chose the Pulitzer Prize winners, he was Editor of the *Cleveland Press*.

THEODORE SHABAD (1922- , Berlin)—Moscow correspondent of the *New York Times*, he won the Polk Award for his reporting on Cambodia in 1975.

KALMAN SIEGEL (1917- , Brooklyn)—As Letter Editor of the *New York Times* for many years, he caused a lot of happiness and a lot of frustration.

ALVIN M. SILVERMAN (1912- , Louisville)—Chief of the Washington Bureau of the *Cleveland Plain Dealer* since 1957.

LEONARD SLOANE (1932- , New York City)—A noted business and financial reporter for the *New York Times*.

LOUIS SOBOL (1896- , New Haven)—Broadway columnist for the *New York Journal American*, 1935–1966.

GEORGE SOLOMON (1940- , New York City)—Sportswriter for the *Washington Post*.

LOUIS STARK (1888-1954)—The famous Pulitzer Prize–winning reporter for the *New York Times* who served in Washington for 20 years and later was on the paper's Editorial Board.

SIMEON STRUNSKY (1879-1948, Russia)—Editor of the *New York Evening Post* and later a noted columnist ("Topics of the Times") for the *New York Times*.

CYRUS L. SULZBERGER (1912- , New York City)—A foreign affairs columnist for the *New York Times*.

HERBERT BAYARD SWOPE (1882-1958)—One of the all-time great reporters and the first winner of the Pulitzer Prize.

JAY G. SYKES (1922- , Philadelphia)—An editorial writer for the *Milwaukee Sentinel*, 1962–1967.

TAD SZULC (1926- , Warsaw)—The noted former *New York Times* reporter who became an outstanding authority on Latin American affairs.

ELIAS TOBENKIN (1882-1963, Russia)—A noted foreign correspondent for the *New York Herald Tribune*.

SEYMOUR TOPPING (1921- , New York City)—Foreign Editor of the *New York Times*, 1966–1969, and then Managing Editor.

HY TURKIN (1915-1955)—A noted New York *Daily News* baseball writer.

SANFORD J. UNGAR (1945- , Wilkes-Barre, Pa.)—A staff writer for the *Washington Post.*

ABIGAIL VAN BUREN (1918- , Sioux City, Iowa)—Born Pauline Friedman. The popular advice columnist ("Dear Abby"). She is the twin of Ann Landers.

GEORGE VASS (1927- , Leipzig, Germany)—A very good sportswriter for the *Chicago Daily News.*

LEO VEIGELSBERG (1846-1907, Nagyboldogasszony, Hungary)—Was Editor in Chief of *Pester Lloyd*, a leading Hungarian paper and the mouthpiece for the government.

JAMES A. WECHSLER (1915- , New York City)—The famous Washington reporter, columnist, and editorial writer of the *New York Post.*

OSCAR WEISS—Edited the official government newspaper in Chile in the early 1970s.

ALEXANDER WERTH (1901-1969, St. Petersburg)—One of the most distinguished newsmen of all time, he was a foreign correspondent for the *New Statesman*, the *New York Nation*, the *London Sunday Times*, the BBC, and the *Manchester Guardian*, not necessarily in that order.

WALTER WINCHELL (1897-1972, New York City)—One of the most powerful—and frequently sued—American newspaper columnists. His column was read by tens of millions.

DAVID ZASLAVASKY (1880-1965, Russia)—A major political writer for both *Izvestiya* and *Pravda.*

PAUL L. ZIMMERMAN (1932- , Philadelphia)—A sportswriter for the *New York Post*, he wrote the very good *A Thinking Man's Guide to Pro Football* in 1970.

NEWSPAPER AND MAGAZINE PUBLISHERS

HARRY C. ADLER (1865-1940, Philadelphia)—Chairman of the Board of the *Chattanooga Times* beginning in 1901.

PHILIP D. ADLER (1902-)—Became Publisher of the *Davenport* (Iowa) *Times.*

GEORGE BACKER (1902- , New York City)—Edited as well as published the *New York Post*, 1939–1942, and was active in New York State politics.

RACHEL BEER (1858-1927, Bombay, India)—Born Richa Sassoon. Owned the *London Sunday Times* from 1893 and edited the *Observer.*

ADOLPHO BLOCH—Owns *Manchete* and *Fatose Fotos*, two of Brazil's largest magazines.

PAUL BLOCK (1877-1941)—Was Publisher and owner of the *Pittsburgh Evening Sun*, the *Pittsburgh Morning Post*, the *Pittsburgh Post-Gazette*, the *Toledo Times*, and the *Toledo Blade.*

RALPH D. BLUMENFELD (1864-1948, Wis.)—Chairman of the London Express Newspaper Company, 1915–1948. He had earlier served as Foreign Editor of the *Daily Express* and as News Editor of the *London Daily Mail.*

JACOB DE CORDOVA (1808-1868, Spanish Town, Jamaica)—Publisher and founder of the *Kingston Daily Gleaner*, the first daily newspaper on the island.

ORVIL E. DRYFOOS (1912-1963)—Succeeded Arthur Sulzberger as publisher of the *New York Times* (and was married to his daughter).

THEODORE FINK (1855-1942, Guernsey, England)—Owned the Herald Newspapers, the largest chain in Australia and the largest publishing enterprise south of the equator.

RALPH GINZBURG (1929- , Brooklyn)—Editor and founder of *Eros*, he served eight months in prison for obscenity in one of the most famous cases of its kind ever to come before the U.S. Supreme Court. He is now Editor and Publisher of *Moneysworth*.

KATHERINE GRAHAM (1917- , New York City)—Present owner of the Washington Post Company, she was the daughter of Eugene Meyer.

MOSES KOENIGSBERG (1878-1945, New Orleans)—Publisher of the *Boston American*. He put together the King Features Syndicate and was at one time Managing Editor of the *Chicago American*.

EDWARD LEVY LAWSON (1833-1916)—Owned the *London Daily Telegraph* and was one of the sponsors of the Stanley expedition to Africa.

JOSEPH M. LEVY LAWSON (1812-1888)—Owned the influential *London Daily Telegraph*. He was the father of Edward Levy Lawson.

ROBERT LAZURICK (1895-1968, Paris)—Founded and served as Editor in Chief of *L'Aurore*, one of the major French newspapers in the post–World War II period. He was also a prominent Socialist party activist and a member of the Chamber of Deputies.

HARRY H. MARKS (1855-1916, London)—Editor of the British *Financial Times*, which he founded. He served two terms as a Member of Parliament.

EUGENE MEYER (1875-1959, Cal.)—Owned the *Washington Post* and built it into a major newspaper. His Washington Post Company owned *Newsweek* and radio and television stations. Meyer also served as Governor of the Federal Reserve Bank and as President of the International Bank for Reconstruction and Development.

SAMUEL I. NEWHOUSE (b. 1895)—One of the great American publishers, he owned numerous newspapers, television and radio stations, and at least a dozen national magazines including *Mademoiselle*, *Vogue*, and *Glamour* (through his control of Condé Nast and the Street and Smith groups). Two of his many newspapers were the *St. Louis Globe-Democrat* and the Portland *Oregonian*.

ARTHUR G. NEWMYER (1885-1955)—Published the *New Orleans Item* and later became Associate Publisher of the *Washington Times-Herald*.

ADOLPH S. OCHS (1858-1935)—Owner of the *Chattanooga Times*, he bought the *New York Times* in 1896 and built it into one of the great newspapers of the world.

MARTIN PERETZ (1922- , Baltimore)—Owner and Publisher of the *New Republic* from 1974.

JOSEPH PULITZER (1847-1911, Mako, Hungary)—Owner of the *St. Louis Post-Dispatch* and later of the *New York World*. The Pulitzer Prizes carry his name. He also served as a congressman.

EDWARD ROSEWATER (1841-1906, Bukoven, Germany)—Editor and owner of the *Omaha Daily Bee*.

DOROTHY SCHIFF (1903- , New York City)—The great owner and Editor of the *New York Post*, which she acquired after her divorce from George Backer.

HENRI SMADJA (1897-1974, Oran, Algeria)—Published *Combat*, one of the leading leftist newspapers in France.

LEOPOLD SONNEMANN (1831-1909, Hochberg, Germany)—Founded the *Frankfurter Zeitung*, one of the great newspapers of Europe.

JULIUS D. STERN (1886-1971, Philadelphia)—Owned the *New York Post*, 1933–1939; the *Philadelphia Record*; and the *Camden* (N.J.) *Courier-Post*.

ARTHUR HAYS SULZBERGER (1891-1968, New York City)—Publisher of the *New York Times*, he also owned one of the largest newsprint companies in the world, the Spruce Falls Power and Paper Company. He was followed as publisher of the *Times* by Orvil Dryfoos, who was in turn followed by Sulzberger's son, **ARTHUR O. SULZBERGER** (1926-).

THE ULLSTEIN FAMILY—LEOPOLD ULLSTEIN (1826–1899) established many German newspapers and magazines and built his company into one of the world's great publication firms. His children established the *Berliner Morgenpost* and developed it into the largest daily paper in Germany. The family's magazine, the *Berliner Illustrierte Zeitung*, had a circulation in the millions. RUDOLF ULLSTEIN led the company after World War II, and his *Berliner Zeitung* was an influential paper in West Germany in the 1950s. The family finally sold out much of their interest to the famous Axel Springer.

MAGAZINE PUBLISHERS AND JOURNALISTS

See also Social Critics; Science Fiction Writers.

SHANA ALEXANDER (1925- , New York City)—Was a columnist for *Life* and *Newsweek* and was featured on CBS's "Spectrum" radio series and on *60 Minutes* on TV. She was also a founding member of the National Women's Political Caucus and received the Golden Pen Award of the American Newspaper Women's Club in 1969.

DAVID M. ALPERN (1942- , Brooklyn)—Became General Editor for National Affairs of *Newsweek* in 1966.

EDWARD ANTHONY (1895-1971, New York City)—Was publisher of the *Women's Home Companion* and of *Collier's* and earlier had served as Publicity Director of Herbert Hoover's victorious 1928 presidential campaign.

JAMES ARONSON (1915- , Boston)—Founder and Editor (up to 1967) of the *National Guardian*.

MAX ASCOLI (1898-1978)—Edited the influential (and now defunct) magazine *The Reporter* for almost 20 years.

JACOB L. CHERNOFSKY (1928- , New York City)—Editor and publisher of the *AB Bookman's Weekly* from 1975.

NORMAN COUSINS (1912- , Union Hill, N.J.)—The famous award-winning Editor of the *Saturday Review*, he became a Unitarian.

EDWIN DIAMOND (1925- , Chicago)—Was a Senior Editor at *Newsweek*, 1962–1969, and later a Contributing Editor to *New York* magazine.

JASON EPSTEIN (1928- , Cambridge, Mass.)—Was a Vice-President at Random House and Director of the *New York Review of Books*.

MARTIN GOLDMAN (1920- , New York City)—Senior Editor at *Time*.

PETER L. GOLDMAN (1933- , Philadelphia)—A Senior Editor at *Newsweek*, he is also author of *The Death and Life of Malcolm X* (1973).

ABEL GREEN (1900-)—Long-time Editor of *Variety*, the bible of show business.

MAXIMILIAN HARDEN (1861-1927, Berlin)—Born Witkowski. Founder and Editor of *Die Zukunft*, one of the most influential magazines in Germany.

GEOFFREY T. HELLMAN (1907- , New York City)—An excellent staff writer for the *New Yorker*.

DAVID HOROWITZ (1939- , New York City)—Was Editor of *Ramparts* from 1968.

RICHARD KAPLAN (1929- , New York City)—Executive Editor of the *Ladies' Home Journal*.

ALLEN KATZMAN (1937- , Brooklyn)—Founder and publisher of the now defunct *East Village Other* in 1965, one of the leading underground newspapers in the U.S.

ANDREW D. KOPKIND (1935- , New Haven)—Editor of *Ramparts* from 1970.

RONALD P. KRISS (1934- , Brooklyn)—A Senior Editor at *Time*.

HAROLD LAVINE (1915- , New York City)—A Senior Editor at both *Newsweek* and *Forbes*.

DAVID LAWRENCE (b. 1888)—One of the most important political commentators in America, he had a nationally syndicated column and was the long-time publisher of *U.S. News and World Report*.

LUDWIG LEWISOHN (1882-1955, Berlin)—The noted novelist and writer was also Associate Editor of the *Nation*, 1919-1926.

MARSHALL LOEB (1929- , Chicago)—The award-winning Senior Editor of *Time*.

EUGENE LYONS (1898- , Uzlain, Russia)—Formerly a UP reporter in Moscow and editor of such magazines as the *American Mercury* and *Pageant*, he became a Senior Editor at *Reader's Digest* in 1952.

MICHAEL J. MALBIN (1943- , Brooklyn)—A Contributing Editor to the *National Journal*.

J. ROBERT MOSKIN (1923- , New York City)—A Senior Editor and then Foreign Editor of *Look*, 1956-1971.

IRA S. MOTHNER (1932- , Brooklyn)—A Senior Editor at *Look* beginning in 1960.

LILLIAN ROSS (1927- , Syracuse)—A staff writer for the *New Yorker* since 1948.

WILLIAM S. RUKEYSER (1939- , New York City)—Has served as editor and staff writer for the *Wall Street Journal*, *Fortune*, and *Money*, and is one of the leading financial commentators in the U.S.

SOL SANDERS (1926- , Atlanta)—South Asia Editor of *U.S. News and World Report*, 1961-1970.

JERROLD L. SCHECTER (1932- , New York City)—Diplomatic Editor of *Time* since 1973.

CHARLES E. SILBERMAN (1925- , Des Moines, Iowa)—A member of the Board of Editors of *Fortune* since 1961.

AL SILVERMAN (1926- , Lynn, Mass.)—Editor in Chief of such magazines as *Sport* and *Saga*.

SIME SILVERMAN (1872-1933, Cortland, N.Y.)—Founded *Variety* in 1905.

ROBERT STEIN (1924- , New York City)—Editor in Chief of *Redbook*, 1958-**1965, and of** *McCall's*, 1965-1967 and from 1972.

I. F. STONE (1907- , Philadelphia)—Born Isidor Feinstein. Became famous through *I. F. Stone's Weekly*, (1953-1967), which he used to comment on American foreign and domestic issues. He later became a Contributing Editor to the *New York Review of Books*.

MARVIN L. STONE (1924- , Burlington, Vt.,)—Editor in Chief of *U.S. News and World Report*.

LESTER TANZER (1929- , New York City)—Associate Executive Editor of *U.S. News and World Report*.

RALPH DE TOLEDANO (1916- , International Zone of Tangier)—A former correspondent for *Newsweek*, be became a syndicated columnist and a leading spokesman for the conservative viewpoint in American life.

GORDON L. WEIL (1937- , Mineola, N.Y.)—President and publisher of *Political Intelligence* from 1974.

LAWYERS

See also Civil Rights Leaders; Feminists; Legal Scholars

MORRIS B. ABRAM (1918- , Fitzgerald, Ga.)—A leading American lawyer, he served as General Counsel of the Peace Corps when it was started.

LEON BERENSON (1885-1943, Warsaw)—A leading lawyer in modern Polish history, he specialized in defending clients charged with political crimes.

JOSEPH E. BRILL (1904-1975)—A noted N.Y. criminal trial lawyer.

ABRAHAM J. DITTENHOEFER (1836-1919, Charleston, S.C.)—A noted copyright lawyer, he was also one of the foremost theatrical lawyers in the U.S.

K. W. EHRLICH (1900-1971)—One of the most famous criminal trial lawyers in the U.S.

LUDWIK ERLICH (1889- , Tarnopol, Russia)—A leading international lawyer, he taught at the U. of Cracow.

MORRIS ERNST (1889-1976)—The lawyer who won the 1933 federal court case exonerating James Joyce's *Ulysses* from charges of obscenity.

JOEL E. GOUDSMIT (1813-1882)—A leading Dutch lawyer, he was a fellow of the Royal Netherlands Academy of Sciences.

MILTON HANDLER (1903- , New York City)—A leading U.S. antitrust lawyer, he also was an expert on trademark law.

WILLIAM B. HERLANDS (1905-1969, New York City)—Although he was Federal District Court Judge in New York, his real contribution was his outstanding work as Chief Trial Assistant in the prosecution of organized crime in New York during Thomas Dewey's anti-crime drive.

ROBERT M. W. KEMPNER (1899- , Freiburg, Germany)—Chief Prosecutor of Nazi war criminals at Nuremberg.

WILLIAM KUNSTLER—*See* Civil Rights Leaders.

SIR GEORGE LEWIS (1833-1911, London)—A leading criminal lawyer in England in the 1800s.

LOUIS MARSHALL (1856-1929, Syracuse, N.Y.)—Probably the leading constitutional lawyer of his generation, he appeared frequently before the Supreme Court.

LEVY MAYER (1858-1922, Richmond, Va.)—An outstanding American corporate lawyer at the turn of the century.

GEORGE Z. MEDALIE (1883-1946, New York City)—A leading crime fighter as U.S. Attorney for the Southern District of New York in the 1930s.

ROBERT M. MORGENTHAU (1919- , New York City)—Served in the same capacity as Medalie, and was noted for his effective and vigorous prosecution of criminals.

HENRY H. MORRIS (1878-1954)—One of the most famous criminal lawyers in the history of South Africa.

SIMON H. RIFKIND (1901- , Meretz, Russia)—A law partner of Adlai Stevenson, he was one of the leading lawyers in the U.S. and a close associate of the Kennedy family.

IRVING SAYPOL (1906-1977)—Later a judge, he prosecuted the Rosenberg spy case for the government.

BERNARD G. SEGAL (1907-)—President of the American Bar Association, 1969-1970.

DAVID SIMONS (1860-1939)—Many consider him to be the leading Dutch criminal lawyer of all time.

SIMON STERNE (1839-1901, Philadelphia)—Broke the power of the Tweed gang in New York politics in the 1870s and helped to establish the Interstate Commerce Commission.

ARNOLD WALD (1932-   , Guanabara, Brazil)—A leading Brazilian lawyer, he served as Secretary General of the Institute of Brazilian Lawyers.

ROBERT G. WOOLF (1928-   , Portland, Maine)—A leading lawyer representing athletes, some of his clients include Thurman Munson and John Havlicek. At one time he represented more than 300 jocks.

DOCTORS AND MEDICAL RESEARCHERS

See also Nobel Prize Winners, Medicine; Psychologists.

ISAAC A. ABT (1867-1955, Wilmington, Ill.)—Served as the President of the American Academy of Pediatrics when it was established.

LAJOS ADAM (1879-1946)—A noted Hungarian physician who made major breakthroughs in the use of anesthesia.

SAUL A. ADLER (1895-1966, Karelitz, Russia)—A world-famous parasitologist who did important research on leishmania diseases and was a leading expert on tropical diseases of all kinds. A member of the British Royal Society, he eventually became an Israeli citizen.

ISIDOR ALBU (1837-1903, Berlin)—A leading authority on eye problems, he became the personal physician to the Shah of Persia.

ALFRED A. ANGRIST (1902-   , Brooklyn)—A leading American pathologist, he helped develop the nomenclature of the field and was an expert on autopsy.

ADOLF A. BAGINSKY (1843-1918, Silesia)—His research laid the groundwork for pediatrics, and his *Textbook of Pediatrics* was one of the most influential books in the field for years.

HEINRICH BANBERGER (1826-1888, Prague)—A leading heart specialist of the 1800s. Banberger's disease is named for him.

SIR LOUIS BARNETT (1865-1946, Wellington, New Zealand)—A great early researcher in the use of X-rays.

SIMON BARUCH (1840-1921, Posen, Prussia)—Credited with being the first physician to take out a ruptured appendix. He served in the Confederate army during the American Civil War.

SEYMOUR BENZER (1921-   , New York City)—Stuart Distinguished Professor at Purdue, he did crucially important research into the mapping of the gene.

ISAAC BERENBLUM (1903-   , Bialystok, Poland)—Author of *Man Against Cancer* and one of the leading authorities in the field, he is now at the Weizmann Institute in Israel.

HIPPOLYTE BERNHEIM (1840-1919, France)—A leading psychotherapist of the 1800s.

JULIUS BERNSTEIN (1839-1917, Berlin)—Widely considered to be the father of modern neurophysiology.

ALEXANDER BESREDKA (1870-1940)—One of the world's leading immunologists and Director of the Pasteur Institute.

IVAN BLOCH (1872-1922)—One of the pioneer scholars on sex, his *Origin of Syphilis* (I always thought I knew where it came from) was an important work, and he is considered a major medical historian.

DAVID BODIAN (1910-   , Chicago)—A world authority on the synaptic functions of the nervous system and a member of the National Academy of Sciences.

GUSTAV BUCKY (1880-1963, Leipzig, Germany)—Bucky rays are named for him, as is the Bucky diaphragm.

LEO BUERGER (1880-1943, Vienna)—A leading American pathologist. Buerger's disease is named for him.

BARON HENRY COHEN (1900- , Birkenhead, England)—Served as President of both the Royal Society of Medicine and the British Medical Association, and played an important role in the development of the National Health Service in Great Britain.

FERDINAND J. COHN (1828-1898, Breslau)—The foremost authority in the world on bacteria, his belief that bacteria were plants revolutionized the field.

JULIUS COHNHEIM (1839-1884, Pomerania)—Proved that tuberculosis was contagious, and did pioneering research on the circulatory system and inflammation. He is considered to be one of the first modern pathologists.

BURRILL B. CROHN (b. 1884, New York City)—The leading expert on regional ileitis. Crohn's disease (granulomatous colitis) is named for him.

WILLIAM DAMESHEK (1900-1969, Voronezh, Russia)—Served as the President of the International and American Societies of Hematology, wrote the standard *Leukemia*, and edited the journal *Blood*, which he founded.

LEO M. DAVIDOFF (1898- , Talsen, Latvia)—Doctor and surgeon on the 1925 Byrd expedition to the Arctic.

JOSEPH B. DE LEE (1869-1942)—His *Principles and Practice of Obstetrics* was the standard work for decades, and he designed many instruments used by doctors all over the world.

LOUIS K. DIAMOND (1902- , New York City)—A leading American hematologist.

ISAAC DJERASSI (1923- , Vienna)—A leading expert on leukemia.

WILLIAM DRESSLER (1890-1969, Austria)—A leading American cardiologist and the author of several major textbooks on the subject. The Dressler syndrome (postmyocardial infarction) is named for him.

LUDWIG EDINGER (1855-1918, Worms, Germany)—A world-famous neurologist. Edinger fibers and Edinger's nucleus are named for him.

GUSTAV EMBIDEN (1874-1933, Hamburg, Germany)—A leading authority on the chemistry of muscular contraction.

BORIS EPHRUSSI (1901-)—One of the leading geneticists in France, he did important research in the heredity of cells.

SIDNEY FARBER (1904-1973)—Did important early research on cancer in children.

HEINRICH FINKELSTEIN (1865-1942, Leipzig, Germany)—One of the leading experts of his generation on children's diseases.

MORRIS FISHBEIN (1889-1976, St. Louis, Mo.)—The famous leader of the American Medical Association and Editor of its journal for many decades.

MAURICE FISHBERG (1872-1934, Russia)—A leading expert on pulmonary tuberculosis.

WILLIAM H. FISHMAN (1914- , Winnipeg, Canada)—Director of Cancer Research at the Tufts–New England Hospital.

ULRICH FRIEDEMANN (1877-1949, Berlin)—A world authority on scarlet fever.

AARON FRIEDENWALD (1836-1902, Baltimore)—A leading U.S. ophthalmologist, he founded the Association of American Medical Colleges.

ALFRED FROEHLICH (1871-1953, Vienna)—The world's foremost expert on adiposo-genetical dystrophy and on the use of hypoglysin in childbirth.

CASIMIR FUNK (1884-1967, Warsaw)—The great biochemist who is considered the father of dietetics, he gave us the word *vitamin*.

JOSEPH GOLDBERGER (1874-1929, Giralt, Hungary)—Pioneered in the use of nicotinic acid in the prevention of pellagra and was one of the leading experts in the world on that disease. He was an American citizen.

RICHARD B. GOLDSCHMIDT (1878-1958, Frankfort)—The leading advocate of the "mutation" theory of evolution. His ideas have not been accepted.

BERNHARD GOTTLIEB (1885-1950, Kuty, Slovakia)—An important dental scientist, he conducted important studies of the epithelial tissue.

DAVID M. GREENBERG (1895-)—Did important early research with radioisotopes and was a member of the Atomic Energy Commission.

MORTON I. GROSSMAN (1919- , Ohio)—Served as an Editor of *Gastroenterology* and is a leader in his specialty.

DAVID GRUBY (1810-1898, Novi Sad, Hungary)—A major 19th-century parasitologist, he did pioneering research on parasitic worms and fungi.

MARTIN GUMPERT (1897-1955, Berlin)—A world authority on geriatrics and the author of *You Are Younger Than You Think*.

ALEXANDER G. GURWITSCH (1874-1954, Poltava, Russia)—Born Gurvish. A winner of the Stalin Prize, he was one of the leading biochemists in the Soviet Union.

ALEXANDER B. GUTMAN (1902- , New York City)—A leading expert on gout, he founded and edited the *American Journal of Medicine*.

ALAN F. GUTTMACHER (1898-1974, Baltimore)—A leading advocate of family planning and population control, he was a long-time President of the Planned Parenthood Association of America.

SIR LUDWIG GUTTMAN (1899- , Germany)—One of the most famous physicians in the world and the holder of the Star of the Grand Cross of the Order of Merit of West Germany, he did crucial research in the treatment of paraplegics at the National Spinal Injuries Center in Great Britain, which he founded and directed.

WALDEMAR M. HAFFKINE (1860-1930)—The Haffkine Institute in India is named for him, as well it should be, since he discovered the vaccine that checked the spread of cholera in the world.

MARKUS HAJEK (1861-1941, in what is now Yugoslavia)—A leading expert on rhinolaryngology and an authority on the treatment of sinus problems.

LUDWIG HALBERSTAEDTER (1876-1949, Silesia)—One of the world's leading researchers of trachoma, he was also an authority on several forms of malaria.

LIPMAN HALPERN (1902-1968, Bialystok, Poland)—Became world-famous for his research on the relationship of posture to organic function. He was an Israeli citizen.

ADOLPH HANNOVER (1814-1894)—A major 19th-century histologist, he did important research on infectious diseases. He was a Dane.

ERNEST A. HART (1836-1898, London)—A leading ophthalmologist, he served as Editor of the *British Medical Journal*.

ISAAC HAYS (1796-1879, Philadelphia)—Was a cofounder of the AMA, developed the standard code of medical ethics for that group, and was a leading researcher in color blindness.

MICHAEL HEIDELBERGER (b. 1888, New York City)—Served as President of the American Association of Immunologists.

MARTIN HEIDENHAIN (1864-1949)—Helped to develop the field of cytology and was a leading histologist at the U. of Tübingen.

RUDOLF HEIDENHAIN (1834-1897, Marienwerder, Germany)—An expert on the secretory process, he is considered among the most important physiologists of his generation.

MILTON HELPERN (1902- , New York City)—One of the foremost forensic pathologists in the U.S., he was Chief Medical Examiner of New York City and also served as President of the National Association of Medical Examiners.

JACOB HENLE (1809-1885)—One of the founders of histology. His theories of the relationship between disease and microorganisms were decades ahead of their time.

AUGUST HIRSCH (1817-1894, Germany)—A founder and President of the German Public Health Association, he did pioneer work in the fields of historical and geographical medicine.

MONROE J. HIRSCH (1917- , New York City)—A leading American optometrist, he was President of the American Academy of Optometry, 1966–1968.

RACHEL HIRSCH (1870-1953)—The Rachel Hirsch Effect, the process whereby corpuscular elements are eliminated from the blood in the human body, is named for her. She was a German.

JULIUS HIRSCHBERG (1843-1925, Potsdam)—A leading ophthalmologist and surgeon, he pioneered in techniques for removing objects from the eye.

ISADOR HIRSCHFELD (1882-1965, Riga, Latvia)—Author of the exciting work *The Toothbrush: Its Use and Abuse*, he was a President of the American Academy of Periodonotology.

IGNAC HIRSCHLER (1823-1891, Pressburg, Hungary)—A great early ophthalmologist, he was a fellow of the Hungarian Academy of Sciences.

LUDWIK HIRSZFELD (1884-1954, Warsaw)—The leading Polish microbiologist. His main research was on the heredity of blood groups.

PHINEAS J. HORWITZ (1822-1904, Baltimore)—Served as the Director of the U.S. Bureau of Medicine and Surgery.

ABRAHAM JACOBI (1830-1919, Hartum, Germany)—A pioneer pediatrician in the U.S.

LUDVIG L. JACOBSON (1783-1843)—One of the leading physicians in Denmark, he won the Prix Monthyon of the French Academy.

THE FATHER OF . . .

the atomic submarine—**HYMAN RICKOVER** (*see* Military Figures: Americans)
communism—**KARL MARX** (*see* Men and Women of the Left: Germans)
cybernetics—**NORBERT WIENER** (*see* Mathematicians)
dietetics—**CASIMIR FUNK** (*see* Doctors)
Esperanto—**LUDWIK ZAMENHOF** (*see* Writers: Poles)
field theory—**KURT LEWIN** (*see* Psychologists)
holography—**DENNIS GABOR** (*see* Nobel Prize Winners: Physics)
the U.S. labor movement—**SAMUEL GOMPERS** (*see* Labor Leaders
logical semantics—**ALFRED TARSKI** (*see* Philosophers)
method acting—**LEE STRASBERG** (*see* Theatrical Directors and Teachers)
modern neurophysiology—**JULIUS BERNSTEIN** (*see* Doctors)
power politics—**HANS J. MORGENTHAU** (*see* Political Scientists)
transactional analysis—**ERIC BERNE** (*see* Psychologists)

JOSEF JADASSOHN (1863-1936, Liegnitz, Germany)—Jadassohn's disease, a very unpleasant skin disorder, is named after him. He also did important research on venereal disease.

HENRY D. JANOWITZ (1915- , Paterson, N.J.)—A former President of the American Gastroenterological Association.

ADRIAN KANTROWITZ (1918- , New York City)—One of the most important cardiovascular surgeons in the world, he pioneered in the use of bioengineering for the heart and developed the auxiliary ventricle and the famous Kantrowitz–General Electric pacemaker.

MORTIZ KAPOSI (1837-1902, Kaposvar, Hungary)—Born Kohn. Kaposi's disease and Kaposi's sarcoma are named for him. He became a Christian.

EPHRAIM KATCHALSKI (1916- , Kiev, Russia)—A world-famous biochemist and authority on proteins, he is an Israeli member of the National Academy of Sciences in the U.S.

LOUIS S. KATZ (1897-1973)—Did pioneer research into hardening of the arteries.

BRUNO Z. KISCH (1890-1966, Prague)—Served as the President of the American College of Cardiology, which he helped to establish. He did important research on the autonomic reflex.

EDMUND KLEIN (1921- , Vienna)—A Canadian, he has done pioneer research in immunotherapy for cancer.

PAUL KLEMPERER (1887-1964, Vienna)—One of the world's leading experts on the spleen.

NATHAN S. KLINE (1916- , Philadelphia)—Served as Chairman of the International Psychiatric Research Foundation and is one of the world's leading psychopharmacologists.

HENRY KOPLIK (1858-1927, New York City)—Koplik's spots, the diagnostic spots of measles in the mouth, are named for him. His *Diseases of Infancy and Childhood* was one of the standard works of the early 20th century.

SAMUEL KRISTELLER (1820-1900, Posen)—Kristeller's method (of ejecting the placenta) was named for him.

HUGO KRONECKER (1839-1914, Silesia)—Did important early work on blood pressure. He was Swiss, and he became a Christian.

LEOPOLD LANDAU (1848-1920, Warsaw)—A leading vaginal surgeon of his time.

OSCAR LASSAR (1849-1907, Hamburg, Germany)—Developed Lassar paste for the treatment of skin afflictions, and was considered a major figure in dermatology in the last half of the 1800s.

GIUSEPPE LEVI (1872-1965, Trieste)—A leading expert on tissue culture and sensory and motor neurons.

PHILIP LEVINE (1900- , Russia)—Discovered numerous blood group factors and was an expert on blood transfusions.

ABRAHAM LEVINSON (1888-1955)—A leading expert on cerebrospinal fluid, he was also one of the world's foremost authorities on meningitis.

LEO LOEB (1869-1959, Mayen, Germany)—A great early cancer researcher, especially in hormonal research.

ALEXANDER R. LURIA (1902- , Kazan, Russia)—A leading Soviet neuropsychologist and the holder of the Order of Lenin.

DAVID L. MACHT (1882-1961, Moscow)—An American, he was a leading authority on the uses of benzyl alcohol.

ALEXANDER MARMOREK (1865-1923, Mielnice, Galicia)—He did pioneering research on typhus and diabetes.

ARTHUR M. MASTER (b. 1895, New York City)—The Master Two-Step test, measuring heart rate and blood pressure, is named for him.

JOSEPH MELNICK (1914- , Boston)—An internationally known virologist at Baylor U. Med. School.

ARYEH L. OLITZKI (1898- , Allenstein, Germany)—An Israeli, he did important research on brucellosa infection in humans.

HERMANN OPPENHEIM (1858-1919, Warburg, Germany)—Was Chairman and founder of the German Neurological Association, wrote a leading neurology textbook, and was one of the world's leading experts on brain tumors.

MEYER A. PERLSTEIN (1902-1969, Chicago)—Served as President of the American Academy of Cerebral Palsy, which he founded, and was a leading authority on the disease.

HUGO C. PLAUT (1858-1928, Leipzig)—The world's leading authority on trench mouth.

ADAM POLITZER (1835-1920, Alberti, Hungary)—Considered the founder of otology and was one of the world's leading authorities on diseases of the ear.

SHEMOOIL RAHBAR (1929- , Hamadan, Iran)—The leading immunologist in the Muslim world and Director of the Abnormal Hemoglobin Research Laboratory of the University of Teheran.

HENRY RAPPAPORT (1913- , Austria)—A leading authority on hematology and reticuloendothelial pathology.

ROBERT REMAK (1815-1865, Germany)—Remak's Ganglion and Remak Fibers carry the name of this pioneer neurologist.

DAVID REUBEN (1933- , Chicago)—Told us everything we ever wanted to know about sex and some things we could have passed up.

MORITZ ROMBERG (1795-1873, Meiningen, Germany)—His *Manual of the Nervous Diseases of Man* is considered to be the first real textbook in the field.

SAMUEL ROSEN (1897- , Syracuse)—An award-winning otologist whose work restored hearing to hundreds.

MAX ROSENHEIM (1908-1972, England)—Onetime President of the Royal College of Physicians and a leading expert on diseases of the kidney. He was a baron.

ALBERT B. SABIN (1906- , Poland)—A member of the National Academy of Sciences, he is the famed developer of the oral polio vaccine that has saved thousands of lives since its introduction.

BERNARD SACHS (1858-1944, Baltimore)—Describer of Tay-Sachs disease and a leading child neurologist.

LEO SACHS (1924- , Leipzig, Germany)—An Israeli, he is one of the world's leading geneticists.

JONAS SALK (1914- , New York City)—The award-winning epidemiologist who developed the polio vaccine that carries his name.

BELA SCHICK (1877-1967, Boglar, Hungary)—His Schick Test for diphtheria proneness has saved countless lives.

VELVA SCHRIRE (1916-1972, Kimberley, South Africa)—A leading cardiologist, he worked with Christiaan Barnard on the first heart transplant.

HARRY M. SELDIN (1895- , Russia)—One of the outstanding oral surgeons in the world.

SIR FELIX SEMON (1849-1921, Danzig, Germany)—Personal physician and long-time friend of Edward VII of England.

ERNEST SIMON (1902-1973, Berlin)—An Israeli, he was a world authority on diabetes.

ADOLPHUS S. SOLOMONS (1826-1910, New York City)—Cofounder of the American Red Cross.

LINA STERN (1878-1968, Lithuania)—Holder of the Soviet Order of Merit and the Stalin Prize, she was one of the leading physiologists in the Soviet Union and was reputedly the first female member of the Soviet Academy of Sciences.

BENEDICT STILLING (1810-1897, Kirchlain, Germany)—A leading expert on color blindness, he did pioneering work on cornea transplants.

IRWIN M. STILLMAN (1896-1975)—One of the most famous "diet doctors" in the U.S. and the author of several best-selling books.

PAUL UNNA (1850-1929, Hamburg, Germany)—The Ducrey-Unna bacillus is partly named for him, and he made a major contribution to the field through his analysis, classification, and description of a variety of skin diseases.

GABRIEL G. VALENTIN (1810-1883, Breslau)—One of the great early physiologists, he was a pioneer researcher of the human lung and authored the then-standard *Textbook of Physiology*. He also did important research on cell theory.

JACOB VAN DERHOEDEN (1891-1968, Utrecht, Netherlands)—Was one of the most important bacteriologists in Holland before settling in Israel.

AUGUST VON WASSERMAN (1866-1925)—A pioneer immunologist and codiscoverer (with Reuben Kahn) of the famous syphilis test that carries his name.

SERGE VORONOFF (1866-1951, Russia)—Did controversial research on the transplanting of glands from animals to humans.

LEON L. WATTERS (1877-1967, Salt Lake City, Utah)—Did important research into the construction of military medical facilities, including portable disinfectors and mobile hospitals.

ISRAEL WECHSLER (1886-1962, Lespedi, Rumania)—Served as President of the American Neurological Association and was a world-famous expert on epilepsy.

CARL WEIGERT (1845-1904, Münsterberg, Germany)—Did important research in tuberculosis and bacteriology.

THEODORE H. WEISENBURG (1876-1934, New York City)—Famed for his book *Adult Intelligence*, he was a President of the American Neurological Association.

CHAIM E. WERTHEIMER (b. 1893, Bühl, Germany)—Winner of the Bunting Prize of the American Association for Diabetes Research, he is a world authority on fat metabolism. He emigrated to Israel.

FERNAND WIDAL (1862-1929, Algeria)—One of the developers of the low-salt diet, he was a pioneer in the treatment of typhoid fever and a fellow of the French Academy of Sciences.

ALEXANDER S. WIENER (1907-1976, New York City)—Codiscoverer of the Rh blood factor.

MAXWELL M. WINTROBE (1901-   , Canada)—Wrote the standard work on clinical hematology.

ABNER WOLF (1902-   , New York City)—Was Editor of the *Journal of Neuropathology and Experimental Neurology* and a President of the American Association of Neurologists.

ABEL WOLMAN (b. 1892, Baltimore)—A President of the American Public Health Association and Editor of the *Journal of Public Health*, he was an internationally recognized authority on environmental pollution and one of the leading sanitary engineers in the U.S.

ARCHITECTS

MAX ABRAMOVITZ (1908-   , Chicago)—His firm designed such famous buildings as Philharmonic Hall (the new one) in New York, the Alcoa Building in Pittsburgh, and the Secretariat building at the UN in New York.

DANKMAR ADLER (1844-1900, Stadtlengsfeld, Germany)—With the great Louis Sullivan, he pioneered in the design of the skyscraper.

CECIL N. BLANKSTEIN (1908- , Manitoba)—A leading Canadian architect who designed the Winnipeg City Hall and the Canadian National Art Gallery.

SIDNEY BREGMAN (1922- , Poland)—Helped design the Niagara Tower and the beautiful Dominion Center in Toronto.

MARCEL BREUER (1902- , Pecs, Hungary)—One the most influential architects in American history. Among his major efforts was New York's Whitney Museum.

ARNOLD BRUNNER (1857-1925, New York City)—The great architect and planner who designed Lewisohn Stadium in New York.

MONTE BRYER (1912- , Bloemfontein, South Africa)—A leading South African architect, he was head designer of Johannesburg's Civic Center.

GORDON BUNSHAFT (1909- , Buffalo)—A leading designer of large office buildings, his masterpiece was the Lever Building in New York.

ROBERTO BURLE-MARX (1909- , Sao Paulo)—One of the world's leading landscape architects.

MICHAEL DE KLERK (1884-1923, Amsterdam)—A leading Dutch architect who specialized in housing projects.

JULIEN ELEGENHEIMER (1880-1938, Geneva)—The world-famous designer of the Palace of the League of Nations and the Belgian Royal Palace.

JOSEF FRANK (b. 1885, Baden, Austria)—Codesigner of the world-famous Karl Marx House in Vienna.

ALEXANDER I. GEGELLO (b. 1891)—Designer of Leningrad's Palace of Culture. He was Vice-President of the Soviet Academy of Architects.

BERTRAND GOLDBERG (1913- , Chicago)—His great work was Marina City towers in Chicago.

PERCIVAL GOODMAN (1904- , New York City)—A Professor at Columbia U. and one of the leading authorities on city planning in the U.S.

HENRY GREENSPOON (1919- , Montreal)—A leading Canadian architect and the designer of Westmount Square in Quebec.

VICTOR D. GRUEN (1903- , Vienna)—A leading American architect, he designed the Northland Shopping Center in Detroit.

MANFRED HERMER (1915- , Volksrust, South Africa)—His great accomplishment was Johannesburg's Civic Theater.

ARNE E. JACOBSEN (1902-1971, Copenhagen)—His many great designs made him the outstanding architect in Denmark.

ALBERT KAHN (1869-1942, Rhaunen, Germany)—One of America's greatest industrial architects, he designed the General Motors Building.

ELY J. KAHN (1884-1972, New York City)—Widely acclaimed as an architectural genius, he specialized in magnificent skyscrapers.

LOUIS I. KAHN (1901-1974, Osel, Estonia)—An internationally known architect, whose greatest achievements were the Richard Medical Research Building at the U. of Pennsylvania and the Yale Gallery of Art.

ROY KANTOROWICH (1917- , South Africa)—A Professor at the U. of Manchester and one of the world's leading authorities on town planning.

MORRIS LAPIDUS (1902- , Odessa)—Designed many magnificent hotels. The Fontainebleau on Miami Beach was not one of his best.

FRED LEBENSOLD (1917- , Poland)—A leading Canadian architect, he designed the National Arts Center in Ottawa.

HAROLD H. LE ROITH (1905- , Grahamstown, South Africa)—An internationally known South African architect.

ERIC MENDELSOHN (1887-1953, Allenstein, Germany)—A leading German architect who specialized in office buildings.

ALFRED MESSEL (1853-1909, Darmstadt, Germany)—One of his great designs was Berlin's Wertheim Department Store.

CLAUDE MEYER-LEVY (1908- , Paris)—A leading French architect famous for the Yachting Pavilion he designed for the 1937 World's Fair.

RICHARD J. NEUTRA (1892-1970, Vienna)—A world-famous American designer of private residences.

SIR NIKOLAUS PEVSNER (1902- , Leipzig, Germany)—One of the world's leading architectural historians and the author of *An Outline of European Architecture.*

EMMANUEL PONTREMILI (1865-1956, Nice, France)—One of his great designs was the Museum of Natural History in Paris.

EUGENE ROSENBERG (1907- , Topolcany, Slovakia)—A leading British architect and a specialist in school and university design, he also designed the U.S. Embassy in London.

MOSHE SAFDIE (1938- , Haifa)—The celebrated Israeli architect whose Habitat was the star of Montreal's Expo.

BRUNO ZEVI (1918- , Rome)—A leading Italian architect.

Part III
Business

BUSINESS LEADERS

ABRAHAM ABRAHAM (1843-1911)—With Joseph Wechsler, he started what ultimately became Abraham & Straus, a great American department store and a Brooklyn landmark.

DAVID B. ADLER (1826-1878)—Helped to found the Chamber of Commerce in Copenhagen and was one of the most important Danish bankers of the mid-1800s.

SIR GEORGE ALBU (1857-1935, Berlin)—A leading figure in the world gold market as head of the General Mining and Finance Corporation of South Africa.

BENJAMIN ALTMAN (1840-1913, New York City)—Creator of B. Altman and Company, the great New York department store.

FRANK ALTSCHUL (b. 1887, San Francisco)—Was a leading banker and Director of Lazard Frères and later of the General American Investors Corporation.

LOUIS V. ARONSON (1923- , Newark, N.J.)—Founder of the Ronson Corporation, his lighters have lit many a cigar.

JULES S. BACHE (1862-1944, New York City)—One of the great investment bankers in American history, his J. S. Bache and Company is still a leading firm.

SIR LEON BAGRIT (1902- , Kiev, Russia)—Served as Chairman of Elliott-Automation and later as Deputy Chairman of English Electric, one of the largest producers of automated control systems in the world. He was also a member of the British Council for Scientific and Industrial Research.

ALBERT BALLIN (1857-1918, Hamburg, Germany)—One of the great shipping tycoons of all time, he took his own life at the end of World War I.

LOUIS BAMBERGER (1855-1944, Baltimore)—A leading American merchant and the head of Bamberger and Company.

BARNEY BARNATO (1852-1897, London)—A Life Governor of De Beers Consolidated Mining Company in South Africa and one of the richest men in the British Commonwealth.

BERNHARD BARON (1850-1929, Rostov-on-Don, Russia)—Owned the huge Carreras tobacco company of Great Britain.

MARCUS S. BEARSTED (1853-1927)—Founder of what became the Shell Oil Company. He was a viscount.

WALTER BEARSTED (1882-1948)—Also a viscount (the British have this thing about heredity), he became Chairman of the Shell Oil Company after his father.

SIR ALFRED BEIT (1853-1906, Hamburg)—A prominent figure in the history of southern Africa, he helped to establish what became Rhodesia. He was a Life Governor of the De Beers Consolidated Mines and a leading mining financier.

SIMON VAN DEN BERGH (1818-1906, Geffen, Germany)—A pioneer in the margarine industry, he was one of the men who helped to establish what became Unilever Limited, now a giant multinational corporation.

EDWARD L. BERNAYS (b. 1891, Vienna)—Was the world's leading authority in public relations. His clients included Thomas Masaryk and Enrico Caruso, and he wrote the pioneering *Crystallizing Public Opinion* (1929). His influence on our social and political culture has been significant, and largely overlooked.

MAURICE BLANK (1848-1921, Pitesti, Rumania)—His Marmorosh, Blank and Company became the second largest bank in Rumania and the largest privately owned bank in the country.

JACOB BLAUSTEIN (1892-1970)—The incredibly wealthy man who built the family American Oil Company into one of the giants of the industry.

LOUIS BLAUSTEIN (1869-1937, Russia)—Established the American Oil Company (AMOCO).

GERSON VON BLEICHROEDER (1822-1893, Berlin)—The fascinating figure who served Bismarck as an adviser on financial matters, he was one of the major bankers in Germany.

THE BLOOMINGDALE BROTHERS (Lyman G., 1841-1905, New York City; and Samuel J., 1873-1968, New York City)—Started the fabulous department store that carries their name. Bloomingdale's is now part of the huge Federated Department Stores.

ALFRED S. BLOOMINGDALE (1916- , New York City)—Of the great merchant family, he was Chairman of the Board and founder of the Diners Club.

CHARLES G. BLUHDORN (1926- , Vienna)—Chairman of the Board and Chief Executive Officer of the huge Gulf and Western Industries, Inc., which operates numerous enterprises.

LUCY BORCHARDT (1878-1969)—Owned and operated the Hamburg Fairplay Tug Company, one of the largest tugboat operations in Europe.

LOUIS H. BOYAR (b. 1898, San Francisco)—A major California real estate developer and the man who constructed Lakewood, Calif., a pioneer planned town.

AUGUST BRENTANO (1831-1886, Austria)—Started the great bookstore chain that carries his name.

ISRAEL BRODSKI (1823-1888, Russia)—In an era when Jews had few rights in Russia, he managed to become the major figure in the refining of sugar in that country, 25 percent of all Russian production deriving from his factories.

SAMUEL BRONFMAN (1891-1971, Brandon, Manitoba)—President of Distillers-Seagrams Limited, one of the largest enterprises of its kind in the world.

SIR ERNEST J. CASSEL (1852-1921, Cologne)—Certainly one of the most powerful men in the world, Cassel built the original Aswan Dam, established the National Bank of Egypt, and developed Vickers-Armstrong into a world leader in arms production. Most important, governments of many countries—from South America to Morocco to China—were dependent upon his loans for their solvency. He became a Catholic.

ANDRE G. CITROEN (1878-1935, Paris)—A pioneer French automobile manufacturer, he was also a leading automotive engineer.

LOUIS S. COHEN (1846-1922, Sydney, Australia)—Head of Lewis' Ltd., a leading British department store chain.

HERMAN CONE (1828-1897)—Head of the family that was among the largest cotton producers in the U.S. and among the world's largest manufacturers of cotton denim and flannel.

BERNIE CORNFELD (1928- , Brooklyn)—The celebrated international financial whiz kid and speculator who outsmarted himself on more than one occasion.

HENRY CROWN (1896- Chicago)—Former owner of the Empire State Building, he had major holdings in many large corporations and was on the Board of Directors of the Hilton Hotel Chain and of General Dynamics.

HENRI D. DEUTSCH (1846-1919, Paris)—Owned one of the two or three largest French petroleum companies and pioneered in the development of aviation fuel.

SHOUL EISENBERG (1921-)—A leading industrialist in both Japan and Korea, and reportedly one of the least known of the truly wealthy men in the world.

MAX FACTOR (1877-1938, Lodz, Poland)—Developed Max Factor and Company into one of the largest cosmetics manufacturers in the world.

ABRAHAM FEINBERG (1908- , New York City)—A leading American business figure, he served as Chairman of the American Bank and Trust Company and as Chairman of the Board of Kayser-Roth.

JOSEPH FELS (1853-1914, rural Virginia)—Founded and developed the Fels-Naphtha Company into one of America's largest soap companies.

EUGENE FERKAUF (1921-   , Brooklyn)—Head of the huge E. J. Korvette chain of department stores and associated supermarkets. The name E. J. Korvette reportedly stood for "eight Jewish Korean [War] veterans."

A. LINCOLN FILENE (1865-1957)—Head of the family that established Boston's largest department store and began many progressive labor-management practices.

SIR WOOLF FISHER (1912-   , Paraparaumu, New Zealand)—Director of New Zealand Steel Limited and other major New Zealand business enterprises and industrial firms.

BENOIT FOULD (1792-1858)—Head of the Fould family, which controlled the huge banking firm that carried their name.

LOUIS FRAENKEL (1851-1911, Germany)—One of the most important financiers in Sweden, he managed the affairs of the Stockholm Handelsbank, one of the country's largest.

LEE K. FRANKEL (1867-1931, Philadelphia)—One of the few Jews to play a major role in American insurance, he helped develop innovative health insurance systems as a Vice-President of the Metropolitan Life Insurance Company.

CARL FÜRSTENBERG (1850-1933, Danzig)—His Berliner Handels-Gesellschaft was one of the major investment banking houses in Germany.

LEWIS GERSTLE (1824-1902, Ichenhausen, Bavaria)—One of the great pioneer merchants in Alaska and the head of the Alaska Commercial Company.

DAVID GESTETNER (1854-1939, Csorna, Hungary)—You can thank him for stencil duplicating, developed by one of his industrial enterprises in Great Britain.

ADAM GIMBEL (1817-1897, Bavaria) **AND FAMILY**—The folks who made Gimbel Brothers and Saks Fifth Avenue into two of the great department store empires in the U.S.

ISAAC H. GLÜCKSTADT (1839-1910)—One of the most famous financiers in Denmark, he directed the Landmandsbanken, the biggest institution of its kind in all of Scandinavia.

MARCUS GOLDMAN (1821-1904) **AND FAMILY**—The great American investment banker family that developed Goldman, Sachs and Company into a leader in the field.

JAKOB GOLDSCHMIDT (1882-1955)—Head of Schwartz, Goldschmidt and Company, an important banking house in Germany before the rise of Hitler.

MEYER GUGGENHEIM (1828-1905, Langnau, Switzerland) **AND FAMILY**—One of the great mining families in America, with major holdings in copper, silver, and lead. Its members are found elsewhere in this book.

EUGEN GUTMANN (1840-1925, Dresden)—Controlled banks in South America and railroads in Turkey as head of the German Dresdner Bank, a leading international operation.

WILHELM R. VON GUTMANN (1825-1895, Lipnik, Moravia)—His Gebrüder Gutmann industries was the largest single factor in the coal industry of the Austro-Hungarian Empire.

SALOMON HABER (1764-1839, Breslau)—The patriarch of S. Haber and Sons, a major European banking house.

LAZARUS HALLGARTEN (d. 1875, Frankfurt)—Head of the family of bankers that played an important role in the trade in gold bullion in America in the mid-1800s.

ARMAND HAMMER (1898-   , New York City)—The enigmatic figure who developed Occidental Petroleum into one of the largest oil companies and who was close to the leadership of the Soviet Union.

SIR VICTOR R. HARARI (1857-1945, Cairo)—A leading financier in Egypt, he served on the board of directors of the National Bank of that country.

JACOB HECHT (1879-1963, Gondelsheim, Germany)—A leading shipping magnate in Europe as head of the Neptun Transport and Navigation Company.

HERMAN W. HELLMAN (1843-1906)—Founder of the Merchants National Bank of California, one of the major early financial institutions in that state.

ISAIAS W. HELLMAN (1842-1920, Rickendorf, Bavaria)—Herman's brother, he owned a large portion of Los Angeles and was one of the city's leading citizens.

HARRY B. HENSHEL (1919- , New York City)—President of the Bulova Watch Company.

LENA HIMMELSTEIN (1881-1951, Lithuania)—Established the Lane Bryant clothing store chain. She was a pioneer in the design and merchandising of maternity clothes and half-sizes.

ARON S. HIRSCH (1858-early 1940s)—A major German industrialist with extensive holdings in the metal industry of that country.

JOSEPH H. HIRSHHORN (1899- , Mitau, Latvia)—A great figure in uranium mining in Canada, he has spent a substantial portion of his fortune in the acquisition of art, which he donated to the American people in the famous museum that bears his name.

MAURICIO HOCHSCHILD (1881-1965, Biblis, Germany)—A major mining industrialist in Latin America, with extensive holdings in Argentina and Chile, he earlier was a dominant force in the Bolivian mining industry.

LOUIS J. HOROWITZ (1878-1956, Czestochowa, Poland)—Became President of the Thompson-Starett Construction Company, one of the major building firms in the U.S.

OTTO J. JOEL (1856-1916, Danzig)—Cofounder and Managing Director of the Banco Commerciale Italiano, a major financial institution in Italy.

SOLOMON B. JOEL (1865-1931)—Chairman of the board of the Johannesburg Consolidated Investment Company and a member of the board of directors of De Beers Consolidated, he was one of the most powerful men in South Africa and a major force in the world's trade in gold and diamonds.

NATHAN S. JONAS (1868-1943, Montgomery, Ala.)—Head of the influential Manufacturers Trust Company.

DAVID N. JUDELSON (1928-)—Head of Gulf & Western Industries, the huge conglomerate that controls (among others) Paramount Pictures, Consolidated Cigar, Kayser-Roth, and Simon & Schuster.

JACOBUS H. KANN (1872-1945, The Hague, Netherlands)—His Lissa and Kann banking house, a major enterprise in Dutch banking, was where the Dutch royal household kept its money.

HARRIS KEMPNER (1837-1894, Russia)—One of the most important bankers in the history of Texas, he was also a major figure in the cotton trade throughout the South.

MAURICIO KLABIN (1860-1923, Posvol, Lithuania)—A major Brazilian industrialist, controlling newsprint and tile factories.

ZSIGMOND KORNFELD (1852-1909, Golcuv Jenikov, Bohemia)—A major Hungarian banker, he served as President of the Budapest Stock Exchange at the turn of the century.

HAROLD KRENSKY (1912- , Boston)—Current head of Federated Department Stores, which includes such firms as Filene's and Bloomingdale's.

ABRAHAM KUHN (1819-1892)—Cofounder of the American investment banking house of Kuhn, Loeb and Company.

LEO LANCZY (1852-1921)—One of the most influential men in Hungarian domestic affairs as Director General of the Hungarian Commercial Bank. He became a Christian.

MAX LANGERMANN (1859-1919, Bavaria)—A great early figure in the development of mining in South Africa.

ALBERT D. LASKER (1880-1952)—Developed Lord and Thomas into one of the great advertising agencies in the world.

ALEXANDRE, SIMON, AND ELIE LAZARD (b. 1800's, Sarreguemines, Lorraine)—Their Lazard Frères became one of the most important banking houses in Europe in the 1800s.

FRED LAZARUS, JR. (b. 1884)—President of Federated Department Stores, the gigantic chain that has played an important role in American retailing.

SAMUEL LEFRAK (1918-   , Brooklyn)—The builder (Lefrak Village and many others) and noted philanthropist who changed the place of residence of hundreds of thousands of middle-class New Yorkers. More people paid rent to him than to any other individual in New York, and perhaps in the U.S.

ROBERT LEHMAN (1891-1969)—The art collector—you can see his collection at the Metropolitan Museum in New York—who led the great banking house of Lehman Brothers.

SAMUEL D. LEIDESDORF (1881-1968, New York City)—His S. D. Leidesdorf and Company became one of the major accounting firms in America. He served as Chairman of the Board of the Institute for Advanced Study at Princeton.

ABRAHAM LEVITT (1880-1962, Brooklyn)—You can thank him for Levittown in N.Y., N.J., and Pa. He and his family revolutionized living patterns in the U.S.

WALTER J. LEVY (1911-   , Hamburg, Germany)—Without doubt the most famous and influential oil expert and consultant in the world.

FREDERICK LEWISOHN (1882-1959)—Helped to found the Anaconda Copper Company and the American Smelting and Refining Company, and had major mining holdings in Latin America.

LEONARD LEWISOHN (1847-1902, Hamburg, Germany)—Cofounder of the United Metals Selling Company, he was a world power in lead and copper. He was the father of Frederick.

SOL M. LINOWITZ (1913-   , Trenton, N.J.)—The famous former Chairman of the Board of the Xerox Corporation, he served with skill as U.S. Ambassador to the OAS.

SOLOMON LOEB (1828-1913)—The other cofounder of Kuhn, Loeb and Company.

THEODOR MANNHEIMER (1833-1900, Copenhagen)—One of the most important figures in the history of banking in Sweden as the director of the Skandinaviska Banken.

STANLEY MARCUS (1905-   , Dallas)—He smokes a pipe and runs a little store called Neiman-Marcus in Dallas, Texas.

LORD SIMON MARKS (1888-1964, Manchester, England)—Half of Marks & Spencer, the huge system of chain stores in England that played a major role in the economic life of the average Britisher. They have no real equivalent in American retailing.

ISRAEL MATZ (1869-1950, Kalvarija, Poland)—Founder and President of a company that produces a vital commodity—Ex-Lax.

ABRAHAM MAZER (1876-1953, Goshecha, Russia)—The Mazer family controlled the Hudson Pulp and Paper Corporation, one of the leading companies of its kind in the U.S.

OTTO MEARS (1841-1931, Lithuania)—President of the Denver and Rio Grande Southern Railway, he built major lines in the American West and served as Lieutenant Governor of Colorado.

HENRY R. MERTON (1848-1929)—The company that bore his name (it later became the Amalgamated Metal Corporation), was one of the leading metal manufacturers in England.

ANDRE MEYER (1900-   , Paris)—Head of Lazard Frerès, still a major force in world banking.

NELSON MORRIS (1839-1907, Germany)—His Morris and Company was a major American meat-packing concern in the 19th century.

SIDNEY MYER (1878-1934, Poland)—One of the leading merchants in Australia and owner of the fabulous Myer Emporium.

NATHAN M. OHRBACH (1885-1972, Vienna)—Head of the department store chain that bears his name.

ADRIANO and CAMILLO OLIVETTI (1901-1960 and 1868-1943)—Son and father, they operated the large Olivetti-Underwood typewriter factories.

HARRY F. OPPENHEIMER (1908-)—The fabulously wealthy South African who dominated the diamond industry of the world. He converted to Christianity.

EMILE PEREIRE (1800-1875)—The Pereire family formed part of the Crédit Mobilier combine, which developed into the leading investment banking firm in France.

ALFRED E. PERLMAN (1902- , St. Paul, Minn.)—Former President of the New York Central Railway, he took over the Penn Central but failed to keep it solvent.

IGNAZ PETSCHEK (1857-1934, Kolin)—He and his family were leading industrialists in central Europe, with particularly extensive holdings in the coal-mining industry.

FRANZ M. PHILIPSON (1851-1925, Magdeburg)—A leading Belgian banker and the man who established the Bank of the Belgian Congo.

SIR LIONEL PHILLIPS (1855-1936, London)—A leading figure in the gold-mining industry in South Africa.

EMIL RATHENAU (1838-1915, Berlin)—An outstanding engineer, he controlled the largest electrical plant in Germany.

CHARLES H. REVSON (1906-1977, Boston)—Built Revlon into the largest producer of cosmetics in the world.

MORRIS RICH (1847-1928, Kaschau, Hungary)—A leading department store operator in the southern U.S.

MESHULAM RIKLIS (1923- , Turkey)—A leading American financier, he controlled the McCrory chain along with many other companies.

JULIUS ROSENWALD (1862-1932, Springfield, Ill.)—The famous President and Chairman of the Board of Sears, Roebuck.

LESSING J. ROSENWALD (1891- , Chicago)—Was Chairman of the Board of Sears, Roebuck after his father, and was a notable figure in American philanthropy.

WALTER N. ROTHSCHILD (1892-1960, New York City)—Chairman of the Board of Federated Department Stores.

SAMUEL RUBIN (1901-1978, Bialystok, Russia)—Founder of Fabergé, a leading manufacturer of perfume.

HELENA RUBINSTEIN (1871-1965, Cracow, Poland)—The world-famous cosmetics expert and industrialist, she was a remarkable person and a tough businesswoman.

VIDAL SASSOON (1928- , London)—The world-famous hair stylist.

AARON SCHEINFELD—Cofounder (with Elmer Winter) of Manpower, Inc., one of the largest personnel placement firms in the world.

RICHARD J. SCHWARTZ (1938- , New York)—Head of Jonathan Logan, a leading apparel firm.

IRVING S. SHAPIRO (1916- , Minneapolis)—The Chairman of the Board and Chief Executive Officer of E. I. du Pont and Company, one of the largest firms in the world.

HERBERT J. SIEGEL (1928- , Philadelphia)—Head of ChrisCraft Industries, a major pleasure boat manufacturer.

NORTON SIMON (1907- , Portland, Ore.)—Head of the huge Norton Simon group of industries.

ALFRED P. SLANER (1918- , New York City)—President of Kayser-Roth, the largest clothing manufacturing establishment in the world.

HANS STERN (1922-   , Essen, Germany)—The largest (or one of the largest) dealers in semiprecious stones in the world.

MAX STERN (1898-   , Fulda, Germany)—President of Hartz Mountain Products, the giant pet food empire.

ISIDOR STRAUS (1845-1912)—The famous owner (with his brother) of Macy's Department Store in New York.

LEVI STRAUSS (1829-1902, Bavaria)—The American inventor of Levis, which have become synonomous with blue jeans.

BENJAMIN H. SWIG (b. 1893)—A real estate tycoon in California, he owned the San Francisco Merchandise Mart.

GERALD SWOPE (1872-1957, St. Louis)—President and Chairman of the Board of International General Electric.

SIR JULES THORN (1899-   , Vienna)—Owner of Thorn Electrical Industries, he was a major force in the television manufacturing business in Great Britain.

LAURENCE A. TISCH (1923-   , New York City)—Head of Loew's Corporation, which controls Lorillard (the tobacco giant), numerous hotels, and CNA Financial Corporation, and is also a leading movie producer.

PERCY URIS (1899-   , New York City)—The Uris family controlled one of the largest construction empires in the U.S. Percy was the firm's President.

SIR ARNOLD WEINSTOCK (1925-   , London)—Managing Director of the British General Electric Company, a huge electronics empire.

SIR ISAAC WOLFSON (1897-   , Glasgow)—His Great Universal Stores were the largest chain (over 3,000) in England, and he had numerous other holdings, including banks, steamships, and considerable property.

ABRAM ZAK—(b. Bobruisk, Russia)—Chairman of the Board of St. Petersburg's Discount and Loan Bank, one of the major banking firms in 19th-century Russia.

JAMES D. ZELLERBACH (1892-1963)—His Crown Zellerbach Corporation was one of the dominating firms in the world paper market. He served as American Ambassador to Italy.

SAMUEL ZEMURRAY (1878-1961, Kishinev, Russia)—Controlled a majority of the stock in the United Fruit Company, which dominated the economies of a number of Central American countries.

Part IV
The Social Sciences

PHILOSOPHERS

MORTIMER J. ADLER (1902- , New York City)—As a philosopher, he was best known for *A Dialectic of Morals*, but his real contribution was as an educator stressing the importance of a knowledge of the great books produced throughout history. He became an editor of the 54-volume series *Great Books of the Western World*.

HENRY D. AIKEN (1912- , Portland, Ore.)—An important historian and expert on ethics, he wrote the widely acclaimed *Age of Ideology* and *Reason and Conduct*.

SAMUEL ALEXANDER (1859-1938, Australia)—The leading British philosopher of metaphysical realism and the author of *Space, Time and Deity*.

HANNAH ARENDT (1906-1975, Hanover)—A major force in political philosophy with (among others) *On Revolution* and her magnificent *Origins of Totalitarianism*, one of the most influential books of modern times.

MAX BLACK (1909- , Baku, Russia)—A Professor at Cornell, he wrote *Language and Philosophy* and was Editor of the *Philosophical Review*. He also served as President of the American Philosophical Society.

GEORGE BOAS (b. 1891)—Author of *The Inquiring Mind* and a Professor at Johns Hopkins, he was one of the foremost historians of ideas in the U.S.

NATHANIEL BRANDEN (1930- , Brampton, Ontario)—Born Blumenthal. A leading popularizer of the objectivist philosophy of Ayn Rand.

JACOB BRONOWSKI (1908-1974, Poland)—Author of *The Western Intellectual Tradition*, he became famous for the *The Ascent of Man*, which was shown on American public television.

MARTIN BUBER (1878-1965, Vienna)—The titanic figure who wrote *I and Thou*, one of the most important religious and philosophical books of all time.

ERNEST CASSIRER (1874-1945)—An original thinker and a very important figure in the history of modern philosophy, he is best known for *The Problem of Knowledge: Philosophy, Science, and History Since Hegel*.

STANLEY L. CAVELL (1926- , Atlanta)—Born Goldstein. Walter M. Cabot Professor of Aesthetics and General Theory of Value at Harvard since 1963.

HAROLD CHERNISS (1904- , St. Joseph, Mo.)—Professor at the Institute of Advanced Study at Princeton and author of *Aristotle's Criticism of Plato and the Academy*.

LEON CHWISTEK (1884-1944, Poland)—A leading Marxist philosopher and author of *The Limits of Science*.

MORRIS RAPHAEL COHEN (1880-1947, Minsk)—One of the foremost American philosophers, he served as President of the American Philosophical Association. Two of his major works are *Reason and Nature* and *The Meaning of Human History*.

JONAS COHN (1869-1947)—A leading neo-Kantian philosopher.

LEON DUJOVNE (1899- , Russia)—One of the leading philosophers in Argentina and the recipient of that country's first National Prize.

IRWIN EDMAN (1896-1954, New York City)—A well-known philosopher and the author of such important books as *Arts and the Man* and *Philosopher's Quest*.

MARVIN FARBER (1901- , Buffalo)—A leading phenomenologist, he founded the International Phenomenological Society and wrote *The Foundation of Phenomenology*.

HERBERT FEIGL (1902- , Reichenberg, Germany)—A leading logical positivist in the U.S.

PHILIPP FRANK (1884-1966, Vienna)—A leading philosopher of science and a biographer of Albert Einstein, Frank is best known for his *Philosophy of Science*, published in 1957.

SEMYON FRANK (1877-1950, Moscow)—One of the most important Soviet philosophers, he converted to Russian Orthodoxy and wrote *Reality and Man.*

MORITZ GEIGER (1860-1937, Frankfurt)—A major figure in aesthetic theory, he had considerable influence within phenomenalistic circles.

NELSON GOODMAN (1906- , Somerville, Mass.)—Important for his work on the concept of simplicity, he is also the author of *Fact, Fiction and Forecast*, one of the most interesting books I have ever read.

ADOLF GRUENBAUM (1923- , Cologne)—Andrew Mellon Professor of Philosophy at the U. of Pittsburgh, he is an important philosopher of mathematics and the author of *Philosophical Problems of Space and Time.*

FRITZ HEINEMANN (b. 1889, Lüneburg, Germany)—Was a professor at Oxford and wrote *Existentialism and the Modern Predicament*, a very influential work.

SIDNEY HOOK (1902- , Brooklyn)—A leading Social Democrat, he wrote *Reason, Social Myths, and Democracy* and has been an outspoken advocate of reasonableness in public affairs.

EDMUND G. A. HUSSERL (1859-1938, Prossnitz, Austria)—One of the most important modern philosophers, he is widely considered the founding father of phenomenology.

HANS JONAS (1903-)—Did important work on the philosophy of religion and wrote the influential *Study on Gnosticism.*

HORACE M. KALLEN (1882-1974, Berenstadt, Silesia)—A leading American philosopher, he was Dean at the New School for Social Research (New York), which he helped establish.

ABRAHAM KAPLAN (1918- , Odessa, Russia)—An important American philosopher, the author of *American Ethics and Public Policy.*

FELIX KAUFMAN (1895-1949, Vienna)—His titanic *Methodology of the Social Sciences* had a tremendous influence after it appeared in English in 1944.

WALTER KAUFMAN (1921- , Freiburg, Germany)—An important humanistic philosopher who wrote *Critique of Religion and Philosophy*, he taught at Princeton University.

RAYMOND KLIBANSKY (1905- , Paris)—A Professor at McGill U., he was President of the International Institute of Philosophy in the mid-1960s.

ERNEST KOLMAN (b. 1892, Prague)—A leading Czech philosopher, he directed the Institute of Philosophy, a division of the Czechoslovakian Academy of Sciences in the early 1960s.

ALEXANDRE KOYRE (1892-1964, Taganrog, Russia)—An important historian of science at the Institute of Advanced Study, he wrote *From the Closed World to the Infinite Universe.*

PAUL O. KRISTELLER (1905- , Berlin)—A Professor at Columbia U. and one of the leading authorities on the philosophy of the Renaissance period, he served as President of the Renaissance Society of America.

RICHARD KRONER (b. 1884)—A German, he was Editor of the important journal *Logos* for 28 years and a leading Hegelian philosopher.

PAUL KURTZ (1925- , Newark)—A Professor at the SUNY Buffalo and the author of *Humanist Manifestos One and Two* (1973).

MORRIS LAZEROWITZ (1907- , Lodz, Poland)—An American philosopher best known for *The Structure of Metaphysics* (1955). He is Sophia and Austin Smith Professor of Philosophy at Smith College.

EMMANUEL LEVINAS (1905- , Lithuania)—A leading French philosopher, he is an authority on the work of Husserl and Heidegger.

ARTHUR LIEBERT (1878-1946, Berlin)—Born Levy. An editor of *Kant-Studien*, a leading publication for Kantian philosophers.

EDUARD LOEWENTHAL (1836-1917, Ernsbach, Prussia)—A leading pacifist philosopher, he dedicated his life to ending war and was considered for a Nobel Peace Prize, but he did not win one.

HERBERT MARCUSE (1898- , Berlin)—Perhaps the most important philosopher of the New Left and one of the founding fathers of Marxist-humanism, he worked for American intelligence in World War II. Three of his books have become classics: *Reason and Revolution, Eros and Civilization*, and *One-Dimensional Man.*

HANS MEYERHOFF (1914-1965, Brunswick, Germany)—Noted for his *Time in Literature*, he taught at UCLA.

EMILE MEYERSON (1859-1933, Lublin, Poland)—One of the leading philosophers of science in France and the author of *Identity and Reality.*

CARLO MICHELSTAEDTER (1887-1910)—He could have been one of the great existentialist philosophers, but he took his own life at the age of 23. An Italian, his limited writings were rediscovered and became influential in Europe in the post–World War II period.

ERNEST NAGEL (1901- , Nove Mesto, Moravia)—One of the greatest philosophers of science of all time, he was President of the Philosophy of Science Association. His most renowned work is *The Structure of Science.*

ROBERT NOZICK (1938- , Brooklyn)—A Professor of Philosophy at Harvard, he won the 1975 National Book Award for *Anarchy, State and Utopia* (1974).

MOSES OSTROGORSKI (1854-1917, Grodno)—A leading political philosopher and a critic of Anglo-American democracy. His writings were widely discussed.

ARTHUR PAP (1921-1959, Zurich)—A very important and influential philosopher in spite of his short life. His fame rests on two major works: *Elements of Analytic Philosophy* and *Semantics and Necessary Truth.*

CHAIM PERELMAN (1912- , Warsaw)—A leading Belgian philosopher known for his work on the philosophy of justice. He was President of the Belgian Philosophical Society and Secretary General of the International Federation of Philosophical Societies.

JOSEF POPPER (1838-1921, Kolin, Bohemia)—One of the most prophetic and original thinkers of his time. Many feel that he laid the groundwork for Freudian analysis, the theory of relativity, and the philosophy of the welfare state.

SIR KARL R. POPPER (1902- , Vienna)—The very influential figure who taught at the London School of Economics. His books *The Logic of Scientific Discovery* and *The Open Society and Its Enemies* have become classics.

AYN RAND (1905- , St. Petersburg, Russia)—Her controversial philosophy of objectivism and rational selfishness, embodied in books such as *The Fountainhead* and *Atlas Shrugged*, have made her a cult figure.

HANS REICHENBACH (1891-1953, Hamburg)—One of the leading philosophers of science in the world, he taught at UCLA. The most important of his many books are *The Philosophy of Space and Time* and *The Rise of Scientific Philosophy.*

MURRAY ROTHBARD (1926- , New York City)—An economist, a leading libertarian spokesman, and the author of *Man, Economy and State* (1962).

EDITH STEIN (1891-1942, Breslau)—An important phenomenologist best known for *On the Problem of Empathy*. She became a devout Catholic and entered a convent, but perished with Jews at Auschwitz.

LEO STRAUSS (1899- , Germany)—One of the most important political philosophers of the 20th century, he taught at the U. of Chicago. His two most important works were *On Tyranny* and *Natural Right and History.*

ALFRED TARSKI (1902- , Warsaw)—The famed father of logical semantics and truly a major intellectual personality, he taught at the University of California and served as President of both the International Union for the History and

Philosophy of Science and the International Association for Symbolic Logic. His textbook *An Introduction to Logic* was widely used all over the world.

JEAN WAHL (b. 1888, Marseilles)—A leading existentialist philosopher and the author of *The Pluralistic Philosophies of England and America*.

SIMONE WEIL (1909-1943, Paris)—One of the most fascinating personalities of modern times, her mystical philosophy of religion has many admirers today. Her major work was *Waiting on God*. She died of starvation, a situation she could have done something about, but chose not to.

OTTO WEININGER (1880-1903, Vienna)—A convert to Christianity, he wrote *Sex and Character*, a vicious anti-Semitic, antifemale polemic. The innate contradictions of his beliefs drove him to suicide at the age of 23.

PAUL WEISS (1901- , New York City)—Editor and founder of the *Review of Metaphysics* and author of *Nature and Man* and *Modes of Being*, he was Sterling Professor of Philosophy at Yale. Among his students was Dick Cavett, who conducted several interesting interviews with him on television.

MORTON WHITE (1917- , New York City)—A leading social and political philosopher, author of *Social Thought in America*, and a Professor at Harvard.

PHILIP P. WIENER (1905- , New York City)—Executive Editor of the *Journal of the History of Ideas*, which he helped to found. His outstanding work was *Evolution and Founders of Pragmatism* (1949).

SOCIAL CRITICS

See also Feminists.

DAVID T. BAZELON (1923- , Shreveport, La.)—Professor of Policy Sciences at SUNY Buffalo and author of *The Paper Economy*.

JULIEN BENDA (1867-1956)—The noted French critic and philosopher who attacked his fellow intellectuals in a brilliant work, *The Great Betrayal* (1928).

IVAN BLOCH (1836-1901, Radom, Poland)—Born Bliokh. His six-volume *Future of War* was a major plea for pacifism as a way of life and an amazingly accurate prediction of modern weaponry. He became a Christian.

NOAM A. CHOMSKY (1928- , Philadelphia)—The brilliant expert in linguistics (*The Sound Pattern of English, Language and Mind, Language and Responsibility*) whose articles in the *New York Review of Books* on social and political issues have thrust him into the center of many controversies.

MIDGE DECTER (1927- , St. Paul, Minn.)—Born Rosenthal. She became Literary Editor of the *Saturday Review/World* in 1972.

WALDO D. FRANK (1889-1967, Long Branch, N.J.)—The very influential liberal Editor of the *New Republic* for 15 years and a perceptive critic of the American scene.

JOSEPH FREEMAN (1897-1965)—A regular contributor to the *Partisan Review* and a cofounder of the *New Masses*, he became disillusioned with the Communist movement at the time of the Hitler-Stalin pact.

EGON FRIEDELL (1878-1938, Vienna)—A major cultural historian whose *Cultural History of the Modern Age* was widely acclaimed. He took his own life.

PAUL GOODMAN (1911-1972, New York)—One of the most influential social critics in the U.S. and the author of *Growing Up Absurd*. He still has a large following.

JEFF GREENFIELD (1943- , New York City)—Coauthor of *A Populist Manifesto*.

ELIE HALEVY (1870-1937)—A noted French philosopher and social critic.

IRVING HOWE (1920- , New York City)—He could just as easily be listed a literary critic because he is a fine one (*Politics and the Novel*, for example), but he is listed here because of his position as Editor of *Dissent*.

HUGO IGNOTUS (1869-1949, Budapest)—A prominent Hungarian social and literary critic. Ignotus was a pen name for Hugo Veigelsberg.

PAUL JACOBS (1918-1978, New York City)—One of the outstanding social critics of his generation.

IRVING KRISTOL (1920- , New York City)—Cofounder and coeditor of *Encounter* and, later, founder and coeditor of *The Public Interest*. He is Henry R. Luce Professor of Urban Values at NYU and a staunch defender of the American system.

GEORGE J. NATHAN (1882-1958, Fort Wayne, Ind.)—The great social and drama critic who was a cofounder of the *American Mercury*.

VICTOR NAVASKY (1932- , New York City)—A prominent critic of the liberal establishment and the author of *Kennedy Justice* and *It Didn't Start with Watergate*.

JACK NEWFIELD (1939- , New York City)—An Editor with the *Village Voice*, he was a leading opponent of the Vietnam war. He is the author of *A Prophetic Minority* and coauthor of *A Populist Manifesto*.

WILLIAM PHILLIPS (1907- , New York City)—Founding Editor of the *Partisan Review* from 1934.

NORMAN PODHORETZ (1930- , Brooklyn)—Editor of *Commentary* and an important member of the critical establishment.

DAVID PRYCE-JONES (1936- , Vienna)—A leading British social and literary critic.

PHILIP RAHV (1908-1973)—Helped to found the *Partisan Review* and was the author of *Image and Ideas*.

HAROLD ROSENBERG (b. 1906, New York City)—One of the most powerful individuals in the art world as Art Critic for the *New Yorker*. His essays were published in all the leading intellectual journals.

SUSAN SONTAG (1933- , New York City)—A noted literary as well as social critic, two of her best books are *Against Interpretation* and *On Photography*.

ROGER STARR (1918- , New York City)—A leading expert and commentator on housing, he served as Commissioner of the Housing and Development Administration of N.Y.C.

HISTORIANS

See also Pulitzer Prize Winners.

HOWARD L. ADELSON (1925- , New York City)—A leading medieval historian and the author of *Medieval Commerce*.

SELIG ADLER (1909- , Baltimore)—An important diplomatic historian and the author of *The Isolationist Impulse*, he is Samuel P. Capen Professor of History at SUNY Buffalo.

GAR ALPEROVITZ (1936- , Racine, Wis.)—A diplomatic historian associated with the "revisionist" school, he wrote *Atomic Diplomacy: Hiroshima and Potsdam*.

WALTER L. ARNSTEIN (1930- , Stuttgart)—A leading American scholar on the history of Great Britain and the author of *Britain, Yesterday and Today*.

BERNARD BAILYN (1922- , Hartford, Conn.)—Winthrop Professor of History at Harvard and one of the leading historians in the U.S., he won the 1968 Pulitzer Prize for *The Ideological Origins of the American Revolution* and the 1975 National Book Award for *The Ordeal of Thomas Hutchinson*.

GEORGE L. BEER (1872-1920, Staten Island, N.Y.)—An important historian of British colonialism and a great admirer of the British system and people, he wrote *The English Speaking Peoples.*

MAX BEER (1864-1949)—The leading historian of socialism in Great Britain.

CAROL R. BERKIN (1942- , Mobile, Ala.)—Professor of History at Baruch College in N.Y.C. and the author of the standard work on Jonathan Sewall.

HARRY BERNSTEIN (1909- , New York City)—An important historian of Latin America, his *Modern and Contemporary Latin America* was one of the best books published on the area in the 1950s.

CAMILLE BLOCH (1865-1949)—For years a major authority and source on the history of the French Revolution, he was the author of the influential *Causes of the World War.*

MARC BLOCH (1866-1944)—A major French historian of feudalism and the author of the important *Feudal Society* and *French Rural Society*. He was killed by the Germans while fighting with the French Resistance.

JEROME BLUM (1913- , Baltimore)—A Professor at Princeton, his *Lord and Peasant in Russia from the Ninth to the Nineteenth Century* is considered a major work of Russian history.

DANIEL J. BOORSTIN (1914- , Atlanta, Ga.)—Director of the National Museum of History and Technology at the Smithsonian, he wrote *America and the Image of Europe*, one of his many excellent books.

WOODROW WILSON BORAH (1912- , Utica, Miss.)—One of the greatest historians of Latin America, he taught at the U. of California.

I. BERNARD COHEN (1914- , Far Rockaway, N.Y.)—Professor of History of Science at Harvard and a former President of the International Union˙ for the History and Philosophy of Science.

LEONARD DINNERSTEIN (1934- , New York City)—Professor of History at the U. of Arizona and author of *The Leo Frank Case.*

MARTIN DUBERMAN (1930- , New York City)—A noteworthy historian of the American Civil War and its aftermath, he is also an important playwright *(In White America)* and a leading advocate of gay rights.

VICTOR L. EHRENBERG (b. 1891, Altona, Germany)—A leading specialist in ancient history, he was cofounder of the Classical Society of London.

LOUIS EISENMANN (1869-1937, Haguenau, France)—A distinguished French historian who was Director of the Center for the Study of Foreign Policy and Secretary General of the Institute for Slavic Studies at the University of Paris.

RICHARD E. ELLIS (1937- , New York City)—Professor of History at SUNY Buffalo and author of *The Jeffersonian Crisis.*

GEOFFREY R. ELTON (1921- , Tübingen, Germany)—Born Ehrenberg. One of the world's major authorities on Tudor England and the author of *The Tudor Revolution in Government.*

HERBERT FEIS (b. 1893, New York City)—One of the foremost American economic historians and a winner of the 1961 Pulitzer Prize. He wrote *Churchill, Roosevelt, Stalin.*

LOUIS FILLER (1912-)—A Professor at Antioch, he is a leading historian of the black experience in the U.S. His major book is *The Crusade against Slavery, 1830-1860.*

PETER GAY (1923- , Berlin)—Durfee Professor of History at Yale, he is a leading cultural historian and the author of *The Age of Enlightenment* and *Weimar Culture.*

LEO GERSHOY (1897- , Russia)—One of the foremost historians of France, he wrote *The French Revolution and Napoleon.*

FELIX GILBERT (1905- , Baden, Germany)—A leading diplomatic historian.

His *To the Farewell Address: Ideas of Early American Foreign Policy* was a major work.

GUSTAVE GLOTZ (1862-1935, Haguenau, France)—A noted authority on Greek history, he served as President of the Institut de France.

ERIC F. GOLDMAN (1915- , Washington, D.C.)—His *Crucial Decade, America 1945-1955* was widely used in American universities. He was a Special Consultant to LBJ, was President of the Society of American Historians, and has been Rollins Professor of History at Princeton since 1962.

THEODOR GOMPERZ (1832-1912, Brünn, Moravia)—An Austrian, he was one of the most important historians of Greek civilization of all time.

LOUIS R. GOTTSCHALK (1899- , Brooklyn)—Served as President of the American Historical Association and wrote the useful *Understanding History: A Primer of Historical Method*. He was Swift Distinguished Service Professor at the U. of Chicago and an expert on Lafayette.

KARL GRUENBERG (1861-1940, Focsani, Rumania)—A noted social historian and Director of the U. of Frankfurt's Institute of Social Research. He was murdered by the SS.

LOUIS M. HACKER (1899- , New York City)—The noted historian and Professor at Columbia whose *U.S. Since 1865* was the leading textbook in the 1930s and '40s.

A. M. HALPERN (1914- , Boston)—A Professor of Asian Studies at Johns Hopkins, he was a Senior Staff Member of the Rand Corporation, 1949-1962.

OSCAR HANDLIN (1915- , Brooklyn)—Won the 1952 Pulitzer Prize for *The Uprooted*.

ELIFILIP HECKSCHER (1879-1952, Stockholm)—A major Swedish historian noted for his study of mercantilism.

LOUIS HENKIN (1917- , Russia)—Hamilton Fish Professor of International Law and Diplomacy at Columbia U.

EMANUEL HERTZ (1870-1940, Bukta, Austria)—A lawyer, he was a leading authority on Abraham Lincoln.

JACK HEXTER (1910- , Memphis, Tenn.)—A leading historian of the development of ideas, he wrote *More's Utopia: The Biography of an Idea*. He is Charles J. Stille Professor of History at Yale.

GERTRUDE HIMMELFARB (1922- , New York City)—Author of *Darwin and the Darwinian Revolution*.

ERIC J. E. HOBSBAWN (1917- , Alexandria, Egypt)—A leading historian of labor and the author of the influential *Industry and Empire*.

RICHARD HOFSTADTER (1916-1970, Buffalo)—A Professor at Columbia, he won Pulitzer Prizes for *The Age of Reform: from Bryan to FDR* and for the excellent *Anti-Intellectualism in American Life*.

HAROLD M. HYMAN (1924-)—A leading historian of Reconstruction in America and the author of *Era of the Oath*.

GABRIEL JACKSON (1921- , Mount Vernon N.Y.)—Professor of History at the U. of California, San Diego, he wrote *The Spanish Republic and the Civil War* for which he won the Herbert Baxter Adams Prize of the American Historial Association, and is a leading authority on Spanish history.

MICHAEL G. KAMMEN (1936- , Rochester, N.Y.)—Newton C. Farr Professor of American History and Culture at Cornell and the author of *A Rope of Sand*.

ERNST H. KANTOROWICZ (1895-1963, Prussia)—A leading medieval historian, he founded the field of political theology.

MORTON KELLER (1929- , New York City)—A major American social historian and the author of the important *Life Insurance Enterprises, 1885-1910*.

MELVIN KRANZBERG (1917- , St. Louis)—Callaway Professor of the History of Technology at Georgia Tech, he was Vice-President of the American Association for the Advancement of Science.

MICHAEL KRAUS (1901- , New York City)—One of the leading cultural historians in the U.S. His *Atlantic Civilization* had great impact.

HYMAN KUBLIN (1919- , Boston)—A leading authority on the history of Japan.

THOMAS KUHN (1922- , Cincinnati)—Professor of the History of Science at Princeton and author of the very influential *Structure of Scientific Revolution*, considered one of the seminal works in the field. He is responsible for the widespread use of the term *paradigm* in the social sciences.

WALTER LAQUEUR (1921- , Breslau, Germany)—Director of the Institute of Contemporary History in London and a welcome voice of reason in the discourse on international affairs.

JOSEPH R. LEVENSON (1920-1969, Boston)—A leading historian of China, his three-volume work *Confucian China and Its Modern Fate* is a landmark study. He taught at the U. of California.

LEONARD W. LEVY (1923- , Toronto)—A major historian of constitutional law and winner of the Pulitzer Prize for his *Origin of the Fifth Amendment*.

BERNARD LEWIS (1916- , London)—Widely considered to be the world's leading Islamic historian, he is a Professor at the U. of London and the author of many notable works, including *Arabs in History*.

ROBERT S. LOPEZ (1910- , Genoa, Italy)—A Professor at Yale and one of the leading medieval historians in the U.S.

FRANK E. MANUEL (1910- , Boston)—A noted historian of ideas and author of *Portrait of Isaac Newton*.

ARNO J. MAYER (1926- , Luxembourg)—A leading diplomatic historian and author of *The Political Origins of the New Diplomacy, 1917–1918*. He teaches at Princeton.

RICHARD B. MORRIS (1904- , New York City)—Gouveneur Morris Professor of History at Columbia and one of the most distinguished American historians, he is the author of *The Peacemakers*.

LOUIS MORTON (1913-1976, New York City)—Daniel Webster Professor of History at Dartmouth, he is a noted military historian and the author of *Strategy and Command*. He served as Deputy Chief Historian of the U.S. Army.

GEORGE L. MOSSE (1918- , Berlin)—A leading cultural historian specializing in Germany, he was an Editor of the *Journal of Contemporary History* and the author of *The Reformation*.

OSKAR NACHOD (1859-1933, Leipzig, Germany)—A pioneer historian of Japan and a noted bibliographer.

SIR LEWIS NAMIER (1888-1960, Galicia)—Born Bernstein-Namierowski. One of the leading historians in England and a famous biographer. He was a member of the British Royal Academy and wrote the important *Structure of Politics at the Accession of George III*.

ABRAHAM P. NASATIR (1904- , Santa Ana, Calif.)—Author of *Before Lewis and Clark* and coauthor of *Latin America*, one of the standard histories of that continent.

GERALD D. NASH (1928- , Berlin)—Professor of History at the U. of New Mexico, he is a prolific historian who serves on the board of editors of several journals.

ARNOLD A. OFFNER (1937- , Brooklyn)—Professor of History at Boston U. and the author of *American Appeasement: United States Foreign Policy and Germany, 1933–1938*.

WALTER PAGEL (1898- , Berlin)—A noted historian of science.

SIR FRANCIS PALGRAVE (1788-1861)—Born Cohen. A premier English historian famed for his multivolume study *The History of Normandy and England*. He converted to Christianity.

RICHARD E. PIPES (1923- , Cieszyn, Poland)—Director of the Russian Research Center at Harvard and author of the important *Formation of the Soviet Union*, he is a leading expert on Soviet nationality groups.

ALFRED F. PIRBRAM (1859-1942, London)—Was professor at the U. of Vienna and a leading authority on the development of the foreign policy of that country.

SIDNEY I. POMERANTZ (1909- , New York City)—One of the first urban historians, his *New York, an American City, 1783–1803* was a widely acclaimed work.

MICHAEL M. POSTAN (1899- , Tighina, Bessarabia)—One of the most important economic historians, he was a Professor at Cambridge U.

THEODORE RABB (1937- , Teplice-Sanov, Czechoslovakia)—Born Rabinowicz. A Professor of History at Princeton and author of the noted *Enterprise and Empire*.

ALEXANDER RABINOWITCH (1934- , London)—Professor of History at the U. of Indiana and Director of its Russian and East European Institute.

ARMIN H. RAPPAPORT (1916- , New York City)—A major diplomatic historian, he wrote *Henry L. Stimson and Japan*.

SIDNEY RATNER (1908- , New York City)—A leading economic historian specializing in the history of taxation in the U.S., he wrote *Taxation and Democracy in America*.

STANLEY R. ROSS (1921- , New York City)—A leading authority on the Mexican Revolution, he became Vice-President of the U. of Texas in 1973.

GUNTHER E. ROTHENBERG (1923- , Berlin)—Professor of Military History at the U. of New Mexico.

JACOB SCHAPIRO (b. 1879, New York City)—Taught at CCNY for many decades and became a well-known expert on 19th-century Europe. He wrote *Condorcet and the Rise of Liberalism* and the widely used text *Modern and Contemporary European History*.

JOSEPH H. SCHIFFMAN (1914- , New York City)—James Hope Caldwell Professor of American Studies at Dickinson College since 1968.

BERNARD SEMMEL (1928- , New York City)—A leading authority on modern Britain and the author of *Imperialism and Social Reform*.

CHARLES J. SINGER (1876-1960)—Author of *From Magic to Science* and one of the leading historians of science in the world, he was President of the International Union of the History of Science.

LOUIS L. SNYDER (1907- , Maryland)—His *Meaning of Nationalism* was a seminal work, and he is regarded as one of the foremost authorities on that phenomenon.

JACOB L. TALMON (1916- , Rypin, Poland)—One of the leading experts on totalitarianism and a major historian of ideas, he wrote the influential *Origins of Totalitarian Democracy*.

FRANK TANNENBAUM (1893-1969, Austria)—One of the leading historians of Latin America and the author of *Ten Keys to Latin America*, he taught at Columbia U.

BARBARA TUCHMAN (1912- , New York City)—One of the world's best-known historians, she received Pulitzer Prizes for General Nonfiction for *The Guns of August* and *Stillwell and the American Experience in China*. Her other books include *The Proud Tower* and *The Zimmerman Telegram*.

IRWIN UNGER (1927- , New York City)—Received the 1965 Pulitzer Prize for *The Greenback Era: A Political and Social History of American Finance, 1865–1879.*

ALLEN WEINSTEIN (1937- , New York City)—Author of the noted work *The Great Fear*, he taught at Smith College.

BERNARD A. WEISBERGER (1932- , New York City)—Author of the excellent work *The Industrial Society*.

BERTRAM D. WOLFE (1896-1977)—A leading scholar, writer, and expert on Marxism, he wrote the widely read *Three Who Made a Revolution*.

HARRY A. WOLFSON (1887- , Belorussia)—A historian of philosophy whose writings had a profound effect on its field.

HENRY R. WINKLER (1916- , Waterbury, Conn.)—Not the Fonz, but a Professor of History and Senior Vice-President at Rutgers U. and Managing Editor of the *American Historical Review*.

STANLEY A. WOLPERT (1927- , Brooklyn)—A Professor of History at UCLA, he wrote *A History of India* and the excellent *Nine Hours to Rama*.

OSCAR ZEICHNER (1916- , New York City)—A major American historian, he served as Dean of Graduate Studies at CCNY and wrote *Connecticut's Years of Controversy, 1750–1776.* He is considered a leading historian of America's colonial period.

POLITICAL SCIENTISTS

GABRIEL A. ALMOND (1911- , Rock Island, Ill.)—Coauthor of *The Civic Culture*, a pioneer work on American political life. He served as President of the American Political Science Association.

DAVID E. APTER (1924-   )—A world-renowned authority on African politics and a Professor at the U. of California, his *Gold Coast in Transition* is considered a landmark work.

SHLOMO AVINERI (1933- , Bielsko, Silesia)—A leading expert on Karl Marx and Marxism, he is Herbert Samuel Professor of Political Science at Hebrew U., Jerusalem.

MAX BELOFF (1913- , London)—One of the most famous British political scientists and a Professor at Oxford, his books on Soviet foreign policy are frequently cited.

SIR ISAIAH BERLIN (1909- , Latvia)—The world-famous British political philosopher and the author of (among others) *Karl Marx* and *Two Concepts of Liberty*.

DAVIS B. BOBROW (1936- , Boston)—An expert on military and defense issues, he is Professor of Government and Politics at the U. of Maryland and a member of the U.S. Air Force Scientific Advisory Board.

WILLIAM D. COPLIN (1939- , Baltimore)—Author of *Introduction to International Relations* (1971, 1974), an outstanding and widely used textbook.

YEHEZKEL DROR (1928- , Vienna)—Born Freeman. An internationally known political scientist and the author of *Crazy States* (1971).

MURRAY EDELMAN (1919- , Nanticoke, Pa.)—George Herbert Mead Professor of Political Science at the U. of Wisconsin.

DANIEL J. ELAZAR (1934- , Minneapolis)—Professor of Political Science at Temple U. and the world's leading authority on federalism. He is active in the Sephardic community in the U.S. and Israel.

HEINZ EULAU (1915- , Offenbach, Germany)—His book *Political Behavior* (1956) made him the leader of behaviorism in modern political science.

HERMAN FINER (1898-1969, Herta, Bessarabia)—Perhaps the leading authority on comparative politics of his time, he was an important figure in British socialism and the author of *Theory and Practice of Modern Government.*

SAMUEL FINER (1915- , London)—A Professor of Government at the U. of Manchester and onetime Vice-President of the International Political Science Association, he was a pioneer student of the role of the military in politics, which he discussed in *The Man on Horseback* (1962) and many other works.

LOUIS L. GERSON (1921- , Poland)—A Professor of Political Science at the U. of Connecticut, he is the author of *John Foster Dulles* (1967).

IRWIN N. GERTZOG (1933- , Brooklyn)—Arthur E. Braun Professor of Political Science at Allegheny College.

MARILYN GITTELL (1931- , New York City)—A Professor of Political Science at Brooklyn College and a leading expert on urban politics.

FRED I. GREENSTEIN (1930- , New York City)—Henry R. Luce Professor of Politics, Law, and Society at Princeton University since 1973, he is famous for *Personality and Politics* (1969), one of the great works on political psychology.

BERTRAM M. GROSS (1912- , Philadelphia)—Distinguished Professor of Urban Affairs at Hunter College and the author of *The Legislative Struggle* (1953).

JACK HAYWARD (1931- , Shanghai)—A Professor of Politics at the U. of Hull, England, he served as Chairman of the Political Studies Association of the United Kingdom.

HERMANN HELLERM (1891-1933, Austria)—A leading political scientist in Germany in the post–World War I period, he was chosen to write the entry for political science in the massive Encyclopedia of the Social Sciences published just after his death.

STANLEY HOFFMAN (1928- , Vienna)—Professor of Political Science at Harvard and a leading expert on both international relations and French politics.

MORTON A. KAPLAN (1921- , Philadelphia)—Professor of Political Science at the U. of Chicago and a leading authority on international relations theory.

OTTO KIRSCHEIMER (1905-1965, Germany)—Renowned for his book *Political Justice* (1961), he taught at Columbia U.

HANS KOHN (1891-1971, Prague)—His work on nationalism made him a respected figure all over the world. *The Idea of Nationalism* (1944) anticipated movements for self-determination after World War II.

WALTER Z. LAQUEUR (1921- , Breslau)—Editor of *Survey*, founder of *Contemporary History*, and a noted authority on Zionism and the Middle East conflict.

WERNER LEVI (1912- , Halberstadt, Germany)—Professor of Political Science at the U. of Hawaii and a leading specialist on Asia.

MARION J. LEVY, JR. (1918- , Galveston, Tex.)—Musgrave Professor of Sociology and International Affairs at Princeton beginning in 1971.

KARL LOEWENSTEIN (1891- , Munich)—Famous for his studies in comparative politics and for *Political Power and the Governmental Process*, he also served as a legal adviser to the American occupation government in Europe after World War II.

THEODORE J. LOWI (1931- , Gadsden, Ala.)—John L. Senior Professor of American Institutions at Cornell U. and author of the widely acclaimed work *The End of Liberalism* (1969).

JOHN MEISEL (1923- , Vienna)—Hardy Professor of Political Science at Queen's U. in Ontario and a leading expert on Canadian politics.

HANS J. MORGENTHAU (1904- , Coburg, Germany)—The father of power politics, he was the single most influential figure in the study of international relations in modern times. His *Politics among Nations* (first edition, 1949) is still the most widely used introductory textbook. He was one of the most important early critics of American involvement in Vietnam.

RICHARD E. NEUSTADT (1919- , New York City)—A noted Professor of Government at Columbia U. and an important adviser to the Kennedy family.

SAUL PADOVER (1905- , Vienna)—Professor of Political Science at the New School for Social Research in N.Y. and author of *The Genius of America* (1960).

ITHIEL DE SOLA POOL (1917- , New York City)—Professor of Political Science at M.I.T. and one of the world's leading experts on political communications.

WILLIAM A. ROBSON (b. 1895, London)—Founder of the *Political Quarterly* and onetime Professor of Public Administration at the London School of Economics. He served as Vice-President of the International Political Science Association and was author of *The Civil Service in Britain and France*.

LLOYD I. RUDOLF (1927- , Chicago)—A Professor of Political Science at the U. of Chicago, he is an expert on problems of political modernization.

HARVEY SHERMAN (1917- , Pittsburgh)—President of the American Society for Public Administration, 1964–1965 and author of *It All Depends: A Pragmatic Approach to Organization* (1966).

KALMAN H. SILVERT (b. 1921, Bryn Mawr, Pa.)—A Professor of Politics at NYU, he was an expert on Latin American Politics and on the theory of political development.

HERBERT SIMON (1916- , Milwaukee)—A leading expert on public administration and behavior and the author of the outstanding *Administrative Behavior*.

EUGENE B. SKOLNIKOFF (1928- , Philadelphia)—Professor of Political Science at M.I.T. and Director of its Center for International Studies.

JOHN G. STOESSINGER (1927- , Austria)—Author of well-known books such as *The Might of Nations* (1962) and *Nations in Darkness* (1971), he is a Professor of Political Science at Hunter College.

FRANK N. TRAGER (1905- , New York City)—Professor of International Affairs at NYU and Director of the National Strategy Information Center.

ADAM ULAM (1922- , Poland)—Professor of Government at Harvard and a noted expert on Soviet politics.

MICHAEL WALZER (1935- , New York City)—Professor of Government at Harvard, he is an important political theorist who wrote books such as *Obligations* (1970).

SIR ALFRED ZIMMERN (1879-1957, London)—Professor of International Relations at Oxford. Perhaps his most important book was *Spiritual Values and World Affairs*, published just before World War II.

LAWRENCE ZIRING (1928- , Brooklyn)—One of the very few Americans who is a Fellow of the Institute of Oriental Studies of the Soviet Academy of Sciences. He is a leading expert on Pakistan.

SOCIOLOGISTS

CHARLES ABRAMS (1901-1970, Vilna)—One of the leading experts in the U.S. on urban and city planning and the author of *Man's Struggle for Shelter*. The development of public housing in America owes much to his work.

THEODOR W. ADORNO (1903-1969, Frankfurt)—Coauthor of *The Authoritarian Personality*, one of the most influential books on social psychology ever published. He returned to Germany in the mid-1950s after having taught for many years at the U. of California.

RAYMOND ARON (1905- , Paris)—A world-famous Professor of Sociology at the Sorbonne, he has written extensively on international affairs as well as on historical sociology.

REINHARD BENDIX (1916- , Berlin)—A former President of the American Sociological Association, he is a leading authority on the work of Max Weber and the author of *Work and Authority in Industry*, for which he received the MacIver Award.

PETER M. BLAU (1918- , Vienna)—An internationally renowned scholar in the field of bureaucracy and formal organizations, his book *Bureaucracy in Modern Society* is one of the field's bibles. He teaches at Columbia U.

ALVIN BOSKOFF (1927- , New York City)—A leading American sociologist and coauthor of *Modern Sociological Theory in Continuity and Change*. His specialty is social change and its ramifications.

WERNER J. CAHNMAN (1902- , Munich)—An important sociological theorist, Cahnman coauthored *Sociology and History* and *How Cities Grew*. He took a great interest in Jewish affairs.

JANET SALTZMAN CHAFETZ (1942- , New Jersey)—Professor of Sociology at the U. of Houston and author of the important *Masculine, Feminine or Human?*.

NATHAN E. COHEN (1909- , Derry, N.H.)—Served as President of the National Association of Social Workers, wrote *Social Work and Social Problems*, and was Dean of the School of Social Work at UCLA in 1968.

LEWIS A. COSER (1913- , Germany)—Perhaps the world's leading authority on conflict theory (*The Functions of Social Conflict*), he also edited the pioneering *Sociology through Literature* and was an Editor of *Dissent*.

PETER F. DRUCKER (1909- , Vienna)—Clarke Professor of Social Science and Management at the Claremont Graduate School since 1971, his *Age of Discontinuity* (1969) was widely acclaimed.

EMILE DURKHEIM (1858-1917, Epinal, France)—Laid the foundation for the entire field of sociology.

S. N. EISENSTADT (1923- , Warsaw)—His books *Political Sociology* and *The Political Systems of Empires* (which won the McIver Award) propelled him to the forefront of modern sociology. He is a Professor at Hebrew U., Jerusalem.

AMITAI W. ETZIONI (1929- , Cologne)—A Professor at Columbia U., he is an important political sociologist and the author of *The Active Society: A Theory of Societal and Political Processes*.

BERNARD FARBER (1922- , Chicago)—Professor of Sociology at Arizona State U. and an expert on the sociology of the family.

LEWIS FEUER (1912- , New York City)—A well-known authority on the sociology of ideas, his most important book was *Psychoanalysis and Ethics* (1955).

GEORGES FRIEDMANN (1902- , Paris)—A leading French sociologist, he served as President of the International Sociological Association.

WILLIAM A. GAMSON (1934- , Philadelphia)—Professor of Sociology at the U. of Michigan and the author of the important and influential *Power and Discontent* (1968).

MORRIS GINSBERG (1889-1970)—An internationally known British sociologist specializing in the comparative study of culture.

NATHAN GLAZER (1923- , New York City)—The famous urban sociologist and critic, and the author of *Beyond the Melting Pot*.

ERVING GOFFMAN (1922- , Canada)—Benjamin Franklin Professor of Anthropology and Sociology at the U. of Pennsylvania since 1968. His book *Stigma* (1963) had a profound effect on the field of social psychology.

SIDNEY GOLDSTEIN (1927- , New London, Conn.)—Professor at Brown U., he was President of the Population Association of America, 1975–1976.

MILTON M. GORDON (1918- , Gardiner, Maine)—Born Goldberg. An expert on social stratification theory and the author of *Social Class in American Sociology*.

ALVIN GOULDNER (1920- , New York City)—Max Weber Professor of Sociology at Washington U. (St. Louis), he was founder and first Editor of *Trans-Action* and the author of *For Sociology.*

LUDWIG GUMPLOWICZ (1838-1909, Cracow)—A pioneer social determinist, he laid the groundwork for the emergence of the field of sociology.

GEORGES GURVITCH (1894-1966, Russia)—A leading French sociologist and Editor of *Political Sociology*, he was one of the first to distinguish between micro- and macro-sociology.

LOUIS GUTTMAN (1919- , New York City)—Developer of the famous Guttman Scale.

MAURICE HALBWACHS (1877-1945)—An important early French sociologist and one of the developers of the concept of "collective memory," he was murdered by the Nazis.

PHILIP M. HAUSER (1909- , Chicago)—A well-known expert on population dynamics (*The Study of Population*), he was a President of the American Sociological Association and also served as Deputy Director of the Bureau of the Census for many years.

MAX HORKHEIMER (b. 1895, Stuttgart)—The institute he headed became the outstanding center for the study of social issues in Germany in the post–World War II era.

IRVING LOUIS HOROWITZ (1929- , New York City)—Professor of Sociology at Rutgers U., he is Editor in Chief of *Trans-Action/Society* and author of *Three Worlds of Development* (1966, 1972).

HERBERT H. HYMAN (1918- , New York City)—Professor of Sociology at Wesleyan U. and a leading authority on public opinion research.

ALEX INKELES (1920- , New York City)—A leading expert on the social structure of the Soviet Union and on comparative social structures in general, he taught at Harvard for many years.

MORRIS JANOWITZ (1919-)—Professor at the U. of Chicago, and the world's leading authority on the sociology of the military (*The Professional Soldier*, 1960, and many others).

NATHAN KEYFITZ (1913- , Montreal)—Professor of Sociology and Demography at Harvard and President of the Population Association of America in 1970.

PHILIP KLEIN (1890- , Hungary)—A leader among the theorists who advocated social action for social workers, he was an important authority on unemployment.

MIRRA KOMAROVSKY (1906- , Russia)—One of the important experts on sex roles and the role of women in society, she was in the first rank of sociologists concentrating on marriage and the family.

SIEGFRIED KRACAUER (1889-1966, Frankfurt)—One of the pioneer sociologists of the film, he is famous for *Caligari to Hitler: A Psychological History of the German Film*, published shortly after World War II.

LEO KUPER (1908- , Johannesburg)—Director of the African Studies Center at UCLA and author of *An African Bourgeoisie* (1965).

PAUL LAZARSFELD (1901- , Vienna)—A leading expert on public opinion research, Lazarsfeld was President of the American Sociological Association and Director of the famed Bureau of Applied Social Research of Columbia U.

SEYMOUR MARTIN LIPSET (1922- , New York City)—A leading political sociologist, he became internationally known for books such as *Political Man* and the coauthored *Union Democracy.*

JOSEPH MAIER (1911- , Leipzig)—One of the world's leading experts on the sociology of religion and the author of *On Hegel's Critique of Kant.*

JULIUS B. MALLER (1901-1959, Vobolniki, Lithuania)—A leading expert in the field of personality testing, he developed the Maller Personality Sketches.

KARL MANNHEIM (1893-1947, Budapest)—One of the great pioneers of the sociology of knowledge. His influence was tremendous.

ROBERT K. MERTON (1910- , Philadelphia)—Author of *Social Theory and Social Structure* and an important scholar on bureaucratic behavior. He was a President of the American Sociological Association.

FRANZ OPPENHEIMER (1864-1943)—Author of the influential work *The State* and Chairman of Sociology at the U. of Frankfurt for many years.

CHESTER RAPKIN (1918- , New York City)—Professor of Urban Planning at Princeton and a noted expert on urban problems.

PHILIP RIEFF (1922- , Chicago)—Benjamin Franklin Professor of Sociology at the U. of Pennsylvania since 1967 and author of *The Triumph of the Therapeutic* (1966).

DAVID RIESMAN (1909- , Philadelphia)—One of the most famous American sociologists. His great contribution was *The Lonely Crowd*.

ARNOLD ROSE (1918-1968, Chicago)—One of America's leading authorities on racial problems, he was also the author of a widely used textbook, *Sociology*.

PETER I. ROSE (1933- , Rochester)—Sophia Smith Professor of Sociology and Anthropology at Smith College and author of *The Study of Society*, which was the standard sociology text for more than a decade.

EDWARD SAGARIN (1913- , Schenectady, N.Y.)—Professor of Sociology City U. of New York and former president American Society of Criminology.

GEORG SIMMIEL (1858-1918, Berlin)—Not raised as a Jew, Simmiel was one of the predominate forces in European sociology in the late 1800s.

NEIL J. SMELSER (1930- , Kahoka, Mo.)—Former Editor of the *American Sociological Review*, Professor at the U. of California, and author of the important *Theory of Collective Behavior* (1962).

WALTER SULZBACH (b. 1889, Frankfurt)—Did pioneer research into the sociology of nationhood and the concepts of national consciousness and nationalism.

MELVIN TUMIN (1919- , Newark)—A leading expert on race relations and social stratification, his book on discrimination, *Social Stratification: The Forms and Functions of Inequity*, received wide attention.

IMMANUEL WALLERSTEIN (1930- , New York City)—Professor at McGill U. and a leading expert on African political and social systems, he has served on the editorial boards of several major sociology journals.

LOUIS WIRTH (1897-1952, Gemünden on the Main, Germany)—One of the foremost sociologists in the U.S., he was President of both the American Sociological Association and the International Sociological Association.

KURT WOLFF (1912- , Darmstadt, Germany)—Yellen Professor of Social Relations at Brandeis U.

MAURICE ZEITLIN (1935- , Detroit)—Professor of Sociology at the U. of Wisconsin and an outspoken critic of Latin American social systems and urbanization.

EDUCATORS

MORTIMER H. APPLEY (1921- , New York City)—Born Applezweig. Named President of Clark U., Mass., in 1974. He became a Unitarian.

WERNER BAUM (1923- , Germany)—Chancellor of the U. of Wisconsin, Milwaukee.

WILLIAM BIRENBAUM (1923- , Macomb, Ill.)—President of Antioch College.

EDWARD J. BLOUSTEIN (1925- , New York City)—Became President of Rutgers U. in 1965.

SIDNEY BOROWITZ (1919- , New York City)—Became Chancellor of NYU in 1972.

LEON BOTSTEIN (1946- , Zurich, Switzerland)—President of Bard College.

ABRAHAM FLEXNER (1866-1959, Louisville, Ky.)—Founder and Director of the Institute for Advanced Study in Princeton, N.J., he was a leading figure in medical education in the U.S.

SAMUEL FREEDMAN (1908- , Russia)—A distinguished Canadian jurist, he served as Chancellor of the U. of Manitoba.

BIRD GANS (1868-1944, Allegheny City, Pa.)—Born Stein. President of the Child Study Association of America.

WILLIAM GLASSER (1925- , Cleveland)—His work on "reality therapy" had a profound effect on American educational practices.

MARVIN L. GOLDBERGER (Chicago)—Became President of the California Institute of Technology in the late 1970s.

ABRAHAM S. GOLDSTEIN (1925- , New York City)—Provost of Yale U. and former Dean of its law school.

SAMUEL B. GOULD (1910- , New York City)—Former President of the State University of New York System, he had earlier been Chancellor of the U. of California, Santa Barbara, and President of Antioch College. He became a Christian.

SIDONIE GRUENBERG (b. 1881)—Long-time Director of the Child Study Association of America. She had considerable influence on American educational practices.

SIR PHILIP J. HARTOG (1864-1947)—Was Vice-Chancellor of the U. of Dacca in India and one of the founders of the famous School of Oriental Studies at the U. of London.

SUSAN S. ISAACS (1885-1948, Bolton, England)—A leading British educational theorist and author of the influential *Intellectual Growth in Young Children*.

LAVOSLAV KADELBURG (1910-)—Director of the Institute of Public Administration in Yugoslavia in the 1970s.

ISAAC L. KANDEL (1881-1965, Rumania)—Author of *Comparative Education*, one of the leading works on cross-cultural education.

PHILIP KAPLAŃ—President of the University of New Haven.

FRITZ KARSEN (1885-1951, Breslau)—Founder and Director of the famous Karl Marx School, which pioneered in innovative educational practices.

PAUL KLAPPER (1885-1952, Jassy, Rumania)—President of Queens College, N.Y., when it was founded.

IRVING LORGE (1905-1961, New York City)—Made major contributions in the education of illiterates and on the nature of the gifted child.

ROBERT E. MARSHAK (1916- , New York City)—President of the City College of New York.

ANNIE NATHAN MEYER (1867-1951, New York City)—A major figure in the establishment of Barnard College of Columbia U.

MARTIN MEYERSON (1922- , New York City)—Served as the President of the U. of Pennsylvania from 1970.

MAURICE B. MITCHELL (1915- , New York City)—The Chancellor of Denver U. from 1967.

NATHANIEL T. NEMETZ (1913-)—A member of the Supreme Court of British Columbia, he became Chancellor of the U. of British Columbia.

AARON H. PASSOW (1920- , Liberty, N.Y.)—A leading expert on urban education, he coauthored *Education of the Disadvantaged* and wrote *Education in Depressed Areas*.

DAVID S. SAXON (1920- , St. Paul, Minn.)—Became President of UCLA in 1975.

JOSEPH J. SCHWAB (1909- , Columbus, Miss.)—Professor at the U. of Chicago and author of the influential *Education and the Structure of the Disciplines*.

MARGARET SELIGMAN (1895-1954)—Cofounder of Bennington College in Vermont.

IRVING SHAIN (1926- , Seattle)—President of the U. of Wisconsin.

MARVIN WACHMAN (1917- , Milwaukee)—President of Temple U.

ROLF WEIL (1921- , Pforzheim, Germany)—President of Chicago's Roosevelt U.

NATHAN WEISS (1922- , Newark, N.J.)—President of Kean College in New Jersey.

ECONOMISTS

See also Nobel Prize Winners: Economics

JULES ABELS (1913- , Taunton, Mass.)—Chief Economist of the Small Business Administration, 1953–1960.

MOSES ABRAMOVITZ (1912- , New York City)—Professor at Stanford U. and an internationally known expert on business cycles.

ALBERT AFTALION (1874-1956, Bulgaria)—Renowned for his research on crises and economic cycles.

OSCAR L. ALTMAN (1909-1968, New York City)—Formerly a Senior Economist with the Securities and Exchange Commission, he became Treasurer of the International Monetary Fund in 1966.

MOSES B. AMZALAK (b. 1892, Lisbon, Portugal)—Chancellor of Lisbon Technical U. and President of the Academy of Sciences of Portugal, he was one of the leading economists in that country.

OTTO ARENDT (1854-1936, Berlin)—A leading conservative in Germany, he helped to found the Colonial Society of Germany and was a strong foe of democracy. He became a Christian.

RICCARDO BACHI (1875-1951)—A great early pioneer in the field of price fluctuations, he was Professor at the Italian Royal Institute of Economic Sciences.

ABRAHAM S. BECKER (1927- , New York City)—A Senior Economist with the Rand Corporation.

GARY S. BECKER (1930- , Pottsville, Pa.)—Professor of Economics at the U. of Chicago and author of *Human Capital*.

ABRAM BERGSON (1914- , Baltimore)—Director of the Russian Research Center at Harvard, 1964–1968, and a noted economist and expert on the Soviet Union.

MARTIN BRONFENBRENNER (1914- , Pittsburgh)—Kenan Professor of Economics at Duke U. and the world's foremost authority on the Japanese economy.

MURRAY BROWN (1929- , Alden, N.Y.)—Goodyear Professor of Economics at the SUNY Buffalo and a leading expert on the economics of production.

KALMAN J. COHEN (1931- , Youngstown, Ohio)—Distinguished Bank Research Professor at Duke U.

JOSEPH DORFMAN (1904- , Russia)—His great work was his multivolume *The Economic Mind in American Civilization*, published over a 12-year period.

VENIAMIN E. DYMSHYTS (1910- , Moscow)—One of the few Jews to serve on the Central Committee of the Soviet Communist party in recent years, he was Deputy Premier and a leading economist.

PAUL EINZIG (1897-)—A leading British economist and the author of *Monetary Reform in Theory and Practice*.

ABRAHAM EPSTEIN (1892-1942, Russia)—His research and recommendations on pensions influenced the enactment of Social Security legislation in the U.S.

MORDECAI EZEKIEL (1899- , Richmond, Va.)—Formerly Assistant Chief Economist of the Federal Farm Board, he later was an important figure in the Agency for International Development (AID) and a leading agricultural economist.

SOLOMON FABRICANT (1906- , Brooklyn)—Served as Director of Research of the National Bureau of Economic Research.

MARTIN FELDSTEIN (1939- , New York City)—A Professor at Harvard, he became a Senior Adviser with the Brookings Panel on Economic Activity in 1975 and won the 1977 John Bates Clark Medal of the American Economic Association.

WILLIAM J. FELLNER (1905- , Budapest)—A leading American economist and the author of *Trends and Cycles in Economic Activity.*

ROBERT FERBER (1922- , New York City)—Professor of Economics and Marketing at the U. of Ilinois, he was President of the American Marketing Association, 1969-1970.

SALLY FRANKEL (1903- , Johannesburg)—A leading South African economist, she served on East African Royal Commission.

STANLEY L. FRIEDLANDER (1938-)—Professor at the City University of New York, he was a Senior Staff Economist on the Council of Economic Advisers to the President, 1966-1967.

ALEXANDER GERSCHENKRON (1904- , Russia)—Walter S. Barker Professor of Economics at Harvard since 1955.

MILTON GILBERT (1909- , Philadelphia)—Author of *Problems of the International Monetary System.*

ELI GINZBERG (1911- , New York City)—A world authority on labor economics, he was Chairman of the National Manpower Council from 1951.

EMANUEL A. GOLDENWEISER (1883-1953, Kiev, Russia)—Director of Research at the Federal Reserve Board, he is considered one of the major architects of the World Bank and the International Monetary Fund.

RAYMOND W. GOLDSMITH (1904- , Brussels)—A major American economist and an expert on banking policies.

EPHRAIM GOMPERTZ (1776-1876)—One of the great early economic theoreticians, his *Discourse on the Nature and Poverty of Money* was a major neglected work in the history of economic thought.

MICHAEL A. HEILPERIN (1909- , Warsaw)—A leading Swiss economist and the author of the influential *Studies in Economic Nationalism.*

MIKHAIL Y. HERZENSTEIN (1859-1906, Odessa)—An advocate of land reform in Russia and a Deputy at the Duma of 1905, he was killed by czarist sympathizers.

JULIUS HIRSCH (1882-1961, Germany)—Secretary of State in the Ministry of Economics in Germany after World War I and a leading expert on quantitative economics.

ALBERT O. HIRSCHMAN (1915- , Berlin)—A Harvard Professor and a leading authority on economic development, he served as Chief of the West European Section of the Federal Reserve Board. His *Strategy of Economic Development* was an influential work.

BERT F. HOSELITZ (1913- , Vienna)—Professor at the U. of Chicago and a leading economic historian. One of his most important books is *Sociological Aspects of Economic Growth.*

NAUM JASNY (1883-1967, Russia)—An important figure in the American intelligence community because his estimates of agricultural production in the Soviet Union were used to extrapolate the military potential of that country. He worked for the Department of Agriculture and was the author of the then-definitive *Soviet Industrialization, 1928–1952.*

LORD RICHARD F. KAHN (1905-)—A leading British economist, he did important research on the "multiplier theory" of economic growth.

MICHAL KALECKI (1899-1970, Lodz, Poland)—A leading Polish economist, he was a member of the State Planning Commission and the Academy of Sciences of Poland.

DAVID S. LANDES (1924- , New York City)—Professor at Harvard and an eminent economic and social historian.

WILLIAM N. LEISERSON (1883-1957, Estonia)—A leading labor economist, he served on the National Labor Relations Board and as Chairman of the National Mediation Board. He was one of the architects of Social Security legislation in the 1930s.

ABBA P. LERNER (1903- , Russia)—A noted economist, he is author of *The Economics of Employment* and is considered a major authority on unemployment questions.

YEVESEY G. LIBERMAN (1897-)—One of the most important economists in the Soviet Union and a champion of incentives in production, he has had a profound effect upon Soviet economic policy and even appeared on a cover of *Time*.

ACHILLE LORIA (1837-1943, Mantua, Italy)—An important economic theorist, his research on the U.S. reportedly influenced the frontier thesis of Frederick Jackson Turner.

ADOLF LOWE (b. 1893, Stuttgart, Germany)—Author of the influential *Classical Theory of Economic Growth.*

FRITZ MACHLUP (1902- , Wiener Neustadt, Austria)—Former President of the American Economic Association and author of *The Political Economy of Monopoly.*

BURTON G. MALKIEL (1932- , Boston)—Gordon S. Rentschler Memorial Professor of Economics at Princeton from 1969.

ARTHUR W. MARGET (1899-1962, Chelsea, Mass.)—Was Director of the International Finance Division of the Board of Governors of the Federal Reserve System.

JACOB MARSCHAK (1898- , Kiev, Russia)—A leading American microeconomist, he wrote *Income, Employment, and the Price Level.*

DAVID I. MEISELMAN (1924-, Boston)—Formerly Frederick R. Bigelow Professor of Economics at Macalester College, he is now at Virginia Polytechnic U.

LUDWIG E. VON MISES (b. 1881, Lemberg, Austria)—A leading free market economist and an important authority on monetary theory.

OSKAR MORGENSTERN (1902-1977, Gorlitz, Germany)—Professor at Princeton and author of *International Financial Transactions and Business Cycles*, he is a leading econometrician.

HANS P. NEISSER (1895- , Breslau)—An important figure in the U.S. Office of Price Administration, he taught at the New School for Social Research.

ARTHUR M. OKUN (1928- , Jersey City)—Chairman of the President's Council of Economic Advisers, 1958–1969 and author of *The Political Economy of Prosperity.*

BERNHARD OSTROLENK (1887-1944, Warsaw)—A leading agricultural economist and the author of *Economic Geography.*

JACOB PERLMAN (1898-1967, Bialystok, Poland)—Directed the Office of Economic and Manpower Studies of the National Science Foundation, where his reports were influential in the determination of governmental economic policy.

KARL POLANYI (1886-1964, Vienna)—An Editor of *Der Oesterreichische*

IN HONOR OF...

Banberger's disease (*see* Doctors and Medical Researchers)
Beer Mountain on the moon (*see* Astronomers)
Belmont Racetrack (*see* Political Figures: Americans)
Bender Gestalt Test (*see* Psychologists)
Blumenfeld Alleys (*see* Psychologists)
Bucky rays (*see* Doctors and Medical Researchers)
Buerger's disease (*see* Doctors and Medical Researchers)
Caro's acid (*see* Chemists)
Crohn's disease (*see* Doctors and Medical Researchers)
Dressler syndrome (*see* Doctors and Medical Researchers)
Dushman vacuum (*see* Physicists)
Edinger Fibers (*see* Doctors and Medical Researchers)
Fejer's theorem (*see* Mathematicians)
Guttman scale (*see* Sociologists)
Grunfeld's defense (*see* Chess)
Goldstein-Sheerer test (*see* Psychologists)
Rachel Hirsch effect (*see* Doctors and Medical Researchers)
Harris Poll (*see* Political Figures: Americans)
Jadassohn's disease (*see* Doctors and Medical Researchers)
Kanner's autism (*see* Psychologists)
Kantrowitz-General Electric Pacemaker (*see* Doctors and Medical Researchers)
Kaposi's sarcoma (*see* Doctors and Medical Researchers)
Koplik's spots (*see* Doctors and Medical Researchers)
E.J. Korvette: Eight Jewish Korean (War) Veterans (*see* Business Leaders: Eugene Ferkauf)
Kristeller's method (*see* Doctors and Medical Researchers)
Levitsky's radical (*see* Mathematicians)
Margules equation (*see* Meteorologists)
Master Two-Step Test (*see* Doctors and Medical Researchers)
Meldola's blue dye (*see* Chemists)
Fort Myers, Fla. (*see* Military Figures: Americans)
Minkowski's Space (*see* Mathematicians)
Pulitzer Prize (*see* Newspaper Publishers)
Remak's Ganglion (*see* Doctors and Medical Researchers)
Rosenheim test (*see* Chemists)
Salk vaccine (*see* Doctors and Medical Researchers)
Toch system of camouflage (*see* Military Figures: Americans)
Traube's rule (*see* Chemists)
Wasserman test (*see* Doctors and Medical Researchers)
Wechsler Adult Intelligence Scale (*see* Psychologists)

Volkswirt, an important economic journal in Austria. His *Great Transformation* was one of the most important books in economics in the immediate period after World War II.

MICHAEL POLANYI (b. 1891, Budapest)—One of the most remarkable intellects in the world, he was a well-known physical chemist at the U. of Manchester who, in midcareer, became an outstanding political economist (he changed departments at the university). He wrote such books as *The Logic of Liberty*, and was a member of the British Royal Society.

KARL PRIBRAM (1897-?, **Prague**)—After fleeing fascism, he worked for the Brookings Institution and several governmental bodies in the U.S. He was an expert on international trade and the author of *Cartel Problems*.

DAVID RICARDO (1772-1823, **London**)—The great pioneer of modern economic thought, his *Principles of Political Economy and Taxation* was one of the most influential works in economics.

JACQUES RUEFF (1896- , **Paris**)—A member of the French Academy and author of *The Age of Inflation*, a subject on which he was an international authority.

WALTER S. SALANT (1911- , **New York City**)—An important staff member on the President's Council of Economic Advisers, he became a Senior Staff Economist with the Brookings Institution in 1954.

EDWIN R. A. SELIGMAN (1861-1939)—A founder and President of the American Economic Society, an important tax economist, and onetime Editor in Chief of the Encyclopedia of the Social Sciences.

ISAIAH SHARFMAN (1886-1969, **Russia**)—A Professor at the U. of Michigan, he wrote the important *Interstate Commerce Commission*.

IRVING H. SIEGEL (1914- , **New York City**)—Senior Staff Economist with the President's Council of Economic Advisers, 1953–1960.

FRANK W. TAUSSIG (1859-1940, **St. Louis**)—A Professor at Harvard and an important adviser on economic matters to President Woodrow Wilson, he wrote *Principles of Economics*, one of the leading textbooks in the field.

YEVGENI S. VARGA (1879-1964, **Hungary**)—Commissar of Finance in the dictatorship of Bela Kun, and then became one of the most influential economists in the Soviet Union.

JACOB VINER (1892-1970, **Montreal**)—An expert on international trade, he was a leading critic of Keynesian economics.

MURRAY WEIDENBAUM (1927- , **Bronx**)—Professor of Economics at Washington U., St. Louis, he was Assistant Secretary of the Treasury, 1969–1971.

HARRY D. WHITE (1892-1948, **Boston**)—An Assistant Secretary of the Treasury and one of its most influential figures on monetary policy, he was charged with aiding Soviet spies in World War II.

FRIEDA WUNDERLICH (1884-1965, **Berlin**)—A refugee from Hitler, she wrote *Labor under German Democracy* and other important books on international labor practices.

ARNOLD ZELLNER (1937- , **New York City**)—H. G. B. Alexander Professor of Economics and Statistics at the U. of Chicago and a leading expert on econometrics.

PSYCHOLOGISTS

KARL ABRAHAM (1877-1925, **Bremen**)—Considered the pioneer psychologist in Germany, he became the foremost expert in the world on manic-depressive behavior. He served as President of the International Psychoanalytical Association.

ALFRED ADLER (1870-1937, **Vienna**)—One of the greatest early figures in modern psychology and a rival of Freud, he founded humanistic psychology.

FRANZ ALEXANDER (1891-1964, **Budapest**)—A President of the American Psychoanalytical Association, he was a world authority on criminal behavior and the author of *The Criminal, the Judge and the Public*. He taught at the U. of Chicago.

MICHAEL BALINT (1896-1970, Budapest)—Onetime President of the British Psychoanalytical Society, author of the very influential *The Doctor, His Patient, and the Illness*, and an expert on human sexuality.

HENRI BARUK (1897-)—Did important research into the roots of aggression as Professor of Psychology at the Sorbonne.

LAURETTA BENDER (1897- , Butte, Mont.)—A leading child psychiatrist, she developed the well-known Bender Gestalt Test and was Editor of Bellevue Studies in Child Psychiatry.

THERESE F. BENEDEK (b. 1892, Eiger, Hungary)—Author of *Psychosexual Functions in Women* and a leading authority on female psychology.

IRVING BERLIN (1917- , Chicago)—Not the songwriter, but President of the Academy of Child Psychiatry, 1973-1975.

ERIC BERNE (1910-1970, Montreal)—Born Bernstein. Considered the father of transactional analysis and the author of the best-selling *Games People Play* (1964).

BRUNO BETTELHEIM (1903- , Vienna)—A leading expert on prejudice and the clinical treatment of children, Bettelheim has been a major figure in psychology for several generations.

WALTER BLUMENFELD (1882-1967, Neuruppin, Germany)—Developer of "Blumenfeld Alleys" and a leading authority on perception, he was Professor of Psychology at the U. of San Marcos in Peru.

CURT BONDY (1894- , Hamburg)—One of the world's foremost experts on adolescent psychology.

JOSEPH BREUER (1824-1925, Vienna)—Considered to have made Freud's work possible, Breuer was the greatest neurophysiologist of his time.

ABRAHAM A. BRILL (1894-1948, Austria)—A leading American psychoanalyst, he brought Freud's work to the attention of American psychologists.

JEROME S. BRUNER (1915- , New York City)—Watts Professor of Psychology at Oxford, he was President of the American Psychological Association, 1964-1965.

CHARLOTTE BUHLER (b. 1893, Berlin)—A leading authority on child development and the author of *The Child and His Family*.

ISIDOR CHEIN (1912-)—His work on race relations and social problems played a role in the Supreme Court desegregation case of 1954.

GERALD COPLAN (1917- , Liverpool)—A Professor of Psychiatry at the Harvard Medical School from 1970, he is one of the leading researchers in the field.

MAX DESSOIR (1867-1947)—A German, he was the first person to use the word *parapsychology*. He was also an important pioneer in the study of the subconscious.

FELIX DEUTSCH (1884-1964, Vienna)—Introduced the concept of posturology and was one of the great early scholars of psychosomatic illness.

HELENE DEUTSCH (b. 1884, Przemysl, Poland)—Her book *Psychoanalysis of the Neuroses* (1932) is considered one of the great works in the field. She did pioneering work in female psychology.

MONTAGUE D. EDER (1865-1936, London)—Cofounder of the British Psychoanalytical Association.

KURT R. EISSLER (1908- , Vienna)—A pioneer scholar in the field of death and dying, he was considered an unorthodox clinician.

LEO S. EITINGER (1912- , Lomnice, Czechoslovakia)—Served as President of the Norwegian Psychiatric Association in the 1960s and received the King's Gold Medal.

MAX EITINGON (1881-1943, Mohilev, Russia)—Cofounder of the famous Berlin Psychoanalytic Polyclinic, he was a central figure in psychoanalysis after World War I.

ERIK H. ERIKSON (1902- , Frankfurt)—One of the world's most famous psychoanalysts, he is the author of such important books as *Insight and Responsibility* and *Childhood and Society*.

NORMAN L. FABEROW (1918- , Pittsburgh)—Clinical Professor of Psychiatry at the U. of Southern California, he is a leading expert on suicide.

PAUL FEDERN (1871-1950, Austria)—Did major work on such diverse subjects as dream analysis, sadism, the psychological roots of revolutionary behavior, and the ego.

OTTO FENICHEL (1897-1946, Vienna)—His textbooks, especially *The Psychoanalytic Theory of Neurosis*, were standard works in the field for many years.

SANDOR FERENCZI (1873-1933, Miskolc, Hungary)—Born Fraenkel. A member of Freud's inner circle and an early scholar of child development and sexuality. If you ever felt that you would like to return to your mother's womb, remember that Ferenczi thought of it first.

JOSHUA FISHMAN (1926- , Philadelphia)—One of the world's most important experts in sociolinguistics.

CHARLES FOX (1876-1964, London)—Was the leading expert on educational psychology in Great Britain.

VICTOR E. FRANKL (1905-)—His book *Man's Search for Meaning* is considered a classic exposition on existential psychology, and he is also credited with founding the movement known as logotherapy.

ABRAHAM N. FRANZBLAU (1901- , New York City)—A popularizer of psychology and the author of such books as *A Sane and Happy Life*.

ALFRED M. FREEDMAN (1917- , Albany)—A noted psychiatrist and a specialist in being a president—for example, he served as President of the American Psychopathological Association, 1971–1972; the American College of Neuropsychopharmacology, 1972–1973; and the American Psychiatric Association, 1973–1974.

ANNA FREUD (1895-)—Despite the handicap of having a world-famous father, she established herself as a major figure in child psychology with books such as *Normality and Psychology in Childhood*.

SIGMUND FREUD (1856-1939, Freiberg)—The titanic figure of modern psychology, he had a fundamental impact on the development and direction of the entire field.

ERICH FROMM (1900- , Frankfurt)—As much a social philosopher as a psychologist, he did important work on the nature of freedom and totalitarianism. Perhaps his major book is *Escape from Freedom*.

JACOB W. GETZELS (1912- , Bialystok, Poland)—A leading educational psychologist and R. Wendell Harrison Distinguished Professor of Educational Psychology at the U. of Chicago.

HAIM G. GINOTT (1922-1973, Tel Aviv)—Became famous for the book *Between Parent and Child*, which I found worked fine if I used it to beat my children.

KURT GOLDSTEIN (1878-1965, Katowice, Poland)—Codeveloper of the famous Goldstein-Sheerer Test, he was an expert on the diagnosis of brain damage.

PHYLLIS GREENACRE (b. 1894, Chicago)—A leading authority on trauma and anxiety, she wrote *Trauma, Growth and Personality* and served as President of the New York Psychoanalytic Institute.

HEINZ HARTMANN (1894-1970, Vienna)—Was President of the International Psychoanalytic Association and a leading scholar on the ego.

EDWARD HITSCHMANN (1871-1957, Vienna)—An unfairly neglected pioneer psychiatrist, he was one of the originators of "psychohistory."

HANS HOFF (1897-1969, Vienna)—Served as President of the World Federation for Mental Health and did important pioneer research into the use of insulin in shock therapy.

WILLI HOFFER (1897-1967, Vienna)—Was a President of the British Psychoanalytic Society and Editor of the *International Journal of Psycho-Analysis*.

IRVING L. JANIS (1918-   , Buffalo)—A Professor of Psychology at Yale and author of *Victims of Groupthink* (1972), which attracted considerable attention.

JOSEPH JASTOW (1863-1944)—President of the American Psychological Association at the turn of the century, he was one of the first academic psychologists to have a syndicated newspaper column.

WILHELM JERUSALEM (1854-1923, Austria)—One of the most important pioneers in the psychology of speech.

LEO KANNER (1894-   , Klekotow, Austria)—Author of the standard textbook *Child Psychiatry*. Kanner's autism is named for him. Some consider him to be the founder of the study of child psychiatry in the U.S.

JACOB R. KANTOR (b. 1888, Harrisburg, Pa.)—Author of the influential *Interbehavioral Psychology*. He challenged conventional theories of stimulus-response.

ABRAM KARDINER (b. 1891, New York City)—A Professor at Columbia U., he was best known for *The Individual and His Society*, published shortly before World War II.

DANIEL KATZ (1903-   , Trenton, N.J.)—An important social psychologist and the coauthor of *The Social Psychology of Organizations*, Katz has conducted work in the psychology of public opinion.

HERBERT C. KELMAN (1927-   , Vienna)—Richard Clarke Cabot Professor of Social Ethics at Harvard since 1968.

KURT KOFFKA (1886-1941, Berlin)—Author of the classic *Principles of Gestalt Psychology*, he is considered one of the pioneers of the discipline.

SAMUEL C. KOHS (b. 1890, New York City)—An expert in the now controversial area of intelligence testing, he developed the Block Design Test.

MELANIE R. KLEIN (1882-1960, Vienna)—A leading British child psychologist and psychoanalyst, famous for her work with play analysis.

ERNST KRIS (1900-1957)—A pioneer in the psychoanalysis of art and Editor of *Imago*.

LAWRENCE KUBIE (1896-1973)—Former Editor of the *Journal of Nervous and Mental Disorders* and author of the important *Practical and Theoretical Aspects of Psychoanalysis* (1936).

DANIEL S. LEHRMAN (1919-1972, New York City)—A leading experimental psychologist focusing on the nature of instinct in animals and man, he was a member of both the National Academy of Sciences and the American Academy of Arts and Sciences.

EDA LESHAN (1922-   , New York City)—A leading "pop" psychologist, she wrote *The Conspiracy Against Childhood* and many other books for a general audience.

LUCIEN LEVY-BRUHL (1857-1939, Paris)—Primarily an anthropologist, he developed controversial views on archetypes and mental processes of early man.

KURT Z. LEWIN (1890-1947, Mogilno, Germany)—Father of group dynamics and field theory and a brilliant psychologist, his *Dynamic Theory of Personality* had a great influence on the field.

SIR AUBREY J. LEWIS (1900-   , Adelaide)—One of the most important psychologists in Australia, he specialized in the study of depression and obsession.

ROBERT JAY LIFTON (1926-   , Brooklyn)—Professor of Psychiatry at Yale, he won the National Book Award for *Death in Life* (1969), a fine and moving study of the survivor.

RUDOLPH M. LOEWENSTEIN (1898- , Lodz, Poland)—An expert on the ego, he served as a President of the American Psychoanalytic Association.

ALEXANDER R. LURIA (1902-)—One of the leading psychologists in the Soviet Union.

MARGARET MAHLER (1897- , Sopron, Hungary)—A leading child psychoanalyst of her generation.

J. MARMOR (1910- , London)—Franz Alexander Professor of Psychiatry at the University of Southern California, he was President of the American Academy of Psychoanalysis, 1965–1966.

ABRAHAM H. MASLOW (1908-1970)—Famed for his book *Toward a Psychology of Being* and for his theories of personality, he was a President of the American Psychological Association.

JULES H. MASSERMAN (1905- , Chudnov, Poland)—Served as President of both the International Association of Social Psychiatry and the American Academy for Psychoanalysis and was the author of the well-known text *The Principles of Dynamic Psychiatry*.

JACOB L. MORENO (b. 1892, Bucharest)—A pioneer in group therapy using psychodrama techniques and the author of *Discovery of Spontaneous Man*.

HUGO MUENSTERBERG (1863-1916, Danzig)—A significant figure in the development of American psychology, he helped develop the first lie detector while a Professor at Harvard and was President of the American Psychological Association (he also was President of the American Philosophical Association). He converted to Christianity.

CHARLES S. MYERS (1873-1946, London)—A noted applied psychologist, he was President of the British Psychological Society and author of one of the leading textbooks in experimental psychology.

MILDRED NEWMAN—Coauthor with Bernard Berkowitz of *How to Be Your Own Best Friend*.

MARVIN K. OPLER (1914- , Buffalo)—Author of *Culture and Social Psychiatry*, Opler works at the interface between psychology and anthropology and is a leading cross-cultural social psychiatrist.

SANDOR RADO (b. 1890, Hungary)—An important psychoanalyst at Columbia U. and elsewhere, he is noted for his research into adaptational psychodynamics.

OTTO RANK (1884-1939, Vienna)—Born Rosenfeld. Did pioneering work on incest, birth, and myths. Perhaps his best-known work is *The Trauma of Birth* (1929).

DAVID RAPAPORT (1911-1960, Hungary)—Director of Research at the Menninger Foundation, he was a leading clinical psychologist and author of *The Structure of Psychoanalytic Theory*.

GREGORY RAZRAN (1901-1973, Slutsk, Russia)—One of the world's leading authorities on conditioning theory.

FRITZ REDL (1902- , Klaus, Austria)—A leading expert on juvenile delinquency and juvenile gang behavior, he wrote *Children Who Hate* and served as the director of Child Research of the National Institute of Mental Health.

WILHELM REICH (1897-1957, Austria)—An important expert on the development of character (somewhat ironic in light of the fact that he was imprisoned for fraud at the time of his death).

THEODOR REIK (1888-1970, Vienna)—Challenged prevailing theories of sexuality in books such as *The Psychology of Sex Relations*.

GEZA REVESZ (1878-1955, Siofok, Hungary)—The world's leading authority on the psychology of blindness, he also conducted important research on the development of language.

ABRAHAM A. ROBACK (1890-1965, Russia)—A leading historian of psychology, he wrote *History of American Psychology* among other works and also did important research on character development.

SIR MARTIN ROTH (1917-   , London)—President of both the World Psychiatry Association and the British Royal Society of Clinical Psychiatry.

SERGEY RUBINSTEIN (1889-1960, Russia)—Winner of the Stalin Prize and one of the leading psychologists in the Soviet Union, he was Director of the Moscow Institute of Psychology during World War II.

HANS SACHS (1881-1947, Vienna)—Two of his books, *Masks of Love and Life* and *The Creative Unconscious*, were major contributions to the psychology of creativity.

MANFRED SAKEL (1900-1957, Nadvorna, Austria)—A leading expert on schizophrenia and its treatment with insulin, he developed the insulin coma treatment, which became standard.

JEROME M. SCHNECK (1920-   , New York City)—A world authority on hypnotherapy.

RENÉ SPITZ (b. 1887, Vienna)—One of the world's leading authorities on growth and development, he developed the concept of anaclitic depression. His most famous book was *The First Year of Life.*

WILHELM STEKEL (1868-1940, Vienna)—Did pioneering work on the importance and role of symbols and symbolism.

ERWIN STENGEL (1902-1973, Vienna)—A leading expert on suicide, he served as President of the International Association for Suicide Prevention.

WILLIAM STERN (1871-1938, Berlin)—Did important work on the testing of intelligence and laid the groundwork for the development of Gestalt psychology.

THOMAS SZASZ (1920-   , Budapest)—Has challenged most of the prevailing theories on mental illness and even the concept itself. He won the 1973 Humanist of the Year Award of the American Humanist Association for books such as *The Age of Madness* and *The Myth of Mental Illness.*

RONALD TAFT (1920-   , Melbourne)—Professor of Social Psychology at Monash U., Victoria, and a leading Australian psychologist, he served as President of the Australian Psychological Association.

VIKTOR TAUSK (1877-1919, Austria)—An important contributor to the theory of schizophrenia. He took his own life.

MORITZ TRAMER (1882-1963, Czechoslovakia)—Founded the first scholarly journal devoted to child psychiatry and is considered one of the founders of the field.

LEV S. VYGOTSKI (1896-1934)—One of the leading psychologists in the Soviet Union, he did important research with the mentally retarded. Vygotski's Blocks carry his name.

DAVID WECHSLER (1869-?, Lespedi, Rumania)—One of the great figures in the history of intelligence testing. The Wechsler Adult Intelligence Scale (WAIS) is widely employed. He was Chief Psychologist at Bellevue Hospital, in N.Y.

ALBERT P. WEISS (1879-1931, Steingrund, Germany)—Noted for his book *A Theoretical Basis of Human Behavior*, he taught at Ohio State U. and may have been the first person to use the term *social status.*

HEINZ WERNER (1890-1964, Vienna)—An expert on the process of perception, Werner taught at Clark U., Worcester, Mass., and was the author of the widely acclaimed *Comparative Psychology of Mental Development.*

MAX WERTHEIMER (1880-1943, Prague)—A great figure in the development of modern psychology, he is considered one of the cofounders of Gestalt psychology.

LEWIS R. WOLBERG (1905-   , Russia)—A leading clinical psychiatrist and therapist, he was the author of *Psychotherapy and the Behavioral Sciences* and helped to found the American Academy of Psychoanalysis.

WERNER WOLFF (1904-1957, Berlin)—Taught at Bard College after fleeing the Nazis and was one of the world's outstanding existential psychologists.

GREGORY ZILBOORG (1890-1959, Kiev)—A leading authority on suicide.

ANTHROPOLOGISTS

DAVID F. ABERLE (1918- , St. Paul, Minn.)—A Professor of Anthropology at the U. of British Columbia and a leading expert on the American Indian.

DAVID BIDNEY (1908- , Russia)—A world-famous anthropologist who taught at the U. of Indiana, he bridged the gap between philosophy and anthropology in such influential books as *Theoretical Anthropology*.

FRANZ BOAS (1858-1942, Minden, Germany)—A titanic figure in the development of anthropology in America, he fought against racial determinism and in favor of culture as the key to understanding mankind. As Professor at Columbia U. he trained two generations of anthropologists. His most noted books were *Race, Language, and Culture*, published at the start of World War II when racism was still at its peak, and *Anthropology and Modern Life*.

RUTH L. BUNZEL (b. 1898, New York City)—A leading expert on the Native American, her book *The Pueblo Potter* has become a classic. She taught at Columbia U.

ALDOPHUS ELKIN (b. 1891)—A pioneer in the development (in Australia) of anthropology as a field of study and the author of the standard *Australian Aborigines*.

VERA ERLICH (b. 1897)—Her *In the Company of Man* was a widely discussed book.

MEYER FORTES (1906- , South Africa)—Did pioneer work in the standard theory of the development of primitive political systems, and carried out important basic research in East Africa.

MORTON H. FRIED (1923- , New York City)—A Professor at Columbia U., he is the author of important anthropology textbooks and a leading expert on Taiwanese culture.

MAX GLUCKMAN (1911- , Johannesburg)—Author of the important *Custom and Conflict in Africa*, he is a leading scholar on the evolution of tribal societies.

JULES HENRY (1904-1967)—Author of the renowned *Culture against Man* and an expert on the culture-personality interface.

MELVILLE J. HERSKOVITS (1895-1963, Bellefontaine, Ohio)—The famed President of the African Studies Association and the outstanding anthropologist on Africa in the U.S. Two of his most important books were *Man and His Works* (a standard textbook) and *The Myth of the Negro Past*.

VLADIMIR JOCHELSON (1855-1937, Vilna, Lithuania)—A noted Russian anthropologist who did pioneering studies of the native populations of Siberia and Alaska.

CLAUDE LEVI-STRAUSS (1898- , Brussels)—Certainly one of the most important figures in the social sciences in the twentieth century. His work on structural anthropology has been widely discussed inside and outside the field.

OSCAR LEWIS (1914-1970, New York City)—His crucial research into the nature of poverty and the culture that accompanies it made him famous. His books, especially *La Vida* and *Five Families*, were tremendously influential. He taught at the U. of Illinois.

ROBERT H. LOWIE (1883-1957, Vienna)—Former Editor of the *American Journal of Anthropology* and a leading scholar on Native Americans. His books *Primitive Society* and *Primitive Religion* broke new ground.

DAVID G. MANDELBAUM (1911- , Chicago)—An important applied anthropologist and ethnologist who taught at the U. of California.

MARCEL MAUSS (1872-1950, Epinal, France)—A noted French anthropologist and sociologist who was also an important historian of religion.

ASHLEY MONTAGU (1905- , London)—A well-known cultural anthropologist who led the academic struggle against racism in books such as *Human Heredity* and *The Direction of Human Evolution.*

MORRIS E. OPLER (1907- , Buffalo)—Professor of Anthropology and Asian Studies at Cornell, he was President of the American Anthropological Association, 1962-1963.

PAUL L. OPPENHEIM (1863-1934)—A leading paleontologist who did important work on Tertiary fossils and fossil invertebrates.

LAWRENCE OSCHINSKY (1921-1965, New York City)—A major physical anthropologist who did important research on human evolution and on the native cultures of North America.

SIEGFRED F. NADEL (1903-1956, Austria)—A leading theorist who held the Chair in Anthropology and Sociology at the Australian National U. His two most significant works were *The Theory of Social Structure* and *The Foundations of Social Anthropology.*

PAUL RADIN (1883-1959, Lodz, Poland)—An important American anthropologist and authority on Native Americans, he wrote *The Road of Life and Death: A Ritual Drama of the American Indians* and *Primitive Man as Philosopher.*

SAUL RIESENBERG (1911- , Newark)—Curator of Anthropology and Senior Ethnologist at the Smithsonian Institution, 1957-1973.

GEZA ROHEIM (1891-1953, Budapest)—Did pioneer work in the relationship between psychology and culture in such books as *The Origin and Foundation of Culture* and *Animism, Magic and the Divine King.*

EDWARD SAPIR (1884-1939, Lauenburg, Germany)—Former Chief of the Geological Survey of Canada and a leading expert on Native American languages and anthropological linguistics in general.

CHARLES SELIGMAN (1873-1940)—Held the first Chair of Anthropology at the University of London and was one of the leading anthropologists in Great Britain.

HARRY L. SHAPIRO (1902- , Boston)—Curator of Physical Anthropology and Chairman of the Department of Anthropology at the American Museum of Natural History, he was President of the American Anthropological Association in 1948 and President of the American Ethnological Society.

LESLIE SPIER (1893-1961, New York City)—A leading authority on the Plains Indians of the U.S.

MELFORD E. SPIRO (1920- , Cleveland)—Professor of Anthropology at the U. of California, San Diego, and President of the American Ethnological Society, 1967-1968.

ALEXANDER SPOEHR (1913- , Tucson, Ariz.)—A leading ethnologist of Pacific cultures, he was President of the American Anthropological Association in 1965 and served as Chancellor of the East-West Center of the U. of Hawaii.

SOL TAX (1907-)—A leading scholar on the Apache, he edited the *American Anthropologist* and *Current Anthropology* while Professor at the U. of Chicago.

LIONEL TIGER (1937- , Montreal)—Professor of Anthropology at the Livingston Campus of Rutgers U., he coauthored the interesting and influential *Men in Groups* (1969).

MISCHA TITIEV (1901- , Kremenchug, Russia)—An important ethnologist of Native Americans and of the Japanese, he taught at the U. of Michigan and wrote *The Science of Man.*

PHILLIP TOBIAS (1925- , Durban, South Africa)—A world-famous paleoanthropologist and associate of Leakey, he served as President of the Royal Society of South Africa.

RICHARD G. VAN GELDER (1928- , New York City)—Curator of the American Museum of Natural History.

FRANZ WEIDENREICH (1873-1948)—A noted German physical anthropologist, he was the first to work on Homo sinanthropus after his discovery in China.

ERIC R. WOLF (1923- , Vienna)—Distinguished Professor of Anthropology at Lehman College, in N.Y., and the author of two exceptional books, *Peasant Wars of the Twentieth Century*, and *Sons of the Shaking Earth*.

LEGAL SCHOLARS

ALEXANDER M. BICKEL (1924-1974, Bucharest)—A leading expert on American Constitutional law before his untimely death. Many believed that he would have been appointed to the Supreme Court.

EDMOND CAHN (1906-1964, New Orleans)—A world authority on the relationship between ethics and law, and author of *Sense of Injustice*.

JEROME A. COHEN (1930- , Elizabeth, N.J.)—Director of East Asian legal studies at Harvard and a leading authority on Chinese law.

EUGEN EHRLICH (1862-1922, Czernowitz)—His *Fundamental Principles of the Sociology of Law* was very influential.

PAUL J. ERRERA (1860-1922, Brussels)—Professor of Constitutional Law and Rector of Brussels U., he was a fellow of the Belgian Royal Academy.

MARIO FALCO (1884-1943, Turin, Italy)—A leading expert on canon law.

SHNEYUR FELLER (1913- , Botosani, Rumania)—A leading Rumanian lawyer, he wrote the great bulk of his country's penal code.

JACOB FINKELMAN (1907- , Russia)—Introduced labor law into the curriculum of Canadian law schools.

ERNST FREUND (1864-1932, New York City)—Served on the National Conference of Commissioners on Uniform State Law for almost 25 years and was a leading expert on public law in the U.S.

PAUL A. FREUND (1908- , St. Louis)—A Harvard Professor and one of the leading constitutional lawyers in the U.S., he was a serious contender for the Supreme Court and was JFK's legal adviser.

RONALD C. GOLDFARB (1933- , Jersey City)—A leading legal scholar and the author of *Ransom: A Critique of the American Bail System*.

ABRAHAM S. GOLDSTEIN (1925- , New York City)—Became Dean of the Yale Law School in 1970 and is William Nelson Cromwell Professor of Law there.

ARTHUR L. GOODHART (b. 1891, New York City)—Was a leading legal scholar, Editor of the *Law Quarterly Review*, and Chairman of the International Law Association. He taught at Oxford U.

LESLIE C. GREEN (1920- , London)—A leading Canadian legal scholar and Professor at the U. of Alberta.

LOUIS L. JAFFE (1905- , Seattle)—Byrne Professor of Administrative Law at Harvard.

MILTON KATZ (1922-)—Director of International Legal Studies at Harvard, he was formerly Chairman of the Board of the Carnegie Endowment for International Peace.

HANS KELSEN (b. 1881, Prague)—One of the most important legal philosophers of modern times, he became a Professor of Political Science at the U. of California after fleeing fascism.

MILTON R. KONVITZ (1908- , Safed, Palestine)—A leading U.S. civil rights scholar, he was Assistant Counsel of the NAACP and Staff Counsel of the American Civil Liberties Union.

LEE KREINDLER (1924- , New York City)—The world's leading authority on aviation accident law.

JOSEF L. KUNZ (1890-1970, Vienna)—A noted international lawyer and the author of *The Changing Law of Nations*.

PAUL LABAND (1838-1918, Breslau)—Considered the leading legal scholar in Germany, and a famed expert on constitutional law.

MANFRED LACHS (1914-)—Served Poland in the UN, was Director of the Legal Department of the Polish Foreign Ministry, and became a judge on the International Court of Justice at The Hague.

SALMON O. LEVINSON (1865-1941, Noblesville, Ind.)—One of the major sponsors of the Kellogg-Briand pact after World War I and one of the authors of the final document.

HENRY G. MANNE (1928- , New Orleans)—Kenan Professor of Law at the U. of Rochester, N.Y.

SOIA MENTSCHIKOFF (1915- , Moscow)—Dean of the U. of Miami Law School, she was the first woman to teach law at Harvard.

ALBERT MOSSE (1846-1925)—Wrote most of the Japanese constitution and was a world authority on administrative law.

LASSA F. L. OPPENHEIM (1858-1919, Windekken, Germany)—Wrote the standard textbook on international law and was considered the world's outstanding expert on the subject. He taught at Cambridge U.

FRITZ E. OPPENHEIMER (1898-1968, Berlin)—A leading international lawyer, he was one of the authors of the surrender documents signed by the Germans at the end of World War II and one of the principal authors of the regulations governing the military occupation of Germany.

LEO PFEFFER (1910- , Hungary)—A leading American constitutional lawyer and the author of *Church and State in the United States*, he taught at Long Island U.

VITTORIO POLACCO (1859-1926, Padua, Italy)—A leading Italian legal scholar, he taught at the Universities of Rome and Padua.

MAX RADIN (1880-1950, Kempen, Poland)—A noted legal realist, he wrote the popular book *The Law and You*.

NORMAN REDLICH (1925-)—Dean of NYU Law School and a leading legal theorist, he helped to investigate the assassination of President Kennedy.

FRED M. RODELL (1907- , Philadelphia)—A Professor at Yale and the author of the very important *Nine Men: A Political History of the Supreme Court 1790-1955*.

HARRY SHULMAN (1903-1955, Krugloye, Russia)—A leading authority on labor law and a famous arbitrator (he settled a famous battle between Ford and the UAW), he became Dean of the Yale Law School shortly before his death.

MICHAEL I. SOVERN (1931- , New York City)—A major legal scholar, he became Dean of Columbia Law School in 1970.

JULIUS STONE (1907- , Leeds, England)—One of the world's leading legal philosophers and the author of *Social Dimensions of Law and Justice* and *Human Law and Human Justice*. He taught at the U. of Sydney after having served as Dean of the U. of New Zealand Law School.

SAMUEL UNTERMYER (1858-1940, Virginia)—Helped to write some of the most famous legislation in American history, including the Clayton Anti-Trust and the Federal Trade Commission acts.

CESARE VIVANTE (1855-1944, Venice)—Wrote the major textbook on Italian commercial law.

HERBERT WECHSLER (1909-   , New York City)—A leading constitutional scholar and lawyer, he wrote *Criminal Law and its Administration* and *Principles, Politics, and Fundamental Law.*

BERNARD WOLFMAN (1924-   , Philadelphia)—A leading expert on tax law and Dean of the U. of Pennsylvannia Law School since 1970. .

Part V
The Physical Sciences

PIONEERS OF ATOMIC ENERGY

See Also Nobel Prize Winners; Physicists.

ROBERT F. BACHER (1905- , Loudonville, Ohio)—Head of the Bomb Physics Division at Los Alamos in the Manhattan Project days, he served as a member of the AEC in the immediate postwar years and later taught at Cal Tech.

ARTHUR BLOK (b. 1882)—Received the Order of the British Empire for his work on nuclear polymers and other efforts during World War II.

LISE MEITNER (1878-1968, Vienna)—A world-renowned physicist who helped discover atomic fission, she fought long and hard to achieve a place in a male-dominated profession.

JOHANN VON NEUMANN (1903-1957, Budapest)—A world-famous mathematician at the Institute for Advanced Study at Princeton, he served on the Atomic Energy Commission in the mid-1950s. His book (written with Oskar Morgenstern) *Theory of Games and Economic Behavior* (1944) was one of the founding texts of what became known as game theory.

J. ROBERT OPPENHEIMER (1904-1967, New York City)—One of the most distinguished physicists in the world, and one who suffered (perhaps needlessly) during the McCarthy period. Director of the Institute of Advanced Study at Princeton for 20 years, he supervised the assembly of the first atomic bomb at Los Alamos and was one of the most important figures in its successful development.

SIR RUDOLF E. PEIERLS (1907- , Berlin)—Coauthor of an important scientific paper on the implications of atomic energy that played a major role in persuading the British to move ahead in atomic research at the start of World War II. He later came to the U.S., where he was an important member of the team that put together the first atomic bomb at Los Alamos.

BRUNO PONTECORVO (1913- , Italy)—Defected to the U.S.S.R. in 1950 and played an important role in Soviet nuclear and thermonuclear research, for which he was awarded both the Lenin Prize and the Order of Lenin. Earlier he had done important research in neutron physics in the U.S. and Great Britain.

EUGENE RABINOWITCH (1901- , St. Petersburg)—An important and neglected member of the Manhattan Project team, he taught biophysics after the war at the U. of Illinois.

SIR FRANCIS E. SIMON (1893-1956, Berlin)—A unique participant in the development of the first atomic bomb because all the while he was working on the project, he was classified as an enemy alien in an effort to deceive German intelligence. He is best known for his work at the low-temperature laboratory at Oxford, which he helped to develop.

LEO SZILARD (1898-1964, Budapest)—He wrote some interesting science fiction stories as a hobby, but they never equaled his 1934 prediction of a nuclear chain reaction. It was Szilard (along with Eugene Wigner) who convinced Albert Einstein of the danger of German atomic research and the promise of nuclear energy, and got him to send his now famous letter to FDR in the fall of 1939 that ultimately led to the Manhattan Project and the development of the bomb.

EDWARD TELLER (1908- , Budapest)—Rightly considered the father of the hydrogen bomb, both for his technical innovations and for his vigorous political efforts on behalf of its development. In recent years he has been associated with a strong defense posture for the U.S. During World II War he played an important role in the Manhattan Project.

VICTOR F. WEISSKOPF (1908- , Austria)—Also involved in the Manhattan Project, but one of his major contributions was as Director General of the European Center for Nuclear Research in the first half of the 1960s, which sought to centralize Western European nuclear research and to share the results among the participating states. He was a professor at M.I.T. for many years.

JERROLD R. ZACHARIAS (1905- , Jacksonville, Fla.)—Another veteran of Los Alamos, Zacharias was responsible for the research that led to the atomic clock. He was the world's leading expert on the radio frequency spectra of atoms.

PHYSICISTS

See also Nobel Prize Winners: Physics.

MAX ABRAHAM (1875-1922, Danzig)—A German, he was an internationally known expert on the electron.

EDWARD N. D. ANDRADE (1887-1971, London)—Andrade's Laws, which describe the flow of metals, are named for him. He is best known for *The Atom and Its Energy*, which appeared after the war and was one of the first books designed to explain atomic energy to a lay audience. He also wrote the outstanding biography of *Sir Isaac Newton* (1954).

LEO ARONS (1860-1919, Berlin)—Discovered the mercury vapor lamp.

DAVID BOHM (1917- , Philadelphia)—Noted for his book *Quantum Theory* (1952), he was one of the few physicists to champion determinism in quantum mechanics.

ISRAEL DOSTROVSKY (1918- , Odessa, U.S.S.R.)—Director General, Israel Atomic Energy Commission, 1965-1971. He was formerly a leading researcher at the Brookhaven National Laboratory.

SAUL DUSHMAN (1883-1954, Rostov, Russia)—Developer of the Dushman vacuum. One of his major contributions was linguistic: He was the first person to use the suffix *tron*, as in *cyclotron*.

PAUL EHRENFEST (1880-1933, Vienna)—A leading expert in the fields of kinetic theory and statistical mechanics.

PAUL S. EPSTEIN (1883-1966, Warsaw)—A noted physicist from Cal Tech and author of a leading textbook on thermodynamics.

JACOB FRENKEL (1894-1952)—One of the first great Soviet theoretical physicists, he achieved international recognition for his theories of nuclear fission.

OTTO R. FRISCH (1904- , Vienna)—Directed the Nuclear Physics Division of the United Kingdom Atomic Energy Establishment. He coined the phrase *nuclear fission*.

HERBERT FROHLICH (1905- , Rexingen, Germany)—A Fellow of the British Royal Society, he taught at the University of Liverpool for many years.

VITALII L. GINZBURG (1916-)—One of the world's leading authorities on the Cerenkov Effect and a holder of the Lenin Prize.

EUGEN GOLDSTEIN (1850-1931, Gleiwitz, Germay)—Discovered "canal rays" and made major contributions to the knowledge of radiant emissions.

HEINRICH R. HERTZ (1857-1894)—The famous discover of electromagnetic waves. His father was born a Jew.

LEOPOLD INFELD (1898-1968, Cracow)—Perhaps the leading Polish physicist of the 20th century, he coauthored *The Evolution of Physics* with Albert Einstein.

ABRAHAM F. JOFFE (1880-1960, Romny, Russia)—A member of the Presidium of the Soviet Academy of Sciences, his book *The Physics of Semiconductors* is still a standard reference work.

PETER L. KAPITZA (1894- , Kronstadt, Russia)—The son of a Jewish mother, he has the distinction of being the first non-British subject to be elected as a fellow of the Royal Society. He was one of the team of researchers who developed Soviet atomic weapons, and served for many years as Director of the Soviet Institute of Physical Problems.

JOSEPH KAPLAN (1902-   , Tapolca, Hungary)—A Professor at UCLA, he is a leading authority on the physics of the upper atmosphere.

FRITZ LONDON (1900-1954, Breslau, Germany)—Did pioneering research on valency.

LEONID I. MANDELSHTAM (1879-1944, Odessa)—A leading Soviet physicist, he was an expert on oscillation theory.

KURT A. G. MENDELSSOHN (1906-   , Berlin)—Served as Editor of the international journal *Cryogenics*, was a member of the Royal Society, and was responsible for the construction of England's first helium liquefaction facility.

YUVAL NE'EMAN (1925-   , Tel Aviv)—Did pioneering research in elementary particle physics. Many feel that he deserved the Nobel Prize for his work.

GIULIO RACAH (1909-1965, Florence)—An immigrant to Israel, he became famous for his research in atomic spectroscopy.

MARKUS REINER (b. 1886)—Rheology became a branch of physics because of his research in the flow of elastic liquid. His name is half of the Buckingham-Reiner equation. He became a citizen of Israel.

DAVID TABOR (1913-   )—A member of the Royal Society, he did important research in the physics of friction lubrication. He taught at Cambridge U. for many years.

IGAL TALMI (1925-   , Kiev)—A resident of Israel, he is one of the world's leading authorities on the nuclear shell model.

SAMUEL TOLANSKY (1907-1973, Newcastle-on-Tyne)—One of a small group of physicists brought in to analyze the rocks and lunar dust from the Apollo flight. He was a member of the British Royal Society and the author of hundreds of research papers.

VLADIMIR VEKSLER (1907-1966, Moscow)—One of the premier physicists in the Soviet Union, the winner of the Lenin Prize and the Atoms for Peace Award. He played a major role in the successful launching of Sputnik and directed the High Energy Laboratory at the Soviet Joint Institute for Nuclear Research.

MATHEMATICIANS

GIULIO ASCOLI (1843-1896)—Developer of "quasi-uniform convergence" and an expert on the theory of functions.

SALOMON BOCHNER (b. 1899, Cracow [then Austria-Hungary])—Henry Burchard Fine Professor of Mathematics at Princeton, 1959-1968.

RICHARD COURANT (b. 1888, Silesia)—His research was instrumental in the development of computers, especially his work on the interface between physics and quantum mechanics.

FERDINAND G. EISENSTEIN (1823-1852)—Did pioneering work in algebra and number theory.

ABRAM ESICOVITCH (b. 1891)—Winner of the Sylvester Medal for his contributions to mathematics and a member of the Royal Society, he worked in a number of branches of the discipline, including number theory.

CHARLES L. FEFFERMAN (1949-   , Washington, D.C.)—A Professor of Mathematics at Princeton, he won the Alan T. Waterman Award.

LEOPOLD FEJER (1880-1959)—Most famous for Fejer's theorem, developed during his doctoral research. He was a member of the Hungarian Academy of Sciences.

MICHAEL FEKETE (1886-1957, Zenta, Hungary)—An Israeli, he discovered the transfinite diameter.

ABRAHAM A. FRAENKEL (1891-1965, Munich)—One of the world's leading experts on set theory.

GUIDO FUBINI (1879-1943, Italy)—An outstanding Italian mathematician, his special interests were in Lie groups and differential geometry.

IZRAIL M. GELFAND (1913-)—Holder of the Stalin Prize and one of the Soviet Union's leading mathematicians, he is most famous for his contributions to the theory of normed algebras. A Professor at Moscow State U., he was a pioneer in functional analysis.

ALEKSANDR O. GELFOND (1906-)—Another leading Soviet mathematician, his book *Transcendental and Algebraic Numbers* is an internationally famous text.

BENJAMIN GOMPERTZ (1779-1865)—A member of a distinguished British family, he produced a method for calculating mortality rates that is still in use today.

A. W. GOODMAN (1915- , San Antonio, Tex.)—Distinguished Professor of Mathematics at the U. of South Florida.

JACQUES S. HADAMARD (1865-1963, Versailles)—The first recipient of the Feltrinelli Prize, he is considered one of the greatest mathematicians who ever lived.

GEORGES-HENRI HALPHEN (1844-1889, Rouen, France)—A member of the French Academy of Sciences, he was an expert on the classification of curves.

FELIX HAUSDORFF (1868-1942, Breslau, Germany)—An internationally recognized authority on set theory. He took his own life.

KARL G. J. JACOBI (1804-1851, Potsdam)—A leading mathematician and a convert to Christianity, he is credited by historians with laying the basis for the study of physics.

SAMUEL KARLIN (1923- , Yonava, Poland)—Professor at Stanford U. and a leading authority on the theory of inventory.

LEOPOLD KRONECKER (1823-1891, Liegnitz)—One of the leading European mathematicians in the mid-1800s. His work, more than that of any other person, led to the theory of commutative fields.

SOLOMON LEFSCHETZ (1884-1972, Moscow)—A Professor at Princeton U. for many years, he was an expert with an international reputation for his work on algebraic geometry and differential equations.

TULLIO LEVI-CIVITA (1873-1942, Padua, Italy)—World-famous for his theory of parallel displacement and winner of the Sylvester Medal of the British Royal Society. His work was fundamental to Einstein's general theory of relativity.

JACOB LEVITSKY (1904-1956, Russia)—A Professor at Hebrew U., Jerusalem, he was the world's leading expert on the laws of rings. The Levitsky radical carries his name.

HYMAN LEVY (b. 1889, Edinburgh)—A leading British mathematician and a political activist, he was an important figure in the Communist party of Great Britain (from which he was eventually expelled), and chaired the Labor party's Science Advisory Committee in the 1920s.

PAUL LEVY (b. 1886)—A noted mathematician, he served as President of the Mathematical Society of France in the mid-1960s.

YOM TOV L. LIPKIN (1845-1875, Russia)—Remembered for his kinematic system, which attracted world-wide attention.

RUDOLF O. S. LIPSCHITZ (1832-1903, Konigsberg, Germany)—Codeveloper of the proof of the equation $dy/dx = (f(x,y,)$, which was of great importance in differential calculus.

HERMANN MINKOWSKI (1864-1909, Alexoten, Lithuania)—"Minkowski Space" refers to his four-dimensional treatment of relativity, and the branch of mathematics known as the geometry of numbers was largely developed from his research.

LOUIS J. MORDELL (1888-1972)—A noted British mathematician and a member of the Royal Society, he was an expert on the theory of numbers.

EMMY NOETHER (1882-1935, Erlangen, Germany)—A distinguished mathematician, she was a pioneer researcher in noncommutative algebra.

ANATOL RAPPOPORT (1911- , Lozovaya, Russia)—A Professor at the U. of Michigan, where he taught mathematical biology for most of his career, he was a leading authority on game theory and the author of *Fights, Games and Debates* (1960).

LOUIS ROSENHEAD (1906- , Leeds, England)—A member of the Council of the British Royal Society, he was an expert on fluid mechanics.

ARTHUR RUBIN—A brilliant mathematician, at 18 he became the youngest graduate student in the history of the California Institute of Technology.

KARL SCHWARZ (1843-1921)—A German, he greatly influenced the field with his work in conformal mapping and potential theory.

BENJAMINO SEGRE (1903-)—A distinguished Italian mathematician best known for his book *Non-Singular Cubic Surfaces*, an important work in geometric theory.

JAMES J. SYLVESTER (1814-1897)—One of Britain's and the world's most famous mathematicians, he was founder and first Editor of the *American Journal of Mathematics*. The medal named for him is one of the most sought-after awards in the field. His major technical contributions were his theories of differential invariants.

OTTO TOEPLITZ (1881-1940)—A German best remembered for his work in matrix algebra.

S. M. ULAM (1909- , Lwow, Poland)—One of America's leading mathematicians, he is a member of the National Academy of Science.

VITO VOLTERRA (1860-1940)—Considered to be responsible for the development of functionals and the creation of the field of mathematical biology. He was the Chairman of the Office for War Inventions in Italy and a Fellow of the British Royal Society.

ANDRE WEIL (1906- , Paris)—A teacher and researcher at the Institute of Advanced Studies in Princeton, he was an expert in group and number theory.

NORBERT WIENER (1894-1964, Columbia, Mo.)—Considered the father of cybernetics, the science that developed the computer and had a profound effect on modern society. Concerned about the implications of his own research, he published *The Human Use of Human Beings* in 1950, a lucid and moral examination of the role of science in society. He was a legend in his own time, and may well be viewed as one of the most important men who ever lived.

OSCAR ZARISKI (1899- , Kobrin, Russia)—Served as President of the American Mathematical Society, edited the *American Journal of Mathematics*, and is renowned for his research on topology and algebraic surfaces.

ASTRONOMERS

ILYA S. ABELMANN (1866-1898, Dvinsk, Russia)—A leading popularizer of astronomy in Russia.

WILHELM BEER (1797-1850)—Did pioneering work in systematically viewing the moon and recording its features. Beer Mountain on the moon carries his name.

LOUIS BERMAN (1903- , London)—A leading American astronomer and an expert on the temperature of stars.

FRITZ COHN (1866-1922, Königsberg, Germany)—A world authority on celestial mechanics.

ERWIN FINLAY-FREUDLICH (1885-1964, Biebrich, Germany)—Applied Einstein's research to astronomy and led a number of important solar eclipse survey parties.

HERMANN GOLDSCHMIDT (1802-1866, Frankfurt)—Held the Gold Medal of the British Royal Astronomical Society for his discovery of many previously unknown asteroids.

JESSE L. GREENSTEIN (1909-)—A leading expert on high-dispersion spectroscopy.

DAVID LAYZER (1925-)—A brillant theorist, he specializes in atomic astrophysics.

MAURICE LOEWY (1833-1907, Pressburg, [Bratislava])—One of the first astronomical photographers, he held the Gold Medal of the British Royal Astronomical Society and was head astronomer of the Paris Observatory.

RUDOLPH MINKOWSKI (1895-)—A leading German, then American, expert on supernovae.

RICHARD PRAGER (1883-1945, Hanover, Germany)—A leading authority of photoelectric stellar photometry.

CARL SAGAN (1934- , New York City)—David Duncan Professor of Astronomy and Space Sciences at Cornell, he won numerous awards for *The Dragons of Eden* and is a leading expert on theories of extraterrestrial life.

FRANK SCHLESINGER (1871-1943, New York City)—A founder and President of the International Astronomical Union, he was Director of the Yale Observatory.

KARL SCHWARZSCHILD (1873-1916, Frankfurt)—One of the great pioneer astrophysicists.

IMMANUEL VELIKOVSKY (1895- , Vitebsk, Russia)—His controversial theories linking events in the Bible to astronomical phenomena made him famous. His best-known book is *Worlds in Collision* (1950).

EDMUND WEISS (1837-1917)—A noted astronomer and onetime Director of the Vienna Observatory.

CHEMISTS

See also Nobel Prize Winners: Chemistry.

EMIL ABEL (1875-1958, Vienna)—Did important research on the battery cell and on homogeneous catalysis.

AARON M. ALTSCHUL (1914-)—A leading nutritional chemist who served the U.S. government in a number of capacities and taught at Tulane.

PAUL ASKENASY (1869-1934, Breslau, Germany)—Did important early research in electrochemistry.

ALFRED L. BACHARACH (1891-1966)—One of the world's leading authorities on vitamins. His work on babies' formulas is credited with eliminating rickets in England.

EUGEN BANBERGER (1857-1932)—A leading German chemist who did important early research in the development of semimicrotechniques.

BASIL BARD (1914-)—A noted lawyer as well as a chemist, he led England's National Research Development Corporation.

ERNST D. BERGMANN (1903- , Karlsruhe, Germany)—Codeveloper of the catarole process. He is an Israeli.

HERMAN S. BLOCH (1912- , Chicago)—One of the most important petroleum chemists in the world and the holder of many patents.

MAX BOBTELSKY (1890-1965, Vladislavov, Lithuania)—One of the early developers of heterometry.

OSCAR BODANSKY (1901- , Russia)—A noted biochemist who was Director of Medical Research for the American Army Medical Corps in World War II and later Vice-President of the Sloan-Kettering Institute for Cancer Research.

ERNEST A. BRAUDE (1922-1958, Germany)—Discoverer of lithium alkenyls and Professor at London's Imperial College, he did important research with radioactive tracers.

ALEKSANDER BRODSKI (1895- , Moscow)—A leading Soviet physical chemist, he won the Stalin Prize.

HERBERT C. BROWN (1912- , London)—An outstanding expert on hydroboration and on steric effects, he worked on uranium compounds during the Manhattan Project.

HEINRICH CARO (1834-1910, Posen)—The famous German chemist who developed Caro's acid and revolutionized and helped develop the German dyestuff industry.

NIKODEM CARO (1871-1935, Lodz)—A major figure in research into acetylene and calcium carbide and their industrial uses.

ERNEST J. COHEN (1869-1944, Amsterdam)—The first President of the Netherlands Chemical Society, he also served as President of the International Union of Pure and Applied Chemistry.

JULIUS B. COHEN (1859-1935, Manchester, England)—His textbooks, especially *Chemistry* (1902), were used all over the world.

MORRIS COHEN (1911- , Chelsea, Mass.)—A leading American metallurgist, he teaches at M.I.T.

EDWIN J. COHN (1892-1953, New York City)—An important biochemist known for his work on fractioning blood plasma, he was a Professor at Harvard.

LASSAR COHN (1858-1922, Hamburg)—Author of the popular *Chemistry in Daily Life.*

MAURICE COPISAROW (1889-1959, Manchester, England)—A major British chemist who continued to do useful research after he became blind.

ZACHARIAS DISCHE (1895- , Sambor, Austria-Hungary)—Did pioneering work on the pentose phosphate cycle and on the metabolic process.

EDUARD DONATH (1848-1932, Westin, Moravia)—One of the leading chemists in Austria. He converted to Christianity.

RALPH I. DORFMAN (1911- , Chicago)—Coauthor of the important *Metabolism of Steroid Hormones.*

CAMILLE DREYFUS (1878-1956, Basel, Switzerland)—Inventor (with his brother) of Celanese, he was President of the Celanese Corporation of America.

HENRY DREYFUS (1876-1945, Basel, Switzerland)—Director of British Celanese Ltd. and the possessor of more than 1,000 patents, considered the most ever held by one person.

KASIMIR FAJANS (b. 1887, Warsaw)—The famous discoverer of element 91, protactinium.

FRITZ FEIGL (1891-1971, Vienna)—A leading chemist in Brazil and an expert on spot tests.

SIR JOHN J. FOX (1874-1944, London)—A member of the British Royal Society and onetime President of the Institute of Chemistry, his main area of research was on the chemistry of diamonds.

ALBERT FRANK (1872-1965, Stassfurt, Germany)—A leading authority on calcium carbide.

ROSALIND FRANKLIN (1920-1957)—One of the world's leading women chemists, she did important work on unraveling the mysteries of DNA.

RAKHIL FREIDLINA (1906-)—A leading Soviet organic chemist, she was a member of the Soviet Academy of Sciences, and did important work on telomerization.

ALESANDR FRUMKIN (1895-)—Winner of the Lenin and Stalin prizes and one of the leading Soviet chemists, he served as Director of the Soviet Institute of Physical Chemistry and later as Director of the Soviet Institute of Electrochemistry.

CHARLES F. GERHARDT (1816-1856, Strasbourg, France)—One of the pioneer organic chemists in France, he developed important systems for classifying organic compounds.

HANS GOLDSCHMIDT (1861-1923, Berlin)—A leading industrial chemist famous for his invention of the Thermit process used in the steel industry.

GUIDO GOLDSCHMIDT (1850-1915, Trieste)—A pioneer in research on the structure of alkaloids.

HEINRICH J. GOLDSCHMIDT (1857-1937, Prague)—Awarded the Norwegian Order of St. Olaf for his contributions to chemistry in Norway. He taught at the U. of Oslo.

VICTOR M. GOLDSCHMIDT (1888-1947, Zurich)—The pioneer of geochemistry and a noted mineralogist.

MOSES GOMBERG (1866-1947, Yelizavetgrad, Russia)—President of the American Chemical Society in the early 1930s and did important work on the Diazo reaction and on the valency of carbon.

JESSE P. GREENSTEIN (1902-1959, New York City)—An internationally known expert on the biochemistry of cancer, he worked at the National Cancer Institute.

NATHAN GRUENSTEIN (1877-1932, Lithuania)—Discovered new methods for extracting acetic acid and acetone by converting acetylene, which greatly helped the German chemical industry.

ERNEST M. GRUNWALD (1923- , Wuppertal, Germany)—Professor at Brandeis and a leading expert in laser chemistry.

PHILIP HANDLER (1917- , New Jersey)—One of the most distinguished biochemists in the U.S., he was a member of the President's Science Advisory Committee, a President of the American Society of Biochemists, Chairman of the National Science Board of the National Science Foundation, and a member of the National Academy of Science.

MILTON HARRIS (1906- , Los Angeles)—Served as Chairman of the American Institute of Chemists and was a leading textile chemist.

WILLIAM Z. HASSID (1897- , Jaffa, Palestine)—Was a Fellow of the National Academy of Sciences and Chairman of the Carbohydrate Division of the American Chemical Society.

SIR IAN M. HEILBRON (1886-1959, Glasgow, Scotland)—Coauthor of *The Dictionary of Organic Compounds*, he was President of the British Chemical Society and one of the leading organic chemists in that country.

REGINALD O. HERZOG (1878-1935, Vienna)—Famous as the first to describe the microcrystalline structure of cellulose.

YEHUDAH HIRSHBERG (1905-1962, Poland)—An Israeli, he was the discoverer of photochromism.

PAUL H. JACOBSON (1859-1923, Konigsberg, Germany)—Coauthor of an important organic chemistry textbook, he was Editor of the influential *Journal of the German Chemical Society* and its General Secretary.

ZVIENRICO JOLLES (1902-1971)—Did pioneer work in the development of flame-resistant materials, which saved thousands of lives, and was an internationally recognized expert on dyestuffs.

MARTIN I. KABACHNIK (1908-)—One of the leading organic chemists in the Soviet Union and a recipient of a Stalin Prize, he did important research on insecticides.

AHARON KATZIR (1914-1972, Lodz, Poland)—Born Katchalski. A noted

Israeli polymer chemist who was murdered in the Japanese Red Army attack at Lod Airport, he had served as President of the International Union of Pure and Applied Biophysics.

ISAAC A. KAZARNOVSKI (b. 1890)—A leading Soviet inorganic chemist and the discoverer of sodium dioxide NaO_2, he won the Stalin Prize.

IZAAK M. KOLTHOFF (b. 1894, Almelo, Netherlands)—The Kolthoff Gold Medal in Analytical Chemistry bears his name. He was President of the Analytical Chemistry Section of the International Union of Pure and Applied Chemistry.

HANS L. KORNBERG (1928- , Herford, Germany)—A leading biochemist in England, he is a member of the British Royal Society and of the Science Research Council.

ALBERT LADENBURG (1842-1911, Mannheim, Germany)—Discovered the molecular weight of ozone and the atomic weight of iodine.

PHOEBUS A. T. LEVENE (1869-1940, Sagor, Russia)—Born Fishel Levin. Chairman of the Chemistry Division of the Rockefeller Institute and a noted structural chemist.

GIORGIO R. LEVI (1895-1965, Ferrara, Italy)—A leading Italian chemist, who later lived in Brazil.

MARIO G. LEVI (1878-1955, Padua, Italy)—A leading Italian industrial chemist.

RAPHAEL LEVINE (1938- , Alexandria, Egypt)—An Israeli, he is one of the world's leading authorities on chemical kinetics.

JULIUS LEWKOWITSCH (1857-1913, Germany)—A leading British chemist and an international expert on the industrial uses of oils and fats.

ADOLPH LIEBEN (1836-1914, Vienna)—His major contributions were research on aliphatic alcohols and the development of an iodoform test for alcohol.

CARL T. LIEBERMANN (1872-1914, Berlin)—President of the German Chemical Society and an expert on the synthesis of alizarin.

EDMUND O. VON LIPPMAN (1857-1940, Vienna)—An expert on the chemistry of sugar and an important chemistry historian.

EDUARD LIPPMANN (1842-1919, Prague)—Did pioneering work in the determination of the level of carbon and hydrogen in various organic compounds.

JACQUES LOEB (1859-1924, Strasbourg, France)—Was Editor of the *Journal of General Physiology*, which he helped found, and a noted physical chemist.

HEINRICH G. MAGNUS (1802-1870, Berlin)—A leading 19th-century German chemist.

WILLY MARCKWALD (1864-1950, Jakobskirch, Silesia)—His research contributed to the discovery of radium. He served as President of the German Chemical Society before the rise of Hitler.

RAPHAEL MELDOLA (1849-1915)—Meldola's blue dye is named for him. He served as President of the British Chemical Society and was Vice-President of the British Royal Society.

L. BENEDICT MENDEL (1872-1935, Delhi, N.Y.)—Served as President of the American Institute of Nutrition and was a Professor at Yale. He did pioneering work on vitamin A.

VICTOR MEYER (1848-1897, Berlin)—Credited with coining the term *stereochemistry*. He took his own life.

LEONOR MICHAELIS (1875-1949, Berlin)—A noted German biochemist.

GUSTAV E. C. NEUBERG (1877-1956, Hanover, Germany)—Director of the Kaiser Wilhelm Institute of Biochemistry until the Nazis threw him out.

CARL OPPENHEIMER (1874-1941, Berlin)—Wrote several important medical chemistry textbooks that were used all over the world.

FRIEDRICH A. PANETH (1887-1958, Vienna)—Director of the Max Planck Institute for Chemistry after World War II, a member of the British Royal Society, and a pioneer in experimentation with radioactive tracers.

DAVID PRESSMAN (1916-   , Detroit)—Has done important work in cancer research.

RALPH A. RAPHAEL (1921-   , London)—A member of the British Royal Society and the author of *Acetylenic Compounds in Organic Synthesis*, he is a Professor at the U. of Glasgow.

DAVID RITTENBERG (1906-1970, New York City)—An influential biochemist who was on the National Academy of Sciences, he did important early research on the movements of molecules.

SIMON ROGINSKI (1900-   )—A leading Soviet physical chemist.

OTTO ROSENHEIM (1871-1955, Germany)—A leading British biochemist who had a number of tests named after him, including one to detect vitamin A.

LOUIS SCHMERLING (1912-   , Milwaukee)—A leading expert on hydrocarbon chemistry and the holder of hundreds of patents.

MURRAY J. SHEAR (1899-   , New York City)—Served as Chief of the Chemical Pharmacology Laboratory at the National Cancer Institute.

ALEXANDER SILVERMAN (b. 1881, Pittsburgh)—One of the world's leading glass chemists.

KARL SPIRO (1867-1932, Berlin)—An important researcher of proteins, he pioneered along the interface between biology and physical chemistry.

FRANZ SONDHEIMER (1926-   , Stuttgart, Germany)—A member of the British Royal Society and a leading authority on steroids.

BARNETT SURE (1891-1960, Vilkomir, Lithuania)—A President of the American Chemical Society.

MICHAEL SZWARC (1909-   , Bedzin, Poland)—A leading expert on the chemistry of wood. An American, he is a member of the British Royal Society.

DAVID L. TALMUD (1900-   )—A member of the Soviet Academy of Sciences and a recipient of the Stalin Prize.

ISIDOR TRAUBE (1860-1943, Hildesheim, Germany)—A noted German chemist. Guess who Traube's rule is named after.

MORITZ TRAUBE (1826-1894, Ratibor, Silesia)—Made major early contributions to the study of osmosis.

ARTHUR I. VOGEL (1905-1966, London)—Renowned for his widely used textbooks, including *Elementary Practical Chemistry*.

JOSEPH J. WEISS (1907-   )—A Briton, he is one of the leading radiation chemists in the world.

LOUIS E. WISE (b. 1888, New York City)—A professor and researcher at the Institute of Paper Chemistry and a leading expert on the chemistry of wood.

PHRASE AND PHRASEMAKERS

catch-22—JOSEPH HELLER (*see* Writers: Americans)
fug—NORMAN MAILER (*see* Writers: Americans)
I Like Ike—HENRY D. SPALDING (*see* Political Figures: Americans)
New Deal—SAMUEL I. ROSENMAN (*see* Political Figures: Americans)
nuclear fission—OTTO R. FRISCH (*see* Physicists)
parapsychology—MAX DESSOIR (*see* Psychologists)
quark—MURRAY GELL-MANN (*see* Nobel Prize Winners: Physics)
stereochemistry—VICTOR MEYER (*see* Chemists)
vitamin—CASIMIR FUNK (*see* Doctors)

BOTANISTS

DANIEL I. ARNON (1910- , Poland)—A leading biochemist, he did important work into the mystery of photosynthesis.

PAUL ASCHERSON (1834-1913, Berlin)—A Professor at the U. of Berlin and a leading botanist.

EUGEN ASKENASY (1845-1903, Odessa, Russia)—A leading expert on chlorophyll and algology.

SHMUEL DUVDEVANI (1903- , Russia)—An Israeli, he developed the standard method for measuring dew.

LEO ERRERA (1858-1905)—The leading botanist in Belgium and a world authority on cells, he was a member of the Belgian Royal Academy and founder of the Belgian Botanical Institute.

MOSES EZEKIEL (1891-1969, Nagpur, India)—One of the leading botanists in Asia, he wrote *A Handbook of Plant Sociology*.

GOTTLIEB HABERLANDT (1854-1945, Ungarisch-Altenberg, Hungary)—One of the great pioneers of plant physiology and the author of the then-standard *Physiological Plant Anatomy*.

PAUL W. MAGNUS (1844-1914)—A German, he was the world's leading authority on algae and chytrids.

HEINZ OPPENHEIMER (1899-1971, Berlin)—A leading expert on citrus. He emigrated to Israel.

ISRAEL REICHERT (b. 1891, Ozorkow, Poland)—A leading plant geographer and an expert on fungi in the Middle East. He became an Israeli citizen.

JULIUS SACHS (1832-1897, Breslau)—Did important pioneering research on photosynthesis and wrote the noted *Textbook of Botany*.

PAUL SORAUER (1839-1916, Breslau)—One of the leading plant pathologists in Europe in the 1800s.

EDUARD STRASBURGER (1884-1912, Warsaw)—Did important research on fertilization and cell biology and helped to establish the field of plant cytology.

JULIUS VON WIESNER (1838-1916, Moravia)—One of the first economic botanists, he did important research on the valuable products that could be extracted from plants.

METEOROLOGISTS

DAVID ATLAS (1924- , New York City)—Flying is much safer because of the storm-detection devices he developed. He is one of the leading radar meteorologists in the world and a Professor at the U. of Chicago.

ARTHUR J. S. BERSON (1859-1942, Neu-Sandec, Galicia)—Did important pioneering research on air pressure and temperature by exploring the atmosphere by balloon. He was an Austrian.

VICTOR CONRAD (1876-1962, Vienna)—Author of *Fundamentals of Physical Climatology*. His research anticipated and predicted the discovery of cosmic rays.

BERNHARD HAURWITZ (1905- , Glogau, Germany)—Former chief meteorologist of Canada.

JOSHUA Z. HOLLAND (1921- , Chicago)—One of the world's leading authorities on radioactive fallout patterns.

EMMIL LESS (1855-1935, Konigsberg, Germany)—Director of the Berlin Weather Bureau for almost 40 years.

FRITZ P. LOEWE (1895- , Berlin)—A leading expert on determining the thickness of ice.

LESTER MACHTA (1919- , New York City)—Director of the Air Research Laboratories of the Environmental Services Administration and a director of the Institute for Atmospheric Sciences, he had earlier been Director of the U.S. Weather Bureau's Meteorological Research division.

MAX MARGULES (1856-1920)—The Margules equation refers to his method of measuring wind velocity and its source, which was revolutionary at the time.

JEROME NAMIAS (1910- , Bridgeport, Conn.)—Assistant Director of the National Meteorological Center, he saved many lives in World War II as the chief forecaster predicting weather in the North Atlantic area. He also established the Weather Bureau's Extended Forecast Division.

JOSEPH PEPPER (1904- , London)—One of the leading meteorologists in England, he was an expert on the wind patterns of the Atlantic.

ROBERT RUBENSON (1829-1902, Stockholm)—The most important Swedish meteorologist of the 19th century, he was Director of his country's Central Meteorological Institute.

MORTON J. RUBIN (1917- , Philadelphia)—Senior Scientist at the Environmental Science Services Administration, he is a leading expert on polar meteorology.

MORRIS TEPPER (1916- , Palestine)—One of the leading planners and administrators in the use of weather satellites, which changed the entire field of weather forecasting. He was associated with NASA.

HARRY WEXLER (1911-1962, Fall River, Mass.)—Research Director of the U.S. Weather Bureau, he helped to organize the activities and research undertaken during the Third International Geophysical Year.

ROBERT M. WHITE (1923- , Boston)—Chief of the U.S. Weather Bureau, he did important research for the U.S. Air Force.

GEOLOGISTS

HUGO BENIOFF (1899-1968, Los Angeles)—One of the world's leading seismologists, he taught at Cal Tech and did crucially important research for the U.S. Navy submarine service.

CESARE D'ANCONA (1832-1901, Pisa, Italy)—A leading Italian geologist and a member of the Italian Royal Geological Association.

MICHAEL FLEISCHER (1908- , Bridgeport, Conn.)—A major figure in American geology, he was Vice-President of the Geological Society of America and President of the Mineralogical Society of America.

BENO GUTENBERG (1889-1960, Darmstadt, Germany)—Was President of the International Association for Seismology, Director of the famed Seismological Laboratory at Cal Tech, and the originator of the hypothesis of continental spreading.

FRANZ Y. LOEWINSON-LESSIG (1861-1939)—One of the leading geologists in the Soviet Union and the world's leading authority on magmatic petrology.

LEO PICARD (1900- , Wangen, Germany)—An Israeli and one of the world's leading experts on ground water.

KARL ROSENBUSCH (1836-1914, Einbeck, Germany)—One of the most prominent early experts on petrography and author of an important textbook.

EDUARD SUESS (1838-1914, London)—Author of the monumental multivolume *Face of the Earth* and one of the leading geologists in the world. His mother was Jewish.

PART V
GEOGRAPHERS

ROBERTO ALMAGIA (1884-1962, Florence)—An Editor of the *Italian Geographical Review*, he served as President of the Italian Geographical Society and wrote a standard text on the geography of Italy.

CARLO ERRERA (1867-1936, Trieste)—Was Vice-President of the Italian National Research Council and an important geographer.

JOSEPH H. GENTILLI (1912-   )—A leading Australian geographer and author of *Australian Climates and Resources.*

NORTON S. GINSBERG (1921-   , Chicago)—Director of the Association for Asian Studies, he is a leading scholar on economic development and a world-famous urban geographer.

JACQUES M. MAY (1896-   , France)—One of the world's leading medical geographers and the author of the standard work in the field.

ALFRED PHILIPSON (1864-1953, Bonn)—An expert on regional geography and one of the leading German geographers of his generation.

EXPLORERS

EMIL BESSELS (1847-1888)—A member of the famous Hall expedition to the North Pole, he was stranded with other explorers and was carried over 1,000 miles on ice until finally rescued by a ship. The expedition had reached the farthest northern point ever attained by ship before their accident.

HERMANN BURGHARDT (1857-1909, Berlin)—Visited places around the world that reportedly had never been seen by a white man. He was murdered by Bedouin tribesmen in Arabia.

NEY ELIAS (1844-1897)—Won the Gold Medal of the British Royal Geographical Society for his trip across an uncharted portion of the Gobi Desert. His explorations were responsible for the present boundaries of Burma and Thailand.

EDOUARD FOA (1862-1901)—One of the first men to cross the African continent from west to east, he also was one of the first to explore the inland sections of what is now Dahomey (Benin).

RAIMONDO FRANCHETTI (1890-1935)—A leading Italian explorer of Africa, especially of the Horn of Africa.

EDUARD GLASER (1855-1908, Deutsch-Rust, Germany)—Conducted important explorations of the Arabian peninsula and especially of Yemen in the late 1800s.

ISAAC I. HAYES (1832-1881, Chester, Pa.)—Discovered Grinnell Land in the Arctic.

ANGELO HEILPRIN (1853-1907)—Helped to resupply Peary in the Arctic in 1892 and also explored Mt. Pelee and other active volcanos.

NATHANIEL ISAACS (1808-1860s)—One of the pioneer explorers and settlers of Natal region in South Africa, he fought with the Zulu people against the Swazis.

EDWARD ISRAEL (1859-1884, Kalamazoo, Mich.)—A member of the famous Lady Franklin Bay Expedition of 1882 that sought to explore the arctic regions of Greenland. The expedition became lost and Israel died and was probably eaten, since the survivors resorted to cannibalism.

GOTTFRIED MERZBACHER (1843-1926, Baiersdorf, Germany)—Climbed mountains (some of which had never been explored or climbed) all over the world.

JULIUS POPPER (1857-1893)—A Rumanian, he became the ruler and dictator of Tierra del Fuego at the tip of Argentina and Chile. He was finally driven off by the authorities.

ALEXANDER SALMON (1822-1866)—One of the first whites to live permanently on Tahiti. He married into royalty there.

RUDOLF SAMOILOVICH (b. 1884, Azov-on-Don, Russia)—Director of the Leningrad Institute for Arctic Research in Leningrad and holder of the Red Banner of Labor, he conducted important explorations on Spitsbergen and rescued Umberto Nobile and others after the crash of their airship in the Arctic.

AVIATORS, ASTRONAUTS, AND OTHERS

See also Military Figures; Inventors, Industrial Designers, and Engineers.

KARL ARNSTEIN (b. 1887)—Designer of the massive dirigibles Akron and Los Angeles. A refugee from the Nazis, he came to the U.S. after a distinguished career as Chief Construction Engineer for the German Zeppelin Company. He rose to the vice-presidency of the Goodyear-Zeppelin firm, America's most important producer of lighter-than-air craft.

HENRY A. BERLINER (b. 1895)—President of Berliner Aircraft, he was a neglected forefather of the helicopter in the first quarter of this century.

ROBERT L. BLUM (1902-   )—An important figure in the automobile industry in France whose role in aviation history derives from his presidency of Hispano-Suiza, one of the most important manufacturers of aircraft engines in Europe; their designs were copied by other companies all over the world.

SELIG BRODETSKY (1888-1954, Olviopol, Russia)—Author of the very influential Mechanical Principles of the Aeroplane (1920), he was a famous mathematician and Professor at the University of Leeds (England) for almost 30 years.

BENEDICT COHN (1913-   , Rumania)—A leading designer of some of the most famous aircraft of all time, including the B-29, the B-47, and practically all of the large transports and bombers of the Boeing Company.

SIDNEY GOLDSTEIN (1903-   , Hull, England)—A noted mathematician, he was Chairman of England's Aeronautical Research Council, 1946-1949, a period during which some of the most innovative aircraft designs in aviation history were developed.

ABRAHAM HYATT (1910-   , Russia)—Became the Chief Scientist for the U.S. Navy Bureau of Aeronautics in 1956. In the 1960s he served as Director of Program Plans and Evaluation of NASA and was one of the leading figures in America's successful drive to put a human being into space.

LEONARD JAFFE (1926-   , Cleveland)—Served NASA in a variety of posts, most importantly as Director of its Communication and Navigation Satellite Programs.

ROBERT JASTROW (1925-   , New York City)—A leading popular science writer, he served as Director of the prestigious Goddard Institute for Space Studies. He received the NASA Medal in 1968.

THEODORE VON KARMAN (1881-1963, Hungary)—One of the most important men in the history of aviation, he was responsible for all research into jet propulsion conducted in the U.S. during World War II. His Aerojet Engineering Corporation did pioneer research into rocket propulsion after the war, although von Karman is regarded most highly for his helicopter propulsion research. Toward the end of his career he led the famous Guggenheim Aeronautical Laboratory of Cal Tech.

ARTHUR KANTROWITZ (1913- , New York City)—Winner of numerous awards and Director of the Avco Corporation, the firm entrusted with the difficult task of designing safe reentry vehicles for U.S. astronauts. In the military sphere, he was instrumental in the development of intercontinental ballistic warheads.

ISRAEL KATZ (1917- , New York City)—His textbook *Combustion Engines* (1952) served as the standard source for many years. He led the Cornell Aircraft Power Laboratory, 1948-1956.

ROBERT KRONFELD (Vienna)—Set a world record in winning the *London Daily Mail* contest in 1931 when he maintained his glider aloft for a then-incredible distance of 93 miles.

JEROME F. LEDERER (1902- , New York City)—One of the world's leading authorities on aviation safety, Lederer became Director of Manned Space Flight Safety for NASA in 1967.

LESTER LEEDS (1920- , New York City)—One of the most famous teachers of aeronautical engineering in the world, he is a Professor at the California Institute of Technology.

CHARLES A. LEVINE—Not as famous as Charles Lindbergh, he has the distinction of being the first airline *passenger* to cross the Atlantic. I wonder what the fare was.

OTTO LILIENTHAL (1848-1896)—A pioneer glider designer and pilot whose work helped lay the groundwork for powered flight. He was killed while piloting one of his own designs.

STEPHEN P. MARAN (1938- , Brooklyn)—Headed the Advanced Systems and Ground Observation Branch of the NASA-Goddard Space Flight Center.

BENJAMIN PINKEL (1909- , Gloversville, N.Y.)—A member of the National Advisory Council for Aeronautics and one of America's most distinguished engineers, he was a director of the Aero-Astronautics Department of the Rand Corporation.

JUDITH RESNIK (1950- , Akron, Ohio)—One of the first women chosen for astronaut training in the U.S.

EDUARD RUMPLER (1872-1940, Vienna)—One of the first aircraft manufacturers in Germany; his planes fought for that country during World War I. His company also produced the first car equipped with a front axle drive.

DAVID SCHWARZ (1845-1897)—A sadly neglected pioneer of manned flight. After his untimely death, Count Zeppelin purchased his designs and became world-famous.

HYMAN SERBIN (1914-)—A leading American aeronautical engineer who worked for a number of major aircraft companies, most notably as Chief Aerodynamics Engineer for the Fairchild Engine and Aircraft Corporation during World War II.

ABRAHAM SILBERSTEIN (1908- , Terre Haute, Ind.)—Director of the NASA Lewis Research Center, he was Director of Space Flight Programs for NASA in the late 1950s and early 1960s.

BORIS VOLYNOV—A Lieutenant Colonel, he is the only known Jew to have traveled in space. He was the Commander of Soyuz Five, the first space vehicle to effect a docking and transfer personnel between ships, a feat accomplished in early 1969.

AL WELSH (1881-1912, Kiev)—A colleague of the Wright Brothers and an instructor at their aviation school. He won the George Campbell Cup for achieving the highest altitude yet attained by an American in 1911, but died the following year in an attempt to better his mark.

ALEC D. YOUNG (1913- , London)—Former head of the Department of Aerodynamics at the College of Aeronautics at Cranfield, England's most prestigious aviation school. He later served as an administrator at the University of London.

MAURICE J. ZUCROW (1899- , Kiev)—His *Principles of Jet Propulsion and Gas Turbines* (1948) was the standard reference work for many years. He taught at Purdue U. after World War II.

INVENTORS, INDUSTRIAL DESIGNERS, AND ENGINEERS

AVRAM BENAROYA (1889-1955, Adrianople)—Developed a system for reducing Turkish to shorthand.

EMILE BERLINGER (1851-1929, Wolfenbüttel, Germany)—"Invented" modern records by using a flat disc, did important research into helicopters, and invented the microphone.

SIR MISHA BLACK (1910- , Baku, Russia)—A leading British industrial designer, he did important work laying out the patterns for the revitalized British railway system.

HENRY DREYFUSS (1904-1972, New York City)—One of the most important industrial designers in the U.S., he designed the interior of trains, ships, and the Boeing 707.

DANIEL C. DRUCKER (1918- , New York City)—Served as President of the Society for Experimental Stress Analysis and was a leading structural engineer who worked on a number of major tunnel projects.

JACOB FELD (1899- , Austria)—A leading American civil engineer, he worked on Yonkers Raceway and the New York Coliseum, among many projects.

WILLIAM FONDILLER (b. 1885, Russia)—Vice-President of Bell Telephone Laboratories and a leading electrical engineer.

ALFRED M. FREUDENTHAL (1906- , Poland)—A leading civil engineer and authority on metal fatigue.

ALEXANDER GOLDBERG (1906- , Vilna)—Invented a system for creating metallic magnesium out of salt water. He is an Israeli.

HARRY GOLDMARK (1857-1941)—A leading civil engineer, he designed the locks of the Panama Canal.

PETER GOLDMARK (1906-1977)—Inventor of the long-playing phonograph and winner of the National Medal of Science. He died in a car crash.

WILLIAM GOLDSMITH (b. 1883, New York City)—A leading construction engineer, he designed the Triborough Bridge in New York.

DORMAN D. ISRAEL (1909- , Newport, R.I.)—Vice-President of Emerson Radio, he was one of the leading radio engineers in the U.S.

WALTER JUDA (1916- , Berlin)—Conducted early and important studies in making fresh water out of salt water.

ISADOR KITSEE (1845-1931, Vienna)—The great Marconi used one of his patents in the development of the wireless.

ARTHUR KORN (1870-1945, Breslau)—A leading electrophysicist, he conducted important research in radio photography.

EDWIN H. LAND (1909- , Bridgeport, Conn.)—Invented the Polaroid camera and became one of the richest men in America.

ROBERT VON LIEBEN (1878-1913, Vienna)—Did important early research on the grid tube that made radio possible.

ABRAHAM LIPSKI (1911- , Lodz, Poland)—A leading Polish engineer and the creator of the preflex construction beam.

SIEGFRIED MARCUS (1831-1898, Malchin, Germany)—Worked on loud-speakers, automobiles, and electric lamps (along with many other devices), and although they were not successful, they contributed to the later success of others.

124 PART V

AUGUSTE MICHEL-LEVY (1844-1911, Paris)—One of the greatest petrologists of his generation, he was the French National Inspector of Mines.

JACOB MILLMAN (1911- , Russia)—A leading electrical engineer and the author of *Vacuum Tube and Semiconductor Electronics.*

MARVIN MINSKY (1927- , New York City)—Professor of Engineering at M.I.T., he is a member of the National Academy of Sciences and one of the leading experts in the world on artificial intelligence.

GEORG SCHLESINGER (1874-1949, Berlin)—Designed some of the most important factories in Germany and was one of the first real industrial psychologists.

ASCHER SHAPIRO (1916- , Brooklyn)—Professor at M.I.T., one of the leading construction engineers in America, and author of *Shape and Flow: The Fluid Dynamics of Drag.*

LESLIE SILVERMAN (1914-1966, Chicago)—A leading industrial hygienist, he taught at Harvard.

JOSEPH SLEPIAN (b. 1891, Boston)—Director of Research at Westinghouse Electric and one of the leading electrical engineers in the U.S.

CHARLES P. STEINMETZ (1865-1923, Breslau)—A President of the American Institute of Electrical Engineers and an important adviser to General Electric.

ARTHUR C. STERN (1909- , Petersburg, Va.)—Served as Assistant Director of the National Center for Air Pollution Control.

BENNO STRAUSS (1873-1944)—Considered to be the inventor of stainless steel, he was employed by the huge Krupp Company in Germany.

JOSEPH WEIL (1897- , Baltimore)—Dean of the College of Engineering at the U. of Florida for many years, he was a leading electrical engineer.

Part VI
The Arts and Entertainment

PART VI

POETS

See also Pulitzer Prize Winners.

AMERICANS

DAISY ALDAN (1923- , New York City)—An award-winning American poet.

JOSEPH AUSLANDER (1897-1965, Philadelphia)—Was Editor of the *North American Review* and author of *Sunrise Trumpets* and other volumes of poetry.

MARVIN BELL (1937- , New York City)—A leading poet and the author of *A Probable Volume of Dreams* and *Residue of Song.*

BABETTE DEUTSCH (1895- , New York City)—A leading critic as well as poet, she wrote *Poetry in Our Time* and *Fire for the Night.*

KENNETH FEARING (1902-1961, Chicago)—One of the most important satiric poets in American history. Two of his best works were *The Big Clock* and *The Loneliest Girl in the World.* He was also a fine novelist.

DONALD FINKEL (1929- , New York City)—Author of *Simeon* and *Adequate Earth.*

DAVID GALLER (1929- , New York City)—His *Leopards in the Temple* was widely acclaimed.

ALLEN GINSBERG (1926- , New Jersey)—A leading contemporary American poet, his *Howl and Other Poems* helped to set the tone for the Beatnik movement and for the 1960s.

ARTHUR GREGOR (1923- , Vienna)—Born Goldberg. Two of his best books are *Selected Poems* and *Figure in the Door.*

ARTHUR GUITERMAN (1871-1943)—A noted poet before and after World War I.

MARILYN HACKER (1942-)—Won the Lamont Poetry Selection Award for *Presentation Piece* and the National Book Award in 1975.

KENNETH KOCH (1925-)—One of the most important American poets, and a teacher of poetry writing. His *Thank You, and Other Poems* was both excellent and influential.

STANLEY J. KUNITZ (1905- , Worcester, Mass.)—A leading American poet, he won the 1959 Pulitzer Prize for *Selected Poems 1928-1958.*

NAOMI LAZARD—Won the 1977 Alice Fay di Castagnola Prize of the Poetry Society of America for her book *Ordinances.*

EMMA LAZARUS (1849-1887, New York City)—The famed poet who wrote "The New Colossus" sonnet that appears on the Statue of Liberty. It has inspired several generations of immigrants to the U.S.

PHILIP LEVINE (1928- , Detroit)—Won the 1977 Lenore Marshall Poetry Prize for his book *The Names of the Lost.*

HOWARD NEMEROV (1920-)—A leading critic as well as poet.

GEORGE OPPEN (1908- , New Rochelle, N.Y.)—Won the 1969 Pulitzer Prize for Poetry for *Of Being Numerous.*

CHARLES REZNIKOFF (1894-1976, Brooklyn)—Author of *By the Waters of Manhattan* and other collections, he was a practicing lawyer.

MURIEL RUKEYSER (1913-)—Her book *A Turning Wind* was widely hailed, and she is considered one of the best poets of the American left.

KARL J. SHAPIRO (1913- , Baltimore)—One of America's leading poets, he won the 1945 Pulitzer Prize for *V-Letter and Other Poems.* He teaches at the U. of Nebraska.

GERALD STERN (1937- , Chicago)—Won the Lamont Poetry Selection of the Academy of American Poets for his collection *Lucky Life.*

BAYLA WINTERS (1921-   , New York City)—Author of *The Tropic of Mother* and *bitchpoems*.

LOUIS ZUKOFSKY (1903-1978)—An important American poet, his major contribution was as a critic.

BRITISH

DANNIE ABSE (1923-   , Cardiff, Wales)—A leading British poet, his best work can be found in *Selected Poems* (1963).

ISAAC ROSENBERG (1890-1918, Bristol)—His poetry was widely acclaimed, especially the work he did while a soldier in World War I. He was killed in action in 1918.

NATHANIEL TARN (1928-   , Paris)—A leading English poet, famed for his collection *Old Savage/Young City*.

CANADIANS

ABRAHAM M. KLEIN (1909-1972, Montreal)—A leading Canadian poet and an innovative force in Canadian literature.

IRVING LAYTON (1912-   , Rumania)—Born Lazarovitch. A leading Canadian poet.

MARK STRAND (1934-   , Summerside, Prince Edward Island)—A leading Canadian poet and the author of *Reasons for Moving* and *Darker*.

MIRIAM DWORKIN WADDINGTON (1917-   , Winnipeg)—One of the most important Canadian poets. Two of her major collections are *The Season's Lovers* and *The Second Silence*.

FRENCH LANGUAGE

EDMOND FLEG (1874-1963)—Born Flegenheimer. A leading playwright as well as poet.

BENJAMIN FONDANE (1898-1944, Jassy, Rumania)—Born Fundoianu. He wrote in French.

HENRI FRANCK (1888-1912, Paris)—Considered one of the leading poets in France during his short and tragic life.

YVAN GOLL (1891-1950, Saint-Die Vosges, France)—Founder of *Surréalisme* and a leading poet.

GUSTAVE KAHN (1859-1936, Metz, France)—A leading symbolist poet and cofounder of the free verse movement.

CATULLE MENDES (1841-1909, Bordeaux)—One of the most heavily published French poets in history.

PIERRE MORHANGE (1901-   , Paris)—A prominent French poet.

TRISTAN TZARA (1896-1963, Moinesti, Rumania)—Born Sami Rosenstein. One of the founders of the Dada school.

GERMAN LANGUAGE

KARL BECK (1817-1879, Hungary)—Beck, who became a Christian, was a leading Hungarian nationalist poet. His work reputedly gave Strauss the idea for his Blue Danube Waltz.

HEINRICH HEINE (1787-1856, Düsseldorf)—Considered one of the outstanding lyric poets of all time. He was a convert to Christianity.

WALTER HEYMANN (1882-1915, Königsberg)—An important early German Expressionist poet. His greatest potential was never realized because he died in combat in World War I.

ELSE LASKER-SCHÜLER (1869-1945, Elberfeld)—One of the great free spirits of German poetry and a leader of the Expressionist movement.

HUNGARIANS

LASZLO BENJAMIN (1915- , Budapest)—A major force in the Communist literary apparatus in Hungary.

JOZSEF KISS (1843-1921, Mezocsat, Hungary)—A major poet, he was the most important force in Hungarian letters for a generation. He was a major literary critic and Editor of *The Week*, Hungary's leading literary journal.

POLES

BOLESLAW LEMIAN (1878-1937, Warsaw)—One of the leading symbolist poets in Poland. His work has been rediscovered in recent years.

ANATOL STERN (1889-1968, Warsaw)—One of the most important futurist poets in Poland.

JULIAN TUWIM (1894-1953, Lodz)—One of the leading Polish poets of his generation.

RUMANIANS

MARIA BANUS (1914- , Bucharest)—Rumania's leading feminist poet.

EMIL DORIAN (1892-1956)—A leading Rumanian poet, he was also a noted novelist.

VERONICA PORUMBACU (1921- , Bucharest)—Born Schwefelberg. A leading Rumanian poet.

RUSSIANS

MARGARITA Y. ALIGER (1915- , Odessa)—Author of the famous "Zova," she won the Stalin Prize in 1943.

EDUARD BAGRITSKI (1895-1934, Odessa)—Born Dzyuba. Author of the famed "The Lay of the Opanas," he was one of the most important Russian poets of his generation.

YOSIF BRODSKY (1940- , Leningard)—Now at the U. of Michigan, he was a leading Soviet poet.

SASHA CHERNY (1880-1932)—Born Alexander Glueckberg. A leading satiric poet and an opponent of the Soviet regime.

YEVGENI DOLMATOVSKI (1915-)—A leading songwriter as well as poet, he won the Stalin Prize for "A Word about Tomorrow."

VERA M. INBER (1890-1972, Odessa)—Won the Stalin Prize and was the author of "The Pulkovo Meridian," one of the most famous poems in Soviet literature.

VLADISLAV F. KHODASEVICH (1886-1939)—A leading Russian poet-in-exile.

SEMYON I. KIRSANOV (1906- , Odessa)—A leading Soviet poet of the ideological school.

OSIP E. MANDELSTAM (1891-late 1930s, Warsaw)—Widely considered to be one of the greatest Russian lyric poets of all time, he died in a Soviet prison.

BORIS SLUTSKI (1919-)—A leading Soviet lyric poet.

JOSEPH P. UTKIN (1903-1944, Manchuria)—A leading Soviet poet. He was killed in an airplane accident.

OTHERS

JOSEF H. GEREZ (1928- , Istanbul)—A leading Turkish poet.

CAMILL HOFFMANN (1878-1944)—A noted lyric poet and Director of the Press bureau of the Czechoslovakian Embassy in Germany.

UMBERTO SABA (1883-1957)—Born Umberto Poli. One of the leading poets in Italy for many years.

BERTA SINGERMAN (1897- , Minsk)—Not a poet herself, she was a famed poetry reader in South America. She was an Argentine citizen.

WRITERS

See also Science Fiction Writers; Nobel Prize Winners; Literature; Pulitzer Prize Winners.

AMERICANS AND CANADIANS

MIMI ALBERT (1940- , New York City)—Born Ginsberg. Author of *The Second Story Man* (1975), a powerful thriller.

MARY ANTIN (1881-1949, Poland)—Best remembered for her commercially successful autobiography, *The Promised Land* (1912).

SAMUEL ASTRACHAN (1934- , New York City)—A fine contemporary novelist. Two of his best works are *An End to Dying* (1956) and *The Game of Dostoevsky*. (1965).

VICKI BAUM (1888-1960, Vienna)—Wrote at least 25 novels, but she will always be known for *Grand Hotel* (1930), the basis for a successful film.

GEORGE BAXT (1923- , Brooklyn)—A leading mystery writer and the author of a number of excellent novels, including *A Parade of Cockeyed Creatures* (1967) and *A Queer Kind of Death* (1966).

SAUL BELLOW (1915- , Lachine, Quebec)—Nobel Prize–winning author of *Herzog, Seize the Day, Henderson the Rain King, The Adventures of Augie March, Mr. Sammler's Planet*, and *Humboldt's Gift* (a Pulitzer Prize winner). One of the leading figures in American and world literature of the twentieth century.

JAY BENNETT (1912- , New York City)—Best known for his wonderful juvenile mysteries, at least two of which won Edgar Awards (given by the Mystery Writers of America) for best juvenile novel: *Long Black Coat* (1974) and *The Dangling Witness* (1975).

MOREY BERNSTEIN (1919- , Pueblo, Colo.)—His purportedly nonfiction book, *The Search for Bridey Murphy*, caused a sensation because of its "documented" claim of proof of reincarnation.

MICHAEL S. BLANKFORT (1907-)—Author of *The Widow-Makers* and *The Juggler*, he has also produced a number of fine screenplays, most notably his treatment of *The Caine Mutiny*.

MAXWELL BODENHEIM (1893-1954, Miss.)—Among the great proletarian writers of the 1930s with novels such as *Roller Skates* and *New York Madness*. A complex personality, his later years were spent in the most abject poverty imaginable, and he was murdered in his skid-row flat.

EDWARD DAHLBERG (1900-)—Dahlberg's talent has only recently been recognized. Among his outstanding novels are *From Flushing to Calvary* (1932) and *Those Who Perish* (1934).

MARCIA DAVENPORT (1903- , New York City)—One of America's leading pre-World War II novelists, she is best known for *Valley of Decision* (1942).

ISAAC DEUTSCHER (1907-1967, Cracow)—One of the leading Marxist historians of all time, he wrote a very famous three-volume work on Leon Trotsky; *Stalin: A Political Biography*; and a controversial work on the Jewish predicament.

MARK DINTENFASS (1941- , New York City)—A leading "black" novelist, he wrote *The Case Against Org* (1970) and *Figure 8* (1973). He is a Professor of English at Lawrence University in Appleton, Wis.

E.L. DOCTOROW (1931- , New York City)—His novel *Ragtime* was a runaway best-seller in 1976. He was Editor in Chief of Dial Press, 1964-1969.

EDWARD JAY EPSTEIN (1935- , New York City)—His *Inquest* (1966) was the best of the numerous books on the Kennedy assassination and the Warren Commission report.

PETER FARB (1929- , New York City)—One of the country's finest writers on conservation and nature, his *Face of North America* achieved widespread attention and respect.

HOWARD FAST (1914- , New York City)—Winner of the Stalin Peace Prize in 1953 and a committed Communist for more than ten years, he severed his relations with the party in the mid-1950s. Best known for *Citizen Tom Paine* and *Spartacus*, he has recently achieved best-seller status with *The Immigrants*. He is also a talented writer of science fiction and fantasy.

JULIUS FAST (1919- , New York City)—Won the Edgar Award for his first novel, the brilliant *Watchful at Night* (1946). Among his other fine works is *The League of Grey-Eyed Women*, (1969).

EDNA FERBER (1887-1968, Kalamazoo, Mich.)—Raised in Appleton Wisc., she became one of America's most beloved novelists with books like *Cimarron*, *Saratoga Trunk*, and *Giant*. She was awarded the Pulitzer Prize for Literature in 1925 for *So Big*.

LOUIS FISCHER (1896-1970, Philadelphia)—An outstanding authority on the Soviet Union and the personal friend of many of that country's leaders, he portrayed the U.S.S.R. in a favorable light in books such as *The Soviets in World Affairs* (1930), but, like so many of the Left, he came to feel betrayed by Stalinism.

ROBERT L. FISH (1912- , Cleveland)—A leading mystery writer, he won the Edgar Award for his novels *The Fugitive* (1962) and *The Snakes* (1963), as well as his short story "Moonlight Gardener."

BRUCE JAY FRIEDMAN (1930- , New York City)—One of the great "black" humorists in American literature, he is best known for his novels *Stern* (1962) and *A Mother's Kisses* (1964).

MERRILL GERBER (1938- , New York City)—Best known for her short stories in *Redbook*. Her novel *An Antique Man* (1967) was critically acclaimed.

HERBERT GOLD (1924- , Cleveland)—A leading novelist with a biting style. One of his best books is *The Optimist* (1959).

WILLIAM W. GOLDMAN (1931- , Chicago)—A fine novelist, he achieved fame with *Boys and Girls Together* (1964).

GERALD GREEN (1922- , Brooklyn)—Previously known primarily for his novel *The Last Angry Man* (1957), he is now a celebrity for his controversial screenplay and novel *Holocaust*.

JOANNE GREENBERG (1932-)—Author of (among others) *I Never Promised You a Rose Garden* (1964).

DAN GREENBURG (1936- , Chicago)—Author of sexy novels such as *Chewsday*, *Philly*, and *Scoring, A Sexual Memoir*.

ALBERT HALPER (1904-)—Now a sadly neglected though excellent writer, he wrote two of the finest proletarian novels—*Union Square* (1933) and *Atlantic Avenue* (1956).

MARK HARRIS (1922-)—One of the best practitioners of the sports novel in the U.S., he achieved his first fame with *Southpaw* (1953).

BEN HECHT (1893-1964, New York City)—Most famous as the coauthor of *The Front Page* (1928), he was an excellent Hollywood script writer. A strong supporter of the Irgun, he was a caustic critic of the Israeli political scene.

JOSEPH HELLER (1923- , Brooklyn)—His novel *Catch-22* (1961) propelled him to fame, and it is surely one of the major novels of this century.

LILLIAN HELLMAN (1905- , New Orleans)—A leading figure in American letters for many years and the subject of considerable controversy for her political views, she has excelled as a novelist, a playwright, and a social critic. Her personal reflections in *Pentimento* were widely discussed.

LAURA ZAMETKIN HOBSON (1900- , New York City)—A best-selling author with books such as *Gentlemen's Agreement*, a scathing indictment of anti-Semitism.

IRVING HOWE—*See* Social Critics.

FANNIE HURST (1889-1968, Hamilton, Ohio)—Most famous for *Back Street*, which was one of the best books of the 1930s, she also served as President of the Authors' Guild during that decade.

RONA JAFFE (1932- , New York City)—Author of sensual novels such as *Family Secrets* and the popular *The Best of Everything* (1974).

RUTH PRAWER JHABVALA (1927- , Cologne, Germany)—Now a resident of India, she is an important satirical novelist best known for her award-winning *Heat and Dust*.

ERICA JONG (1942- , New York City)—Born Mann. Caused a sensation with frank and explicit books such as *Fear of Flying* (1973) and *How to Save Your Own Life* (1977).

MATTHEW JOSEPHSON (1899-1978, Brooklyn)— His books on American history and society (*The Robber Barons, The Politicos*, and *The President Makers*) were worthy of a professional historian. He was also a noted biographer (*Victor Hugo* and others).

ROGER KAHN (1927- , Brooklyn)—A writer and sportswriter for *Sports Illustrated* and *Esquire*. His book *The Boys of Summer* (1972) brought joy to the hearts of Dodger fans everywhere. Where is Clem Labine when we need him?

JUSTIN KAPLAN (1925- , New York City)—A noted literary and social historian, his book *Mr. Clemens and Mark Twain* won both the National Book Award and the Pulitzer Prize for Biography in 1967.

BEL KAUFMAN (Berlin)—Taught in the New York City public schools and wrote the famous *Up the Down Staircase*.

HARRY KEMELMAN (1908- , Boston)—Famed for his mystery novels featuring Rabbi Small and his Nicky Welt series in *Ellery Queen's Mystery Magazine*.

ARTHUR KOESTLER (1905- , Budapest)—One of the few major writers who was successful in more than one language (he wrote in German, Hungarian, and English). His *Darkness at Noon* (1940) is considered one of the most important personal and political statements in modern literature. *The God That Failed* is the best of an excellent group of self-revelatory books by disillusioned Marxists. In many respects he is the prototypical humanist of the 20th century.

ROBERT KOTLOWITZ (1924- , New York City)—His novel *Somewhere Else* (1972) deserved the critical acclaim it received.

JONATHAN KOZOL (1936- , Boston)—Winner of the 1968 National Book Award for *Death at an Early Age*. His books on contemporary American educational practices became the focus of both admiration and controversy.

JOSEPH P. LASH (1909- , New York City)—National Book Award and 1972 Pulitzer Prize-winning biographer of Franklin D. Roosevelt.

G. LEGMAN (1917- , Scranton, Pa.)—Author of *The Horn Book* and other wild and erotic works, his books have been banned in many places.

ALAN LELCHUCK (1938- , Brooklyn)—An English professor at Brandeis U., he is a rapidly rising novelist with books such as *American Mischief* (1973).

MILTON LESSER (1928- , New York City)—Author of several dozen mystery novels credited to "Stephen Marlowe," as well as the creator of the "Chester Drum" series.

IRA LEVIN (1929- , New York City)—One of America's most popular novelists for works such as *Rosemary's Baby, The Stepford Wives,* and *The Boys from Brazil.* He won an Edgar for *A Kiss Before Dying* in 1953.

MEYER LEVIN (1905-   , Chicago)—Achieved fame with *Compulsion* (1956), which was based on the Leopold-Loeb murder. He has also published a series of novels on modern Jewish and Israeli life.

NORMAN MAILER (1923-   , Long Branch, N.J.)—Considered one of the country's premier writers, both for his novels (*The Deer Park* and many others) and for his journalism. He won the 1969 Pulitzer Prize for General Nonfiction.

BERNARD MALAMUD (1914-   , New York City)—One of the few "major novelists" who actually deserves the praise he has received, his entire corpus of work is outstanding, particularly his National Book Award and 1967 Pulitzer Prize-winning *The Fixer* (1966).

ARTHUR MALING (1923-   , Chicago)—*Decoy* (1969), *Loophole* (1971), and *The Snowman* (1973) have made him a leading mystery writer.

WALLACE MARKFIELD (1926-   , Brooklyn)—Finally receiving the critical attention he richly deserves for books such as *To an Early Grave* (1964) and *You Could Live If They Let You* (1974).

NICHOLAS MEYER (1945-   , New York City)—His novel featuring Sherlock Holmes, *The Seven-Per-Cent Solution,* was a best-seller and an excellent movie.

LEONARD MICHAELS (1933-   , New York City)—Professor of English at the University of California since 1968, he is the author of *I Would Have Saved Them If I Could* and other fine books.

ROBERT NATHAN (b. 1894, New York City)—A prolific writer, best remembered for *Portrait of Jennie* (1940).

JAY NEUGEBOREN (1938-   , Brooklyn)—A still rising and underappreciated talent. One of his best books is *Big Man* (1966).

SAMUEL B. ORNITZ (1890-1957, New York City)—A leading left-wing author, his book *Haunch, Paunch, and Jowl* became famous.

CYNTHIA OZICK (1928-   , New York City)—Her story "The Pagan Rabbi" was one of the best I have ever read.

GRACE PALEY (1922-   , New York City)—Born Goodside. Author of *The Little Disturbances of Man* (1959) and the very effective *Enormous Changes at the Last Minute* (1974).

DOROTHY PARKER (1893-1967)—The famed writer of many pieces for the *New Yorker,* she had a Jewish father and was a regular member of the New York literary scene at the Algonquin Hotel.

S. J. PERELMAN (1904-   , Brooklyn)—One of the funniest men in America, he was an institution in the pages of the *New Yorker* for decades. He is one of the greatest punsters of all time, and was responsible for many of the wonderful one-liners in several Marx Brothers movies.

ZELDA POPKIN (1898-   , Brooklyn)—Author of a number of excellent mystery novels in the early 1940s (especially *Murder in the Mist,* 1940), her *Death of Innocence* (1971) was adapted for television.

CHAIM POTOK (1929-   , New York City)—Author of *The Chosen* (1967) and other novels.

ELLERY QUEEN—Frederic Dannay (1905-   , Brooklyn) and Manfred B. Lee (1905-1971, Brooklyn), born Daniel Nathan and Manford Lepofsky respectively. These two cousins created one of the most famous detectives of all time. They wrote more than 40 books and edited some 75 mystery anthologies. One of the major contributions (largely Dannay's) was the establishment and editorship of *Ellery Queen's Mystery Magazine,* the leading publication in the field.

MORDECAI RICHLER (1931-   , Montreal)—Certainly one of the two or three most outstanding authors in Canada, he is best known for *The Apprenticeship of Duddy Kravitz* (1959; also a film), although it is not his best work.

HAROLD ROBBINS (1912-   )—Born Rubin. One of the best-selling authors of all time.

JUDITH ROSSNER (1935-   , New York City)—Born Perelman. Caused a sensation with *Looking for Mr. Goodbar* (1975), which was made into a film.

LEO ROSTEN (1908-   , Lodz)—Best known for *The Joys of Yiddish* and *The Education of H*Y*M*A*N* K*A*P*L*A*N*. His best book is without question *Captain Newman, M.D.* (1962).

HENRY ROTH (1906-   , Tysmenica, Austria-Hungary)—One of those writers who will always be remembered for one book—in this case *Call It Sleep* (1934), possibly the best American novel of the 1930s.

PHILIP ROTH (1933-   , Newark)—Although he upset quite a few people with *Portnoy's Complaint*, the fact remains that he is a great novelist. Possibly his best book was *Goodbye, Columbus* (1959).

J(EROME) D. SALINGER (1919-   , New York City)—The author of *Franny and Zooey* (1961) and the classic *Catcher in the Rye* (1951), one of the most widely taught books in American universities.

RICHARD SAPIR (1936-   , New York City)—Coauthor of the "Destroyer" series of thrillers.

SUSAN FROMBERG SCHAEFFER (1941-   , Brooklyn)—Professor of English at Brooklyn College and the author of *Falling* (1973) and the excellent *Anya* (1974).

BUDD SCHULBERG (1914-   , New York City)—A leading American author and screenwriter, with works like *On the Waterfront* (screenplay), *The Harder They Fall*, and *What Makes Sammy Run?*

ERICH SEGAL (1937-   , Brooklyn)—Author of the runaway best-sellers *Love Story* (1970) and *Oliver's Story* (1977), he also wrote the screenplay for the Beatles movie *Yellow Submarine*. He was a professor of classics at Yale U. when he published *Love Story*.

LIONEL SHAPIRO (1908-1958, Montreal)—An important Canadian novelist with strong political convictions, the author of *The Sealed Verdict* (1947) and other books.

IRWIN SHAW (1913-   , Brooklyn)—An outstanding short story writer (and considerably better at that length than when working with the novel), he has been a big-name novelist from *The Young Lions* to *Rich Man, Poor Man*.

LOUIS SHEAFFER (1912-   , Louisville, Ky.)—Born Slung. Won the 1974 Pulitzer Prize for Biography for *O'Neill: Son and Artist*.

SIDNEY SHELDON (1917-   , Chicago)—Best-selling novelist of books such as *The Other Side of Midnight*. His work will not live forever.

ALIX KATES SHULMAN (1932-   , Cleveland)—Author of several excellent novels, including *Memoirs of an Ex-Prom Queen*.

MAX SHULMAN (1919-   )—One of America's funniest writers, he is best known for *Rally Round the Flag, Boys* (1957), which was made into fair film.

ISAAC BASHEVIS SINGER (1904-   , Radzymin, Poland)—Perhaps the finest writer to have emerged from the Yiddish tradition, he won the Nobel Prize for Literature in 1978.

DAVID SLAVITT (1935-   , White Plains, N.Y.)—As "Henry Robbins" he produced several of the more controversial novels of the 1960s: *The Exhibitionist* (1967) and *The Voyeur* (1968).

AARON M. STEIN (1906-   )—As "George Bagby" and "Hampton Stone," he was a much better than average mystery writer.

GERTRUDE STEIN (1874-1946, Allegheny, Pa.)—An important influence on the literary and artistic life of the 1920s and '30s, her *Autobiography of Alice B. Toklas* is a stunning accomplishment.

IRVING STONE (1903-   )—Born Tennenbaum. A best-selling author whose books, including *Lust for Life* and *The Agony and the Ecstasy* have frequently been filmed.

JACQUELINE SUSANN (1921-1974, Philadelphia)—The famous best-selling author of such books as *Once Is Not Enough* and *Valley of the Dolls*.

HARVEY SWADOS (Died 1972, Holyoke, Mass.)—Novelist, social critic, and the author of *Standing Fast* and *False Coin*.

STUDS TERKEL (1912-   , New York City)—One of the finest exponents of the nonfiction book in the U.S., his bibliography is uniformly excellent: *Working*, *Division Street: America*, and *Hard Times* are three of the best.

ALVIN TOFFLER (1928-   , New York City)—His *Future Shock* (1970) is required reading at hundreds of colleges. It gave "futurism" a tremendous push and started a growth industry.

LAWRENCE TREAT (1903-   , New York City)—Born Goldstone. An excellent mystery writer, winner of the 1965 Edgar Award for best short story, and author of many novels, including *The Leather Man*, *V as in Victim*, and *Over the Edge*.

LEON URIS (1924-   , Baltimore)—With *Battle Cry*, *Topaz*, *QB VII*, and *Exodus*, he is one of the best of the best-selling authors.

IRVING WALLACE (1916-   , Chicago)—The popular author of such books as *The Chapman Report*, *The Prize*, and *The Man*.

EDWARD L. WALLANT (1926-1962)—He never achieved great fame during his too-short life, but books such as *The Human Season* and *The Pawnbroker* deserved it.

JEROME WEIDMAN (1913-   , New York City)—Although he has written many excellent books, he will always be remembered primarily for *I Can Get It for You Wholesale*, published during the Depression. The title still has great meaning.

NATHANIEL WEST (1903-1940)—Born Nate Weinstein. He was killed in an auto wreck, but during the 1930s he showed them all with *Miss Lonelyhearts*, *A Cool Million*, and especially *The Day of the Locust*. He told it as he saw it.

ELIE WIESEL (1928-   , Sighet, Transylvania)—Novelist and playwright on Holocaust and Jewish themes.

THYRA WINSLOW (1893-1961, Ark.)—Born Samter. Her book *My Own, My Native Land* is one of the neglected masterpieces of the 1930s.

HERMAN WOUK (1915-   , New York City)—An internationally acclaimed best-selling author with books such as *The Winds of War*, he has a real feel for the impact of war on society. *The Caine Mutiny* (for which he won the Pulitzer Prize) is one of the great character studies in the English language.

SOL YURICK (1925-   , New York City)—A novelist with terrific technique. Both *The Bag* (1968) and *Fertig* (1966) are excellent.

BRITISH

GRACE AGUILAR (1816-1847)—A member of a famous Sephardic family, she made her reputation with *The Days of Bruce* (1852).

HENRY CECIL (1902-   , London)—Born Henry Leon. His books *Alibi for a Judge* and *Brothers in Law* received critical acclaim.

LIONEL DAVIDSON (1922-   )—Author of *Making Good Again*, one of the best British novels of 1968.

WALTER L. EMANUEL (1869-1915)—One of England's cleverest humorists. His work appeared frequently in *Punch*.

BRIAN GLANVILLE (1931-   , London)—One of the best writers of sports fiction in the world (he is also a sportswriter), he wrote *The Olympia* (1969) and other novels.

LOUIS GOLDING (1895-1958, Manchester)—An outstanding novelist who frequently treated Jewish themes, he is best known for *Magnolia Street* and *Mr. Emmanuel*, which was made into an excellent film.

PHILIP GUEDALLA (1889-1944)—A renowned biographer.

STEPHEN HUDSON (1869-1944)—Born Sydney Schiff. Remembered for the excellent novel *Richard Kurt* (1919).

GERALD KERSH (1909-1968)—A former professional wrestler and Hollywood scriptwriter, he was a fine novelist and an excellent writer of fantasy.

ADA LEVERSON (1865-1936)—An excellent satirist who poked fun at Victorian life-styles in her novels.

LEWIS MELVILLE (1874-1932)—Born Lewis Benjamin. His books on the life and works of Thackeray have become standard sources.

LEONARD MERRICK (1864-1939, London)—Born Miller. A widely acclaimed short story writer. One of his best collections is *The Man Who Understood Women* (1908).

EDWARD H. W. MEYERSTEIN (1889-1952)—Famous for his trilogy *Trence Duke*, three of the best psychological novels of the 1930s.

CHAIM RAPHAEL (1908- , Middlesborough)—A stylistic craftsman in his fiction and his scholarly books, he also produced a number of excellent suspense novels (as "Jocelyn Davy"), including *The Naked Billany*.

FREDERIC RAPHAEL (1931- , Chicago)—Author of numerous movie scripts, he is also an important novelist. One of his best books is *The Earlsdon Way*.

SIEGFRIED SASSOON (1886-1967)—A world-renowned poet, his novel *Memoirs of an Infantry Officer* has become justly famous. A member of the famous English-Jewish family, he was raised as a Protestant and later became a Roman Catholic.

RONALD SEGAL (1932- , Capetown)—Driven into exile in England for his anti-apartheid views, he became Editor of the Penguin African Library series and the author of many books.

PAUL TABOR (1908- , Hungary)—Born Tabori. A noted translator and the author of *Salvatore*.

ISRAEL ZANGWILL (1864-1926, London)—A world-famous stylist of the English language.

FRENCH

ROMAIN GARY (1914- , Vilna)—Born Kacew. Part Jewish, he is the author of *The Roots of Heaven* and *The Ski Bum*, both of which were filmed.

JOSEPH KESSEL (1898- , Clara, Argentina)—Best known for his work during the 1920s, he became famous for *The Pure in Heart*.

ANDRÉ MAUROIS (1885-1967, Elbeuf)—Born Emile Herzog. The world-famous novelist and critic. He was a member of the prestigious French Academy.

ALBERT MEMMI (1920- , Tunis)—One of the most distinguished authors to come out of North Africa, he could just as easily be listed under Sociology for his insightful studies of Jewish and Arab culture.

IRENE NEMIROWSKY (1903-1944, Kiev)—Author of several excellent novels, including *David Golder*. She was killed by the Nazis.

MARCEL PROUST (1871-1922, Paris)—The tremendously influential French novelist was the son of a Jewish mother.

ANDRÉ SCHWARZ-BART (1928- , Metz)—Won the Prix Goncourt for the powerful and beautiful *The Last of the Just* (1961).

ELSA TRIOLET (1903- , Moscow)—Born Blick. Won the Prix Goncourt for *A Fine of 200 Francs*.

VERCORS (1902- , Paris)—Vercors was the pseudonym of Jean Bruller, author of *Put Out the Light* and the wonderful *Sylva*.

GERMANS AND AUSTRIANS

HERMAN BROCH (1886-1951)—Best known for his novels *The Death of Vergil* (1945) and *The Sleepwalkers* (1932). He was saved from the Nazis through the help of writers all over the world.

LION FEUCHTWANGER (1884-1958, Munich)—Famous for his historical novels.

EFRAIM FRISCH (1873-1942, Russia)—His novel *Zenobi* (1927) has attained the status of a classic. He was an Austrian citizen.

HANS HABE (1911- , Budapest)—Born Janos Bekessy. A major novelist and writer (*A Thousand Shall Fail*, 1941) who wrote a very interesting book on the assassination of JFK, *The Wounded Land*.

STEFAN HEYM (1913- , Chemnitz)—Born Helmut Flieg. After finding sanctuary in the U.S., he returned to East Germany where he won the Heinrich Mann Prize and the National Prize for Arts and Literature. He eventually fell into disfavor with the Communist regime. His finest work is *The Crusaders*, considered by some critics to be the best single literary work on World War II.

HEINRICH E. JACOB (1889-1967, Berlin)—Among his many books and plays are excellent biographies of Strauss and Haydn.

FRANZ KAFKA (1883-1924, Prague)—Clearly one of the most significant writers of this century. His impact on all Western artistic expression has been immense. *The Metamorphosis* and *The Penal Colony* have been imitated hundreds of times, but never equaled.

EMIL LUDWIG (1881-1948, Breslau)—A leading biographer of the 1930s and '40s. Lincoln, Cleopatra and Stalin were among his subjects.

ARTHUR LANDSBERGER (1876-1933, Berlin)—A pioneer German mystery writer. He took his own life.

ERNEST LOTHAR (b. 1890, Brünn)—Born Mueller. His novel *Beneath Another Sun* was an international success. He became a Catholic.

ALFRED NEUMANN (1895-1952, Lautenburg, Germany)—An important historical novelist, he wrote masterpieces such as *The Patriot*.

FELIX SALTEN (1869-1947, Budapest)—I bet you didn't know that Bambi, that cute little deer in the Disney film, was Jewish. Well, he was a creation of Felix Salten, who was born Siegmund Salzmann and became a noted critic and writer in Austria before World War II.

ANNA SEGHERS (1900- , Mainz)—Another member of that group of writers that returned to (East) Germany after World War II, she was awarded the Lenin Peace Prize for books such as *The Seventh Cross*, which became internationally famous.

FRANZ WERFEL (1890-1945, Czechoslovakia)—A major force among the German Expressionist writers, he wrote the novel *The Song of Bernadette*, as well as poems and plays. An Austrian, he came to the U.S. in 1939.

ARNOLD ZWEIG (1887-1968, Gross-Glogau, Germany)—Achieved an international reputation for *The Case of Sergeant Grischa* and his books on Germany in the twentieth century before World War II. He returned to that country after the war, received the Lenin Peace Prize, and became the President of the East German Academy of Arts.

STEFAN ZWEIG (1881-1942, Vienna)—An outstanding biographer who had a huge international following in the 1920s and '30s. Perhaps his finest book was *Magellen* (1938). He took his own life during World War II.

ITALIANS

GIORGIO BASSANI (1916- , Bologna)—Renowned for the novel *The Garden of the Finzi Contini*. His *Gold-Rimmed Spectacles* is just as moving.

ANNIE VIVANTI CHARTRES (1868-1942, London)—Best known for her excellent novel *The Devourers* (1910), she escaped from persecution in Italy only to die in London during a German air attack.

CARLO LEVI (1902-1975, Turin)—His *Christ Stopped at Eboli* caused a sensation after World War II. During the 1960s he was a member of the Italian Senate under the Communist party banner.

ALBERTO MORAVIA (1907- , Rome)—Born Pincherle. A writer of international reputation, acquired through books such as *Two Women* (the film version of which won Sophia Loren an Academy Award) and *The Conformist*. He is certainly one of the two or three most important Italian writers of the postwar period.

ITALO SVEVO (1861-1928)—Born Ettore Schmitz. His *Confessions of Zeno* catapulted him to fame. This book is widely considered to be one of the outstanding works of Italian literature in the 20th century.

POLES

KAZIMIERZ BRANDYS (1916- , Lodz)—A noted novelist who was one of the most influential forces in Polish literature and letters in the post–World War II period.

BRUNO JASIENSKI (1901-1939, Klimentow)—Born Zyskind. A committed Communist who spent the 1930s in the Soviet Union. He was an organizer of the Union of Soviet Writers.

TADEUSZ PEIPER (b. 1891, Cracow)—A poet, dramatist, and noted critic, he was one of the most influential figures in Polish literature in the 1920s and '30s.

ANTONI SLONIMSKI (b. 1895)—Many consider him to be the single most influential figure in Polish literature in modern times. He was also an outstanding theater critic. He was not raised as a Jew.

JULJAN STRYJKOWSKI (1905- , Stry)—Born Pesach Stark. An important personality in Polish letters after World War II. Widely translated, he is most famous for *Run to Fragala* (1951).

LUDWIK ZAMENHOF (1859-1917, Bialystok)—Attempted to change all of writing by developing an entirely new, international language, which he called Esperanto. The language works, is reasonably easy to learn—but when was the last time you heard someone curse in it?

RUSSIANS

MARK ALDANOV (1889-1957, Kiev)—Born Landau. Fled Russia after the revolution and became a noted historical novelist. One of his major works was *The Fifth Seal* (1943).

ISAAC BABEL (1894-194?, Odessa)—A rediscovered genius, he is one of the many hundreds of thousands who disappeared during and after the purges. His short stories, collected in *Red Cavalry* and *Odessa Tales*, live on.

YULI DANIEL (1925-)—Imprisoned more than once, he is one of the great literary heroes of the new Soviet resistance. Best known for *This Is Moscow Speaking and Other Stories*, he used science fiction to attack the Soviet system in stories such as "The Life of a Dog."

ILYA G. EHRENBURG (1891-1967, Kiev)—The great Soviet writer whose best work was his first—*The Extraordinary Adventures of Julio Jurenito*.

YURI P. GERMAN (1910- , Riga)—Famed Soviet novelist whose most noteworthy book was *Antonina* (1937).

DANIEL A. GRANIN (1918- , Petrograd)—One of the first intellectuals in the Soviet Union to take advantage of (and to celebrate) the new freedoms available after the death of Stalin, he is best known for his story "One's Own Opinion."

VASILI S. GROSSMAN (1905-1964, Berdichev)—Wrote *The People Is Immoral*, one of the great early novels of World War II.

ILYA ILF (1897-1937, Odessa)—Born Ilya A. Fainzilberg. One of the most popular humorists in the Soviet Union.

LEV A. KASSIL (1905-   )—Quite possibly the most widely read author in the U.S.S.R., he has produced a long string of books for young adult readers, an area of publishing taken very seriously in the Soviet Union.

BENJAMIN A. KAVERIN (1902-   , Pskov)—Born Zilberg. A pioneer Soviet crime and mystery writer, best known for *The Unknown Artist* (1947).

EMMANUIL G. KAZAKEVICH (1913-1962, Kremenchug)—Won two Stalin Prizes for books such as *The House on the Square*.

YURI N. LIBEDINSKI (1898-1959, Odessa)—An ideological writer who reflected the party line. His best book was his first—*A Week* (1923). His work still enjoys great popularity.

BORIS L. PASTERNAK (1890-1960, Moscow)—Although the novel *Doctor Zhivago* made him world-famous, he was also one of the finest poets in all of Russian history. He twice refused the Nobel Prize for Literature, and not because he didn't want it.

SOUTH AFRICANS

NADINE GORDIMER (1923-   , Springs)—Best known for *A World of Strangers*. A number of her best books cannot be sold in her native land.

DAN JACOBSON (1929-   , Kimberley)—Almost all his books, including *A Dance in the Sun* and *The Evidence of Love*, are concerned with the immorality of his country's racial policies.

SARAH GERTRUDE MILLIN (1889-1968, Lithuania)—Born Liebson. Two of her many major novels are *Mary Glenn* and *God's Step-children.*

OTHERS

FELIX ADERCA (1891-1962, Puiesti, Rumania)—Noted for his outstanding war novel, *1916*, he was one of Rumania's leading writers.

ELIAS CANETTI (1905-   , Russe, Bulgaria)—Although he wrote in German, Canetti is the most famous author in the world of Bulgarian origin. His most noteworthy book is *Auto da Fe* (1946).

OSCAR DAVICO (1919-   , Sabac, Yugoslavia)—Won Yugoslavia's highest national literary award three times.

SOPHIE ELKAN (1853-1921)—One of Sweden's most famous female novelists and author of *John Jall* (1899) and *The King* (1904).

ALBERTO GERCHUNOFF (1884-1950, Proskurov, Russia)—Argentinian writer renowned for *The Jewish Gauchos of the Pampas*, he founded and led the Argentine Writers Association.

EGON HOSTOVSKY (1908-   )—A leading Czech novelist. Two of his most important works are *The Midnight Patient* (1954) and *The Charity Ball* (1957).

JORGE ISAACS (1837-1895, Cali, Colombia)—His novel *Maria* (1867) is considered one of the finest works produced in South America in the 19th century. His father was of Jewish origin.

FERENC KORMENDI (1900-   , Budapest)—Renowned for his powerful novel *Escape to Life* (1933), which won several awards.

DAVID MARTIN (1918-   , Hungary)—An émigré to Australia, where he won fame for books such as *Tiger Bay* (1946, made into a film) and *The Young Wife* (1962).

NESTORAS MATSAS (1932-   , Athens)—A noted film director as well as a novelist, he won the Greek National Prize for Literature for *The Fairy Tale of Theophilos*. He was baptized.

HARRY MULISCH (1927- , Haarlem, Netherlands)—One of the leading existentialist writers in Europe, his novel *The Black Light* (1956) was widely discussed. His mother was Jewish.

ISAAC PELTZ (1899- , Bucharest)—Considered one of Rumania's finest novelists, he has received suprisingly little attention in the West.

KAREL POLACEK (1892-1944)—One of the leading humorists and satirists in Czechoslovakia, he was murdered in a Nazi concentration camp.

SCIENCE FICTION WRITERS AND EDITORS

ISAAC ASIMOV (1920- , Soviet Union)—The incredibly prolific author of such masterpieces as *The Foundation Trilogy*; *I, Robot*; and *The Gods Themselves* (1973 Hugo Award winner). He is also a leading science writer and one of the very best after-dinner speakers.

ALFRED BESTER (1913-)—One of the all-time greats, with books such as *The Demolished Man* and *The Stars My Destination*. His short stories are also excellent.

ROBERT BLOCH (1917-)—Although best known as the author of *Psycho*, he is a fine science fiction and fantasy writer.

JACK DANN—An excellent writer and the editor of *Wandering Stars* and several other collections.

AVRAM DAVIDSON (1923- , Yonkers, N.Y.)—Author of *Rogue Dragon* and other novels, he is one of the very best short story writers in the business, and one of the most original.

JUDY LYNN BENJAMIN DEL REY—Editor of Del Rey Books (Ballantine), she is one of the leading forces in the publishing of science fiction in the U.S.

HARLAN ELLISON (1934-)—The dynamic author who has won numerous Hugo and Nebula awards, he is a legend in the science fiction community and one of the top television and film writers in Hollywood.

HUGO GERNSBACK (1884-1967)—The father of American science fiction as founder and Editor of *Amazing Stories*, the first magazine in the field.

H. L. GOLD (1914- , Montreal)—An excellent writer who never wrote enough, his major contribution was as Editor of *Galaxy Science Fiction*, which he built into the best magazine in the field in the 1950s.

C. M. KORNBLUTH (1923-1958, New York City)—Was one of the best science fiction writers. He often wrote with Frederik Pohl (*The Space Merchants*, *Gladiator-at-Law*, and others). He also left us *The Syndic* and a host of excellent short stories.

HENRY KUTTNER (1914-1958, Los Angeles)—A major science fiction writer who died too young. His later work was usually in collaboration with his wife, C. L. Moore. His short stories, usually featuring series characters, were often excellent.

BARRY N. MALZBERG (1938-)—A master of "psychological" science fiction, he won the John W. Campbell Memorial Award for *Beyond Apollo*, and was at one time the most prolific writer in the field.

JUDITH MERRIL (1923-)—Born Grossman. A leading writer at one time and then one of the field's most influential editors, she has been relatively inactive in recent years. Her first story, "That Only a Mother" is considered a classic.

ROBERT SHECKLEY (1928- , New York City)—His short stories are among the finest in science fiction. His novels include *Mindswap* and *Journey beyond Tomorrow*.

ROBERT SILVERBERG (1936- , New York City)—One of the greatest science fiction writers of all time, he wrote *Dying Inside, Thorns, Tower of Glass, Shadrach in the Furnace*, and *The Stochastic Man*.

NORMAN SPINRAD (1940-)—A leading writer of the 1960s and '70s with books such as *Bug Jack Barron* and *The Iron Dream*. His short stories are also notable.

WILLIAM TENN (1920-)—Born Phillip Klass. Noted for his beautifully crafted and frequently funny short stories, which can be found in collections such as *Of All Possible Worlds* and *The Square Root of Man*.

STANLEY G. WEINBAUM (1900-1935, Louisville, Ky.)—His brilliant career was cut short by an early death, but many feel that he revolutionized the field with his sympathetic treatment of aliens.

DONALD A. WOLLHEIM (1914- , New York City)—One of the leading editors in the field, first at Ace Books and then under his own DAW Books (NAL) imprint.

PLAYWRIGHTS

See also Pulitzer Prize Winners

S. N. BEHRMAN (b. 1893, Worcester, Mass.)—The brilliant author of *No Time for Comedy* and other wonderful plays.

TRISTAN BERNARD (1866-1947, Besançon, France)—A great novelist and playwright who wrote some of the funniest dialogue ever performed on the stage.

VLADIMIR BILL-BELOTSERKOVSKI (1885-1966, Russia)—The leading Soviet dramatist specializing in Marxist propaganda.

PADDY CHAYEFSKY (1923- , Bronx)—The wonderful author of *The Catered Affair, The Bachelor Party* and *Marty*. He answered Vanessa Redgrave in a famous exchange during the Academy Award ceremonies of 1978.

JEROME COOPERSMITH (1925- , New York City)—A leading playwright and television writer.

ALDO DE BENEDETTI (1892-1970)—Although he was a major Italian playwright, his best work was as a screenwriter.

GEORGES DE PORTO-RICHE (1849-1930, Bordeaux)—A member of the French Academy and one of the leading playwrights in his country.

BRUNO FRANK (1887-1945, Stuttgart, Germany)—A leading playwright in Germany for more than 20 years. He was at his height when the rise of Hitler cut short his career.

MOSS HART (1904-1961, New York City)—George S. Kaufman's famous collaborator, he shared the 1937 Pulitzer prize for *You Can't Take It With You* and was the coauthor of *The Man Who Came to Dinner*.

HERMAN HEIJERMANS (1864-1924, Rotterdam)—A leading Dutch dramatic playwright, he was also an important novelist.

HENRIK HERTZ (1798-1870)—One of the leading Danish playwrights of the 19th century, he became a Christian.

ISRAEL HOROVITZ (1939- , Wakefield, Mass.)—An excellent American playwright, he wrote *The Indian Wants the Bronx*.

EUGENE IONESCO (1912- , Rumania)—A member of the French Academy and one of the major playwrights of the 20th century, he founded what became known as the theater of the absurd. His most play famous is *Rhinoceros*. He is the son of a Jewish mother.

JEROME KASS (1937- , Chicago)—A playwright and screenwriter, he wrote the excellent TV drama *Queen of the Stardust Ballroom* (1975).

GEORGE S. KAUFMAN (1889-1961, Pittsburgh)—Although he always worked with collaborators, he became one of America's most famous playwrights. In addition to the plays mentioned in connection with Moss Hart, he coauthored *The Solid Gold Cadillac* and the Pulitzer Award–winning *Of Thee I Sing* (with Morrie

Ryskind and Ira Gershwin). He also wrote several of the Marx Brothers' best films.

VLADIMIR M. KIRSHON (1902-1938)—A leading Soviet playwright who never deviated from the party line, he was nevertheless executed during the Great Purge.

ARTHUR KOBER (1900-1975, Brody, Galicia)—A leading American playwright who specialized in comedy, he wrote *Having a Wonderful Time.*

BERNARD KOPS (1926- , London)—One of the best and most influential of contemporary British playwrights, he wrote such works as *The Dream of Peter Mann, The Hamlet of Stepney Green,* and *Yes from No-Man's Land.*

JOSEPH KRAMM (1907-)—Author of the powerful drama *The Shrike,* which won a Pulitzer Prize.

FRANTISEK LANGER (1888-1965)—Considered to be one of the greatest Czechoslovakian playwrights of all time.

ARTHUR LAURENTS (1918-)—Many feel that his first play was his best—the powerful *Home of the Brave.* He also wrote a number of excellent filmplays.

JEROME LAWRENCE (1915-)—Born Schwartz. An excellent American playwright, he wrote *Inherit the Wind* and many others.

FRANK MARCUS (1928- , Breslau, Germany)—A major playwright and the author of the suspenseful *Killing of Sister George* (1965).

MURRAY MEDNICK (1939- , Brooklyn)—Author of the interesting play *The Hawk,* he won an Obie Award for *The Deer Kill.*

SIDNEY MICHAELS (1927- , New York City)—Among his fine plays are *Dylan* and *Ben Franklin in Paris.*

ARTHUR MILLER (1915- , New York City)—One of the most important playwrights in the world, his *Death of a Salesman* is among the most significant plays of the 20th century. He won the Pulitzer Prize several times (*see* Pulitzer Prize Winners). He was the screenwriter for *The Misfits,* Clark Gable's last film, which also starred his wife, Marilyn Monroe.

FERENC MOLNAR (1878-1952, Budapest)—Born Neumann. Enjoyed an international reputation for plays such as *The Tale of the Wolf* and *The Devil.*

CLIFFORD ODETS (1906-1963, Philadelphia)—The distinguished playwright who gave us *Golden Boy* among others.

HAROLD PINTER (1930- , London)—A leading British playwright, he wrote *The Homecoming, The Birthday Party,* and the excellent *The Caretaker.*

RONALD RIBMAN (1932- , New York City)—Author of *The Ceremony of Innocence* and the Obie Award–winning *Journey of the Fifth Horse.*

ELMER L. RICE (1892-1967, New York City)—Born Reizenstein. A major figure in the American theater by virtue of plays such as *Love among the Ruins, Between Two Worlds,* and the Pulitzer Prize–winning *Street Scene.*

STANLEY RICHARDS (1918- , Brooklyn)—Born Myers. A noted playwright and critic.

HOWARD SACKLER (1929- , New York City)—Won the Pulitzer Prize, the New York Drama Critics Circle Award, and the Antoinette Perry Award, all for *The Great White Hope.*

PETER SCHAFFER (1926- , London)—A leading British playwright and author of *Five-Finger Exercise* and the wonderful *Equus.*

EDMOND SEE (1875-1959, Bayonne, France)—A leading French playwright specializing in comedy.

NEIL SIMON (1927- , New York City)—One of the premier commercial playwrights. Some of his work is outstanding, including *Plaza Suite* and *The Odd Couple.* Most of his plays have been filmed.

THE SPEWACKS: BELLA (1899-) **and SAMUEL** (1899-1971)—The popular playwrights who wrote *Boy Meets Girl* and others.

YALE M. UDOFF (1935- , Brooklyn)—An excellent playwright, television, and film writer.

PETER WEISS (1916- , Berlin)—Author of the brilliant *Persecution and Assassination of Jean-Paul Marat as Performed by the Inmates of the Asylum of Charenton Under the Direction of the Marquis De Sade.*

ARNOLD WESKER (1932- , London)—Another of that brilliant group of British-Jewish playwrights, he is the author of *Roots* (the other one) and *Barley.*

LITERARY AND DRAMA CRITICS AND AGENTS

LIONEL ABEL (1910-   )—Born Abelson. A leading dramatic playwright and drama critic. He won the Obie Award for *Absalom* in 1956 and is the author of *Metatheatre: A New View of Dramatic Form.*

M. H. ABRAMS (1912- , Long Branch, N.J.)—F. J. Whiton Professor of English at Cornell and the author of *Natural Supernaturalism.*

CHARLES ANGOFF (1902- , Russia)—Served as Editor of the *American Mercury*, and as an editor of the *Literary Review*, and, in 1969, as President of the Poetry Society of America. He also is an excellent novelist.

LEOPOLD AVERBAKH (1903-late 1930s)—A leading Soviet literary critic who perished during the purges.

ARKADII V. BELINKOV (1921-1970, Moscow)—One of the most influential literary critics in the Soviet Union and the author of *Rough Copy of Feelings*, he served more than a decade in prison for his views. He eventually came to the U.S.

WALTER BENJAMIN (1892-1940, Berlin)—A tremendously important critic who is still widely read, he combined philosophy and literary criticism with skill and grace.

BERNARD BENSTOCK (1930- , New York City)—Professor of English and Comparative Literature at the U. of Illinois and a leading Joyce scholar.

ALBERT BERMEL (1927- , London)—Professor of Theatre at Lehman College, N.Y.C. and a noted drama critic.

NAOMI BLIVEN (1925- , New York City)—A major book reviewer for the *New Yorker.*

HAROLD BLOOM (1930- , New York City)—DeVane Professor of the Humanities at Yale and the author of *The Visionary Company* and *Yeats*, among other major works.

FREDERICK S. BOAS (1862-1957)—A leading authority on the Elizabethan period and the author of *Christopher Marlowe.*

GEORG BRANDES (1842-1927)—Born Morris Cohen. One of the most influential literary critics in Europe, he was a Dane.

OSIP N. BRIK (1888-1945, Moscow)—A noted Soviet literary critic and expert on the sociology of art.

ROBERT S. BRUSTEIN (1927- , New York City)—The long-time Theatre Critic of the *New Republic* and the author of *The Theatre of Revolt.*

DAVID DAICHES (1912- , Sunderland, England)—One of the leading British literary critics of the 20th century and the author of *Poetry and the Modern World* and *The Novel and the Modern World.*

ARTHUR ELOESSER (1870-1938, Berlin)—A noted German critic and the author of *Modern German Literature.*

CLIFTON FADIMAN (1904-   )—Book Editor of the *New Yorker* for ten years and was known to millions for his radio show, *Information Please.*

LESLIE FIEDLER (1917- , Newark)—The very influential literary critic and author of *Love and Death in the American Novel.*

GILBERT W. GABRIEL (1890-1952)—Served as Literary Editor and Music and Drama Critic for the *New York Evening Sun.*

JOHN GASSNER (1903-1967)—A Professor at Yale, he was the author of the very important *Theater in Our Times.*

MIKHAIL O. GERSHENZON (1869-1925, Kishinev, Russia)—One of the leading literary historians and philosophers in Russia.

ISAAC GOLDBERG (1887-1938, Boston)—A leading American scholar on Latin American literature and the author of *Brazilian Literature* and *Studies in Spanish-American Literature.*

LUCIEN GOLDMANN (1913-1970, Bucharest)—A noted French expert on the work of Racine and Pascal.

EDUARD GOLDSTUECKER (1913-   )—President of the Czechoslovakian Writer's Union and an important literary historian.

SIR ISRAEL GOLLANCZ (1864-1930)—A world-famous authority on Shakespeare, he was one of the founders of the British Royal Academy.

MARTIN GOTTFRIED (1933-   , New York City)—The influential Drama Critic of *Women's Wear Daily* and later of the *New York Post* and the author of *A Theater Divided.*

STEPHEN J. GREENBLATT (1943-   , Cambridge, Mass.)—Author of *Three Modern Satirists* and *Sir Walter Raleigh*, he teaches at the U. of California.

FRIEDRICH GUNDOLF (1880-1931)—The pen name of Friedrich Gundelfinger. A noted German Shakespearean scholar.

WILLY HAAS (b. 1891, Prague)—A major critic in Germany after World War II, he was founder and Editor of *Die Literärische Welt*, one of the leading German literary journals before the rise of Hitler.

ERNEST HEILBORN (1867-1941, Berlin)—The influential Drama Critic of the *Frankfurter Zeitung.*

HENRI HERTZ (1875-1966, Norgent-sur-Seine, France)—A major French literary and political critic for decades.

MILTON HINDUS (1916-   , New York City)—Wolkenstein Professor of English at Brandeis U. and a leading expert on Walt Whitman.

CLIVE HIRSCHHORN (1940-   , Johannesburg)—Theater Critic of the London *Sunday Express.*

RUDOLF KAYSER (1889-1964)—One of the most influential literary critics before the rise of Hitler as Editor of *Die Neue Rundschau.*

ALFRED KAZIN (1915-   , Brooklyn)—A leading book reviewer and critic, his *On Native Ground* was a very influential work. He served as an editor of the *New Republic.* His recent book, *New York Jew*, makes fascinating reading.

ALFRED KERR (1867-1948, Breslau, Germany)—Born Kempner. His work became the prototype of modern literary criticism. He was Drama Critic for the *Berliner Tageblatt* and *Der Tag.*

ROBERT R. KIRSCH (1922-   , Brooklyn)—A gifted novelist, he is Literary Editor of the *Los Angeles Times.*

ALADAR KOMLOS (b. 1892, Alsosztregova, Hungary)—Born Kredens. The noted Hungarian critic who wrote *The New Hungarian Lyrics*, he served as Chairman of the Hungarian Literary Society.

LOUIS KRONENBERGER (1904-   , Cincinnati)—The long-time Drama Critic of *Time* and a noted author (*Kings and Desperate Men*).

DOROTHEA KROOK (1920-   , Riga, Latvia)—One of the world's leading experts on the work of Henry James and the author of *The Elements of Tragedy*, she teaches at Tel Aviv U.

MARTIN LAMM (1880-1950, Stockholm)—A member of the Swedish Royal Academy, he was an important critic and literary historian.

ROBERT LANGBAUM (1924-   , New York City)—James Branch Cabell

Professor of English at the U. of Virginia and the author of *The Poetry of Experience*.

HERBERT A. LEIBOWITZ (1935- , Staten Island, N.Y.)—An excellent and influential poetry critic.

J. C. LEVENSON (1922- , Boston)—Edgar Allan Poe Professor of English at the U. of Virginia and the author of *Stephen Crane*.

OSCAR I. LEVERTIN (1862-1906, Gryt, Sweden)—The noted literary critic of the Swedish newspaper *Svenska Dagbladet* and and important poet.

M. M. LIBERMAN (1921- , New York City)—Oakes Ames Professor of English Literature at Grinnell College and the author of the important *Practice of Criticism*.

STEVEN MARCUS (1928- , New York City)—An Associate Editor of the *Partisan Review* and a Professor of English at Columbia U., he is one of the leading literary critics in the U.S. One of his best books is *The Other Victorians*.

JOSEPH H. MAZO (1938- , Bronx)—The Dance and Theatre Critic of *Women's Wear Daily* and the author of the very good *Dance Is a Contact Sport* (1974).

SCOTT MEREDITH (1923- , New York City)—Born Feldman. One of the world's leading literary agents.

MICHELE MURRAY (1933-1974, Brooklyn)—Born Freedman. Book Review Editor of the *National Observer* before her tragic death.

NORMAN PODHORETZ (1930- , Brooklyn)—The noted literary critic and Editor of *Commentary*, he let it all hang out in *Making It* (1968).

ALFRED POLGAR (1873-1955, Vienna)—One of the leading drama critics in Austria.

ERIC S. RABKIN (1946- , Queens)—A Professor of English at the U. of Michigan, he is a leading scholar in the field of speculative literature. Two of his most important books are *Science Fiction* (coauthored) and *Narrative Suspense*.

PAUL ROSENFELD (1890-1946, New York City)—Coeditor of the annual *American Caravan* and the author of *Discoveries of a Music Critic*.

HILARY RUBENSTEIN (1926- , London)—A partner of A. P. Watt and Sons, one of Britain's most important literary agencies.

ARTHUR SAINER (1924- , New York City)—Literary Critic and Book Editor of the *Village Voice*, 1961-1965, he became Drama Critic for that paper in 1969.

DELMORE SCHWARTZ (1913-1966, Brooklyn)—An Editor of the *Partisan Review*, he was an important critic and one of the most important (and relatively neglected) poets and writers in the U.S.

MARC SLONIM (1894-1976)—One of the leading authorities in the world on Russian literature, his *Soviet Literature* has become a standard work.

THEODORE H. SOLOTAROFF (1928- , Elizabeth, N.J.)—A leading American critic and Editor of the late and lamented *New American Review*.

STEPHEN SPENDER (1909- , London)—Coeditor of *Encounter* and one of the world's most important literary critics.

JEAN STAROBINSKI (1920- , Geneva)—A major authority on structural criticism and French literature, his work has been tremendously influential.

GEORGE STEINER (1929- , Paris)—The widely acclaimed literary critic and the author of *The Death of Tragedy*.

DIANA TRILLING (1905-)—Born Rubin. An important literary critic.

LIONEL TRILLING (1905-1975, New York City)—Influenced a generation of students as a Professor at Columbia U. His *Liberal Imagination* is considered a major work.

YURI TYNYANOV (1894-1943, Rezhitsa, Latvia)—Considered the foremost literary theorist in the Soviet Union until his death.

LOUIS UNTERMEYER (1885-1977)—The very prolific poet and critic, whose anthologies helped establish the reputations of numerous writers.

JUDAH WATEN (1911- , Odessa, Russia)—A leading literary critic in Australia and a major figure of the Australian Left, he is also a novelist of note.

AVRAHM YARMOLINSKY (1890- , Russia)—A leading American scholar and literary critic and the author of such important books as *Dostoevsky, A Life*, and *Russian Poetry*.

HELEN YGLESIAS (1915- , New York City)—Born Bassine. A notable critic, novelist, and book reviewer who served as Literary Editor of the *Nation*.

COMPOSERS

GEORGE ANTHEIL (1900-1959, Trenton, N.J.)—A leading avant-garde composer and an excellent pianist.

VICTOR A. BELY (1904- , Russia)—An important Soviet composer who became popular for his songs sung by troops during World War II, he was a recipient of the Stalin Prize.

RALPH BENATZKY (1884-1957)—It has been estimated that he wrote the incredible total of 5,000 songs and numerous operettas. He was also a noted composer of film music.

ARTHUR V. BERGER (1912- , New York City)—A noted critic as well as a composer.

MATVEY I. BLANTER (1903- , Pochep, Russia)—A leading composer of musical comedies in the Soviet Union and author of the song "Katyusha" about the famous artillery rockets.

MARC BLITZSTEIN (1905-1964, Philadelphia)—One of the best "proletarian" composers, he wrote several excellent operas of the working class. He was killed in a street fight.

ERNEST BLOCH (1880-1959, Geneva)—The noted composer of *America* and *Symphony in C Sharp Minor*, he wrote many other excellent works.

HENRY D. BRANT (1913- , Montreal)—A leading experimental composer who has used electronic apparatus in his compositions.

MARIO CASTELNUOVO-TEDESCO (1895-1968)—A leading Italian composer who wrote film scores after fleeing fascism in his native country.

FRANCIS CHAGRIN (1905-1972, Bucharest)—A noted French composer.

AARON COPLAND (1900- , Brooklyn)—The acclaimed composer of *Billy the Kid*, and the magnificent *Piano Concerto*, he was awarded the Medal of Freedom by a grateful American government. He won the 1945 Pulitzer Prize.

DAVID DIAMOND (1915-)—A prominent American composer.

SEM DRESDEN (1881-1957, Amsterdam)—Served as President of the Dutch Society of Composers and was Director of the Dutch Royal Conservatory.

PAUL DUKAS (1865-1935, Paris)—The celebrated composer of *Ariane et Barbe-Bleue* and many other notable works.

ISAAC DUNAYEVSKI (1900-1955, Lokhvitsa, Russia)—An important Soviet popular-song composer who wrote the "Song of Stalin"; it is not surprising that he won the Stalin Prize.

HANNS EISLER (1899-1962, Leipzig, Germany)—Fled Germany during the Hitler era and came to America where he wrote film music. Returning to Germany after the war (he was asked to leave the U.S.), he wrote the German Democratic Republic's National Anthem.

CAMILLE ERLANGER (1863-1919, Paris)—A leading French composer.

LEO FALL (1873-1925, Olomouc, Moravia)—A world-famous composer of light operas.

SAMUEL Y. FEINBERG (1890-1962, Odessa, Russia)—Winner of the Stalin Prize and a noted composer of piano concertos.

MORTON FELDMAN (1926- , New York City)—A leading avant-garde composer.

BENJAMIN FRANKEL (1906-1973, London)—One of the top filmscore composers in England.

REINHOLD M. GLIERE (1874-1956, Kiev, Russia)—A noted Soviet composer who won both the Lenin and Stalin prizes, he was also Chairman of the Union of Soviet Composers for more than a decade.

MIKHAIL F. GNESIN (1883-1957, Rostov-on-Don, Russia)—A Soviet composer who was one of the most important music educators in that country.

MORTON GOULD (1913- , Richmond Hill, N.Y.)—Excels in both popular and "serious" music and has produced such works as the Broadway musical *Billion Dollar Baby*, and the excellent *Fall River Legend*. He also conducted the orchestra at the Radio City Music Hall for many years.

LOUIS GRUENBERG (1884-1964, Poland)—Used Black themes very effectively in the opera *Emperor Jones* and was a prize-winning composer.

HENRI HERZ (1802-1888, Vienna)—Composed more than 200 works for the piano and was an outstanding pianist. He will always be remembered in Mexico, for he wrote its national anthem.

FERDINAND HILLER (1811-1885, Frankfurt, Germany)—Born Hildesheim. A noted composer/conductor who wrote a standard text on musical theory. He became a Christian.

VICTOR HOLLAENDER (1866-1940)—A famous composer of light opera, he also wrote "Annemarie," a popular song during World War I.

GEORG JACOBI (1840-1906, Berlin)—A world-famous composer of ballet music, most notably for *The Beauty and the Beast*.

EMMERICH KALMAN (1882-1953, Siofok, Hungary)—A leading composer of light operas such as *Gypsy Princess*.

LEON KIRCHNER (1910- , Brooklyn)—One of the America's leading composers and the winner of many awards, including the Pulitzer Prize and the New York Music Critics' Circle Award. He is the Walter Bigelow Rosen Professor of Music at Harvard.

ERICH W. KORNGOLD (1897-1957, Brno, Czechoslovakia)—Composed excellent music while still a child. Many feel he never fulfilled his promise.

WOLF LIEBERMANN (1910- , Zurich)—A fine composer, he became General Manager of the Hamburg State Opera.

ERNEST LISSAUER (1882-1937, Berlin)—Although he was an important poet and dramatist, he appears here because he wrote the infamous "Hymn of Hate," a favorite of German soldiers in World War I.

GUSTAV MAHLER (1860-1911, Kalischt, Bohemia)—The world-famous composer, conductor, and administrator (he was Director of the Vienna Opera). He became a Catholic.

FELIX MENDELSSOHN (1809-1847, Hamburg)—Without doubt the greatest working composer of the first half of the 19th century. He was baptized.

GIACOMO MEYERBEER (1791-1864, Berlin)—Born Jacob Liebmann-Beer. The great operatic composer.

DARIUS MILHAUD (1892-1974, Aix-en-Provence, France)—One of the famed "Les Six," he was a brilliant and innovative composer of operas.

SERGIU NATRA (1924- , Bucharest)—A noted Israeli composer.

JACQUES OFFENBACH (1819-1880, Cologne)—The great French operatic composer.

FRANZ REIZENSTEIN (1911-1968, Nuremberg, Germany)—An excellent pianist as well as composer.

RUDOLF RETI (1885-1957, Uzhitse, Serbia)—A fine composer. His real contribution was as a musical theorist who wrote such important books as *The Thematic Process in Music*.

VITTORIO RIETI (1898- , Alexandria, Egypt)—A noted composer and music theorist.

ROLAND-MANUEL (1891-1966, Paris)—Born Roland A. M. Levy. A noted composer who became President of the International Music Council of UNESCO.

SIGMUND ROMBERG (1887-1951, Nagykanizsa, Hungary)—The world-famous composer of *The Desert Song, The Student Prince,* and dozens of other popular operettas.

HENRY RUSSELL (1813-1900, Sheerness, England)—Born Levy. One of the most popular composers and song writers in England in the 19th century.

ARNOLD SCHOENBERG (1874-1951, Vienna)—The famed composer who developed the twelve-tone method of composition.

GUNTHER SCHULLER (1925- , New York City)—One of the most successful composers who mixed jazz forms with classical composition.

WILLIAM SCHUMAN (1910- , New York City)—A leading American composer (*Symphony for Strings* and many others), he served as President of Lincoln Center in New York after directing the Juilliard School of Music for more than 17 years.

MATYAS SEIBER (1905-1960, Budapest)—An important Hungarian composer, he was killed in an auto wreck.

ROBERT STARER (1924- , Vienna)—An important composer of ballet music.

OSCAR STRAUS (1870-1954, Vienna)—Born Strauss. A noted composer of light operas, perhaps best known for *The Chocolate Soldier.*

ALEXANDER TANSMAN (1897- , Lodz, Poland)—An outstanding pianist and conductor.

ERNEST TOCH (1887-1967, Vienna)—A Pulitzer Prize–winning composer who had fled the Nazis and continued his work in the U.S.

MOISSEY S. VEINBERG (1919- , Warsaw)—A noteworthy Soviet composer.

EMIL WALDTEUFEL (1837-1915, Strasbourg, France)—Well known as a composer of popular waltzes.

JAROMIR WEINBERGER (1896-1967, Prague)—A leading Czech composer.

CONDUCTORS

MOSE ATZMON (1931- , Hungary)—An Israeli, he became Conductor of the Sydney (Australia) Symphony in the early 1960s.

DANIEL BARENBOIM (1942- , Buenos Aires)—An Israeli and a prominent pianist, he has recently turned to conducting and enjoyed great success.

LEONARD BERNSTEIN (1918- , Lawrence, Mass.)—The famed Conductor of the New York Philharmonic, known for *West Side Story* and for his Young People's Concerts.

GARY BERTINI (1927- , Bessarabia)—An Israeli, he is an important composer as well as conductor.

LEO BLECH (1871-1958, Germany)—Former Conductor of the Berlin State Opera, he served as Conductor of the Stockholm Royal Opera after leaving Germany.

ARTHUR BODANZKY (1877-1939, Vienna)—A noted conductor of operas at the New York Metropolitan and elsewhere.

GUSTAV BRECHER (1879-1940)—Music Director of the famed Leipzig Opera, 1924–1933. He took his own life.

THEO BUCHWALD (1902- , Vienna)—Conductor of the National Symphony Orchestra of Peru.

EMIL COOPER (1877-1960)—Born Kuper. Conductor of the New York Metropolitan Opera, 1944-1950, and, earlier, Director of the Petrograd Philharmonic.

SIR MICHAEL COSTA (1808-1884, Naples)—One of the greatest opera conductors of the 19th century, he directed the Royal Italian Opera at Covent Garden for over 20 years.

LEOPOLD DAMROSCH (1832-1885, Posen, Poland)—The world-famous composer and conductor, he worked at the Metropolitan as well as many other posts.

WALTER J. DAMROSCH (1862-1950, Breslau, Germany)—The famed Conductor of the New York Metropolitan Opera.

ISSAY A. DOBROVEN (1894-1953)—Directed the Bulgarian State Opera in the late 1920s and was Conductor of the Imperial Opera.

ANTAL DORATI (1906- , Budapest)—One of the most famed conductors and musical directors in the world. Some of his major podiums were the Minneapolis Symphony, the Dallas Symphony, the B.B.C. Symphony, the National Symphony (Washington, D.C.) and the Stockholm Philharmonic.

ARTHUR FIEDLER (1894-1979, Boston)—The celebrated Conductor of the Boston Pops and a genuine national treasure of the U.S.

GRZEGORZ FITELBERG (1879-1953, Dvinsk, Latvia)—Served as the Conductor of the Bolshoi Ballet in Moscow and as Conductor of the Warsaw Philharmonic.

LUKAS FOSS (1922- , Berlin)—Conductor of the Buffalo Philharmonic, he is also a noted composer' and pianist.

EDWIN FRANKO GOLDMAN (1878-1950, Louisville, Ky.)—One of the greatest figures in the development of bands and band music in America, he served as President of the American Bandmasters' Association, which he helped found.

VLADIMIR GOLSCHMANN (1893-1972, Paris)—Long-time Conductor of the St. Louis Symphony and later Conductor of the Denver Symphony.

SIR GEORGE HENSCHEL (1850-1934, Breslau)—Conductor of the Boston Symphony and later Conductor of the Scottish Symphony. He became a Christian.

ELIAHU INBAL (1936- , Jerusalem)—A leading Israeli conductor with an international reputation.

JACOB A. JOSEPHSON (1818-1880, Stockholm)—An important Swedish conductor and composer who established the famed Uppsala Philharmonic Society.

ISTVAN KERTESZ (1929-1973, Budapest)—An outstanding talent, he was Musical Director of the Cologne Opera and simultaneously Conductor of the London Symphony.

OTTO KLEMPERER (b. 1885, Breslau)—Conductor of the Berlin State Opera until the rise of Hitler, he later served as Director of the Los Angeles Philharmonic and the Pittsburgh Symphony, and then became Musical Director of the Budapest Opera. He is considered one of the outstanding conductors of the 20th century.

ANDRE KOSTELANETZ (1901- , St. Petersburg)—One of the most widely acclaimed conductors of his generation.

SERGE KOUSSEVITZKY (1874-1951, Tver, Russia)—The famed Musical Director of the Boston Symphony, he established the concert series at Tanglewood and served as President of the Berkshire Music Center. His contribution to American classical music is incalculable.

JOSEF KRIPS (1902- , Vienna)—Became Conductor of the London Symphony after serving as Conductor for the Vienna State Opera.

ERICH LEINSDORF (1912- , Vienna)—The famed Conductor of the Boston Symphony and the New York Metropolitan Opera.

HERMANN LEVI (1839-1900, Giessen, Germany)—The brilliant Conductor of the Royal Munich Opera.

JAMES LEVINE (1943- , Cincinnati)—The brilliant young Director of the New York Metropolitan Opera.

WALTER BURLE MARX (1902- , Sao Paulo)—Conductor and founder of the Rio de Janeiro Philharmonic.

PIERRE MONTEUX (1875-1964, Paris)—One of the premier conductors of his time, he held the baton at the Boston Symphony, the New York Metropolitan, and the San Francisco Symphony.

FELIX J. MOTTL (1856-1911, Vienna)—Was Conductor of the Munich Opera and a noted composer.

EUGENE ORMANDY (1899- , Budapest)—The famed Conductor of the Philadelphia Philharmonic.

EGON POLLACK (1879-1933, Prague)—Conductor of the Hamburg Opera, 1917-1932.

ANDRE PREVIN (1929- , Berlin)—Born George Previn. Widely considered one of America's outstanding conductors, he won several Academy Awards for his film music before becoming Conductor of the Pittsburgh Symphony.

EVE QUELER (1936- , New York City)—One of the very few women conductors in the U.S., and considered one of the best.

FRITZ REINER (1888-1963, Budapest)—The famed Conductor of the Chicago Symphony, he had previously been Conductor at the Met.

JOSEPH ROSENSTOCK (b. 1895, Cracow, Poland)—Most recently with the Met, he had earlier served as Musical Director of the Cologne Opera.

MANUEL ROSENTHAL (1904- , Paris)—A fine talent, he was Conductor of the Seattle Symphony for several years.

ARTUR RODZINSKY (1892-1958, Split, Dalmatia)—Conductor of the New York Philharmonic, 1943-1947.

MAX RUDOLF (1902- , Frankfurt)—Conductor of the Cincinnati Symphony, 1958-1970.

SIR LANDON R. RUSSELL (1873-1938, London)—A leading British conductor of his generation.

KURT SANDERLING (1912- , Germany)—Codirector of the Leningrad Philharmonic for almost 20 years, he later became the Conductor of the Berlin (East Germany) Symphony.

RUDOLF SCHWARZ (1905- , Vienna)—Chief Conductor of the B.B.C. Symphony in the late 1950s and early '60s.

FABIEN SEVITZKY (1893-1967, Vichny-Volotchok, Russia)—Conductor of the Indianapolis Symphony for more than 20 years.

LEONARD SLATKIN—Conductor of the New Orleans Philharmonic.

SIR GEORG SOLTI (1912- , Budapest)—Musical Director of Covent Garden, 1961-1969, he became Conductor of the Chicago Symphony and the Paris Symphony.

TOSSY SPIVAKOVSKY (1907- , Odessa)—Conductor of the Berlin Philharmonic.

WILLIAM STEINBERG (1899-1978, Cologne)—Director and Chief Conductor for a number of distinguished orchestras, including the Buffalo Philharmonic, the Pittsburgh Symphony, and most recently, the Boston Symphony.

JULIUS STERN (1820-1883)—Conductor of the Berlin Symphony in the late 1860s.

JOSEPH STRANSKY (1872-1936, Humpolec, Bohemia)—A noted Conductor of the New York Philharmonic and the New York State Symphony.

WALTER SUSSKIND (1913- , Czechoslovakia)—Conductor of the Cincinnati Symphony.

GEORGE SZELL (1897-1970, Budapest)—The great Conductor of the Berlin State Opera and later of the Metropolitan and the Cleveland Philharmonic.

MICHAEL TILSON THOMAS (1944- , Hollywood)—The young genius who served as Conductor of the Buffalo Philharmonic in 1971 after winning the Koussevitzky Prize.

ARNOLD VOLPE (1869-1940, Kovno, Lithuania)—Conductor of the University of Miami Symphony for almost 15 years.

ALFRED WALLENSTEIN (1898- , Chicago)—A noted cellist with the New York Philharmonic, he became Conductor of the Los Angeles Philharmonic and Musical Director of the Hollywood Bowl.

BRUNO WALTER (1876-1962, Berlin)—Conductor of the New York Philharmonic after World War II, he had been Director of the Munich Opera before the rise of Hitler.

ALBERT L. WOLFF (b. 1884, Paris)—Conductor of the famed Opéra Comique in Paris before World War I, he later served as Musical Director of the Théâtre des Champs Elysées.

PIANISTS

CHARLES ALKAN (1813-1888, France)—Born Morhange. An excellent composer whose work has recently enjoyed renewed popularity and respect, he stopped playing at the height of his powers.

VLADIMIR D. ASHKENAZY (1937- , Russia)—One of the world's leading pianists and winner of several major competitions, he has been performing since he was six.

VICTOR BABIN (1908-1972, Moscow)—A noted composer as well as a pianist.

FANNY BLOOMFIELD-ZEISLER (1863-1927, Vienna)—She toured all over the world and amazed audiences wherever she went.

JACOB BLUMENTHAL (1829-1908, Hamburg, Germany)—Performed regularly for the court of Queen Victoria of Great Britain.

ALEXANDER BOROVSKY (b. 1889)—An excellent soloist, he performed all over the world.

ALEXANDER BRAILOWSKY (1896-1976, Russia)—Concert pianist.

JOHN BROWNING (1933- , Denver)—A famed soloist and winner of the 1954 Steinway Centennial Award.

IGNAZ BRUELL (1846-1907, Prossnitz, Moravia)—One of the leading concert pianists at the turn of the century.

ABRAHAM CHASINS (1903- , New York City)—An outstanding composer as well as a pianist.

SHURA CHERKASSKY (1911- , Odessa, Russia)—A world-renowned pianist, still in demand.

HARRIET COHEN (1901-1967)—Considered the finest pianist of her generation in Great Britain.

MISHA DICHTER (1945- , Shanghai)—One of the top young pianists, he nearly won the 1966 Tchaikovsky Competition.

LEON FLEISHER (1928- , San Francisco)—A leading pianist and the winner of important international competitions, he later conducted the Annapolis Symphony.

OSIP S. GABRIELOVITCH (1878-1936, St. Petersburg, Russia)—A pianist of international stature, he was better known as the husband of Mark Twain's daughter, Clara, and Conductor of the Detroit and Philadelphia Symphony Orchestras.

EMIL G. GILELS (1916- , Odessa, Russia)—The greatest contemporary

Soviet pianist, he was awarded both the Lenin and Stalin prizes.

LEOPOLD GODOWSKY (1870-1938, Soshly, Lithuania)—A leading pianist of international repute.

GARY GRAFFMAN (1928-   , New York City)—One of the finest pianists in the U.S.

MARK HAMBOURG (1879-1960, Russia)—A world-renowned virtuoso.

CLARA HASKIL (1895-1960, Bucharest)—A world-renowned pianist. A major international prize carries her name.

STEPHEN HELLER (1813-1888, Budapest)—Famous as a pianist and for his numerous compositions for piano.

DAME MYRA HESS (1890-1956)—The great virtuoso performer who was one of the finest women pianists in history.

VLADIMIR HOROVITZ (1904-   , Kiev, Russia)—The master who stopped playing for a long time and then made a spectacular return. He is probably the best-known pianist in the world.

ERICH I. KAHN (1905-1956, Germany)—A specialist in chamber music, he was also a noteworthy composer.

JOSEPH KALICHSTEIN (1946-   , Tel Aviv)—Winner of the 1969 Leventritt Award, he is one of the leading young pianists in the world.

MINDRU KATZ (1925-   , Bucharest)—An Israeli and the winner of several major piano competitions.

LOUIS KENTNER (1905-   , Karwin, Galicia)—A prominent concert pianist.

LEO KESTENBERG (1882-1962, Rozsahegy, Hungary)—A prominent music educator (he was responsible for "Kestenberg-Reform" movement), he was also an excellent pianist.

WANDA LANDOWSKA (1877-1959, Warsaw)—Her wonderful Baroque technique made her and the harpsichord familiar to a modern audience.

MISCHA LEVITSKY (1898-1941, Kremenchug, Russia)—Renowned for his renditions of Chopin, he performed all over the world.

LAZARE LEVY (1882-1964, Brussels)—An internationally known concert soloist.

RAYMOND LEWENTHAL (1926-   , San Antonio, Tex.)—Badly injured when mugged (in New York, where else?), he made a remarkable comeback against great odds.

JOSEF LHEVINNE (1874-1944, Orel, Russia)—One of the world's finest pianists at the turn of the century.

BENNO MOISEIWITSCH (1890-1963, Odessa, Russia)—One of the great interpreters of Chopin.

MORITZ MOSZKOWSKI (1854-1925, Breslau)—A major concert performer.

MURRAY PERAHIA (1947-   , New York City)—He became a major figure after winning the Leeds International Competition in 1972.

MICHAEL ROLL (1946-   , Leeds, England)—Won the Leeds International Competition and is one of the finest young pianists in Great Britain.

MORIZ ROSENTHAL (1862-1946, Lvov)—An internationally known pianist who had a long and successful career.

ANTON RUBINSTEIN (1829-1894, Vyjgvatinetz, Podolia)—One of the great pianists of the 19th century, and one of the most famous. His technique established new standards that have rarely been equaled.

ARTUR RUBINSTEIN (b. 1886, Lodz, Poland)—One of the great pianists of the 20th century.

PNINA SALZMAN (1922-   , Tel Aviv)—An internationally acclaimed Israeli virtuoso.

HAROLD SAMUEL (1879-1937, London)—Known all over the world for his expertise on and interpretations of Bach.

ARTUR SCHNABEL (1882-1951, Lipnik, Moravia)—A leading concert performer, he was also a noted teacher and a famed child prodigy.

JULIUS SCHULHOFF (1825-1898, Prague)—A noted 19th-century concert pianist and composer.

RUDOLF SERKIN (1903- , Eger, Germany)—One of the greatest all-around talents in the world for decades, his repertoire is incredibly extensive.

SOLOMON (1902- , London)—One of the great British pianists. His full name is Solomon Cutner.

KARL TAUSIG (1841-1871, Warsaw)—One of the greatest technical virtuosos of the 19th century.

SIGISMUND THALBERG (1812-1871, Geneva)—Quite possibly the finest virtuoso of the first half of the 19th century.

ROSALYN TURECK (1914- , Chicago)—One of the great interpreters of Bach and one of the finest concert pianists in the world.

CESARE VALABREGA (1898-1965, Pesaro, Italy)—A great Italian master who had an international reputation.

ALEXIS WEISSENBERG (1929- , Sofia, Bulgaria)—One of the strongest contemporary performers, he has appeared all over the world.

PAUL WITTGENSTEIN (1887-1961, Vienna)—A famous one-armed pianist. (He lost an arm in World War I.)

VIOLINISTS

LICCO AMAR (1891-1959, Budapest)—A fine violinist, he was the Berlin Philharmonic's Concertmaster, 1915–1920.

LEOPOLD AUER (1845-1930, Veszprem, Hungary)—The outstanding violin teacher of his generation (Heifetz and Milstein were among his students) and a great technician. He was baptized.

ADOLF BRODSKY (1851-1929, Taganrog, Russia)—Founder of the famous Brodsky Quartet and an internationally known performer.

FERDINAND DAVID (1810-1873, Hamburg)—The outstanding violin teacher before Auer.

MISCHA ELMAN (1891-1967, Talnove, Russia)—Acknowledged as one of the world's finest violinists.

CARL FLESCH (1873-1944, Moson, Hungary)—A leading violinist and a noted teacher.

MIRIAM FRIED (1946- , Rumania)—An Israeli, she won several important violin competitions and is considered one of the leading female violinists in the world.

IDA HAENDEL (1924- , Chelm, Poland)—One of the major female violinists of the current generation, she has performed all over the world.

EMIL HAUSER (1893- , Budapest)—The famous founder of the equally famous Budapest String Quartet.

GUSTAV HOLLAENDER (1855-1915)—A leading violinist of the late 1800s.

JASCHA HEIFETZ (1901- , Vilna, Lithuania)—The great virtuoso who became world-famous.

BRONISLAW HUBERMAN (1882-1947, Czestochowa, Poland)—A star from the time he was a child.

JOSEPH JOACHIM (1831-1907)—One of the major violinists and teachers of the 19th century (many would argue that he was *the* greatest).

LEONID B. KOGAN (1924- , Dniepropetrovsk, U.S.S.R.)—One of the two or three leading violinists in the Soviet Union and the recipient of the Lenin Prize.

RUDOLF KOLISCH (1896- , Klamm, Austria)—A noted violinist who directed the Pro Arte Quartet.

YEHUDI MENUHIN (1916- , New York City)—The great child prodigy who became one of the premier soloists of all time.

NATHAN MILSTEIN (1904- , Odessa, Russia)—Another great child prodigy and soloist.

TIVADAR NACHEZ (1859-1930, Pest, Hungary)—Born Theodor Naschitz. A leading violinist with an international reputation.

DAVID F. OISTRAKH (1908-1974, Odessa, Russia)—The greatest Soviet violinist of all time and a master of technique.

MICHAEL RABIN (1937-1972)—One of America's leading young violin virtuosos before his untimely death.

EDUARD REMENY (1830-1898, Heves, Hungary)—Born Hoffman. One of the most unusual and innovative performers of his generation.

ALEXANDER SCHNEIDER (1908-)—A brilliant soloist, he was one of the most famous members of the Budapest String Quartet.

ISAAC STERN (1920- , Kremenetz, U.S.S.R)—The internationally famous star who provided the violin music in *Fiddler on the Roof.* He was a child prodigy.

HENRYK SZERYING (1918- , Warsaw)—An underrated virtuoso.

JOSEPH SZIGETI (1892- , Budapest)—The internationally known virtuoso who has thrilled audiences since he was seven.

HENRI TEMIANKA (1906- , Greenock, Scotland)—The internationally famous soloist who starred with the Paganini Quartet for over 20 years.

LIONEL TERTIS (b. 1876, Great Britain)—Perhaps the most famous violist of all time.

HENRI WIENIAWSKI (1834-1880, Lublin, Poland)—A master of technique, he served as the personal soloist of the Czar.

EFREM ZIMBALIST (b. 1889, Rostov-on-Don, Russia)—A leading violinist with an international reputation. He became a Christian.

PINCHAS ZUCKERMAN (1948- , Israel)—An outstanding violinist, he also was Conductor of the Utah Symphony.

PAUL ZUKOFSKY (1943- , Brooklyn)—Yet another child prodigy and one of the most distinctive violinists in the world.

CELLISTS

KARL DAVYDOV—(1838-1889, Goldingen, Courland)—Born Davidhof. A noted performer who is credited with starting the first cello academy in Russia.

JACQUELINE DU PRÉ (1945- , Oxford, England)—The great cello soloist who converted to Judaism when she married Daniel Barenboim.

EMANUEL FEUERMANN (1902-1942, Kolomea, Galicia)—A great talent who died prematurely. He was an internationally famous cellist, quite possibly one of the greatest in history.

GREGOR PIATIGORSKY (1903-1976, Yekaterinoslav, Russia)—A wonderful cellist with the Berlin Philharmonic, he was also a leading chess patron.

DAVID POPPER (1843-1913)—A leading soloist and composer for the cello.

LEONARD ROSE (1918- , Washington, D.C.)—One of the greatest contemporary cellists.

CLASSICAL AND OPERA SINGERS

MARIO ANCONA (1860-1931, Leghorn, Italy)—A leading baritone with the Metropolitan Opera in the 1890s.

RAFAEL ARIE (1922- , Sofia, Bulgaria)—A world-famous basso, he has won many prizes and performed as a soloist throughout Europe and North America.

LUCIENNE BREVAL (1869-1935, Männedorf, Switzerland)—Born Berthe Schilling. A world-famous opera star for three decades.

ALMA GLUCK (1884-1938, Bucharest)—Born Reba Fiersohn. A great soprano of the Metropolitan Opera, she was active in the formal organization of musical performers in the U.S.

ALEXANDER KIPNIS (1891-1978, Zhitomir, Russia)—One of the greatest male singers in the history of opera, he was a regular with the Berlin State Opera before the rise of fascism. He was both a bass and a baritone during his long career.

NINA KOSHIETZ (1894-1965, Kiev, Russia)—A leading soprano.

EVELYN LEAR (1910-   , New York City)—The noted American soprano who has sung with several major opera companies in the U.S. and abroad.

ADELE LEIGH (1928-   , New York City)—An outstanding lyric soprano of the British stage.

EMANUEL LIST (1891-1967, Vienna)—A prominent performer with the New York Metropolitan.

GEORGE LONDON (1920-   , Montreal)—One of the great bass-baritones of the 20th century, he became an important administrator, serving with the John F. Kennedy Center for the Performing Arts and as Director of the Los Angeles Opera Association.

PAULINE LUCCA (1841-1908, Vienna)—One of the great opera singers of the late 19th century, she excelled as Carmen.

ELAINE MALBIN (1932-   , New York City)—An outstanding American opera singer.

MARGARETE MATZENAUER (1881-1963, Temesvar, Hungary)—A noted contralto and soprano who performed all over Europe.

MIKHAIL MEDVEDEV (1852-1925)—Born Meyer Y. Bernstein. One of the great Russian opera stars at the turn of the century, he performed at the Bolshoi and for the St. Petersburg Imperial Opera Company.

ROBERT MERRILL (1917-   , New York City)—The great baritone of the Metropolitan and one of the leading singers in the U.S., he may have been responsible for the Yankees winning the 1978 World Series, since they won when he sang the national anthem.

OTTILIE METZGER (1878-1943, Frankfurt)—A foremost dramatic singer, she was a contralto.

GUIDITTA PASTA (1798-1865, Saronno, Lombardy)—One of the great sopranos of her time.

ROSA PAULY (b. 1894, Eperies, Hungary)—Born Rose Pollak. A wonderful soprano.

JAN PEERCE (1904-   , New York City)—Born Jacob Perelmuth. Became one of America's great operatic tenors and performed regularly for the Metropolitan.

ROBERTA PETERS (1930-   , New York City)—Born Peterman. A leading opera singer and performer of classical music.

REGINA RESNIK (1921-   , New York City)—One of the most famous Carmens of all time, she was a mezzo-soprano at the New York Metropolitan.

JOSEPH SCHMIDT (1904-1942, Davideni, Bukovina)—A celebrated operetta singer before World War II and a recording star in Europe.

LOTTE SCHOENE (b. 1891, Vienna)—Born Charlotte Bodenstein. A leading soprano.

FREDRICH SCHORR (1888-1953, Nagyvarad, Hungary)—A bass-baritone who starred at the Met, he specialized in Wagner.

BEVERLY SILLS (1929-   , New York City)—Born Belle Silverman. One of the world's leading operatic sopranos.

RICHARD TAUBER (1892-1948, Linz, Austria)—A very famous operetta star before World War II.

JENNIE TOUREL (1910-1973, Montreal)—The star mezzo-soprano of the Metropolitan.

RICHARD TUCKER (1914-1975, New York City)—The amazing lyric tenor of the Metropolitan.

OTHER FIGURES IN CLASSICAL MUSIC

LARRY ADLER (1914-   , Baltimore)—Without question the finest harmonica virtuoso in history. He was persecuted during the McCarthy era and spent a large portion of this career outside of the U.S.

SIMEON BELLISON (1881-1953)—The famed clarinetist of the New York Philharmonic.

HENRICH CONRIED (1848-1909, Austria)—Born Cohn. Manager of the Metropolitan Opera after the turn of the century.

RUBIN GOLDMARK (1872-1936)—The famed Professor of Composition at the Juilliard School of Music who trained a generation of composers.

HERBERT GRAF (1904-1973, Vienna)—One of the leading producers and administrators of operas and opera companies of the 20th century.

REYNALDO HAHN (1875-1947, Caracas, Venezuela)—The famous music critic of the newspaper *Le Figaro,* he later became the chief administrator of the Paris Opera.

OTTO H. KAHN (1867-1934, Mannheim, Germany)—Onetime Chairman of the Board and President of the Metropolitan.

ROBERT LEVIN (1912-   , Norway)—Rector of the Norwegian Academy of Music in the 1970s.

JULIUS RUDEL (1921-   , Vienna)—The noted Musical Director of the New York City Opera, he later held the same position at the Kennedy Center for the Performing Arts.

POPULAR MUSIC COMPOSERS AND LYRICISTS

See also Musical Comedy Figures; Composers of Film Scores.

DAVID ARKIN (1906-   , New York City)—A noted painter as well as a songwriter, his "Black and White" (as recorded by Three Dog Night) was a number one song in 1973.

BURT BACHARACH—*See* Rock, Pop, and Folk Artists.

IRVING BERLIN (1888-   , Kirghizia, Russia)—Born Baline. The tremendously prolific songwriter who wrote "God Bless America," the music for shows such as *Call Me Madam* and standards like "Alexander's Ragtime Band," and became a legend in his own time.

LEW BROWN (1893-1958, Odessa, Russia)—Born Louis Brownstein. A member of the songwriting team of Da Sylva, Brown, and Henderson, who turned out many hits of the 1920s—"The Birth of the Blues," "Sonny Boy," and "The Best Things in Life Are Free," to name a few. He was a cousin of Leon Trotsky.

SAMMY CAHN (1913-   )—The wonderful lyricist who often worked with Jimmy Van Heusen, he won Academy Awards for "Call Me Irresponsible," "High Hopes," and "Three Coins in the Fountain."

CY COLEMAN (1929-   )—Born Seymour Kaufman. Wrote "Hey, Look Me Over" and the music for a number of Broadway shows.

GEORGE GERSHWIN (1898-1937, New York City)—Born Jacob Gershvin. The enormous talent who left us *Porgy and Bess, An American in Paris, Rhapsody in Blue,* "Swanee," and many other gifts.

IRA GERSHWIN (b. 1896)—A noted lyricist and the brother of George Gershwin.

OSCAR HAMMERSTEIN II (1895-1960, Doylestown, Pa.)—The great librettist who with various partners, often Richard Rodgers, gave us such musicals as *Oklahoma, South Pacific, The King and I, Show Boat, Rose Marie,* and many others.

YIP HARBURG (1898-   )—Won Academy Awards for "Happiness Is a Thing Called Joe" and "Over the Rainbow" (he was the lyricist for *The Wizard of Oz),* and wrote the great "Brother, Can You Spare a Dime?" One of the great figures in American popular music, he was still going strong in the late 1970s.

LORENZ HART (1895-1943, New York City)—The tormented talent who worked with Richard Rodgers on *Pal Joey* and *The Boys from Syracuse.*

JEROME KERN (1885-1945, New York City)—Produced at least 1,000 songs for movies and the stage, the best known of which are "Smoke Gets in Your Eyes" and "Ol' Man River."

BURTON LANE (1912-   , New York City)—Born Burt Levy. A leading composer of popular music and coauthor of "On a Clear Day You Can See Forever."

ALAN JAY LERNER (1918-   , New York City)—The wonderful lyricist who helped give us such shows and films as *Paint Your Wagon, My Fair Lady, Camelot,* and *An American in Paris.* He usually worked with Frederick Loewe.

FRANK LOESSER (1910-   , New York City)—A leading popular composer, he wrote *Guys and Dolls* and *How to Succeed in Business without Really Trying,* and he won the New York Drama Critics' Award several times. Among his famous songs was "Praise the Lord and Pass the Ammunition."

FREDERICK LOEWE (1901-   , Vienna)—The composer who worked with Alan Jay Lerner on the shows mentioned above and on many others.

RICHARD RODGERS (1902-   , New York)—One of America's most honored composers, his work with Oscar Hammerstein II will live forever. His shows include *Carousel, South Pacific, The King and I,* and *Annie Get Your Gun.* It should also be remembered that he wrote the beautiful score for *Victory at Sea.*

STEPHEN SONDHEIM (1930-   , New York City)—One of the biggest names among contemporary composers.

KURT WEILL (1900-1950, Dessau, Germany)—The noted composer of light operas and Broadway shows who wrote *One Touch of Venus, Knickerbocker Holiday, The Threepenny Opera,* and many others.

ROCK, POP, AND FOLK ARTISTS (AND OTHERS)

HERB ALPERT (1935-   , Los Angeles)—His "Tijuana Brass" sound made him famous. He is also a gifted composer and an important record company executive.

ED AMES (1929-   , Boston)—The most famous of the singing Ames Brothers, he had hit singles and a good part as an Indian on TV's *Daniel Boone.*

BURT BACHARACH (1928-   , Kansas City, Mo.)—One of America's leading songwriters (along with Hal David, with whom he used to work regularly), with tunes like "Raindrops Keep Fallin' on My Head," "Alfie," and "The Look of Love."

THEODORE BIKEL—*See* Entertainers.

MIKE BLOOMFIELD (1942-   , Chicago)—One of the leading rock guitarists in the business, he also led the influential Electric Flag rock group.

DAVID BLUE (1941-   )—Born David Cohen. A talented singer and composer.

GEORGIA BROWN (1933-   )—Born Lillian Klot. A leading British singer and also an excellent actress.

LEONARD COHEN (1934-   , Montreal)—One of the premier songwriters and singers. His "Suzanne" was a popular song of the 1960s. Also a poet and novelist, his book *Beautiful Losers* is excellent.

HAL DAVID (1921-   , New York City)—A top lyricist best known for his collaborations with Burt Bacharach.

SAMMY DAVIS, JR.—*See* Entertainers.

NEIL DIAMOND (1941-   , Brooklyn)—A top singer/songwriter of the contemporary pop music scene, and one of the most original.

BOB DYLAN (1941-   , Duluth, Minn.)—Born Robert Zimmerman. Became a legend in his own time and the major figure in folk rock music in the world. His protest songs of the 1960s inspired millions of young (and not so young) people.

CASS ELLIOT (1941-1974, Baltimore)—Born Ellen Cohen. Sang with the Mamas and the Papas and as a single before her accidental death.

BRIAN EPSTEIN (1934-1967, England)—His managing of the Beatles brought him fame and wealth and helped to revolutionize popular music.

ALAN FREED (1922-1965, Johnstown, Pa.)—One of the most important disc jockeys in the history of rock 'n' roll, he helped to establish the form in the U.S.

ART GARFUNKEL (1941-   , Newark)—With Paul Simon, one of the most effective and popular duos of all time. He later had hit records on his own and became an actor *(Carnal Knowledge)*.

EDDIE FISHER (1928-   , Philadelphia)—One of the leading pop singers in the U.S.

GEORGIA GIBBS (1926-   , Worchester, Mass.)—Born Fredda Lipson. Had hit songs in the 1950s ("Rock with Me Henry" and others) by "covering" songs by Black rhythm and blues artists.

GERRY GOFFIN (1939-   , Queens)—A leading songwriter, he often worked with Carole King.

EYDIE GORME (1932-   , Bronx)—Had a number of hits and is a leading nightclub performer with her husband, Steve Lawrence.

LOU GOTTLIEB (1923-   , Los Angeles)—The bass player with the Limelighters, one of the leading folk groups of the 1960s.

ARLO GUTHRIE (1947-   , New York City)—A leading folk-rock singer ("Alice's Restaurant"), he is the son of the famed Woody Guthrie and a Jewish mother. He reputedly had a folk-song bar mitzvah.

JANIS IAN (1950-   , New York City)—Born Fink. Had a number of highly original hit songs with considerable social content, including "Society's Child" and "At Seventeen."

KITTY KALLEN (1926-   , Philadelphia)—The lovely singer who had several major hits, including "Little Things Mean a Lot."

MURRAY KAUFMAN—Known as Murray the "K," he was the top disc jockey in New York.

LAINIE KAZAN (1940-   , New York City)—A leading night club singer.

CAROLE KING (1938-   , Brooklyn)—Born Klein. A leading rock songwriter of the 1950s and '60s, she is now a very successful singer as well. As a songwriter, she worked with Gerry Goffin, Jerry Leiber, and Mike Stoller.

AL KOOPER (1944-   , Brooklyn)—A top songwriter, he became one of the most influential record producers in the U.S.

TULI KUPFERBERG (1923- , New York City)—Cofounder of the incredible singing group the Fugs. His songs, such as "Nothin," had a wide following in the 1960s.

STEVE LAWRENCE (1935- , Brooklyn)—Born Sidney Liebowitz. One of the leading popular singers in America and with his wife, Eydie Gorme, a leading nightclub act.

JERRY LEIBER (1933- , Baltimore)—With Carole King and Mike Stoller, he wrote many of the top rock hits of the 1950s, including "Kansas City" and "Hound Dog."

GARY LEWIS (1945- , Los Angeles)—Son of Jerry Lewis, his group, Gary Lewis and the Playboys, had several top-ten hits in the 1960s, and he was chosen as the top male singer of 1966.

GODDARD LIEBERSON (1911- , Hanley, England)—Served as President of the Record Industry Association and was President of Columbia Records.

ENRICO MACIAS (1938- , Constantine, Algeria)—The leading male pop singer in France.

BARRY MANILOW (1946- , Brooklyn)—One of the leading pop singers in the U.S., and one of the most creative.

TONY MARTIN (1913- , San Francisco)—Born Alvin Morris. A major singing star before the rock era. He also acted.

BETTE MIDLER (1945- , Paterson, N.J.)—A fabulous entertainer, she is one of the most versatile singers in the business. She grew up in Hawaii.

MITCH MILLER (1911- , Rochester, N.Y.)—Millions of people sang along with Mitch each week on TV.

OLIVIA NEWTON-JOHN (1947- , Cambridge, England)—The very popular singer is the granddaughter of the Nobel Laureate Max Born.

PHIL OCHS (1941-1976, El Paso, Tex.)—One of the foremost protest singers and composers ("I Ain't Marching Anymore" and many others) in folk music of the mid-1960s. He lived in the shadow of the young Bob Dylan, and never received the recognition due him. He died by suicide.

DOC POMUS (1925- , Brooklyn)—With Mort Shuman, he wrote some of the biggest hits in the history of rock 'n' roll, including "Young Love" and "Teenager in Love."

EMPEROR ROSKO (1936-)—Born Mike Pasternak. A leading disc jockey in Great Britain.

NEIL SEDAKA (1939- , Brooklyn)—One of the top songwriter/singers in the U.S., he is still turning out hits.

MORT SHUMAN (1936- , New York City)—Writer of hit songs with Doc Pomus.

IRWIN SILBER (1925- , New York City)—Editor of *Sing Out!*, the leading publication devoted to folk music in the U.S.

CARLY SIMON (1945- , New York City)—One of the leading female singers in the U.S.

PAUL SIMON (1941- , New York City)—The songwriting half of Simon and Garfunkel, he has continued to be successful since they decided to go their own ways. He is regarded as one of the most talented and influential performers in contemporary popular music.

MAYNARD SOLOMON (1930- , New York City)—Cofounder of Vanguard Records, one of the most important folk and pop labels in the country.

PHIL SPECTOR (1940- , Bronx)—One of the leading record producers in the U.S., he discovered and developed many stars.

MIKE STOLLER (1933- , New York City)—With Jerry Leiber, wrote many hits and scored a number of Elvis Presley films.

BARBRA STREISAND—*See* Film Stars.

LOUIS TEICHER (b. Wilkes Barre, Pa.)—Teamed with Arthur Ferrante to form a very successful piano duo. Some of their hits were "Theme from *The Apartment*" and "Tonight."

JAZZ PERFORMERS

LEE ABRAMS (1925-)—A leading jazz drummer.

RAY ABRAMS (1920-)—A fine jazz saxophonist.

BARRY ALTSCHUL (1943- , Bronx)—The noted drummer.

DAVID AXELROD (1936- , Los Angeles)—An important jazz producer and composer.

LEONARD (RED) BALABAN (1929- , Chicago)—A noted bass player who also sings. He is the son of theatre magnate Barney Balaban.

TEDDY CHARLES (1928-)—Born Theodore Cohen. One of the leading exponents of the vibes.

ALVIN G. COHN (1925- , Brooklyn)—Tenor sax player and composer, he is a leading Broadway arranger.

ALBERT M. DROOTIN (1916- , Boston)—One of the leading clarinetists in the 1940s and '50s.

BENJAMIN DROOTIN (1920- , Russia)—A top drummer.

ZIGGY ELMAN (1914-1968)—Born Harry Finkleman. Led one of the best of the big bands.

VICTOR S. FELDMAN (1934- , London)—A leading performer on piano and vibes, he is also an outstanding composer.

JERRY FIELDING (1922-)—Born Gerald Feldman. A leading jazz composer.

ARNOLD FISHKIN (1919-)—Born Fishkind. One of the best base players in all of jazz.

DAVID FRIEDMAN (1944- , New York City)—One of the leading vibraphone players in the country.

HERB GELLER (1928- , Los Angeles)—Alto sax player, he is also a composer.

STAN GETZ (1927- , Philadelphia)—One of the greatest tenor saxophonists of all time and one courageous man.

TERRY GIBBS (1924- , Brooklyn)—Born Julius Gubenko. Widely considered to be one of the greatest vibraphonists of all time.

BENNY GOODMAN (1909- , Chicago)—The world-famous King of Swing and the best known clarinetist in the world. His positive role in race relations has been largely ignored.

STEVEN GROSSMAN (1951- , Brooklyn)—A top sax man.

MORT HERBERT (1925-)—Born Pelovitz. A leading jazz performer.

ART HODES (1904- , Nikoliev, Russia)—One of the top jazz pianists for many years, he won an Emmy.

MARTY HOLMES (1925-)—Born Hausman. A noted jazz musician.

PAUL HORN (1930- , New York City)—A top flutist who also plays other instruments, he is also a composer.

DAVID HOROWITZ (1942- , Brooklyn)—Best known for his work with the synthesizer, he is also a fine jazz pianist.

MAX KAMINSKY (1908- , Brockton, Mass.)—A long-time and very good trumpet man.

DICK KATZ (1924- , Baltimore)—Piano player and composer, he is also a noted jazz scholar.

MOE KOFFMAN (1928- , Toronto)—One of the top flute players for many years.

ROMAN KUNSMAN (1941- , Kuibishev, U.S.S.R.)—One of the best sax players in the Soviet Union, he emigrated to Israel in 1970.

ARNIE LAWRENCE (1938- , Brooklyn)—Born Arnold L. Finkelstein. A big-time saxophone player.

MARC L. LEVIN (1942- , Bayonne, N.J.)—An excellent cornet man.

ALAN LEVITT (1932- , New York City)—A noted drummer.

HANK LEVY (1927- , Baltimore)—One of the leading jazz composers.

LOU LEVY (1928- , Chicago)—A fine pianist, he worked with Ella Fitzgerald for many years.

MEL LEWIS (1929- , Buffalo)—Born Mel Sokoloff. A great jazz drummer.

DAVE LIEBMAN (1946- , Brooklyn)—A solid sax man, he also plays the flute.

HARVEY MANDEL (1945- , Detroit)—A top jazz guitarist.

SHELLY MANN (1920- , New York City)—The well-known drummer and composer.

HERBIE MANN (1930- , Brooklyn)—Born Herbert Solomon. One of the best-known jazz flutists in America.

STEVE MARCUS (1939- , New York City)—A leading saxophonist.

MEZZ MEZZROW (1899-1972, Chicago)—Born Milton Mesirow. A major exponent of New Orleans jazz, and an interesting clarinetist.

BUDDY MORROW (1919-)—Born Muni Zudekoff. At one time the leading jazz trombonist in the world.

ABE MOST (1920- , New York City)—A top clarinetist.

BEN POLLACK (1903-1971, Chicago)—Had one of the top bands for many years and was an outstanding drummer. He took his own life.

BUDDY RICH (1917- , Brooklyn)—One of the all-time great drummers, he is still terrific.

JOSHUA RIFKIN (1944- , New York City)—One of the great interpreters of Scott Joplin.

ROD RODNEY (1927-)—Born Robert Chudnick. A leading jazz trumpeter.

JOE SAYE (1923-)—Born Shulman. A leading jazz pianist in Britain.

IRA SCHULMAN (1926- , Newark)—One of the great all-around musicians.

BERNIE SENENSKY (1944- , Winnipeg)—A solid pianist and a talented composer.

ARTIE SHAW (1910- , New York City)—Born Arthur Arshawsky. The often-married band leader and clarinetist.

HANK SHAW (1926-)—Born Henry Shalofsky. A noted jazz trumpet player.

MICKEY SHEEN (1927-)—Born Milton Scheinblum. One of the finest jazz drummers in the U.S.

EDDIE SHU (1918-)—Born Edward Shulman. A great all-around jazz performer.

PHOEBE SNOW (1952- , Teaneck, N.J.)—Born Laub. One of the best jazz and popular singers.

LEW SOLOFF (1944- , New York City)—One of the very best trumpet players around.

DICK SUTTON (1928-)—Born Schwartz. An important jazz composer as well as a fine trumpet player.

HARVIE SWARTZ (1948- , Chelsea, Mass.)—A top bass player and composer.

ALEXANDER TSFASSMAN (1906-1971, Zaporozhe, Russia)—Was Director of the Jazz Orchestra of Radio Moscow and fought a lifetime struggle to get jazz accepted in the Soviet Union.

RUTH KOMANOFF UNDERWOOD (1946- , New York City)—A fine percussionist and marimba player who worked with the Mothers of Invention.

JERRY WALD (1919- , Newark)—Led a good big band in the swing era and was a fine clarinetist.

GEORGE T. WEIN (1925- , Boston)—The famous producer of the Newport Jazz Festival.

SOL YAGED (1922- , Brooklyn)—A noted clarinetist.

DENNY ZEITLIN (1938- , Chicago)—A top piano player and a well-known psychiatrist.

BARRY K. ZWEIG (1942- , Detroit)—One of the top jazz guitarists.

MICHAEL ZWERIN (1930- , New York City)—A trumpet player who was Jazz Critic for the *Village Voice* in the late 1960s.

ARTISTS

JULES ADLER (1865-1952)—A leading French realist painter, he specialized in scenes of industrial life.

SAMUEL M. ADLER (1898-)—A leading American symbolist painter.

YAACOV AGAM (1928- , Rishon le-Zion, Israel)—Born Gipstein. One of the most famous kinetic artists.

PIERRE ALECHINSKY (1927-)—A noted Belgian realist painter of the "Cobra" group.

JOHN H. AMSHEWITZ (1882-1942, Ramsgate, England)—One of the leading muralists in Great Britain.

MORDECAI ARDON (b. 1896, Tuchow, Poland)—Born Bronstein. An internationally known Israeli painter.

JEAN ATLAN (1913-1960, Constantine, Algeria)—One of the leading abstract painters in the world.

LEON BAKST (1867-1924, St. Petersburg)—Born Lev Rosenberg. Rediscovered, he is now considered to be an artistic genius of the first rank.

ROBERT BERENY (1887-1953, Budapest)—A widely acclaimed graphic artist.

PETER BLUME (1906- , Russia)—His often fantastic murals have brought him a large following in the U.S. and throughout the world.

AARON BOHROD (1907- , Chicago)—One of the leading American painters.

ISAAC BRODSKY (1884-1930, St. Petersburg)—The leading portrait painter in Russia, he did a famous one of Lenin.

JUDITH CASSAB (1920- , Australia)—A leading nonrepresentational painter.

MARC CHAGALL (1887-)—Born Segal. One of the most famous painters of the 20th century.

JACQUES CHAPIRO (b. 1887)—One of the leading members of the Paris school.

PAUL CITROEN (1896- , Berlin)—One of the leading painters in Holland, he specializes in pencil drawings.

JEAN DAVID (1908- , Bucharest)—A well-known Israeli graphic artist.

ENRICO DONATI (1909- , Milan)—One of the leading abstract painters in Italy.

BEDRICH FEIGL (1884-1966)—One of the most influential Czech artists of his generation.

ADOLF FENYES (1867-1945, Budapest)—A noted Hungarian painter.

BARNETT FREEDMAN (1901-1958, London)—One of the leading book illustrators in England, he also designed postage stamps.

OTTO FREUNDLICH (1878-1943)—A leading German painter and sculptor, he died in a German concentration camp.

MARK GERTLER (1891-1939, London)—A noted British artist. He took his own life.

RUTH GIKOW (1914- , Russia)—A noted graphic artist, she achieved a major reputation as a muralist.

MILTON GLASER—*See* Miscellaneous Awards.

ENRICO GLICENSTEIN (1870-1942, Turek, Poland)—A leading artist who excelled in printmaking and sculpture as well as painting.

GLUCK (1895- , London)—Born Gluckstein. One of the most interesting British artists, she dropped out of the British art scene for more than 30 years and did not reemerge until 1973.

ADOLPH GOTTLIEB (1903-1974)—One of the famous "Ten" Expressionist painters.

SOLOMON A. HART (1806-1881)—A member of the British Royal Academy and a noted artist.

JOSEF HERMAN (1911- , Warsaw)—A leading British realist painter.

LEOPOLD HOROVITZ (1838-1917, Slovakia)—A noted Hungarian portrait painter.

GERSHON ISKOWITZ (1921- , Poland)—A leading Canadian landscape painter.

ISAAC ISRAELS (1865-1934)—Famed for his paintings of urban scenes.

JOZEF ISRAELS (1824-1911, Groningen, Netherlands)—Among the most important Dutch painters of his time.

ERNST A. JOSEPHSON (1851-1906)—One of the great early anticipators of the Expressionist movement, he was a leading artist in Scandinavia.

ALFRED JUSTITZ (1879-1934, Nova Cerekev, Slovakia)—One of the most influential artists in Czechoslovakia.

LOUIS KAHAN (1915- , Vienna)—One of the leading portraitists in Australia.

HOWARD KANOVITZ (1929- , Fall River, Mass.)—One of the leading exponents of Photorealism in the U.S.

IVAN C. KARP (1926- , New York City)—Considered the father of pop art, he is the author of *Diibue Doo*, and Director of the Leo Castelli Gallery.

JIRI KARS (1882-1945, Kralupy, Bohemia)—Born Jiri Karpeles. A noted graphic artist. He took his own life.

FRANZ M. KEMPF (1928- , Melbourne)—A noted Australian artist.

WOLF KIBEL (1903-1938, Warsaw)—A leading artist in South Africa.

MICHEL KIKOINE (1891-1968, Gomel, Russia)—A noted French painter.

MOISE KISLING (1891-1953, Cracow, Poland)—An important French painter.

YVES KLEIN (1928-1962, Nice, France)—One of the leading New Realist painters.

FRANZ KLINE (1910-1962, Wilkes-Barre, Pa.)—An "action painter," now considered a major figure in American art.

HUGO KRAYN (1885-1919, Berlin)—One of the best German urban artists of his time.

MAURICIO LASANSKY (1913- , Buenos Aires)—One of the most important and influential figures in the graphic arts field and the inventor of the Lasansky method of color printing.

JACK LEVINE (1915- , Boston)—One of the leading realist painters in the U.S.

ISAAC I. LEVITAN (1861-1900, Wirballen, Lithuania)—One of the greatest landscape painters in Russia in the 19th century.

JAN LE WITT (1907- , Czestochowa, Poland)—A leading graphic artist.

SOL LE WITT (1928- , Hartford, Conn.)—Sculptor and conceptual artist.

MAX LIEBERMANN (1847-1935, Berlin)—A noted painter and President of the Academy of Art in Berlin.

LILIAN LIJN (1939- , New York City)—A leading American kinetic artist.

EL(EAZER) LISSITZKY (1890-1941, Russia)—A highly underrated and influential figure in 20th century art, he was a painter, draftsman, and printmaker.

MANE-KATZ (1894-1962, Kremenchug, Russia)—Became one of the leading French painters. His work is still highly regarded.

LOUIS MARCOUSSIS (1883-1941, Warsaw)—Born Marcous. A French painter famed for his engravings.

LUDWIG MEIDNER (1884-1966)—A leading Expressionist painter of Europe.

AMEDEO MODIGLIANI (1884-1920, Leghorn, Italy)—Considered one of the great modern masters.

THEODORE S. MOISE (1806-1883)—A well-known American portrait painter.

HENRY MOSLER (1841-1920, New York City)—A highly acclaimed American painter, he is represented in many museums.

MELA MUTER (1873-1967, Warsaw)—Born Mutermilch. One of those "lost" artists, she was "found" only two years before her death.

YEHUDAH NEIMAN (1931-   , Warsaw)—An Israeli, he is one of the most important luminist painters in the world.

BARNETT NEWMAN (1905-1970, New York City)—A leading abstract painter of the post–World War II era.

JULES PASCIN (1885-1930, Viddin, Bulgaria)—Born Pincus. A noted artist. He took his own life.

GEORGE D. PEIXOTTO (1859-1937, Cleveland)—An underappreciated painter of considerable talent.

CAMILLE PISSARRO (1830-1903, Bordeaux)—One of the great painters of the 19th century.

MAN RAY (1890-1976)—A member of the early Dadaists and one of the first Surrealists, he was a painter and a noted photographer.

SIR JOHN ROTHENSTEIN (1901-   )—Director of the famed Tate Gallery for more than 15 years.

SIR WILLIAM ROTHENSTEIN (1872-1945, Bradford, England)—A leading British Impressionist painter.

MARK ROTHKO (1903-1970, Russia)—One of the most famous abstract painters in the U.S.

MAURICE SENDAK (1928-   , Brooklyn)—One of the leading illustrators of childrens books in the world.

BEN SHAHN (1898-1969, Kaunas, Lithuania)—A superb painter and a wonderful printmaker.

URI SHULEVITZ—*See* Miscellaneous Awards.

CHAIM SOUTINE (1893-1943, Smilovitchi, Lithuania)—One of the great oil painters. His work commands attention (and very high prices).

MOSES SOYER (1907-   )—A leading painter, brother of Raphael.

RAPHAEL SOYER (1899-   )—A leading American painter, he is a member of the U.S. National Institute of Arts and Letters.

SAUL STEINBERG (1914-   , Ramaicol-Sarat, Rumania)—The highly original artist best known for his drawings in the *New Yorker*.

PHILIP SUTTON (1928-   , London)—A leading British painter.

LESSER URY (1861-1931, Birnbaum, Germany)—A leading German painter who achieved international recognition.

MAX WEBER (1881-1961, Bialystok, Poland)—One of the greatest (and earliest) innovative painters in America.

MARK ZHITNITSKI (1903-   , Mogilev, Russia)—A leading Soviet painter.

SCULPTORS

MARK ANTOKOLSKI (1843-1902, Vilna)—One of the foremost sculptors in Russia.

NAUM L. ARONSON (1872-1943, Dreslavka, Latvia)—One of the most innovative sculptors in France.

ZACHARIE ASTRUC (1839-1907)—One of the most famous French sculptors of the 19th century.

SAUL BAIZERMAN (1899-1957, Vitebsk)—He did superb, original work.

LEONARD BASKIN (1922- , New Brunswick, N.J.)—A noted printmaker as well as sculptor, he specializes in works of wood.

LEOPOLD BERNSTEIN-SINAIEFF (1867-1944, Vilna)—A leading French sculptor who received the Legion of Honor. He was murdered in a German concentration camp.

ANDRE BLOC (1896-1966, Algiers)—One of the most innovative sculptors of the 20th century. His "constructions" and "habitacles" received international attention.

ANTHONY CARO (1924- , Kingston-upon-Thames, England)—A leading abstract sculptor in Europe.

JOSEPH M. DA COSTA (1863-1939, Amsterdam)—Specialized in animal figures and was the great pioneer of 20th-century sculpture in Holland.

JO DAVIDSON (1883-1952, New York City)—A leading U.S. sculptor.

BENNO ELKAN (1877-1960, Dortmund, Germany)—One of the leading portrait sculptors, he did a famous figure of Winston Churchill.

JOZSEF ENGEL (1815-1901, Satoraljaujhely, Hungary)—A prominent Hungarian sculptor, he did a number of busts of royalty, including one of Queen Victoria.

SIR JACOB EPSTEIN (1880-1959, New York City)—One of the most famous sculptors in the world. His work in bronze has been widely acclaimed.

MOSES J. EZEKIEL (1844-1917)—An American, he won the Italian Michael Beer Prize for sculpture.

HERBERT FERBER (1906-)—A leading American sculptor.

ILYA Y. GUENZBURG (1860-1939, Vilna)—A prominent Russian sculptor.

OTTO GUTFREUND (1889-1927)—A Czech, he was one of the great early exponents of Cubism and was famous for his *Hamlet* and *Don Quixote*.

MENASHE KADISHMAN (1932- , Tel Aviv)—A leading Israeli sculptor with an international reputation and following.

GYULA KOSICE (1924- , Kosice, Czechoslovakia)—Born Fernando Falik. One of the most noted Latin American sculptors (he is an Argentine), he has pioneered in the use of Plexiglas in sculpture.

IBRAM LASSAW (1913- , Alexandria, Egypt)—One of the leading abstract sculptors, he was President of the American Abstract Artists.

JACQUES LIPCHITZ (1891-1973, Druskieniki, Lithuania)—One of the most famous sculptors in the world and a leading Cubist.

SEYMOUR LIPTON (1903-)—A leading American sculptor, his work can be seen all over the U.S.

ELIE NADELMAN (1882-1946, Warsaw)—An American, he was a leading Cubist sculptor.

NAUM NEHEMIA (b. 1890)—One of the great pioneers of the constructivist movement in sculpture.

ERNEST NEIZVESTNY (1926-)—One of the leading sculptors in the Soviet Union.

CHANA ORLOFF (1888-1968, Staro-Konstantinov, Russia)—One of the leading sculptors in France.

ANTON PEVSNER (1886-1962)—A leader in the constructivist movement.

NICHOLAS SCHOEFFER (1912- , Kalosca, Hungary)—One of the leading kinetic artists in the world and an outstanding sculptor.

BERNARD SCHOTTLANDER (1924- , Mainz, Germany)—An internationally renowned British sculptor.

PHOTOGRAPHERS

DIANE ARBUS (1923-1971)—A leading American photographer who has had major exhibits throughout the country.

RICHARD AVEDON (1923-)—Some consider him the leading American photographer.

CORNELL CAPA (1918- , Hungary)—Became famous through his work for *Life*.

ROBERT CAPA (1913-1954, Budapest)—Born Andrei Friedmann. The leading combat photographer of all time, he was a cofounder of Magnum Photos, a major agency in the field. He died in Vietnam while covering the war between the French and the Indochinese rebels.

ALFRED EISENSTAEDT (1898- , Germany)—One of the world's great photographers, he worked for *Life* magazine for many years.

PHILIPPE HALSMAN (1906- , Riga, Latvia)—A world-famous photographer. His *Jump Book* featured photos of celebrities jumping (it is much better than it sounds). He served as President of the American Society of Magazine Photographers.

IZIS (1911- , Mariampol, Lithuania)—Born Israel Bidermanas. A leading French photographer whose work was featured in *Paris Match*.

SIMPSON KALISHER (1926- , New York City)—A leading free-lance photographer whose work hangs in all the major museums and galleries.

JILL KREMENTZ (1940- , New York City)—One of the leading contemporary photographers, she specializes in children and young adults.

ARNOLD NEWMAN (1919- , New York City)—A leading portrait photographer.

IRVING PENN (1917-)—One of the most prominent commercial photographers, he makes manufactured products look like works of art.

JOE ROSENTHAL (1912-)—A photographer for the Associated Press, he became immortal by taking the famous picture of American troops raising the flag on Iwo Jima in World War II.

ERICH SALOMON (1886-1944)—One of the leading photographers in Europe. He was killed in a German concentration camp.

DAVID SEYMOUR (1911-1956, Warsaw)—Before his death while on assignment in the Sinai Campaign, he was a cofounder of Magnum Photos and a leading American photographer.

AARON SISKIND (1903- , New York City)—A leading Expressionist photographer.

ALFRED STIEGLITZ (1864-1946, Hoboken, N.J.)—The great pioneer who helped to establish photography as an art form.

ROMAN VISHNIAC (1897- , St. Petersburg, Russia)—One of the world's leading scientific cinematographers, he is famous for his photographs taken through a microscope.

CARTOONISTS AND CARICATURISTS

DAVID BERG (1920- , Brooklyn)—Wrote for *Mad* magazine and was a cartoonist on both *Captain Marvel* and *Archie*.

HERBERT L. BLOCK (1909- , Chicago)—Known to millions as Herblock, the Pulitzer Prize-winning political cartoonist of the *Washington Post*.

AL CAPP (1909- , New Haven)—Born Alfred Caplin. His *Li'l Abner* comic strip became world-famous and was used as the basis for a Broadway play, a movie, and several TV specials.

ALSO KNOWN AS...................................

FRANCOISE DREYFUS	ANOUK AIMEE
MELVIN ISRAEL	MEL ALLEN
ALLEN KONIGSBERG	WOODY ALLEN
BEATRICE FRANKEL	BEATRICE ARTHUR
LEV ROSENBERG	LEON BAKST
RONA BURSTEIN	RONA BARRETT
BENJAMIN KUBELSKY	JACK BENNY
MILTON BERLINGER	MILTON BERLE
JOEY GOTTLIEB	JOEY BISHOP
MEL KAMINSKY	MEL BROOKS
JOYCE BAUER	DR. JOYCE BROTHERS
LEONARD SCHNEIDER	LENNY BRUCE
SAMILE DIANE FRIESEN	DYAN CANNON
ISIDOR ISKOWITCH	EDDIE CANTOR
CATHERINE HOLZMAN	KITTY CARLISLE
MARC SEGAL	MARC CHAGALL
IRA GROSSEL	JEFF CHANDLER
HOWARD COHEN	HOWARD COSELL
HOWARD SILVERBLATT	HOWARD DA SILVA
DANILOVICH DEMSKY	KIRK DOUGLAS
ROBERT ZIMMERMAN	BOB DYLAN
JULIUS GARFINKLE	JOHN GARFIELD
MARIAN LEVEE	PAULETTE GODDARD
ELLIOT GOLDSTEIN	ELLIOT GOULD
LYOVA ROSENTHAL	LEE GRANT
LAURENCE SKIKNE	LAURENCE HARVEY
LESLIE STAINER	LESLIE HOWARD
DANNY KAMINSKY	DANNY KAYE
MICHAEL OROWITZ	MICHAEL LANDON
EMILE HERZOG	ANDRE MAUROIS
IVO LEVI	YVES MONTAND
MUNI WEISENFREUND	PAUL MUNI
ARTHUR TEICHMAN	ARTHUR MURRAY
MICHAEL PESCHKOWSKY	MIKE NICHOLS
MARIA PEISER	LILY PALMER
JOAN MOLINSKY	JOAN RIVERS
JILL OPPENHEIM	JILL ST. JOHN
SIMONE KAMINKER	SIMONE SIGNORET
BELLE SILVERMAN	BEVERLY SILLS
PHIL SILVERSMITH	PHIL SILVERS
ISADOR FEINSTEIN	I.F. STONE
LEV BRONSTEIN	LEON TROTSKY
MIKE WALLACH	MIKE WALLACE
GENE SILVERSTEIN	GENE WILDER
SHIRLY SCHRIFT	SHELLY WINTERS
ISAIAH LEOPOLD	ED WYNN

WILL EISNER (1917-　, New York City)—Cartoonist and creator of *The Spirit*.

JULES FEIFFER (1929-　, New York City)—The multitalented cartoonist whose work always contained a great amount of social commentary. His work has appeared for years in the *Village Voice*.

MAX FLEISCHER (1885-1972, Vienna)—Creator of *Betty Boop* and *Popeye*. *See* Film Producers.

FRANTISEK GELLNER (1881-1914, Mlada, Czechoslovakia)—A great satirical cartoonist and a fine poet, he was killed in World War I.

REUBEN L. (RUBE) GOLDBERG (1883-1970)—In addition to the incredible machines that made him world-famous, he also created Boob McNutt and Mike and Ike. His name became part of the English language. In addition, he was one of the founders of the National Cartoonist Society and won a Pulitzer Prize.

MILT GROSS (1895-1970, Bronx)—Among his cartoon strips was *Banana Oil*.

LEO HAAS (1901-　)—An important political cartoonist for the East European left-wing press.

IRWIN HASEN (1918-　, New York City)—Creator of the popular strip *Dondi*.

THOMAS T. HEINE (1867-1947)—A famous German caricaturist who often attacked the pretensions of the government and army, he helped to found *Simplicissimus*, one of the leading German satirical journals.

HERBLOCK—*See* Herbert Block.

ALBERT HIRSCHFELD (1903-　, St. Louis)—The great caricaturist whose portraits of theatrical personalities are a feature of the *New York Times*.

IMRE KELEN (1895-　, Gyor, Hungary)—Became Director of the UN Television Service, but was earlier known as one of the great cartoonists of Europe.

TED KEY (1912-　, Fresno, Calif.)—Creator of the popular *Hazel*.

DAVID LANGDON (1914-　)—One of the most popular cartoonists to appear in the *New Yorker*, he had earlier been a contributor to the British satirical magazine *Punch*.

MEL LAZARUS (1927-　, New York City)—Creator of *Miss Peach* and *Momma*.

RANAN LURIE (1932-　, Egypt)—The internationally known cartoonist who is syndicated in many American papers and has won numerous awards for his creative political cartoons.

FREDERICK B. OPPER (1857-1937)—One of the great American political cartoonists for the *New York Journal* and the Hearst papers, he is considered to be one of the creators of the modern comic strip.

JOE SHUSTER (1914-　, Toronto)—One of the two men who created *Superman*.

JERRY SIEGEL (1914-　, Cleveland)—The other man who created *Superman*. Neither man saw a great deal of money from their creation.

OTTO SOGLOW (1900-1975, New York City)—His strip *The Little King* ran in hundreds of papers for decades.

SAUL STEINBERG—*See* Artists.

VICTOR WEISZ (1913-1966, Berlin)—Known as Vicky, he was a famous cartoonist and caricaturist for London's *Evening Standard* and the *New Statesman*.

OTHER FIGURES IN ART

BERNARD BERENSON (1865-1959, Baltramentz, Lithuania)—Born Valvrojenski. A major art historian and the author of important books such as *Italian Pictures of the Renaissance*. He converted to Catholicism.

GEORGE BLUMENTHAL (1858-1941)—Was President of the Metropolitan Museum of Art, New York.

LORD JOSEPH DUVEEN (1869-1939, Hull, England)—One of the most famous art dealers in the British Empire.

RICHARD ETTINGHAUSEN (1906- , Germany)—A leading authority on Islamic art and Hagop Kevorkian Professor of Islamic Art at NYU, he earlier served as Head Curator of the Freer Gallery of the Smithsonian Institution.

PEGGY GUGGENHEIM (1898- , New York City)—One of the world's greatest patrons of modern art.

RUDOLF HALLO (1896-1933)—A leading art historian.

ERWIN PANOFSKY (1892-1968, Hanover, Germany)—A leading American art historian. *Pandora's Box: The Changing Aspects of a Mythical Symbol*, which he coauthored with his wife, is considered a major work in the field.

HAROLD ROSENBERG (1906-1978)—Art Critic at the *New Yorker*, he was a champion of the Abstract Expressionist painters.

DANCERS

JEAN BABILEE (1923-)—Born Gutmann. A noted soloist for the Ballets des Champs Elysées after World War II.

ADOLPH BLOM (1884-1951, St. Petersburg)—Danced all over Europe with the Imperial Ballet and later was a star in America.

RENE BLUM (1878-1944)—Founder of the Ballets Russes de Monte Carlo, he was long-time Director of the famous Ballet de l'Opéra de Monte Carlo.

RUTHANNA BORIS (1918-)—A noted American dancer and teacher with the Metropolitan Opera Ballet and others.

JOHN CRANKO (1927-1973, Rustenburg, South Africa)—The noted Director of the Stuttgart (Germany) Ballet.

EDOUARD ESPINOSA (1872-1950, London)—Creator of the British Ballet Company, he served as Ballet Master at Covent Garden.

ELIOT FELD—One of the outstanding male dancers in the U.S., he is also a noted choreographer.

SONJA GASKELL (1904- , Kiev, Russia)—Served as Artistic Director of the Het National Ballet of Amsterdam.

ARNOLD L. HASKELL (1903-)—One of the most famous dance critics in the world (*Balletomania* and *The Making of a Dancer* were two of his outstanding books), he directed the Royal Ballet School of Great Britain.

MELISSA HAYDEN (1928- , Toronto)—Born Mildred Herman. Has been one of the great dancers of the world and a featured performer with the New York City Ballet.

NORA KAYE (1920-)—One of the great dramatic dancers of all time, she performed with such companies as the Ballet Theater and the New York City Ballet.

LINCOLN KIRSTEIN (1907- , Rochester, N.Y.)—Cofounder of the New York City Ballet, he produced many outstanding ballets.

DAVID LICHINE (1910-1972, Russia)—Born Lichtenstein. The wonderful dancer and choreographer who worked with the Ballets Russes de Monte Carlo.

ALICIA MARKOVA (1910-)—Born Lilian Marks. One of the world's finest dancers.

ARTHUR MURRAY (1895-)—Born Teichman. The famous dancing teacher and developer of dancing schools.

VALERY PANOV—One of the greatest Soviet dancers. His successful struggle to leave the Soviet Union with his wife made headlines.

MAYA PLISETSKAYA (1925-   , Moscow)—A "People's Artist of the U.S.S.R." and the recipient of the Lenin Prize, she is prima ballerina of the famed Bolshoi Ballet.

DAME MARIE RAMBERT (b. 1888, Warsaw)—Born Miriam Rambach. One of the most famous of all ballet teachers.

JEROME ROBBINS (1918-   , New York City)—Born Rabinowitz. A leading choreographer.

HERBERT ROSS (1926-   )—One of the greatest choreographers in Broadway history, he worked on many hit shows.

IDA RUBENSTEIN (1885-1960, St. Petersburg)—The noted ballerina of the Diaghilev Ballet.

ARTHUR SAINT-LEON (1815-1870)—Ballet Master of Russia's Imperial Ballet and an outstanding dancer in his own right.

ANNA SOKOLOW (1915-   )—Formerly a leading performer with the Martha Graham troupe, she became one of the leading dance teachers in the U.S.

HELEN TAMIRIS (1905-1966, New York City)—Born Becker. Cofounder of the Dance Repertory Theater and one of the major early figures in the development of modern dance in America, she choreographed many Broadway shows and led the WPA Dance Theater during the Depression.

THEATRICAL PRODUCERS

DAVID BELASCO (1859-1931, San Francisco)—Born Valasco. One of the great producers in the history of theater, he was responsible for over 350 productions. Also a noted playwright, he wrote the original nonoperatic *Madame Butterfly*.

KERMIT BLOOMGARDEN (1905-1976)—Broadway producer.

ALEXANDER H. COHEN (1920-   )—A major "angel" and one of the leading American producers.

JOHN GOLDEN (1874-1955)—A leading producer, he was also an excellent songwriter.

MAX GORDON (b. 1892)—Among his most famous productions were *The Solid Gold Cadillac* and *The Women.*

JED HARRIS (1900-   , Vienna)—Born Jacob Horowitz. Long-time partner of George M. Cohan, he was associated with such hits as *You Can't Take It with You* and *The Jazz Singer.* He was a Pulitzer Prize winner.

JOHN HOUSEMAN (1902-   , Bucharest)—Also a noted stage director, he was a founder of the famed Mercury Theater and in 1936 produced one of the most famous productions of *Hamlet* ever staged.

LEON M. LION (1879-1947, London)—A leading British producer, he specialized in the work of John Galsworthy.

DAVID MERRICK (1912-   )—Has been one of the dominant forces on the American stage for decades.

HERMAN SHUMLIN (1898-   )—Another major force in American theater.

FLORENZ ZIEGFELD (1869-1932, Chicago)—His "Follies" captured the hearts and imagination of America, and made him one of the most famous showmen of all time.

THEATRICAL DIRECTORS AND TEACHERS

STELLA ADLER (1902-   )—A founder of the legendary Group Theater in New York.

JOSEPH ANTHONY (1912- , Milwaukee)—Born Joseph Deuster. Also directed films.

HERBERT BLAU (1926- , New York City)—Cofounder of San Francisco's Actors' Workshop and one of the directors of the former Lincoln Center Repertory Theater in New York.

HAROLD CLURMAN (1901- , New York City)—The noted Drama Critic of the *New Republic* and *The Nation*, he was one of the founders and a Director of the Group Theater.

JULES IRVING (1925-)—A founder of the Actors' Workshop and a former Director of the Lincoln Center Theater, N.Y.

LEOPOLD JESSNER (1878-1945)—The leading German Expressionist director.

JONATHAN MILLER (1934-)—A very creative stage and television director and a talented actor.

OTA ORNEST (1912-)—Born Ornstein. A leading Czechoslovakian theatrical director.

MAX REINHARDT (1873-1943, Baden, Austria)—Born Max Goldmann. One of the outstanding and most influential directors and producers in history.

ALAN SCHNEIDER (1917- , Russia)—A leading director who specialized in the work of Edward Albee.

LEE STRASBERG (1901- , Budanov, Austria-Hungary)—Cofounder and a major figure of the Group Theater. The father of "method" acting as the Artistic Director of the Actors' Studio from 1948.

JOHN ZACHARIAS (1917-)—One of the leading theatrical directors in Sweden.

THEATER MANAGERS AND OWNERS

LILIAN BAYLIS (1874-1937)—Founded the world-famous "Old Vic" theater, the site of some of the greatest productions of Shakespeare ever staged in England. She also managed the Sadler's Wells Theater, which became legendary for its operatic and ballet productions.

BERNARD DELFONT (1909- , Russia)—Born Winogradsky. One of the leading theatrical managers in England and also a major film and television producer.

CHARLES FROHMAN (1860-1915)—The major figure in the Frohman family of theater owners who controlled most of the major theaters in the U.S. He died when the *Lusitania* was sunk by a German U-boat.

LAWRENCE LANGNER (1890-1962, England)—One of the founders of the Washington Square Players of New York, which later developed into the famed Theater Guild.

BARNETT LEVY (1798-1837)—Constructed and owned Australia's first legitimate theater, the Theatre Royal.

THE SHUBERT FAMILY: JACOB J. (1877-1963); **LEE** (1876-1953); and **SAM** (1875-1905), all born in Syracuse, New York—Owned at least 17 Broadway theaters and an estimated half of the theaters in the U.S. during the 1950s. They also produced hundreds of plays.

STARS OF THE THEATER

LUDWIG BARNAY (1842-1924)—A leading German Shakespearean actor.

OSZKAR BEREGI (1876-1966)—Perhaps the leading Shakspearean actor in Hungary, he later had a modest career as a film actor in the U.S.

HERSCHEL BERNARDI (1923- , New York City)—An outstanding American legitimate actor with roots in the Yiddish theater.

SARAH BERNHARDT (1844-1923)—The French star who became one of the most famous actresses of all time and a legend in her lifetime.

LOUIS BOUWMEESTER (1842-1925)—An outstanding Dutch Shakespearean actor.

FANNY BRICE (1891-1951, New York City)—The great star of *Fanny* and a leading stage comedienne. Barbra Streisand portrayed her in the film *Funny Girl*.

MORRIS CARNOVSKY (1897- , St. Louis)—A noted Shakespearean actor whose career was harmed during the McCarthy period.

BOGUMIL DAWISON (1818-1872, Germany)—Born Davidson. One of the premier actors of the mid-1800s, he specialized in Shakespeare.

LUDWIG DESSOIR (1810-1874)—Born Leopold Dessauer. A leading Shakespearean actor at Berlin's Royal Theater.

ERNST DEUTSCH (1890-1969)—A famous German Expressionist actor.

JANE FREIDMANN (1931-)—One of the leading ladies of the Swedish stage.

MARTIN GABEL (1912- , Philadelphia)—An excellent legitimate actor. He is married to Arlene Francis.

JACK GILFORD (1907- , New York City)—Born Gellman. One of the stars of *A Funny Thing Happened on the Way to the Forum* and other productions.

PALLE GRANDITSKY (1923-)—A noted Swedish actor and an excellent director.

LILY HANBURY (1875-1908)—During her short life she achieved stardom on the British stage.

ANNA HELD (1873-1918, Paris)—One of the leading French actresses at the turn of the century.

STEVEN HILL (1924-)—Born Solomon Berg. Is seen frequently on TV as well as on the stage.

DAVID JAMES (1839-1893, Birmingham, England)—Born Belasco. One of the major stars of the British stage in the 19th century.

DAVID KNIGHT (1927-)—Born Mintz. Appears frequently on the British stage.

VERA KORENE (1901- , Paris)—One of the stars of the Comédie Française.

FRITZ KORTNER (1892-1970, Vienna)—Widely considered to be the finest German actor of his generation. His career was cut short by the rise of Hitler.

GERALD LAWRENCE (1873-1957, London)—A noted British actor.

EUGENIE LEONTOVICH (1900- , Odessa)—A fine actress, she also appeared in a number of memorable film roles.

LUCIE MANNHEIM (1905- , Berlin)—One of the leading German actresses before the rise of fascism.

ADAH MENKEN (1835-1868)—One of the leading American actresses of the mid-19th century, she caused a sensation by donning tights.

YVONNE MITCHELL (1925- , London)—A star of the London classical stage, she also acted in some notable films, including *Woman in a Dressing Gown*.

ZERO MOSTEL (1915-1977, Brooklyn)—One of the few actors blacklisted in the McCarthy era to go on to stardom, he will always be remembered for his roles in *A Funny Thing Happened on the Way to the Forum* and *Rhinoceros*.

PAUL MUNI—*See* Film Stars.

MAX PALLENBERG (1877-1934, Vienna)—One of the leading German actors associated with Max Reinhardt. He died in an airplane crash.

RACHEL (1821-1858, Switzerland)—Born Eliza Rachel Felix. One of the greatest actresses of all time as a performer on the French stage. A free spirit, she had two children but no husband.

ADA REEVE (1874-1966)—A noted British actress who had a long and successful career.

RUDOLF SCHILDKRAUT (1862-1930, Istanbul)—One of the few actors to have major careers on both the American and European stage.

ADOLF SONNENTHAL (1834-1909)—A great classical actor specializing in Shakespeare.

MUSICAL COMEDY FIGURES

LIONEL BART (1930-   , London)—Born Begleiter. A leading British writer and composer. One of his biggest hits was *Oliver!*

ABE BURROWS (1910-   , New York City)—Wrote an incredible string of hits, including *Can-Can, Silk Stockings, Guys and Dolls,* and the Pulitzer Prize–winning *How to Succeed in Business without Really Trying.*

BETTY COMDEN (1919-   , Brooklyn)—Worked with Jule Styne and Adolph Green on such hits as *Wonderful Town* and *Bells Are Ringing.*

VIVIAN ELLIS (1904-   , London)—A leading composer-lyricist for the British musical stage.

ADOLPH GREEN (1915-   , Bronx)—One of America's leading lyricists, he wrote the words for the songs in such hits as *Singing in The Rain* and *Wonderful Town* and did the writing on the film *Auntie Mame.*

JOEL GREY (1932-   )—One of America's top musical comedy stars, he is best known for his role in *Cabaret.* He is the son of the noted Yiddish star Mickey Katz.

MICHAEL KIDD (1917-   , New York City)—Born Greenwald. One of the leading choreographers in the U.S., he worked on such productions as *Seven Brides for Seven Brothers* and *Guys and Dolls.*

FRITZI MASSARY (1882-1969, Vienna)—Born Friederike Massarik. A great German actress, she starred in both dramatic roles and in musical comedies.

HAL PRINCE (1928-   , New York City)—The great producer of musical comedies on Broadway. He has a magic touch.

JULE STYNE (1905-   , London)—Wrote the music for such hits as *Gentlemen Prefer Blondes, Gypsy, Funny Girl,* and *Peter Pan.*

DALE WASSERMAN (1917-   , Rhinelander, Wis.)—Won the Tony Award and the New York Drama Critics' Circle Award for *Man of La Mancha.*

COMEDIANS

See also Entertainers; Film Stars; Stars of the Theater;
Television Performers.

DON ADAMS (1927-   , New York City)—The very funny star of TV's *Get Smart!*

MOREY AMSTERDAM (1914-   , Chicago)—An excellent stand-up comic who used to work with a cello, he is best known for his role on the old *Dick Van Dyke Show.*

JACK BENNY (1894-1974, Waukegan, Ill.)—Born Benjamin Kubelsky. One of the great and most beloved comedians in American history, he was even more popular on radio than on television.

SHELLY BERMAN (1926-   , Chicago)—One of the great social comics of the 1960s.

JOEY BISHOP (1919-   , Bronx)—Born Gottlieb. Had his own TV show and is a very effective talk show host.

VICTOR BORGE (1909- , Denmark)—Born Borge Rosenbaum. Specialized in one-man shows and was a popular TV personality for many years. He used a piano in his act and was a fine pianist.

DAVID BRENNER (1945- , Philadelphia)—One of the fastest-rising young comedians of the 1970s.

MEL BROOKS—*See* Film Directors.

LENNY BRUCE (1926-1966)—Born Schneider. The great and tragic talent who died of an overdose of drugs. He broke new ground in the use of sexual and ethnic material, much of which is accepted as commonplace today.

GEORGE BURNS (1896- , New York City)—Born Nathan Birnbaum. Still one of the country's top comedians and a first-rate actor. He became a legend when teamed with his wife, Gracie Allen.

EDDIE CANTOR (1892-1964, New York City)—Born Isidor Iskowitch. A top vaudeville and then TV comedian, he also started the Screen Actors' Guild.

JACK CARTER (1923- , New York City)—A solid TV and nightclub comedian, still working regularly in the 1970s.

MYRON COHEN (1902- , Grodno, Poland)—One of the most successful "Jewish" comedians, he has one of the greatest deliveries of them all.

BILL DANA (1924- , Quincy, Mass.)—"Jose Jimenez" is Jewish.

RODNEY DANGERFIELD (1921- , Babylon, N.Y.)—Famous for his commercials, he is a terrific nightclub comedian. He does not get the respect he deserves.

TOTIE FIELDS (1931-1978, Hartford)—The very funny and very brave comedienne who laughed at herself along with her audiences.

LARRY FINE (1902-1975)—The frizzy-haired member of the Three Stooges, and a sadly ignored comedy genius. He and his partners snuck quite a bit of Yiddish into their films.

BUD FLANAGAN (1896-1968)—Born Weinthrop. One of the great British music hall comics (in partnership with Chester Allen).

DAVID FRYE (1934- , Brooklyn)—For a brief period he was at the top and one of the most talented impersonators in the business.

BUDDY HACKETT (1924- , Brooklyn)—Born Leonard Hacker. The rotund comic is still one of the funniest men in America, in many ways too sophisticated for a mass audience.

CURLY HOWARD (1907-1952)—The fat member of the Three Stooges, he was a master of the facial expression.

MOE HOWARD (1897-1975)—The mop-haired member of the Three Stooges, he had some of the greatest facial expressions of all time and was a master of the double-take.

SHEMP HOWARD (1895-1955)—The best actor of the Three Stooges, he was terrific in films such as *The Bank Dick*.

LOU JACOBI (1913- , Toronto)—Born Jacobovitch. A very funny comic actor.

MILT KAMEN (1924- , Harleyville, N.Y.)—A very funny TV comedian, he was at his best in a talk show format.

ALAN KING (1924- , Brooklyn)—Born Irwin Kniberg. A leading nightclub and TV comedian, he always works with a cigar in hand.

JACK KRUSCHEN (1922- , Winnipeg, Manitoba)—A very funny man, he is primarily a character actor on stage and TV.

PINKY LEE (1916- , St. Paul, Minn.)—Born Pincus Leff. A wild sight-gag comedian.

JACK E. LEONARD (1911-1973)—Worked out of Chicago and was an excellent "insult" comedian, a predecessor of (and also much better than) Don Rickles.

JERRY LESTER (1911- , Chicago)—A comedian who used to be seen frequently on TV, he was also in films such as *The Rookie*.

SAM LEVENSON (1914- , Russia)—Star of numerous panel shows on TV and a very Jewish comedian.

JACKIE MASON (1931- , Sheboygan, Wis.)—A smash hit on the Ed Sullivan Show until an errant finger got him in trouble. He is one of the leading creative comedians around.

ELAINE MAY (1932- , Philadelphia)—Wrote terrific material and teamed with Mike Nichols in one of the great acts of recent years. She is also a fine actress and a director. Her daughter is the actress Jeannie Berlin.

JAN MURRAY (1917- , New York City)—Made his reputation on TV, but is also an excellent nightclub performer.

HOWARD MORRIS—*See* Television Stars.

MIKE NICHOLS—*See* Film Directors.

CARL REINER (1922- , Bronx)—Better as a comedy writer than a performer, he was effective on the *Dick Van Dyke Show*. He has become a first-rank screenwriter, but I miss him the most as Sid Caeser's pal on TV. His son is TV actor Rob Reiner.

DON RICKLES (1926- , New York City)—The talented "insult" comic. People either love him or hate him.

THE RITZ BROTHERS: AL (1901-1965); **JIM** (1903-); and **HARRY** (1906-)—Their real name was Joachim and they were all born in Newark. Their style and routines set the pattern for comedy today. They were true pioneers, especially Harry.

JOAN RIVERS (1935- , Brooklyn)—Born Molinsky. A leading comic, both as a performer and as a writer.

MORT SAHL (1927- , Montreal)—One of the greatest social comedians. Few individuals or institutions have escaped his satiric barbs.

SOUPY SALES (1925- , Franklinton, N.C.)—Born Milton Hines and raised in North Carolina, he is popular with kids and adults alike.

DICK SHAWN (1929- , Buffalo)—Born Schulefand. A badly underrated comedian in the physical tradition. He became a regular on the *Mary* show in 1978.

ALLAN SHERMAN (1924-1973)—The chubby comedian who wrote humorous lyrics to well-known tunes. He scored a tremendous success as "My Son, the Folksinger."

PHIL SILVERS—*See* Television Performers.

SMITH AND DALE: JOSEPH SELTZER (b. 1884) and **CHARLES MARKS** (b. 1882)—Much more than just ethnic comedians. Their routines are among the funniest of all time.

DAVID STEINBERG (1942- , Winnipeg)—One of the bright young comedians on the American scene.

LARRY STORCH (1925- , New York City)—A great comedian whose considerable talent has been largely wasted on TV.

JOHNNY WAYNE (1918-) and **FRANK SCHUSTER** (1916-)—From Toronto and one of Canada's top acts. Excellent writers, they never achieved great success in the U.S.

LARRY WILDE (1928- , Jersey City)—Born Wildman. An excellent nightclub comedian before becoming the leading author of joke books in the U.S.

ED WYNN (1886-1966, Philadelphia)—Born Isaiah Leopold. One of the great early stars of TV after his *Wizard of Oz* performance. His son is the film actor Keenan Wynn.

HENNY YOUNGMAN (1906- , Liverpool, England)—The all-time King of the One-Liners—"Take my wife—please."

ENTERTAINERS

See also Comedians; Film Stars; Television Performers.

JOEY ADAMS (1911- , New York City)—Born Joseph Abramowitz. A leading nightclub entertainer before becoming President of the American Guild of Variety Artists in 1959.

NORA BAYES (1868-1928)—Born Dora Goldberg. One of the great singing stars of vaudeville.

THEODORE BIKEL (1924- , Vienna)—The versatile star of screen (*The Russians Are Coming, The Russians Are Coming* and other films) and stage (*The Sound of Music*) and a wonderful folksinger in many languages.

SAMMY DAVIS, JR. (1925- , New York City)—The popular black entertainer and singer converted to Judaism.

LOTTIE COLLINS (1866-1910)—One of the leading music hall singers in England in the 19th century.

URI GELLER (1946- , Tel Aviv)—The Israeli performer famous for his "psychokinetic" effects.

CHARLES A. W. GROCK (1880-1959, Moulin de Loverse, Switzerland)—One of the leading clowns in the world. His father was Jewish.

HARRY HOUDINI (1874-1926, Budapest)—Born Erich Weiss and raised in Appleton, Wis., where his father was the rabbi. A legend in his own time, he was the greatest escape artist who ever lived.

SOL(OMON) HUROK (1890-1974, Pogar, Russia)—The impresario who handled the negotiations that brought Soviet performers to the U.S.

GEORGE A. JESSEL (1898- , New York City)—Georgie is the Toastmaster General of the United States. Just ask him.

AL JOLSON (1886-1950)—Born Asa Yoelson. A leading American entertainer, he starred in the first "talkie," *The Jazz Singer*, in 1927.

BERT LAHR (1895-1967, New York City)—Born Irving Lahrheim. One of America's greatest burlesque performers, he will always be remembered as the scared lion in the movie *The Wizard of Oz*.

TED LEWIS (1889-1971)—Born Theodore Friedman. Was a leading American nightclub performer.

MARCEL MARCEAU (1923- , Strasbourg)—The greatest mime of all time.

JULES PODELL (1899-1973)—Owned the famous Copacabana night club in New York.

ARKADI RAYKIN (1911-)—The leading mime in the Soviet Union.

BILLY ROSE (1899-1966, New York City)—Born William Rosenberg. Wrote hundreds of songs, was the legendary husband of Fanny Brice, and built the Diamond Horseshoe into one of America's most famous nightspots. He invested his money well and was reported to have owned more stock in AT&T than any other individual.

AL SCHEAN (1868-1949, Dornum, Germany)—One of America's great vaudeville performers.

BERNARD "TOOTS" SHOR (1904-1977)—His restaurants in New York were favorite spots for the political and entertainment elites.

GEORGE SIDNEY (1878-1945)—Born Sammy Greenfield. One of America's leading vaudeville comedians.

THE THREE STOOGES—*See* Larry Fine; Curly, Moe, and Shemp Howard—all in "Comedians."

SOPHIE TUCKER (1884-1966)—Born Kalish. The great American vaudeville singer who was the self-proclaimed "last of the red-hot mamas."

PART VI

FRANKIE VAUGHAN (1928-   , Liverpool, England)—Born Frank Abelson. One of the leading singers and entertainers in England for many years.

LOU WALTERS (1896-1977)—Established the Latin Quarter as one of the leading nightclubs in the U.S. He was the father of Barbara Walters.

Part VII
Motion Pictures and
Television

FILM EXECUTIVES

BARNEY BALABAN (1887-1971, Chicago)—Became President of Paramount Pictures in 1936 and led the company to the heights of success.

LAJOS BIRO (1880-1948, Vienna)—Born Blau. Helped start the famed London Film Production Company and was also a talented writer (screenplays for *The Private Life of Henry VIII* and *The Way of All Flesh*).

VICTOR M. CARTER (1910- , Rostov, Russia)—Served as President and Chairman of the Board of Republic Pictures.

WILLIAM E. CHAIKIN (1919- , Cleveland)—President of Avco Embassy Pictures Corp.

HARRY COHN (1891-1956, New York City)—The legendary mogul who was President of Columbia Pictures Corp.

BERNARD DONNENFELD (1926- , New York City)—President of the Film-makers Group since 1970.

ROBERT EVANS (1930- , New York City)—An important executive at Paramount Pictures and one of the most controversial figures in the business.

EDWARD S. FELDMAN (1929- , New York City)—President of the Motion Picture Division of Filmways.

WILLIAM FOX (1879-1952, Hungary)—Born Fuchs. One of the pioneer tycoons in the film business. One wonders whether Twentieth Century Fuchs would have been as successful.

DAVID F. FRIEDMAN (1923- , Birmingham, Ala.)—President of Entertainment Ventures.

SAMUEL GOLDWYN (1882-1974, Warsaw)—Born Goldfish. The titanic figure who was the Goldwyn in Metro-Goldwyn-Mayer.

SHELDON GUNSBERG (1920- , Jersey City)—Chief Executive Officer and President of the Walter Reade Organization.

PAUL M. HELLER (1927- , New York City)—Co-owner, with Fred Weintraub, of Sequoia Pictures.

NEWTON P. JACOBS (1900- , Pittsburgh)—Chairman of the Board of Crown International Pictures.

LEO JAFFE (1909-)—President, Chairman, and Chief Executive Officer of Columbia Pictures Industries.

JAY KANTER (1927-)—Senior Vice-President in charge of production at Twentieth Century Fox.

NORMAN B. KATZ (1919- , Scranton, Pa.)—Chief Executive Officer and Vice-President of Warner Brothers.

ARTHUR B. KRIM (1910- , New York City)—Chairman of the Board and President of United Artists, he is an important fund raiser for the Democratic party.

HOWARD W. KOCH (1916- , New York City)—Vice-President in Charge of Production at Paramount in the mid-1960s, he produced *The Odd Couple* and *Come Blow Your Horn*.

CARL LAEMMLE (1867-1939, Laupheim, Germany)—Founder of Universal, he created the "star" system and was responsible for the first genuine movie (*Traffic in Souls*).

ALAN LANDSBURG (1933- , New York City)—President of Alan Landsburg (what else?) Productions.

JESSE L. LASKY (1880-1958, San Jose, Calif.)—The pioneer film executive who produced many excellent biographies including *The Adventures of Mark Twain*. He was as much a legend as Harry Cohn.

MARCUS LOEW (1872-1937, New York City)—Owner of the huge string of Loew's theaters, he controlled MGM at one time.

LOUIS B. MAYER (1885-1957, Russia)—The Mayer in Metro-Goldwyn-Mayer, he was Vice-President in Charge of Production there. He produced the Andy Hardy series and helped to shape the movie industry.

DANIEL MELNICK (1932-)—President and Chief Operating Officer at Columbia Pictures, he had earlier been Head of Production at both Columbia and MGM.

DAVID V. PICKER (1931- , New York City)—Became President of Paramount Pictures in 1976.

ERIC PLESKOW (Vienna)—Became Chief Executive Officer and President of United Artists in 1973.

FRANK E. ROSENFELT (1921- , Peabody, Mass.)—Chief Executive Officer and President of MGM.

HAROLD SUGERMAN (1905- , New York City)—Executive Director of Chancellor Films.

TONY TENSER (1920-)—Managing Director of Tigon Pictures.

IRVING G. THALBERG (1899-1936)—Chief of Production at MGM, he produced *Ben Hur*, *Mutiny on the Bounty*, and many other famous films. He was known as the "boy wonder" of the film industry.

THE WARNER BROTHERS: ALBERT (1883-1967, Baltimore); **HARRY** (1881-1958, Poland); **JACK** (1892-1978, London, Ont.); and **SAM** (1884-1927, London, Ont.)—The famous family who started Warner Brothers and began it all with the first sound film, *The Jazz Singer*.

FRED WEINTRAUB (1928- , Bronx)—Half of Weintraub-Heller Productions (Sequoia Pictures).

EMANUEL L. WOLF (1927- , Brooklyn)—President and Chairman of the Board of Allied Artists Industries.

ADOLPH ZUKOR (1873-1976, Ricse, Hungary)—Began Paramount Pictures and served as its President and Chairman of the Board of Directors.

FILM PRODUCERS

BUDDY ADLER (1908-1960)—Head of the Studio at Fox from the mid-1950s until his death and also worked at Columbia. He won an Academy Award for *From Here to Eternity* and also produced *Love Is a Many-Splendored Thing* and *The Inn of the Sixth Happiness*.

IRVING ALLEN (1905- , Poland)—Worked mostly in England, where he helped to start Warwick Films. He produced *Zarak*, *Cockleshell Heroes* and many others.

IRWIN ALLEN (New York City)—The film and TV producer who specialized in "catastrophes," as in *The Towering Inferno* and *The Poseidon Adventure*.

EDWARD L. ALPERSON (1896-1969)—An independent producer of second features and B films, although he did produce *Black Beauty* and the memorable *Invaders from Mars*.

SAMUEL Z. ARKOFF (1918-)—One of the leading executive producers in the business, he was founder of American-International Pictures.

SIR MICHAEL BALCON (1896- , Birmingham, England)—One of the leading producers in Great Britain and Chairman of British Lion Films. Among his productions were *The Lavender Hill Mob* and *Kind Hearts and Coronets*.

JEAN BENOIT-LEVY (1888-1959)—A leading producer and director in France.

MONTY BERMAN (1913- , London)—A leading producer of British B films, he produced the very good *The Hellfire Club* (1961).

PANDRO S. BERMAN (1905- , Pittsburgh)—A leading producer at MGM and RKO, his films included *the Blackboard Jungle, The Three Musketeers, National Velvet,* all of the Rogers-Astaire films, and *The Hunchback of Notre Dame.*

JULIAN BLAUSTEIN (1913- , New York City)—A major Hollywood producer (*Bell, Book and Candle; Broken Arrow; The Day the Earth Stood Still*).

JERRY BRESLER (1912- , Colorado)—An independent producer with some commercially successful films to his credit, including *Diamond Head, The Vikings,* and *Another Part of the Forest.*

HERMAN COHEN (1928- , Detroit)—One of the leading horror movie producers. One of his productions was the never-to-be-forgotten *I Was a Teenage Werewolf.*

ARTHUR COHN (1928-)—One of the leading producers in Switzerland, he won an Academy Award for *The Garden of the Finzi-Continis.* He was also the producer of *The Sky Above, The Mud Below.*

ANATOLE DE GRUNWALD (1910-1967, St. Petersburg)—One of the leading producers and writers in England. Two of his most famous productions were *Spitfire* and *The Way to the Stars.*

DAVID DEUTSCH (1926- , Birmingham, England)—A leading British producer, of films such as *Nothing but the Best.*

MORRIS ENGEL (1918- , New York City)—Specialized in nontraditional films made on a meager budget, such as the widely acclaimed *The Little Fugitive.*

SAMUEL ENGEL (1904-)—Among his many films were *Boy on a Dolphin* and *Sitting Pretty.*

CHARLES K. FELDMAN (1904-1968)—Producer of such notable films as *Red River* and *The Big Sleep.*

BENJAMIN FISZ (1922- , Poland)—Produced several good films, including *The Battle of Britain* (1969).

MAX FLEISCHER (1889-1973, Austria)—One of the leading producers of cartoons and the creator of Popeye the Sailor Man.

ALEXANDER FORD (1908- , Lodz, Poland)—One of the leading producers in Poland (*Border Street, Five Boys of Barski Street*). He emigrated to Israel.

ARTHUR FREED (1894- , Charleston, S.C.)—Born Grossman. An outstanding songwriter as well as a producer. He produced many of the greatest musicals in film history (*Singin' in the Rain; An American in Paris; On the Town*).

BERT I. GORDON (1922- , Kenosha Wis.)—An independent producer and director of horror films, some of them quite good.

HAROLD HECHT (1907- , New York City)—Made a number of memorable films starring Burt Lancaster (*Vera Cruz; Trapeze*) and also produced *Marty; Cat Ballou;* and *Separate Tables.*

MARCEL HELLMAN (1898- , Rumania)—British producer of many films, including *Moll Flanders.*

KENNETH HYMAN (1928- , New York City)—A leading executive producer of hit films (*The Dirty Dozen; The Roman Spring of Mrs. Stone*).

ARTHUR P. JACOBS (1918-1973, Los Angeles)—The independent producer who gave us *Planet of the Apes.*

MARTIN JURNOW (1914- , New York City)—Among his productions were *The Great Race* and *Breakfast at Tiffany's.*

SAM KATZMAN (1901- , New York City)—The famous producer of the Jungle Jim series and of the culturally important *Rock around the Clock.*

SIR ALEXANDER KORDA (1893-1956, Hungary)—One of the most famous producers of all time. Among his more than 100 films were *Catherine the Great* and *The Private Life of Henry VIII.*

STANLEY KUBRICK (1928-   , New York City)—A major American producer (*2001: A Space Odyssey*; *Lolita*; *Dr. Strangelove*).

ELY LANDAU (1920-   , New York City)—The noted producer of many films (*The Pawnbroker*; *Long Day's Journey into Night*).

MERVYN LEROY (1900-   , San Francisco)—A major figure among American producers, he made *The Wizard of Oz*, *Quo Vadis*, and *Mister Roberts*, among others.

SOL LESSER (1890-   , Spokane, Wash.)—He gave us most of the Tarzan films as well as *Kon Tiki*.

JOSEPH E. LEVINE (1905-   , Boston)—The famed producer of such films as *Harlow*, *The Carpetbaggers*, and *Hercules*.

RAOUL LEVY (1922-1967)—The noted French producer whose film *And God Created Woman* (which he also wrote) catapulted Brigitte Bardot to fame.

ANATOLE LITVAK (1902-   , Kiev, Russia)—A noted director as well as producer, he made many excellent movies including *Anastasia* and *Sorry, Wrong Number*.

ERNST LUBITSCH (1892-1947, Berlin)—The famous producer of *Ninotchka*; *The Merry Widow*, and a host of others.

MARTIN MELCHER (1915-1968)—Coproducer of all the films of Doris Day from the time of their marriage.

THE MIRISCH BROTHERS: HAROLD (1907-   ); **MARVIN** (1918-   ); **and WALTER** (1921-   ), all born in New York City—The famous family that produced dozens of noted films including *The Children's Hour*, *West Side Story*, and *Some Like It Hot*.

SEYMOUR NEBENZAL (1899-1961)—One of the most famous producers in pre-Nazi Germany, he was much less successful in the U.S.

JOE PASTERNAK (1901-   , Szilagy-Somlyo, Hungary)—Produced many musicals, including *The Great Caruso*; *Jumbo*; and *One Hundred Men and a Girl*. One of best productions was *Destry Rides Again*.

WILLIAM PERLBERG (1899-1968)—Among his many famous productions were *The Country Girl*; *Forever Amber*; and *The Song of Bernadette*.

ERICH POMMER (1889-1966)—The famed German producer who was associated with some of the most noted films in German film history: *The Blue Angel*; *Metropolis*; and *The Cabinet of Dr. Caligari*.

HARRY POPKIN (New York City)—Among his many productions were *The Well* (an important film with a message of racial brotherhood) and *Champagne for Caesar*.

HANS RICHTER (b. 1888, Berlin)—A noted producer of off-beat and surrealistic films, his 1946 release *Dreams That Money Can Buy* has been widely discussed.

AARON ROSENBERG (1912-   , New York City)—The well-known producer for Universal who has also been active in television, two of his best-known films are *The Great Man* and *The Glenn Miller Story*.

ROBERT ROSSEN (1908-1966, New York City)—An excellent director as well as a noted producer. His films *The Hustler* and *Body and Soul* both won Academy Awards.

HARRY SALTZMAN (1915-   , St. John, Canada)—Coproducer of the very successful James Bond films, he also produced *The Ipcress File*.

DORE SCHARY (1905-   , Newark, N.J.)—Producer of close to 300 films, including *The Asphalt Jungle* and *King Solomon's Mines*, he was the author of the play *Sunrise at Campobello*.

WALTER SELTZER (1914-   , Philadelphia)—His productions included *Skyjacked* and *The War Lord*.

DAVID O. SELZNICK (1902-1965, Pittsburgh)—One of the leading producers of all time (*Duel in the Sun*; *Gone with the Wind*; *King Kong*; *David Copperfield*).

SOL C. SIEGEL (1903- , New York City)—Produced some of America's top hits, including *Les Girls*; *No Way to Treat a Lady*; and *Call Me Madam*.

MILTON SPERLING (1912- , New York City)—Two of his best films were *The Battle of the Bulge* and *Murder, Inc.*

SAM SPIEGEL (1901- , Austria)—In many respects the epitome of the Hollywood producer, he has produced a long line of successful movies including *The African Queen*; *The Bridge over the River Kwai*; *On the Waterfront*; and *The Night of the Generals*.

MILTON SUBOTSKY (1921- , New York City)—A writer as well as a producer. Some of his horror flicks have become the object of cult adoration—for example, *Torture Garden* (1967).

MIKE TODD (1909-1958, Minneapolis)—Born Avrom Goldbogen. Introduced Cinerama to the screen and produced *Around the World in 80 Days*. He was the husband of Elizabeth Taylor at the time of his death.

JERRY WALD (1912-1962, Brooklyn)—A writer as well as a producer, he left us *Johnny Belinda*; *Destination Tokyo*; and *Peyton Place*.

WALTER WANGER (1894-1968)—Born Walter Feuchtwanger. A leading American film producer.

LAWRENCE WEINGARTEN (1895-1975, Chicago)—His productions included *Cat on a Hot Tin Roof*; *The Unsinkable Molly Brown*; and *The Tender Trap*.

DAVID WEISBART (1915-1967)—Produced *Valley of the Dolls*; *Love Me Tender*; and *Rebel without a Cause*.

DAVID WOLPER (1928- , New York City)—One of the leading producers of documentaries in the world and more recently a movie producer, his *Hellstrom Chronicle* was widely acclaimed.

SAM ZIMBALIST (1904-1958)—An important producer whose films included *Ben Hur*.

FILM DIRECTORS

LUDWIG BERGER (1892-1969, Germany)—Born Bamberger. Directed a number of films, including *The Thief of Baghdad*.

CLAUDE BERRI (1935-)—Born Langman. A noted French director and writer.

MEL BROOKS (1926- , New York City)—Born Kaminsky. One of the great comic geniuses of all time.

RICHARD BROOKS (1912- , Philadelphia)—Also a fine writer, he directed *Cat on a Hot Tin Roof* and received an Academy Award for *Elmer Gantry*.

EDWARD L. CAHN (1899-1963)—One of his notable directing jobs was on the 1932 production of *Law and Order*. He specialized in B films.

WILLIAM CASTLE (1914- , New York City)—Born Schloss. Made a string of sometimes excellent horror and science fiction movies.

PIERRE CHENAL (1903-)—Born Cohen. A noted French director.

HUBERT CORNFIELD (1929-)—Among the films he directed were *The Third Voice* and *Pressure Point*.

GEORGE CUKOR (1899- , New York City)—One of the great American directors (*A Star Is Born*; *My Fair Lady*; *Gaslight*; *Camille*; and *Little Women*).

JULES DASSIN (1911- , Middletown, Conn.)—He left the country because of Joe McCarthy and directed such films as *Rififi*; *Never on Sunday*; and before going to Europe, *Naked City*.

ARTHUR DREIFUSS (1908- , Frankfurt)—Directed numerous B films, including *Riot on Sunset Strip*.

FILM DIRECTORS 183

SERGEI EISENSTEIN (1898-1948)—The great Soviet director of *Battleship Potemkin* and *Alexander Nevsky* (for which he received the Order of Lenin). He is considered one of the finest directors of all time. His father was Jewish.

JEAN EPSTEIN (1897-1953, Warsaw)—The great French director who may have been the first person to use slow motion in his films.

RICHARD FLEISCHER (1916- , Brooklyn)—A noted American Director.

THEODORE J. FLICKER (1929-)—Among his films were *The President's Analyst*.

MILOS FORMAN (1932-)—The great Czech director who came to prominence with *Loves of a Blonde* and won an Academy Award for *One Flew Over the Cuckoo's Nest*.

JOHN M. FRANKENHEIMER (1930- , New York City)—Part Jewish, he has directed many notable films including *The Train* and *The Young Savages*.

WILLIAM FRIEDKIN (1939- , Chicago)—Widely considered one of the most important current directors, he won an Academy Award for *The French Connection* and also directed *The Exorcist*.

JACK GARFEIN (1930-)—Among his many films was *Something Wild*, which starred his wife, Carroll Baker.

HUGO HAAS (1901-1968, Czechoslovakia)—Directed a series of films starring the unforgettable Cleo Moore (*Pick-Up* and many others).

VICTOR HALPERIN (1895-)—Director of B films such as *Revolt of the Zombies*.

JOSEPH HEIFITS (1904-)—A leading Soviet director (*Baltic Deputy*; *The Lady with the Little Dog*).

MONTE HELLMAN (1931-)—Directed dozens of quickies, including the very good *Two Lane Blacktop*.

JAN KADAR (1918-1979, Budapest)—The wonderful Czech director who gave us *The Shop on Main Street*, which received an Academy Award.

GARSON KANIN (1912- , Rochester, N.Y.)—One of the top screenwriters in the U.S., he wrote *Adam's Rib*, directed and wrote *Born Yesterday* (the theatrical production), and directed *The Great Man Votes*.

PHIL KARLSON (1908- , Chicago)—Born Philip Karlstein. His directorial credits include *Five Against the House*; *Walking Tall*; and *The Silencers*.

IRVIN KERSHNER (1923- , Philadelphia)—Director of *Up the Sandbox* and *The Flim Flam Man*.

ZOLTAN KORDA (1895-1961)—Two of his finest efforts were *The Macomber Affair* and *Cry the Beloved Country*.

HENRY KOSTER (1905- , Germany)—Born Hermann Kosterlitz. Directed many important films (*The Robe; The Singing Nun; The Inspector General*).

STANLEY E. KRAMER (1913- , New York City)—A producer as well as a director and one of the major figures in American movies (*Death of a Salesman; Home of the Brave; High Noon; On the Beach*).

HARRY LACHMAN (b. 1886)—Worked in both America and England, directing films such as *Dante's Inferno*.

LEW LANDERS (1901-1961)—Born Louis Friedlander. Directed dozens of films in his long career.

FRITZ LANG (1890-1976, Vienna)—Perhaps the leading director in pre-Nazi Germany (*Metropolis; M;* and *Dr. Mabuse*). After he came to America he directed *You Only Live Once* and *The Big Heat*, among others. His mother was Jewish.

ARNOLD LAVEN (1922- , Chicago)—The American director of *Rough Night in Jericho* and the 1958 version of *Anna Lucasta*.

HERBERT I. LEEDS (1901-)—Born Levy. The American director.

CLAUDE LELOUCH (1937- , Paris)—Shot to fame with his 1960 film *A Man and a Woman* and has been a major French director ever since.

IRVING LERNER (1909- , New York City)—One of his best efforts was *Studs Lonigan.*

RICHARD LESTER (1932- , Philadelphia)—Although born in the U.S., he has worked primarily in England, directing such films as *Petulia; The Knack;* and *A Hard Day's Night.*

PAOLO LEVI (1919- , Genoa)—Primarily known as a playwright, he was also a better-than-fair film director.

ARTHUR LUBIN (1901- , Los Angeles)—Best remembered for his comedies (he directed the Francis the Talking Mule films), he also directed the 1943 production of *The Phantom of the Opera.*

SIDNEY LUMET (1924- , Philadelphia)—One of America's premier directors. His credits include *The Pawnbroker; Funny Girl;* and *Long Day's Journey into Night.*

DANIEL MANN (1912- , New York City)—A leading American director (*The Rose Tattoo* and *Come Back Little Sheba*).

DELBERT MANN (1920- , Lawrence, Kans.)—The creative director of *Separate Tables; Dark at the Top of the Stairs;* and *Marty.*

JOE MAY (1880-1954)—Born Mandel. An important German film director who worked in this country after fleeing Hitler.

PAUL MAZURSKY (1930- , Brooklyn)—A leading writer and director of Hollywood films.

JIRI MENZEL (1938-)—One of the greatest Czech directors of all time, his *Closely Watched Trains* won an Academy Award in 1966.

LEWIS MILESTONE (b. 1895, Chisinau, Russia)—Hollywood director of such films as *A Walk in the Sun; Halls of Montezuma;* and *Pork Chop Hill.*

LEONIDE MOGUY (1899-)—Born Magulevsky. One of the leading directors in the Soviet Union, he directed *Prison without Bars* and *Tomorrow Is Too Late.*

SAM NEWFELD (1900-1964)—One of the leading directors of B movies, including the very good *Queen of Burlesque.*

JOSEPH M. NEWMAN (1909- , Logan, Utah)—Director of *This Island Earth* and many other films.

MIKE NICHOLS (1932- , Berlin)—Born Michael I. Peschkowsky. The director of such famous films as *Barefoot in the Park; Catch-22;* and *The Graduate,* he earlier teamed with Elaine May in a top comedy act.

MAX OPHULS (1902-1957, Germany)—The well-known director whose work on *Lola Montes* made him and the film famous.

IRVING PICHEL (1891-1954)—Among his directorial efforts were *A Medal for Benny* and *Destination Moon.*

SYDNEY POLLACK (South Bend, Ind.)—A first-rank director (*They Shoot Horses, Don't They?* and *The Slender Thread*).

OTTO L. PREMINGER (1906- , Vienna)—The famous director of *The Man with the Golden Arm; Laura;* and *Advise and Consent,* he was also an important producer. He was neither as good nor as bad as people say he was.

ROBERT RAFELSON (1935-)—Rapidly becoming one of America's top directors with films such as *Five Easy Pieces.*

ALAN RAFKIN—American director of many films, including *The Shakiest Gun in the West.*

IRVING RAPPER (1904- , London)—One of Warner Brothers' regular directors. His films include *Marjorie Morningstar* and *Deception.*

IRVING REIS (1906-1953)—Directed *All My Sons; The Fourposter;* and *The Bachelor and the Bobby Soxer* in his too-short career.

MARTIN RITT (1919- , New York City)—The very talented director of *Paris Blues; The Great White Hope; Hud;* and *The Long Hot Summer.*

ABRAM ROOM (1894-)—A well-known Soviet director.

PHIL ROSEN (1888-1951, **Russia**)—Directed dozens of B films in the 1930s and '40s.

STUART ROSENBERG (1925- , **New York City**)—A major director (*Cool Hand Luke*).

HERBERT ROSS (1927- , **New York City**)—Went from being a leading choreographer to being a leading director and worked on such films as *Play It Again Sam* and *The Owl and the Pussycat.*

BORIS SAGEL (1923-)—A film director who also works frequently in television.

GENE SAKS (1921-)—A major talent, he directed *Mame; The Odd Couple;* and *Barefoot in the Park.*

SIDNEY SALKOW (1909- , **New York City**)—A major B film director, he worked on all or almost all of the Lone Wolf movies and also directed *Sitting Bull.*

LUIS SASLAVSKY (1908- , **Sante Fe, Argentina**)—An important film director in Argentina.

FRANKLIN SCHAFFNER (1920- , **Tokyo**)—One of the top American directors, he worked on *Planet of the Apes; Papillon; Patton;* and *The Best Man.*

JOHN SCHLESINGER (1926- , **London**)—The great British director of *Darling; Billy Liar;* and many other excellent films.

LEE SHOLEM (1900-)—Among his films were *Emergency Hospital* and *That Redhead from Wyoming.*

DON SIEGEL (1912- , **Chicago**)—Went from B movies to major hits, from *Riot in Cell Block Eleven* and the great original version of *Invasion of the Body Snatchers* to *Two Mules for Sister Sara* and *Dirty Harry.*

ELIOT SILVERSTEIN (1925-)—A prominent American director of *A Man Called Horse* and *Cat Ballou,* among others.

ALEXANDER SINGER (1932-)—Directed *Love Has Many Faces* and *A Cold Wind in August,* among many others.

ROBERT SIODMAK (1900-1973, **Memphis, Tenn.**)—His effort on *The Killers* was outstanding, and he has been unfairly neglected.

STEVEN SPIELBERG (1946-)—The hottest young or old director in the business (*Jaws; Duel; Close Encounters of the Third Kind*).

JOSEF VON STERNBERG (1894-1969, **Vienna**)—One of the top directors in the world for more than 20 years. His work on *Underworld* and *The Blue Angel* will live forever. Truly a legend in his own time.

JOSEPH STRICK (1923- , **Pittsburgh**)—The very sophisticated director of *The Balcony* and other films.

ERICH VON STROHEIM (1885-1957, **Austria**)—From *Greed* in 1923 to *Sunset Boulevard* in 1950, he was the epitome of the motion picture director.

DZIGA VERTOV (1896-1954)—Born Dennis Kaufman. A prominent Soviet director.

EDGAR G. ULMER (1900-1972, **Austria**)—A leading director of B films after he came to the U.S., he directed *The Black Cat* and *The Man From Planet X.*

JIRI WEISS (1913-)—A prominent Czech director.

JULES WHITE (1900- , **Budapest**)—Director of numerous shorts, he worked with the Three Stooges for more than ten years.

BILLY WILDER (1906- , **Vienna**)—Certainly one of the major figures in American film. He and his collaborators wrote such films as *Sunset Boulevard; The Lost Weekend; Witness for the Prosecution;* and others. He won many Academy Awards both as a director and as a writer.

ROBERT WISE (1914- , **Winchester, Ind.**)—A major director, he produced and directed *West Side Story,* directed *The Sand Pebbles* and *I Want to Live* (for which he won an Academy Award), and was one of the directors of *The Sound of Music.*

WILLIAM WYLER (1902- , **Mulhouse, France**)—The great director of *The*

Best Years of Our Lives; Ben-Hur; Mrs. Miniver; and *Funny Girl*, he won many Academy Awards.

FRED ZINNEMANN (1907- , Vienna)—Won several Academy Awards for films such as *A Man for All Seasons; From Here to Eternity;* and *High Noon.*

ALBERT ZUGSMITH (1910- , Atlantic City, N.J.)—A producer as well as a director, he produced *Fanny Hill* and directed such winners as *Teacher Was a Sexpot* and *The Private Life of Adam and Eve* (now we know).

FILM STARS

See also Comedians; Entertainers; Television Performers.

DAVID ABRAHAM (1909- , Bombay)—One of leading actors in India and a veteran of well over 100 movies, he acted under the single name David.

LUTHER ADLER (1903- , New York City)—A fine stage actor as well as a film performer, he starred in *Wake of the Red Witch* and portrayed Hitler in *The Magic Face.*

ANOUK AIMÉE (1932- , Paris)—Born Francoise Dreyfus. She appeared in *La Dolce Vita* and is best known for her role in *A Man and a Woman* (1966).

HARDIE ALBRIGHT (1904-1975)—A very big star for a short period in the 1930s, in films such as *Young Sinners.* He was part Jewish.

WOODY ALLEN (1936- , Brooklyn)—Born Allen Konigsberg. One of the great comic geniuses of all time, he is a director, an actor, and a writer, and plays jazz clarinet.

ALAN ARKIN (1934-)—The multitalented star of *Catch-22* and *The Russians Are Coming, The Russians Are Coming.*

LAUREN BACALL (1924- , New York City)—The beautiful actress who starred in such films as *The Big Sleep* and *Key Largo.* Her recent autobiography made her a best-selling author as well.

CARROLL BAKER (1931- , Johnstown, Pa.)—Had leads in *Giant, Baby Doll, The Carpetbaggers;* and *Harlow.* She converted to Judaism.

MARTIN BALSAM (1919- , New York City)—A great supporting actor in *A Thousand Clowns* and many other films.

THEDA BARA (1890-1955, Cincinnati)—Born Goodman. The greatest vamp of all time. Her most famous role was in *Camille* (1918).

BINNIE BARNES (1905-)—A terrific second lead, she starred in such films as *The Private Life of Henry VIII* and *The Three Musketeers* (1939). She became a Catholic.

HARRY BAUR (1891-1943)—A star in French films, he was particularly outstanding in *The Golem.*

RICHARD BENJAMIN (1939- , New York City)—A very talented actor who excels in both comedy and drama. He can be a very nasty character (on the screen).

ROBBY BENSON (1957- , Dallas)—A fine young actor (*The End; Ode to Billy Joe;* and others) who is one of the darlings of the teens and preteens. He is the son of director Don Siegel.

ELIZABETH BERGNER (1897-)—Although she never equaled her stage fame on the screen, she was one of Europe's finest actresses. Two of her major films were *Stolen Life* and *As You Like It.*

MEL BLANC (1908- , San Francisco)—The wonderful man who was the voice of Bugs Bunny, Donald Duck, and a host of other animated characters.

CLAIRE BLOOM (1931- , London)—The British actress who starred in *The Spy Who Came in from the Cold* and many other films. She was at one time married to Rod Steiger.

LLOYD BOCHNER (1924-)—A noted Canadian character actor.

GERALDINE BROOKS (1925-1977, New York City)—An outstanding movie and Broadway actress. Her films include *An Act of Murder*; *The Reckless Moment*; and *Mr. Ricco*.

RED BUTTONS (1919- , New York City)—Before winning an Academy Award for *Sayonara* and starring in such films as *They Shoot Horses, Don't They?*, he was a leading TV comic.

JAMES CAAN (1940- , New York City)—The handsome leading man who starred in *Cinderella Liberty* and many other films.

DYAN CANNON (1938- , Tacoma, Wash.)—Born Samile Diane Friesen. A vastly underrated actress. Her marriage to Cary Grant made headlines.

JEFF CHANDLER (1918-1961, New York City)—Born Ira Grossel. One of the best-looking leading men on the American screen. Hollywood typecast him as an American Indian (*Cochise* and several others). He died during a back operation.

LEE J. COBB (1911-1972, New York City)—A wonderful actor (*On the Waterfront*, for example), he shot to fame on the basis of his performance in the stage production of *Death of a Salesman*. He was also a regular on TV's *The Virginian*.

TONY CURTIS (1925- , Bronx, N.Y.)—Born Bernie Schwartz. Not taken seriously as an actor for years, he finally received the critical acclaim due him for films such as *The Boston Strangler* and *Some Like It Hot*.

LILI DARVAS (1906- , Budapest)—Frequently portrayed sultry European types on the American screen.

HOWARD DA SILVA (1909- , Cleveland)—Born Silverblatt. Lost most of his prime working years because of Joseph McCarthy.

LUDWIG DONATH (1900-1967, Vienna)—Typecast by the Hollywood geniuses as a Nazi, and he had the title role in *The Strange Death of Adolf Hitler*.

KIRK DOUGLAS (1916- , Amsterdam, N.Y.)—Born Issur Danilovich Demsky. A champion amateur wrestler before becoming one of Hollywood's top leading men, he starred in such films as *Paths of Glory*; *Champion* (one of his best performances); and *Lust for Life*.

MELVYN DOUGLAS (1901- , Macon, Ga.)—An Academy Award winner, he also acted on the stage. He was unforgettable in *The Best Man*. He is married to Helen Gahagan Douglas.

RICHARD DREYFUSS (1949- , Brooklyn)—One of the leading film actors in the U.S., he starred in *Jaws* and *Close Encounters of the Third Kind*.

MARTY FELDMAN (1933- , England)—One of the funniest men in the world (who else can make you laugh so hard by just looking at you?), he appears frequently in Gene Wilder productions. He was one of England's top music hall performers before his film career.

CARRIE FISHER (1956- , Beverly Hills, Ca.)—The Princess in *Star Wars*, she is the daughter of Eddie Fisher and Debbie Reynolds.

JOHN GARFIELD (1913-1952, New York City)—Born Julius Garfinkle. A product of the Group Theater in New York, he became famous for his performance in *Body and Soul* in 1947 but was hounded mercilessly by the Red baiters and never achieved the fame due him.

HERMIONE GINGOLD (1897- , London)—A very funny lady, she played some choice roles, including parts in *Gigi* and *The Music Man*.

PAULETTE GODDARD (1911- , Great Neck, N.Y.)—Born Marian Levee. She never quite became the top star she wanted to be, but she had some excellent roles, including a bitchy lady in *The Women*. She was frequently married (one of her husbands was Charlie Chaplin).

BRUCE GORDON (1919-   )—One of the screen's leading heavies and a solid character actor, he has appeared in many films but is best known for his rendition of Frank Nitti on TV's *The Untouchables*.

ELLIOT GOULD (1938-   , Brooklyn)—Born Goldstein. One of the top leading men.

LEO GORCEY (1915-1969)—One of the original "Dead End Kids" and the leader of the "Bowery Boys" he led one of the strangest lives of any Hollywood personality.

LEE GRANT (1929-   , New York City)—Born Lyova Rosenthal, she is simply one of the best actresses on the American screen and is frequently seen on TV.

LAURENCE HARVEY (1928-1973, Yonishkis, Lithuania)—Born Skikne. Made some excellent movies, including *Room at the Top* and *Darling*.

GOLDIE HAWN (1945-   , Washington, D.C.)—Shot to prominence as the "dumb blonde" on TV's *Laugh-In* and then went on to stardom as an Academy-Award-winning film actress.

ROBERT HIRSCH (1925-   )—An excellent French actor who is also a noted director.

DUSTIN HOFFMAN (1937-   , Los Angeles)—A leading American actor, he starred in such films as *Little Big Man*; *Midnight Cowboy*; *The Graduate*; and *Papillon*.

JUDY HOLLIDAY (1923-1965, New York City)—Born Judith Tuvim ("holiday" in Hebrew). One of the greatest film comedians, she won an Academy Award for *Born Yesterday*. She lost a brave struggle to cancer.

OSCAR HOMOLKA (1898-1978, Vienna)—One of the best-known actors in Germany before the rise of the Nazis, he became a successful character actor in the U.S. He played the part of Gestapo General on the TV show *Hogan's Heroes*.

JOHN HOUSEMAN (1902-   , Bucharest, Rumania)—The son of a Jewish father, he is a great character actor, and can be seen on *Paper Chase* on TV.

LESLIE HOWARD (1893-1943, London)—Born Stainer. A major British leading man (*Pygmalion* and *Gone with the Wind*). His plane disappeared over the English Channel during World War II.

CARL JAFFE (1902-   )—A refugee from Hitler, he appeared frequently in British films.

SAM JAFFE (1897-   , New York City)—The great character actor who starred in (the original) *Lost Horizon; Ben Hur; Gunga Din*; and many other films.

SIDNEY JAMES (1913-   )—A delightful British character actor, he was featured in the "Carry On" movies. Perhaps his most memorable performance was in *The Lavender Hill Mob*.

CAROLYN JONES (1932-   , Amarillo, Tex.)—A fine actress, she is a convert to Judaism. She was married to Aaron Spelling.

MADELINE KAHN (1942-   , Boston)—One of the funniest ladies on the screen and a regular in Mel Brooks films.

KURT KATCH (1896-1958, Poland)—Born Isser Kac. A fine character actor who gave a wonderful performance in *The Mask of Dimitrios* (1944).

DANNY KAYE (1913-   , Brooklyn)—Born Kaminsky. One of the all time great movie comics. All of his films had merit, but two of the best were *The Inspector General* and *The Secret Life of Walter Mitty*. He was also a successful TV performer.

STUBBY KAYE (1918-   )—A fine legit actor, he was terrific in *Guys and Dolls* and *Li'l Abner*.

HARVEY KEITEL (1941-   , Brooklyn)—An excellent actor in such films as *Welcome to L.A.*; *Buffalo Bill and the Indians*; and *Alice Doesn't Live Here Anymore*.

FILM STARS 189

ABBE LANE (1932- , Brooklyn)—She made a few films, but is best known as the band singer for (and former wife of) Xavier Cugat.

HARVEY LEMBECK (1923- , New York City)—A very funny man, he was featured as a hood in the "Beach Party" pictures of the 1960s. His son, Michael, is "Captain Kool" on TV.

SAM LEVENE (1905- , Russia)—Appeared in numerous films and Broadway plays, but he will always be remembered as Nathan Detroit.

JERRY LEWIS (1926- , Newark, N.J.)—Teamed with Dean Martin and then branched out on his own. Although not highly regarded by American critics, in France he is considered a comic genius on a par with Chaplin.

MAX LINDNER (1883-1925, St. Loubes, France)—A major star in French silent films.

HERBERT LOM (1917- , Prague)—Had some notable roles in such films as *Spartacus* and *War and Peace*.

PETER LORRE (1904-1964, Hungary)—One of the great actors of all time, he will always be remembered as the deranged murderer in *M* and for his roles in *Casablanca* and *The Maltese Falcon*.

PAUL LUKAS (1895-1971, Budapest)—A wonderful actor in films such as *Berlin Express* and *Watch on the Rhine*.

MALA (1906-1952)—Born Ray Wise, he was part Jewish and part Eskimo. He had a brief cup of tea at the top in serials such as *Hawk of the Wilderness*, and then later had parts in such films as *The Tuttles of Tahiti*. He had one of the best builds of any Hollywood actor before or since.

HANK MANN (1887-1971)—Born David Liebermann. An overweight supporting actor in many silent films, including *The Great Dictator*, he was also one of the famed Keystone Cops.

JANET MARGOLIN (1943-)—An excellent actress frequently seen on TV movies, she starred in *David and Lisa*.

THE MARX BROTHERS: CHICO (Leonard, 1891-1961); **HARPO** (Arthur, 1893-1964); the rarely seen **GUMMO** (Milton, 1894-1978); **GROUCHO** (Julius, 1895-1977); and **ZEPPO** (Herbert, 1901-)—Most of their movies have become classics, especially *Animal Crackers* and the wonderful *A Night at the Opera*. Groucho was a genius.

WALTER MATTHAU (1920- , New York City)—The Academy Award–winning actor who is always a delight to watch. His films include *The Fortune Cookie*; *The Sunshine Boys*; *The Odd Couple*; and many others.

SID MELTON (1920- , Brooklyn)—Although he is frequently seen, few people could tell you his name.

MIROSLAVA (1930-1955)—Born Stern. The Greek-American actress whose short career included *The Brave Bulls*.

MARILYN MONROE (1926-1962, Los Angeles)—The famous Hollywood star was a convert to Judaism.

YVES MONTAND (1921-)—Born Ivo Levi. The famous French actor, he is married to Simone Signoret.

RON MOODY (1924-)—Born Moodnick. A well-known British character and comic actor.

PAUL MUNI (1895-1967, Lemberg, Poland)—Born Muni Weisenfreund. A veteran of the Yiddish theater, he became one of the finest actors in the history of American film. His many fine performances included the title role in the Academy Award–winning *Story of Louis Pasteur*; *The Life of Emile Zola*; and the powerful *I Am a Fugitive from a Chain Gang*.

JULES MUNSHIN (1915-1970)—He was the "other" sailor in *On the Town*.

ALLA NAZIMOVA (1879-1945, Yalta, Russia)—A fine character actress in both the silent and sound eras.

ANTHONY NEWLEY (1931- , London)—The British star of *Oliver Twist* and

Cockleshell Heroes. He is also a fine singer.

PAUL NEWMAN (1925- , Cleveland)—One of the premier leading men in American films, he starred in such hits as *The Hustler*; *The Long Hot Summer*; *Butch Cassidy and the Sundance Kid*; and *Cat on a Hot Tin Roof.*

LILLI PALMER (1914- , Pojer, Poland)—Born Maria Peiser and at one time married to Rex Harrison. A leading lady in many films.

ELEANOR PARKER (1922- , Cedarville, Ohio)—A leading lady in many films, she is a convert to Judaism.

LARRY PARKS (1914-1975)—Born Samuel Klausman. A second lead in a number of films.

NEHEMIAH PERSOFF (1920- , Jerusalem)—He often portrayed a gangster (in *On the Waterfront*, for example), both in films and on TV (*The Untouchables* and others).

LUISE RAINER (1912- , Vienna)—Won an Academy Award for the 1937 film *The Good Earth.*

HARRY REEMS (1947- , New York City)—Born Herbert Streicher. One of the biggest (you should excuse the expression) stars of pornographic films. He "played" the doctor in *Deep Throat.*

EDWARD G. ROBINSON (1893-1973, Bucharest)—The premier film gangster in *Little Caesar*, he had a tremendous acting range, which he exhibited in films like *Dr. Ehrlich's Magic Bullet.*

OSSIP RUNITSCH (1889-1947, St. Petersburg)—One of the leading film personalities in the Soviet Union.

JILL ST. JOHN (1940- , Los Angeles)—Born Oppenheim. Works regularly in films and on TV and is very nice to look at.

JOSEPH SCHILDKRAUT (1895-1964)—Although he won two Academy Awards, his talent was largely wasted in Hollywood.

GEORGE SEGAL (1934- , New York City)—The immensely popular film star, he was terrific in *A Touch of Class* and *King Rat*. He has a wonderful feel for light comedy.

PETER SELLERS (1925- , Southsea, England)—One of the great comic actors of all time, his Pink Panther films are nothing compared to his performances in *Dr. Strangelove* and *I'm All Right, Jack.*

SYLVIA SIDNEY (1910- , New York City)—Born Sophia Kossow. Wonderful in films such as *Street Scene* and *The Searching Wind.*

SIMONE SIGNORET (1921- , Wiesbaden, Germany)—Born Kaminker. The superb French actress who starred in many excellent films including *Room at the Top.*

ROD STEIGER (1925- , Westhampton, N.Y.)—Another of the great stars of *On the Waterfront* (he played Brando's brother), he became one of the great stars of Hollywood in films such as *The Pawnbroker* and *In the Heat of the Night* (he won the Academy Award for both).

ELAINE STEWART (1929- , New Jersey)—Born Elsy Steinberg. One of the most beautiful women in films.

HAROLD J. STONE (1911-)—A wonderful character actor in films and TV. His considerable talents have largely been wasted.

SUSAN STRASBERG (1938- , New York City)—A member of the great acting family, she has appeared in dozens of films, including *The Brotherhood*; *Kapo*; and most memorably, *Picnic.*

ROBERT STRAUSS (1913-1975)—A character actor and comedian. He never equaled his great performance in *Stalag 17.*

BARBRA STREISAND (1942- , Brooklyn)—A true superstar, both as an actress and as a singer, she was terrific in *Funny Girl*, the film that won her an Academy Award.

ELIZABETH TAYLOR (1932- , London)—The beautiful actress who converted to Judaism because she always wanted to.

KENT TAYLOR (1907-)—Born Louis Weiss. A solid supporting actor.

SID TOMACK (1907-1962)—A great character actor in dozens of films, he had one of the all-time great Brooklyn accents.

CHAIM TOPOL (1935-)—The great Israeli actor who had the lead in *Fiddler on the Roof.*

GEORGE VOSKOVEC (1905- , Sazava, Czechoslovakia)—An excellent supporting actor, he gave a memorable performance in *The Spy Who Came in from the Cold.*

ANTON WALBROOK (1900-1967, Vienna)—Born Wohlbruck. One of the leading Austrian actors, he appeared in several English-language films including *Colonel Blimp* and *Victoria the Great.*

ELI WALLACH (1915- , Brooklyn)—A veteran of many films and TV shows. Perhaps his greatest performance was in *The Rose Tattoo.*

JESSE WHITE (1918-)—Born Wiedenfeld. A great comedy performer who appeared in dozens of films.

CORNEL WILDE (1918- , New York City)—A Hollywood leading man and now an excellent director, he starred in such films as *A Song to Remember; Forever Amber; Storm Fear; No Blade of Grass;* and many others.

GENE WILDER (1935- , Milwaukee)—Born Silberstein. The crazy, wonderful comic talent (*Young Frankenstein* and several others).

SHELLEY WINTERS (1923- , St. Louis)—Born Shirley Schrift. She has had her share of great and terrible parts over the years. She won Academy Awards for *A Patch of Blue* and *The Diary of Anne Frank.*

JOSEPH WISEMAN (1919-)—His great acting talents have been largely ignored by Hollywood. He was great in *The Night They Raided Minsky's* and as the sinister *Dr. No.*

KEENAN WYNN (1916- , New York City)—A solid actor and the son of Ed Wynn, his film credits include *Dr. Strangelove* and *The Americanization of Emily.*

SCREENWRITERS

GEORGE AXELROD (1922- , New York City)—A leading comedy writer, he scripted such hits as *Will Success Spoil Rock Hunter?; Breakfast at Tiffany's;* and, in a noncomic mood, *The Manchurian Candidate.*

IRVING BRECHER (1941- , New York City)—Formerly a top radio writer, he wrote the films *Meet Me in St. Louis; Bye, Bye, Birdie;* and many others. He also wrote two Marx Brothers films.

JEROME CHODOROV (1911-)—Wrote or adapted such hits as *Junior Miss; Louisiana Purchase;* and *My Sister Eileen.* He often worked with Joseph Fields.

NORMAN L. CORWIN (1910- , Boston)—Now a screenwriter, his real fame resides in his radio career, for he was perhaps the most outstanding scriptwriter in commercial radio in the 1930s and '40s.

I. A. L. DIAMOND (1920- , Ughemi, Rumania)—Largely neglected because he wrote with the great Billy Wilder, some of his (their) great films were *Irma La Douce; One Two Three;* and *The Apartment,* three of the biggest hits of the 1960s.

HENRY EPHRON (1912-) and **PHOEBE EPHRON** (1914-1971)—A wonderful team that wrote such films as *Captain Newman, M.D.; The Jackpot;* and *Desk Set.*

JULIUS J. EPSTEIN (1909-) and **PHILIP G. EPSTEIN** (1909-1952), both born in New York City—Twins, they practically dominated the 1940s with (among others) *The Man Who Came to Dinner; Arsenic and Old Lace*; and *Four Daughters*. They won an Academy Award for the immortal *Casablanca*.

CARL FOREMAN (1914-   , Chicago)—A leading writer who also produced and directed, he wrote many major pictures including *High Noon; Champion; Home of the Brave* (which broke new ground with its racial theme); *The Men*; and *Young Winston*.

MELVIN FRANK (1917-   )—A producer and director who also wrote, two of his biggest hits were *My Favorite Blonde* (with Norman Panama) and *Mr. Blandings Builds His Dream House*.

JULES FURTHMAN (1888-1966)—Wrote the script for the original *Mutiny on the Bounty; The Big Sleep*; and *Nightmare Alley*.

JAMES A. GOLDMAN (1927-   , Chicago)—A novelist as well as screenwriter, he won an Academy Award for *The Lion in Winter* in 1968 and also wrote *Nicholas and Alexandra*.

LUKAS HELLER (1930-   , Germany)—Among his many scripts were *Whatever Happened to Baby Jane?* He coauthored *The Dirty Dozen* and *Hush, Hush Sweet Charlotte*.

MICHAEL KANIN (1910-   , Rochester, N.Y.)—Won an Academy Award in 1942 for his screenplay *Woman of the Year*.

HAL KANTER (1918-   , Savannah, Ga.)—Coauthor of *Pocketful of Miracles*, he is also a top producer and director and has been very active in TV.

HARRY KLEINER (1916-   , Teplic, Russia)—Among his biggest hits were *Bullitt; Ice Palace*; and *Carmen Jones*. He also did the screenplay for *Fantastic Voyage*, which Isaac Asimov later novelized.

NORMAN KRASNA (1909-   , New York City)—A writer/director/producer, he wrote *Bachelor Mother* and *Indiscreet* and wrote and directed the Academy Award–winning *Princess O'Rourke*.

HARRY KURNITZ (1907-1968)—Among his many fine scripts were *The Inspector General* and *Witness for the Prosecution*.

CHARLES LEDERER(1906-   )—Wrote the film version of *The Front Page* and the 1962 version of *Mutiny on the Bounty*.

ERNEST LEHMAN (1920-   , New York City)—A producer as well as a writer, he wrote *The Sweet Smell of Success*, wrote and produced *Hello Dolly*, and produced, directed, and wrote the script for *Portnoy's Complaint*.

M. LENGYEL (b. 1880, Balmazujvaros, Hungary)—A noted Hungarian playwright, his film scripts include *Ninotchka; Catherine the Great*; and the famous *The Blue Angel*.

SONYA LEVIEN (1888-1960)—Wrote the Academy Award–winning *Interrupted Melody*; and *Jeanne Engels*, and served as Story Editor for most of the major studios, including Paramount, MGM, and Fox.

ALBERT LEWIN (1895-1968)—The multitalented producer, writer, and director. He wrote and directed *The Picture of Dorian Gray* and wrote, produced, and directed *Pandora and the Flying Dutchman*, among others.

RICHARD MAIBAUM (1909-   , New York City)—Scripted many fine movies, including *Thunderball; Goldfinger*; and *From Russia with Love*. He also wrote *Cockleshell Heroes*, for my money one of the best war films ever made.

ALBERT MALTZ (1908-   , Brooklyn)—His career was almost ruined during the McCarthy period, when he was one of the "Hollywood Ten" and served a prison term. He wrote such fine films as *Naked City; Destination Tokyo*; and *Pride of the Marines*. More recently, he wrote *Two Mules for Sister Sara*.

BERTRAM MILLHAUSER (1892-1958)—Wrote many "second feature" films as well as the memorable *Tokyo Joe*.

HERMAN MANKIEWICZ (1897-1953)—Long-rumored to have been the "real" writer of *Citizen Kane*, he had a long list of credits, including *Pride of St. Louis*.

JOSEPH L. MANKIEWICZ (1909- , Wilkes-Barre, Pa.)—Received Academy Awards for writing *All About Eve* and *Letter to Three Wives,* and is also a noted director (*Suddenly Last Summer* and many others).

WOLF MANKOWITZ (1924- , London)—A novelist of some note (he wrote *Expresso Bongo*), he has become an outstanding screenwriter.

GEORGE OPPENHEIMER (1900- , New York City)—A leading screenwriter, he wrote such hits as *Libeled Lady* and *A Day at the Races*. He also wrote for the TV show *Topper*.

ABRAHAM POLONSKY (1910- , New York City)—Another victim of the McCarthy witch hunts, he was one of the most talented men in Hollywood. He wrote and directed *Force of Evil* and *Tell Them Willie Boy Is Here*.

SAMSON RAPHAELSON (1896- , New York City)—A leading scripter, he wrote many films, most notably *Heaven Can Wait* and *Green Dolphin Street*.

IRVING REVETCH (1915-)—Writer and producer of the excellent *The Reivers*, he was the coauthor of *Hombre* and *Hud*.

ROBERT RISKIN (1897-1955)—A superb writer. Among his great scripts were those for *Meet John Doe*; *You Can't Take It With You*; and *Mr. Deeds Goes to Town*.

MORRIE RYSKIND (b. 1895)—One of the all-time great comedy writers whose scripts include *My Man Godfrey*; *Animal Crackers*; and the classic *A Night at the Opera*.

HARRY SEGALL (b. 1897)—Wrote a number of excellent fantasy films in the 1940s, including *For Heaven's Sake* and *Angel on My Shoulder*.

MAXWELL SHANE (1905- , Paterson, N.J.)—An excellent writer and director, he wrote, directed, and produced *City Across the River*, one of the best proletarian films of the 1940s.

STANLEY SHAPIRO (1925-)—A producer as well as a writer, he specializes in comedies. He was coauthor of *Pillow Talk* (which won an Academy Award) and *That Touch of Mink*, and wrote and produced *Bedtime Story*, all of which starred Doris Day.

MELVILLE SHAVELSON (1917- , Brooklyn)—Wrote and directed many films, including *Houseboat* and *Beau James* and was the producer and director of *Cast a Giant Shadow*.

JACK SHER (1913- , Minneapolis)—An excellent scriptwriter, he coauthored the scripts for *Move Over, Darling* and *Paris Blues*.

CURT SIODMAK (1902-)—A German, he was a solid writer and director with a good touch for science fiction and fantasy.

JO SWERLING (1894- , Russia)—The writer of such famous films as *Blood and Sand* and *Lifeboat*.

MALVIN WALD (1917- , New York City)—Among his finest efforts were the screenplays for *Al Capone* and *The Naked City*.

CINEMATOGRAPHERS

STANLEY CORTEZ (1908- , New York City)—Born Kranz. One of America's greatest cinematographers, he worked on such films as *Night of the Hunter* and *The Magnificent Ambersons*.

KARL FREUND (1800-1969, Czechoslovakia)—The cinematographer for some of the greatest German films ever made, including *Metropolis*. After fleeing to the U.S., he won an Academy Award for *The Good Earth* and worked on many other important films, including *Key Largo*.

MAX GREENE (1896-1968)—Born Mutz Greenbaum. A leading cinematographer in both Germany and Great Britain.

BORIS KAUFMAN (1906- , Bialystok, Poland)—One of the world's leading cinematographers, he received an Academy Award for his work on *On the Waterfront* (1954).

MILTON KRASNER (1898-)—A major cinematographer, he won an Academy Award for *Three Coins in the Fountain*.

SAM LEAVITT (1917-)—A leading American cinematographer, he worked on many films, including *The Defiant Ones*.

JERZY LIPMAN (1922-)—The leading cinematographer in Poland and one of the finest in the world, he is best known for his work on *Kanal* and *Knife in the Water*.

JOSEPH RUTTENBERG (b. 1889, Russia)—Won at least four Academy Awards for *Gigi*; *Somebody Up There Likes Me*; *and Mrs. Miniver*.

HASKELL WEXLER (1926-)—One of the best-known cinematographers in the world, he won an Academy Award for *In the Heat of the Night* and also worked on *The Thomas Crown Affair* and *The Best Man*.

ART DIRECTORS AND DESIGNERS

SAUL BASS (1920- , New York City)—A leading Hollywood title designer.

MAURICE BINDER (1925-)—A leading Hollywood title designer. He did the great titles for *Dr. No* and set the pattern for the James Bond films.

NATHAN JURAN (1907- , Austria)—A leading Hollywood art director, he won an Academy Award for *How Green Was My Valley*. He later became a director of mostly action films.

BORIS LEVEN (1900- , Russia)—A leading production designer, he won an Academy Award for *West Side Story* and worked on such films as *The Sound of Music* and *The Sand Pebbles*.

COMPOSERS OF FILM SCORES

ELMER BERNSTEIN (1922- , New York City)—Simply one of the best in the business. He won an Academy Award for *To Kill a Mockingbird*.

HOWARD DIETZ (b. 1896)—Long associated with MGM, he wrote the score for *The Band Wagon*, among other films.

JOSEPH GERSHENSON (1904- , Russia)—Led the Music Department at Universal Pictures after 1941.

ERNEST GOLD (1921- , Vienna)—The well-known composer who won an Academy Award for *Exodus*.

JERRY GOLDSMITH (1930-)—A prominent American composer.

BERNARD HERMANN (1911-1975, New York City)—A leading film composer, he scored such films as *Psycho* and *Citizen Kane*.

FREDRICH HOLLAENDER (1896- , London)—In America as Frederick Hollander, he was a pioneer film scorer. He did the music for *The Blue Angel*.

ERIC W. KORNGOLD (1897-1957, Czechoslovakia)—Won Academy Awards for his music in *Anthony Adverse* and *The Adventures of Robin Hood*.

IRWIN KOSTAL (1915-)—Won an Academy Award for *The Sound of Music*.

LOUIS LEVY (b. 1893)—A noted British film composer best known for his score for *Nanook of the North*.

ALFRED NEWMAN (1901-1970)—One of the leading film composers of all time with over 275 scores, he has won at least five Academy Awards for films like

Love Is a Many Splendored Thing; Call Me Madam; Tin Pan Alley; and *With a Song in My Heart.*

MAX STEINER (1888-1971, Vienna)—The renowned composer who won Academy Awards for "Since You Went Away"; "Now Voyager"; and "The Informer".

MORRIS STOLOFF (1893- , Philadelphia)—A noted composer and musical director, he won Academy Awards for *Cover Girl* and *The Jolson Story.*

DIMITRI TIOMKIN (1899-)—One of the world's best-known film composers with credits such as *High Noon; The High and the Mighty;* and *The Old Man and the Sea.*

FRANZ WAXMAN (1906-1967, Germany)—Born Wachsmann. Won Academy Awards for the scores of *A Place in the Sun* (1951) and *Sunset Boulevard* (1950).

TELEVISION EXECUTIVES, PRODUCERS, DIRECTORS, AND WRITERS

MORT ABRAHAMS (1916- , New York City)—A major TV producer and writer.

DANNY ARNOLD (1925- , New York City)—Born Arnold Rothman. A top TV writer.

ROBERT L. BENDICK (1917- , New York City)—A leading producer, he won the Peabody Award in 1948 for *The United Nations in Action* and Emmy Awards for *The Great American Dream Machine.*

HARVE BENNETT (1930- , Chicago)—Born Fischman. A leading TV writer, he was executive producer of *Rich Man, Poor Man* and *The Bionic Woman.*

LORD SIDNEY L. BERNSTEIN (1899- , Ilford, England)—A leading TV pioneer in England and head of the huge Granada group of TV and publishing companies.

HERBERT BRODKIN (1912- , New York City)—A leading TV producer of dramatic shows and specials.

RUPERT CAPLAN (b. 1896, Montreal)—Was Senior Drama Producer for the Canadian Broadcasting Corporation's television division.

MURRAY CHERCOVER (1929- , Montreal)—A tremendous power in Canadian TV, he is President and Director of CTV (Canadian Television).

ALVIN COOPERMAN (1923- , Brooklyn)—A prominent TV producer.

NORMAN CORWIN (1910- , Boston)—Has been one of the leading radio, TV, and theatrical producers for decades. His awards (including the Peabody) run into the dozens.

LOUIS COWAN (1910-1976)—Formerly the President of CBS-TV.

FRED FREED (1921-1974)—A leading producer of TV documentaries, he won a total of seven Emmys during his distinguished career.

FRED W. FRIENDLY (1915-)—Born Wachenheimer. Was Head of the News Department at CBS beginning in 1964 and had earlier helped produce such shows as *CBS Reports* and, on radio, *Hear It Now.* He is also one of the leading critics of the age of television. He received at least ten Peabody Awards.

BRUCE GELLER (1931-1978, New York City)—The creator of such popular shows as *Mannix* and *Mission Impossible* before his tragic death in a plane crash.

LEONARD GOLDENBERG (1905- , Scottsdale, Pa.)—The long-time head of ABC, he finally built it to the point of overtaking the other two American giants.

MARK GOODSON (1915- , Sacramento, Calif.)—Of the famed team of Goodson-Todman, he is one of the leading TV producers.

SIR LEW GRADE (1906- , Russia)—Born Winogradsky. Was Managing Director of Associated Television and Incorporated Television Company, two of the largest operations in England. He is also a major force in the film industry, as Chairman of A.P. Films and associated companies.

ROBERT KAUFMAN (1931-)—A writer for screen and TV and the winner of the Emmy and Peabody awards for *The Bob Newhart Show*. His film plays include *Divorce American Style* and the campy *Dr. Goldfoot and the Bikini Machine*.

PETER KORTNER (1924- , Berlin)—Emmy-winning writer son of the noted German actor Fritz Kortner.

NORMAN LEAR (1922- , New Haven, Conn.)—The major producer of such shows as *All in the Family* and *Maude*, he is one of the most influential men in the history of American TV.

HARRIS L. KATLEMAN (1928- , Omaha)—President of MGM-TV.

RICHARD L. LEVINSON (1934- , Philadelphia)—The Emmy award-winning creator of such shows as *Columbo* and *The Bold Ones*, he was the cocreator of *Mannix*.

DAVID LEVY (1913- , Philadelphia)—Producer and Executive Vice-President of Network Programs at NBC, 1959-1961, and the creator of *The Addams Family*.

LORING MANDEL (1928- , Chicago)—A noted writer for screen and TV, he worked all of the great dramatic shows of the "Golden Age" of the 1950s.

DON M. MANKIEWICZ (1922- , Berlin)—Another major figure of the "Golden Age" and a top writer, he wrote the pilot shows for the *Marcus Welby, M.D.* and *Ironside* series.

SUSAN MILLER (1942-)—Born Spivak. Creator of the very popular *Soap*.

NEWTON N. MINOW (1926- , Milwaukee)—A lawyer who worked with Adlai Stevenson, he was the most famous Chairman of the Federal Communications Commission in the history of that agency. His 1961 description of TV as "a vast wasteland" had national impact but has not resulted in very much positive change.

WILLIAM S. PALEY (1901- , Chicago)—The dynamic Chairman of the Board of CBS for almost 30 years.

PIERRE PARAF (b. 1893, Paris)—Served as Chief Editor of the national radio and television companies of France.

MARTIN A. RAGAWAY (1928- , Brooklyn)—One of the leading comedy writers in the business and an Emmy Award winner, he wrote for such stars as Dick van Dyke and Red Skelton.

ALVIN RAKOFF (1927- , Canada)—A leading TV director in Great Britain.

MARTIN RANSHOHOFF (1927-)—Became Chairman of Filmways and produced such TV successes as *The Addams Family* and *The Beverly Hillbillies*, and also produced *The Cincinnati Kid* and the great *Americanization of Emily*.

LEONARD RUSKIN (1923-1973)—A leading TV producer, he was one of the founders of *TV Guide*.

RICHARD SALANT (1914- , New York City)— Former president of CBS News.

DAVID SARNOFF (1891-1971, Uzlian, Russia)—President of RCA and founder of NBC. RCA became the biggest industrial empire of its kind in the world. Sarnoff was also the wireless operator who first heard the call for help from the *Titanic*.

ROBERT SARNOFF (1918- , New York City)—President and later Chairman of the Board of NBC after his father, he also led RCA.

ALEX SEGAL (1915-1977)—One of the great early directors of live dramatic American television.

ROD SERLING (1924-1975)—The justly famous creator of *The Twilight Zone.*

LAWRENCE SPIVAK (1900- , Brooklyn)—Creator and long-time producer of *Meet the Press.*

SHIMON WINCELBERG (1924- , Kiel, Germany)—A leading TV writer, he wrote some of the best episodes of *Gunsmoke*; *Naked City*; and *Route 66.*

TELEVISION PERFORMERS

See also Comedians; Entertainers; Film Stars.

JACK ALBERTSON (1910- , Malden, Mass.)—Won an Academy Award for *The Subject Was Roses* in 1968 and gained fame as the Man on *Chico and the Man.*

BEATRICE ARTHUR (1924- , New York City)—Born Frankel. Best known in the title role of *Maude.*

EDWARD ASNER (1929- , Kansas City)—A fine actor, he portrayed Lou Grant on the *Mary Tyler Moore Show.*

JOHN BANNER (1910-1973, Austria)—A refugee from Hitler, he played the friendly German prison guard on *Hogan's Heroes*, 1965-1969.

GENE BARRY (1922- , New York City)—Born Klass. He had plenty as TV's Bat Masterson and Amos Burke.

JACK BARRY (1918- , Lindenhurst, N.Y.)—The well-known game show host.

MILTON BERLE (1908- , New York City)—Born Berlinger. He was Mr. Television and the first TV superstar. He was such a big star that it obscured his real comic genius and the critics did not take him as seriously as they should have.

WARREN BERLINGER (1937- , Brooklyn)—Frequently seen on TV and in the movies, he is a fine character actor.

JOYCE BROTHERS (1929- , New York City)—Born Bauer. One of the leading "pop" psychologists on TV and radio. She is not on a par with Adler and Jung.

KITTY CARLISLE (1914- , New Orleans)—Born Catherine Holzman. A fine operatic singer who became a well-known TV personality as a panelist on *To Tell the Truth.*

SID CAESAR (1922- , Yonkers, N.Y.)—His *Your Show of Shows* was one of the great events in the history of television. He is a tremendous comic talent.

STUART DAMON (1937-)—Born Stu Zonis. A frequent performer on TV and in films.

MICHAEL DOUGLAS (1945- , New Brunswick, N.J.)—The son of Kirk Douglas and one of the stars of the late and lamented *Streets of San Francisco.* He produced the Academy Award-winning film *One Flew over the Cuckoo's Nest.*

HERB EDELMAN (1933- , Brooklyn)—A very talented character actor.

PETER FALK (1927- , New York City)—The great star of *Columbo*, he is one of the very best actors seen regularly on television.

ALLEN FUNT (1914- , New York City)—Creator and host of the very entertaining *Candid Camera.*

VIRGINIA GRAHAM (1913- , Chicago)—Born Komiss, she is a popular radio and television talk show hostess.

BEN GRAUER (b. 1908- , New York City)—One of the great television and radio announcers, he was known to millions for his New Year's Eve countdowns from Times Square.

LORNE GREEN (1915- , Ottawa)—The great leader of the family on

Bonanza (as Ben Cartwright) and a terrific dramatic actor, he was founder of Toronto's Academy of Dramatic Arts.

MONTY HALL (1923-   , Winnipeg)—The host of the disgusting but very popular *Let's Make a Deal*. He deserves better.

MARTY INGELS (1936-   , Brooklyn)—The very funny character actor.

SCOTT JACOBY—A talented young dramatic actor who has appeared on a number of excellent TV specials, including *That Summer*.

GABE KAPLAN (1945-   , Brooklyn)—A great stand-up comedian, he became a major star on *Welcome Back Kotter*.

MARVIN KAPLAN (1924-   )—One of the very few actors who can make you laugh just by standing there.

WERNER KLEMPERER (1919-   , Cologne, Germany)—Colonel Klink on *Hogan's Heroes*. Many of the Germans on that show were Jews.

JACK KLUGMAN (1922-   , Philadelphia)—The messy one of the *Odd Couple*, he was great in *Twelve Angry Men* and *Quincy*.

HARVEY KORMAN (1927-   , Chicago)—The wonderful comic actor and a star of the *Carol Burnett Show*, he was great in *High Anxiety*.

MARTIN LANDAU (1933-   , Brooklyn)—The capable actor and star of *Mission Impossible*. He is married to his costar, Barbara Bain.

MICHAEL LANDON (1937-   , Forest Hills, N.Y.)—Born Orowitz, he became famous as Little Joe on *Bonanza* before starring on *Little House on the Prairie*.

LOUISE LASSER (1942-   , New York City)—Star of the wild *Mary Hartman, Mary Hartman* and a former wife of Woody Allen.

MICHELE LEE (1942-   , Los Angeles)—Born Dusiak. A lovely comic actress, she was terrific in the film *How to Succeed in Business without Really Trying*.

SHELDON LEONARD (1907-   , New York City)—Born Bershad. Was terrific in often funny gangster roles on TV and films before becoming a top television producer.

OSCAR LEVANT (1906-1972, Pittsburgh)—A fine pianist, he was a cynical panelist on many TV shows in the 1950s.

ROBERT Q. LEWIS (1924-   , New York City)—Appeared on a bewildering array of TV game shows.

SHARI LEWIS (1934-   , New York City)—The popular puppeteer who appears frequently on television and in nightclubs.

HAL LINDEN (1931-   , New York City)—An excellent Broadway performer and actor, he achieved his greatest popular success as *Barney Miller*.

PEGGY LIPTON (1948-   , Lawrence, N.Y.)—Became a star on *The Mod Squad*.

TINA LOUISE (1934-   , New York City)—Born Blacker. Ginger on *Gilligan's Island* and one of the most beautiful women on TV.

HAL MARCH (1921-1970)—Best known as the host of the ill-fated *$64,000 Question*, he also made a number of movies, including *It's Always Fair Weather*.

ROSS MARTIN (1920-   , Poland)—Born Martin Rosenblatt. An excellent character actor, he played Robert Conrad's sidekick on *The Wild, Wild West*.

MITCH MILLER (1911-   , Rochester, N.Y.)—Millions sang along with Mitch each week. Whatever happened to him?

HOWARD MORRIS (1919-   , New York City)—The underrated sidekick on *Your Show of Shows*, he is an excellent writer. He directed *With Six You Get Eggroll* and was great in *High Anxiety*.

BESS MYERSON (1924-   , New York City)—Miss America in 1945, she is now frequently seen on TV. She was also the official greeter of the City of New York.

BARRY NEWMAN (1938-   , Boston)—One of the fastest rising stars on television.

FUNNY, YOU DON'T LOOK JEWISH!

BAMBI—*See* Felix Salten (Writers: Germans and Austrians).
BETTY BOOP—*See* Max Fleischer (Cartoonists and Caricaturists).
BUGS BUNNY—*See* Mel Blanc (Film Stars).
DONDI—*See* Irwin Hasen (Cartoonists and Caricaturists).
DONALD DUCK—*See* Mel Blanc (Film Stars).
JOSE JIMENEZ—*See* Bill Dana (Comedians).
LI'L ABNER—*See* Al Capp (Cartoonists and Caricaturists).
SUPERMAN—*See* Joe Shuster and Jerry Siegel (Cartoonists and Caricaturists).

PHYLLIS NEWMAN (1935- , Jersey City)—A stage actress, she became a vivacious panelist on many game shows and frequent guest on talk shows.

LEONARD NIMOY (1931- , Boston)—Mr. Spock of *Star Trek* is one of TV's most popular stars and a very underrated actor.

ROB REINER (1946- , Bronx)—Meathead on *All in the Family*, he is the son of Carl Reiner and the husband of Penny Marshall.

MARK RICHMAN (1927-)—An excellent actor frequently seen on TV.

AVERY SCHREIBER (1935- , Chicago)—A comic character actor on TV, he had a great bit as a New York cab driver in comedy skits.

WILLIAM SHATNER (1931- , Montreal)—Captain Kirk on *Star Trek* and a fine dramatic actor, he has not received roles equal to his considerable talent.

DINAH SHORE (1917- , Winchester, Tenn.)—The only Jewish star of the Grand Ole Opry, she became a major star on television, with her own show. Recently she has become an effective talk show hostess.

PHIL SILVERS (1912- , Brooklyn)—Born Silversmith. The fabulous Sergeant Bilko and a top comedian, he was terrific in the film *A Funny Thing Happened on the Way to the Forum*.

ARNOLD STANG (1925- , Chelsea, Mass.)—The delightfully funny comedian and character actor, he has the weakest chin in the business.

PETER STRAUSS (1947- , New York City)—A top young actor, he portrayed Rudy Jordache in *Rich Man, Poor Man*.

DAVID SUSSKIND (1920- , New York City)—One of the leading producers in the business, his network and public TV talk shows have been very popular.

ROY THINNES (1938- , Chicago)—Star of *The Invaders* on TV, he is a convert to Judaism.

ABE VIGODA (1922- , New York City)—The great character actor who was "Fish" on TV.

HENRY WINKLER (1945- , New York City)—The fabulously popular Fonz on *Happy Days*, he was terrific in *The Lords of Flatbush*. He is one of the hottest properties in Hollywood.

STEPHEN YOUNG (1939- , Canada)—Born Levy. Starred on *Judd for the Defense*.

TELEVISION NEWSCASTERS

ELIE ABEL (1920- , Montreal)—An outstanding NBC newscaster, he received both the Peabody Award and the Award of the Overseas Press Club and became the Dean of the School of Journalism at Columbia University.

MEL ALLEN (1913-   , Birmingham, Ala.)—Born Melvin Israel. One of the most famous sports announcers of all time and the long-time voice of the New York Yankees

HOWARD COSELL (1920-   , Winston-Salem, N.C.)—Born Cohen. A legend in his own time and one of the best-known men in the U.S. He single-handedly changed the face of American national sportscasting.

BETTINA GREGORY (1946-   , New York City)—Born Friedman. A TV news reporter for ABC and the only woman military correspondent in the business.

GEORGE HERMAN (1920-   , New York City)—The veteran CBS news correspondent and the moderator of *Face the Nation.*

IRVING R. LEVINE (1922-   , Pawtucket, R.I.)—Economic Correspondent for NBC, he was the first television correspondent to be accredited by the Soviet authorities.

EDWIN NEWMAN (1919-   , New York City)—A leading reporter and commentator for NBC and their Critic-at-Large, he has won several Emmys and Peabody Awards. A champion of good English, he is the author of the best-selling books *Strictly Speaking* and *A Civil Tongue.*

BERT QUINT (1930-   , New York City)—A CBS news reporter who frequently reports from Rome.

BERNARD REDMONT (1918-   , New York City)—CBS Bureau Chief in Moscow from 1976, he was the Paris Bureau Chief of the Westinghouse Broadcasting Company, 1962–1976.

ALVIN ROSENFELD (1919-   , St. Louis)—The veteran NBC newsman who served that network as Israel and Madrid Bureau Chief in his long career.

MORLEY SAFER (1932-   , Toronto)—CBS reporter and cohost of *60 Minutes.*

RICHARD J. SCHAAP (1934-   , New York City)—A TV sports commentator, he was a leading sports reporter and Sports Editor of *Newsweek,* 1956–1963.

DAVID SCHOENBRUN (1915-   , New York City)—One of the great figures in news broadcasting, he was Chief Correspondent for CBS and Chief of its Washington Bureau. He won an Emmy in 1958.

MIKE WALLACE (1918-   , Brookline, Mass.)—Born Wallach. Cohost of *60 Minutes* and a leading CBS correspondent and investigative reporter.

BARBARA WALTERS (1931-   , Boston)—One of the best-known television personalities, she switched from NBC (where she had been a mainstay of the *Today Show*) to co-anchor the ABC evening news.

Part VIII
Sports

AUTO RACING

RENE DREYFUS (1905-   )—The winner of over 30 races and one of the most popular figures in France, he won the French Driving Championship in 1938.

ROBERT GROSSMAN (1923-   )—One of the leading drivers in the U.S. during the 1960s.

PETER REVSON—One of the top American drivers of the 1970s, he was killed in a crash in South Africa. He finished second at the 1971 Indianapolis 500 classic and won many important events, including the Canadian–American Challenge Cup and the British Grand Prix.

MAURI ROSE (1906-   , Dayton, Ohio)—One of the all-time great race drivers, he was America's National Driving Champion in 1936 and won the Indy 500 in 1941, 1947, and 1948.

JODY SCHECKTER (1951-   , East London, South Africa)—One of the leading drivers in the world, he has won numerous major races.

SHEILA VAN DAMM (1922-   , Gloucester Terrace, England)—A leading woman driver and the European Champion in 1954 and 1955.

BASEBALL

CAL ABRAMS (1924-   , Philadelphia)—An outfielder for the Dodgers, Reds, Pirates, Orioles, and White Sox (1949–1956). He played in 567 games and hit .269.

MORRIE ARNOVICH (1910-1959, Superior, Wis.)—Played for the Phillies, Reds, and Giants (1936-1941) and played in 590 games and hit .287. He hit .324 in 1939.

JACOB H. ATZ (1879-1945, Washington, D.C.)—Considered one of the greatest minor league managers of all time. He became a Catholic.

ROBERT "BO" BELINSKY (1936-   , New York City)—Part Jewish, he played for the Angels, Phillies, and others. He pitched a no-hitter in 1962.

WILLIAM E. BENSWANGER (b. 1892, New York City)—President of the Pittsburgh Pirates, 1932-1946.

MOE BERG (1902-?, New York City)—The famous American spy who was also a major league catcher for several teams. He played in 663 games and hit .243. The phrase "good field, no hit" reportedly referred to him.

RON BLOMBERG (1948-   , Atlanta)—Nagged by injuries, he had all the tools to be a great one. He was the Number One Draft Choice in Major League Baseball in 1967. An outfielder with the Yankees, he hit .329 in 100 games in 1973 and .311 in 90 games in 1974.

SAMUEL A. BOHNE (1896-   , San Francisco)—Born Sam Cohen. Outfielder and infielder for Cincinnati and other teams, he played in 663 games and hit .261.

LEO J. BONDY (1883-1944, Pottsville, Pa.)—Vice-President of the New York Giants, 1934-1944.

ROD CAREW (1945-   )—All-Star infielder of the Minnesota Twins and the California Angels, six-time American League batting champion, and a sure bet for the Hall of Fame. He is a convert to Judaism.

ANDY COHEN (1904-   , Baltimore)—An infielder with the New York Giants, he played in 262 games and hit .281. He was later a coach with the Phillies.

HARRY DANNING (1911-   , Los Angeles)—Catcher with the Giants, 1933-1942. He played in 890 games and hit .285. He was on the NL All-Star team in 1939, 1940, and 1941.

MYRON W. "MOE" DRABOWSKY (1935-   , Ozanna, Poland)—Pitcher with the Cubs, Milwaukee, the Reds, and Kansas City in the 1950s and 1960s. His mother was Jewish. He pitched two no-hitters in the majors.

BARNEY DREYFUSS (1865-1932, Freiberg, Germany)—Owned the Pittsburgh Pirates for 32 years and is considered the father of the World Series.

HARRY EISENSTADT (1915- , Brooklyn)—Pitcher with the Dodgers, Tigers, and Indians (1935-1942). He won a total of 25 games.

HARRY FELDMAN (1919-1962, New York City)—Pitcher with the Giants (1942-1946), he won a total of 35 games.

JULIUS (1872-1925, Cincinnati) and MAX (1877-1951, Cincinnati) FLEISCH-MANN—Owned the Cincinnati Reds.

ALLEN S. FORMAN (1928- , Morristown, N.J.)—An umpire in the National League in the 1960s.

MURRAY FRANKLIN (1914- , Chicago)—Although he played the infield briefly for the Tigers, he is best known for hitting .439, the highest average in baseball in 1938. He was playing in the Mountain States League at the time.

ANDREW FREEDMAN (1860-1915, New York City)—Owned the New York Giants, 1894-1902.

JUDGE EMIL E. FUCHS (1878-1961, New York City)—Owned and managed the Boston Braves.

MILTON GALATZER (1909- , Chicago)—Played 251 games and hit .268 for the Indians and Reds between 1933 and 1939.

JOE GINSBERG (1926- , New York City)—Catcher for a bunch of teams between 1948 and 1962, he played in 695 games and hit .241.

HARRY GOLDMAN (1857-1941)—One of the founders of the American League.

SID GORDON (1918- , Brooklyn)—Played for the Giants, Braves, and Pirates (1941-1955) and hit .283 in 1,475 games. Twice an All-Star, including in 1950 when he had 27 homers, hit .304 and drove in over 100 runs.

HANK GREENBERG (1911- , New York City)—The great Detroit Tiger first baseman who played in 1,394 games and hit .313. His best year was 1940, when he hit .340. He hit 58 home runs in 1938. He was MVP in the American League on two occasions and is a member of Baseball's Hall of Fame.

LOUIS W. HEILBRONER (1861-1933, Fort Wayne, Ind.)—Managed the St. Louis Cardinals in 1900.

KEN HOLTZMAN (1945- , St. Louis)—An outstanding pitcher, he threw two no-hitters. He starred for the Cubs and Oakland, and won 21 games in 1973. He also won four World Series games.

JEROLD C. HOFFBERGER (1919- , Baltimore)—Owner of the Baltimore Orioles for many years.

EDWIN I. HYNEMAN (1869-1946, Philadelphia)—Co-owner of the Philadelphia Phillies in the first quarter of the century.

BENJAMIN M. KAUFF (1891-1961, Middleport, Ohio)—Played for several major league teams as an outfielder and hit .310 in 859 games. He led the Federal League in hitting with .366 and stole 75 bases in 1914. For the Giants, he hit .308 in 1917.

JOHNNY KLING (1875-1947, Kansas City, Mo.)—Considered one of the greatest catchers in baseball history, he spent most of his career with the Cubs. He played in 1,228 games and hit .271.

SANDY KOUFAX (1935- , New York City)—The great Hall of Fame pitcher for the Dodgers, he won over 100 games, pitched four no-hitters (one a perfect game), led the league in strikeouts many times, and was MVP in 1963. He struck out 269 men in 1961, and won 25 games and struck out 306 in 1963. He was the youngest player ever to make the Hall of Fame.

LOUIS C. KRAMER (1848-1922, Cincinnati)—Helped found the Cincinnati

Reds and served as President of the American Association when it was one of the major leagues.

BARRY LATMAN (1936-   , Los Angeles)—Pitched for the White Sox, Indians, and Angels and won more than 50 games. He was 13 and 5 in 1961.

JAMES J. LEVEY (1906-   , Pittsburgh)—Infielder for the Browns, 1930-1933, he hit .230 in 440 games.

ERSKINE MAYER (1891-1957, Atlanta, Ga.)—Known as "Scissors," he pitched for the Phillies and other teams and won 91 and lost 70. He won 21 games in 1914 and 1915.

NATHAN MENDERSON (1820-1904, Germany)—President of the Cincinnati Reds in 1880.

CHARLES S. "BUDDY" MYERS (1904-   , Ellisville, Miss.)—Played the infield for Washington and Boston, led the American League in hitting with .349 in 1935, and led the league in steals with 30 in 1928. He played in 1,923 games and hit .303.

GABE PAUL (1910-   )—Formerly Vice-President of the White Sox, he became President of the Cleveland Indians and is considered one of the leading front office men in baseball. He is now with the New York Yankees.

BARNEY PELTY (1880-1939, Farmington, Mo.)—A pitcher with the Browns and Washington, his record was 92 and 118. He won 17 games in 1906.

LIPMAN E. PIKE (1845-1893, New York City)—Considered to have been the first professional baseball player in history.

JACOB A. PITLER (1894-   , New York City)—Played briefly for Pittsburgh but is best known as the long-time coach of the Brooklyn Dodgers.

JAMES H. REESE (1904-   , Los Angeles)—Born Solomon. Played for the Yankees and Cards from 1930 to 1932 and hit .278 in 232 games as an infielder. He hit .346 in 1930 (for half a season).

EDWARD M. REULBACH (1882-1961, Detroit)—Pitched for the Cubs, Dodgers, and Braves and won 181 and lost 105. He won 24 games in 1908 and 21 in 1915 and also won two World Series games. He was part Jewish.

SAUL W. ROGOVIN (1922-   , Brooklyn)—A fine pitcher who played for the Tigers, White Sox, Baltimore, and the Phillies from 1949 to 1957. He won 48 of the 154 games he appeared in. His best year was 1951, when he led the league in ERA (2.78).

JAMES J. ROSEMAN (b. 1856, New York City)—Played outfield and first base and pitched for many major league teams. He played in 678 games and had a lifetime average of .271.

AL ROSEN (1925-   , Spartanburg, S.C.)—The great third baseman of the Indians from 1947 to 1956, he played in over 1,000 games, hit .285, led the league in homers twice, was MVP in 1953 (.336 and 43 homers), and was an All-Star selection at least four times.

GEORGE ROSEN (1913-   , Toronto)—Known as "Goody," he played for the Dodgers and Giants, 1937-1946, and hit .291 in 551 games. His best year was 1945, when he hit .325.

AL SCHACHT (1892-   , New York City)—Won 14 games total for the Senators between 1919 and 1921 but is best known as the Clown Prince of Baseball.

DICK SHARON (1950-   , Redwood City, Calif.)—Part Jewish, he played the outfield for several teams in the 1970s, including the Angels and Cardinals.

LARRY SHERRY (1935-   , Los Angeles)—An ace Dodger pitcher in the 1960s, he won 14 games in 1960 but is best known for his great relief work during the 1959 season and in the World Series that year.

NORM SHERRY (1931-   , New York City)—Played for the Dodgers and Mets in the late 1950s and early '60s and hit .215 in 194 games. He managed the Angels in 1976.

ALEXANDER B. SMITH (1871-1919, New York City)—Known as "Broadway," he played almost every position for the New York Giants, the Red Sox, the Cubs, and other teams. He played in 278 games and had a lifetime average of .278.

AARON S. STERN (1853-1920)—Owned the Cincinnati Reds, 1882-1890.

"SILENT GEORGE" STONE (1876-1945, Lost Nation, Nebr.)—St. Louis Browns outfielder, he played in 848 games and hit .301. He led the league in hitting with .358 in 1906.

STEVE STONE (1947-   , Cleveland)—A pitcher with the Giants and Cubs, he was 12-8 with the Cubbies in 1975.

MICKEY WEINTRAUB (1907-   , Chicago)—He played for the Giants, the Reds, and the Phillies from 1933 to 1938 and hit .295 in 450 games. His best year was 1941 (.316).

BASKETBALL

See also Olympic Medalists.

RED AUERBACH (1918-   , Brooklyn)—The legendary head coach and General Manager of the Boston Celtics. His teams won many titles in the 1950s, '60s, and '70s.

MAC BAKER (1898-   , New York City)—An AAU All-America in 1919 and a retrospective All-America in 1920 and 1921 from NYU.

MOE BECKER (1917-   )—A great star at Duquesne (he was selected for their all-time team), he played pro ball with the Bullets, Pittsburgh, Boston, Detroit, and other teams in the 1940s. He was a First Team All-America pick in 1941.

JULES BENDER (1914-   , New York City)—Pro player with the Baltimore Bullets and other teams, he played at Long Island University (LIU). He was First Team All-America in 1937.

LULU BENDER (1910-   , New York City)—A star at Columbia U., and the leading scorer in the Ivy League in 1930-1931, he played the pro game with a number of clubs. He was First Team All-America in 1930 and 1932.

MARK BINSTEIN—An All-America Honorable Mention from the U.S. Military Academy in 1955, he coached in both National and American Basketball associations.

HARRY BOYKOFF (1922-   , New York City)—From St. John's, he was one of the first dominating big men (6'9") in the game. He played pro ball with Boston and other teams. He was a First Team All-America in 1943 and a Second Team All-America in 1946.

TANHUM COHEN-MINTZ (1939-   , Palestine)—An outstanding, 6'8" basketball player from Israel, he was a First Team European All-Star in 1964.

GEORGE FEIGENBAUM (1929-   )—Played pro ball with Baltimore and Milwaukee in the early 1950s after a college career at both LIU and the U. of Kentucky.

JEROME FLEISHMAN (1922-   )—From NYU, he played pro ball with Philadelphia, 1947–1950. He was a Second Team All-America in 1943.

DONALD J. FORMAN (1926-   )—From NYU, he played one year (1949) with the Minneapolis Lakers. He was a Second Team All-America in 1948.

MARTY FRIEDMAN (b. 1889, New York City)—Another great pioneer of the pro game (the New York Whirlwinds), he is a member of the Hall of Fame.

LAWRENCE FRIEND (1935-   )—A star at the U. of California, he played with the Knicks in 1958. He was a First Team All-America in 1957.

JACK GARFINKEL (1920-   )—Won the Haggerty Award in 1941 as the leading basketball player in the New York area. He starred at St. John's and played with the Royals and Boston in the pro ranks in the late 1940s.

EMANUEL GOLDBLATT (1904-   , Philadelphia)—Played at the U. of Pennsylvania and also played pro ball and was elected to the Helms Hall of Fame. He was chosen as a retrospective Third Team All-America in 1925.

MOE GOLDMAN (1913-   , Brooklyn)—A star at CCNY in the early 1930s, he played pro ball for almost a decade. He was Second Team All-America in 1934.

EDWARD B. GOTTLIEB (1900-   )—Head Coach of the Philadelphia Warriors, 1947–1955, he owned the club from 1952 to 1962 and is a member of the Hall of Fame.

NORMAN GREKIN (1930-   )—MVP at the NIT in 1952, he starred at LaSalle and then played one year (1954) with the Warriors.

SONNY HERTZBERG (1922-   )—A star at CCNY, he played with the Knicks, Washington, and the Celtics in the late 1940s and early '50s.

ARTHUR HEYMAN (1941-   , New York City)—College Basketball Player of the Year and NCAA Tournament MVP in 1963, he starred at Duke before playing for the Knicks in the 1960s. He made the NBA All-Rookie Team in 1964, but never realized his great potential as a pro. He was his own worst enemy. He was a Second Team All-America in 1961, a First Team All-America in 1962, and a First Team All-America in 1963.

NAT HOLMAN (1896-   , New York City)—Long-time Coach of CCNY and one of the greatest basketball players of all time. He was an original Celtic, and one of the greatest of all pro players.

RED HOLZMAN (1920-   , New York City)—A CCNY star, he played pro ball with Rochester, 1946–1954, before turning to coaching with Milwaukee and St. Louis. He was one of the most famous head coaches in the history of the New York Knicks. He was a Third Team All-America in 1942.

RALPH KAPLOWITZ (1920-   )—From NYU, he played with the Warriors in 1947 and 1948.

BARRY KRAMER (1942-   , Schenectady, N.Y.)—Winner of the Haggerty Award in 1963 and a great star at NYU, he finished as second leading scorer in the country in 1963. He played with the Knicks and with San Francisco in the mid-1960s. He was a First Team All-America in 1963 and a First Team All-America in 1964.

BENJAMIN KRAMER (1913-   , Chelsea, Mass.)—A second team All-America pick in 1936 from LIU and a pro player for a decade. He also coached the Baltimore Bullets. They called him Red.

RUDY LARUSSO (1937-   , Brooklyn)—The great All-Star forward of the Los Angeles Lakers in the 1960s. He starred at Dartmouth.

BARRY LEIBOWITZ—From LIU, he played with New Jersey and Pittsburgh of the ABA, in Europe, and in Israel in the late 1960s and early '70s. He was an All-America Honorable Mention in 1967.

PINKY MATCH (1904-1944)—A Third Team retrospective All-America pick from CCNY for 1925.

SAMUEL MELITZER (b. 1888, New York City)—Chosen as a Second Team retrospective All-America for 1909 from Columbia U.

JERRY NEMER (1912-   , Chicago)—Voted Most Valuable Player in the history of the U. of Southern California in 1960, he starred on that team in the early 1930s and was a Second Team All-America in 1933.

DAVE NEWMARK—7'1" from Columbia U., he played with the Atlanta Hawks in the early 1970s.

BERNARD OPPER (1918-   , New York City)—Played at the U. of Kentucky and then pro ball with the Detroit Eagles and other teams. He was a First Team All-America in 1939.

MAURICE PODOLOFF (b. 1890, Russia)—The famous and powerful Commissioner of the National Basketball Association.

LEONARD R. ROSENBLUTH (1933- , New York City)—One of the all-time great college players, he was Helms College Player of the Year and the MVP of the NCAA Tournament in 1957. He played only one year in the pros, with the Warriors in 1958. He was a First Team All-America in 1956 and 1957, and a Third Team All-America in 1955.

MENDY RUDOLPH (1928-)—One of the most famous referees in the history of the NBA, he is now an announcer.

LEONARD SACHS (1897-1942, Chicago)—One of the great coaches, he led Loyola of Chicago for almost 20 years (1924–1942) and won 224 games. Elected to both the Naismith Memorial Hall of Fame and the Helms Hall of Fame, he became a Catholic.

ABE SAPERSTEIN (b. 1901-?, London)—The great personality who started and coached the fabulous Harlem Globetrotters. His contribution to race relations in the U.S. is enormous.

ADOLPH SCHAYES (1928- , New York City)—One of the all-time great pro players, this 6′8″ star was an NBA All-Star on 12 occasions, all as a member of the Syracuse five (1949–1963). He spent one year with the Warriors and then became their Head Coach. He was a First Team All-America in 1948 and is in the Hall of Fame.

BARNEY SEDRAN (b. 1891, New York City)—Born Sedransky. A CCNY graduate, he is considered one of the greatest early pro players.

ALBERT STARK (b. 1897)—Won 102 games as Head Coach of Dartmouth before and after World War II.

IRA STREUSAND (1890-1964, Austria)—One of the great early college and pro players, he instituted the practice of foul shooting by the fouled player rather than by somebody else. He was selected as a retrospective All-America from CCNY for 1908.

LOUIS L. SUGARMAN (1890-1951, New York City)—A pioneer pro player and, later, Head Coach at Princeton U. for one year (1921).

SIDNEY H. TANENBAUM (1925- , Brooklyn)—A great NYU guard, he was elected to the Helms Hall of Fame and played with the Knicks and the Bullets in the late 1940s. He was a First Team All-America from NYU in 1946 and a First Team All-America selection in 1947.

DAVID TOBEY (b. 1898, New York City)—An early pro player, he became one of the leading referees in basketball and was the author of the standard work on the subject.

NEAL WALK (1948- , Brooklyn)—From the U. of Florida, he was an All-America center in the late 1960s. He played pro ball with the Suns and Knicks, and averaged over 20 points per game and had over 1,000 rebounds in 1972–1973. He was also outstanding the previous and following years, but his play declined dramatically when he became a vegetarian and lost 35 pounds (he was 6′11″ and 250). He is the only graduate of Miami Beach High School to play pro basketball.

RON WATTS—From Wake Forest, he was an All-America selection in the 1960s and played with the Boston Celtics.

GEORGE WOLFE (1908-)—Played at St. John's and in the pros, and coached LIU, 1944–1945.

MAX ZASLOFSKY (1925- , Brooklyn)—One of the great pro stars of his era (1947–1956), playing with Chicago, the Knicks, Baltimore, Milwaukee, and Fort Wayne. He was the NBA's leading scorer in 1948. At one time, he was the third-highest scorer in the history of the NBA.

BOWLING

MORT LINDSEY (1888-1959, Newark)—Won many major tournaments and was a leading bowler during the first quarter of this century. He is a member of the American Bowling Congress Hall of Fame.

SYLVIA WENE MARTIN (1928- , Philadelphia)—A five-time All-America, she was one of the leading bowlers in American history.

MORRIE OPPENHEIM (1936- , Chicago)—Was selected as an All-America in 1959–1960.

MARK ROTH (1952- , Brooklyn)—The leading bowler in the world in the late 1970s, he was also the leading money winner on the Pro Tour.

LOUIS B. STEIN (1858-1949, Winstorten, Holland)—One of the founders of the American Bowling Congress, he was responsible for many standard rules, including the 16-pound limit for the ball and the 300-pin scoring system.

ROSE M. WEINSTEIN (1937- , Wilkes Barre, Pa.)—Selected as an All-America in 1962–1963.

BOXING

See also Olympic Medalists

WORLD CHAMPIONS

ABRAHAM W. ATTELL (b. 1884, San Francisco)—World Featherweight Champion, 1901–1912. One of the greatest fighters of his division, he was elected to Boxing's Hall of Fame.

MAX BAER (1909-1959, Omaha, Neb.)—Heavyweight Champion of the World, 1934–1935. His father was of Jewish origin.

BENNY BASS (1904- , Kiev, Russia)—Featherweight Champion of the World, 1927–1928, and Junior Lightweight Champion of the World, 1929–1931. He won 140 fights in his long career.

JACKIE BERG (1909- , London)—Born Judah Bergman. Junior Welterweight Champion of the World, 1930–1931. He won 162 fights.

JACK BERNSTEIN (1899-1945, New York City)—Born John Dodick. Junior Lightweight Champion of the World in 1923. He won 67 fights and lost only 7.

MUSHY CALLAHAN (1905- , New York City)—Born Vicente M. Scheer. Junior Welterweight Champion of the World, 1926–1930.

ROBERT COHEN (1930- , Bone, Algeria)—Bantamweight Champion of the World, 1954–1956.

ABE GOLDSTEIN (1900- , New York City)—Bantamweight Champion of the World in 1924. He won 89 fights.

ALPHONSE HALIMI (1932- , Constantine, Algeria)—Bantamweight Champion of the World, 1957–1959. He is an Orthodox Jew.

HARRY HARRIS (1880-1959, Chicago)—Bantamweight Champion of the World, 1901–1902. He never lost the title—he had to give it up when he outgrew the division.

BEN JEBY (1907- , New York City)—Born Morris B. Jebaltowsky. Middleweight Champion of the World, 1932–1933.

LOUIS "KID" KAPLAN (1902- , Russia)—Featherweight Champion of the World, 1925–1927. Considered one of the all-time greats at that weight, he won 101 fights in his career.

SOLLY KRIEGER (1909- , New York City)—Middleweight Champion of the World, 1938–1939. He won a total of 80 fights.

BENNY LEONARD (1896-1947, New York City)—Born Benjamin Leiner. One of the greatest lightweights in history, he was Lightweight Champion of the World, 1917-1925.

BATTLING LEVINSKY (1891-1949, Philadelphia)—Born Barney Lebrowitz. Light Heavyweight Champion of the World, 1916-1920, and one of the finest fighters in his division in the history of the sport.

TED LEWIS (b. 1893, London)—Born Gershon Mendeloff. Welterweight Champion of the World, 1915-1919, and an all-time great. He won 155 fights.

AL McCOY (1894, Rosenhayn, N.J.)—Not the real McCoy—he was born Al Rudolph. Middleweight Champion of the World (and the first lefty ever to win a world title) 1914-1917.

DANIEL MENDOZA (1764-1836, Aldgate, England)—The great early English champion, he was the unofficial heavyweight champion of the world between 1792 and 1795.

BOB OLIN (1908-1956, New York City)—Light Heavyweight Champion of the World, 1934-1935.

VICTOR PEREZ (1911-1942, Tunis)—Flyweight Champion of the World, 1931--1932. He won a total of 89 fights. Perez, who fought as "Young Perez", was murdered by the Germans.

CHARLEY PHIL ROSENBERG (1902- , New York City)—Bantamweight Champion of the World, 1925-1927. He was born Charles Green, but his name was not Jewish enough for the New York fans (or so he thought).

"SLAPSIE" MAXIE ROSENBLOOM (1904-1976, New York City)—Light Heavyweight Champion of the World, 1930-1934, and one of the most colorful men in the game. He won 208 fights. His flaky attitude has obscured his great talent. He is in Boxing's Hall of Fame.

BARNEY ROSS (1909-?, New York City)—Born Barnet Rasofsky. Lightweight and the Junior Welterweight Champion of the World, 1933-1935, and then the Welterweight Champion of the World, 1934-1938. One of the all-time great welterweights and elected to the Hall of Fame, Ross fought his greatest fight against drug addiction acquired as a result of wounds during World War II. He won the struggle.

MIKE ROSSMAN—Son of a Jewish mother, he was Light Heavyweight Champion of the World in 1978.

CORPORAL IZZY SCHWARTZ (1902- , New York City)—Flyweight Champion of the World, 1927-1929.

AL SINGER (1907-1961, New York City)—Lightweight Champion of the World in 1930. His record included 60 wins and 8 losses.

OTHER BOXERS

ABE THE NEWSBOY (b. 1888)—Born Abraham Hollandersky. It is claimed that he fought more often than any other boxer—1,309 professional fights in 13 years.

MONTE ATTELL (1885-1960, San Francisco)—Bantamweight Champion of the U.S., 1909-1910.

PHIL BLOOM (b. 1894, London)—A lightweight, he fought all the leading men in his division. He had 175 fights, 99 of which were declared no contests.

NEWSBOY BROWN (1904- , Russia)—Born David Montrose. Was Bantamweight Champion of the Far East in the 1930s, fought for the World Flyweight Championship, and was a helluva good fighter.

JOE CHOYNSKI (1886-1943, San Francisco)—Fought all the great heavyweights at the turn of the century and held his own. He won 50 fights.

LEACH CROSS (1886-1957, New York City)—One of the leading lightweights, he had 154 fights. As Louis C. Wallach, he became a noted physician.

NAT FLEISCHER (b. 1887, New York City)—The noted boxing historian who established the ranking system used today.

RUBY GOLDSTEIN (1907- , New York City)—A leading lightweight who had a 50–5 record, he became a leading referee, frequently working championship fights.

BOBBY HALPERN (1933-)—An ex-convict, he boxed professionally at the age of 44 and was knocked out. He was later shot gangland-style.

SIG HART (1872-1963)—A leading bantamweight who once claimed the world title, he later became a famous manager.

WILLIE JACKSON (1897-1961, New York City)—Born Oscar Tobler. A leading lightweight, he had 158 fights.

JOE JACOBS (1896-1940, New York City)—One of the all-time great fight managers, he handled Max Schmeling and other boxers.

HARRY LEWIS (1886-1956, New York City)—A very tough welterweight who had 163 fights, he was a leading contender for the title.

DAVE ROSENBERG (1901- , New York City)—National AAU Welterweight Champion in 1919. He also had 57 pro fights.

JOHNNY ROSNER (b. 1895, New York City)—A leading flyweight who once claimed the title in that division.

LEW TENDLER (b. 1898, Philadelphia)—One of the truly great lightweights (he also fought as a welterweight), he had 167 fights and was elected to the Hall of Fame.

SID TERRIS (1904- , New York City)—National AAU Lightweight Champion as a youth and later had an outstanding pro career, winning 85 fights and losing only 12.

MATT WELLS (1886-1953, London)—Welterweight and Lightweight Champion of Great Britain and also Welterweight Champion of the British Empire.

CHARLEY WHITE (b. 1891, Liverpool, England)—Born Charles Anschowitz. A leading lightweight, he had 170 pro fights.

YOUNG OTTO (b. 1886, New York City)—Born Otto Susskind. A leading lightweight who had 196 fights, he knocked out 17 consecutive opponents in 1905.

YOUNG MONTREAL (b. 1898, Russia)—Born Morris Billingkoff. A leading flyweight who had over 100 fights.

CHESS

MANUEL AARON (1935- , India)—An International Master, he won the championship of India in 1959 and 1961.

LEV ARONIN (1920-)—A Soviet International Master, he is particularly noted for his creative contributions to opening theory.

YURY AVERBACH (1922-)—A leading Soviet endgame authority, he is an International Master who won the Soviet Championship in 1954.

G. ROSAMARIA BAUMSTARK (1941-)—A Rumanian International Woman's Master.

BELA BERGER (1931- , Hungary)—An International Master, he emigrated to Australia.

OSSIP BERNSTEIN (1882-1962, Jitomir, Russia)—An International Grandmaster, he was one of the few players to successfully compete at an advanced age.

ARLOS BIELICKI (1940-)—World Junior Champion in 1959, he is an International Master from Argentina.

ARTHUR B. BISGUIER (1929- , New York City)—U.S. Champion several times, he is an International Grandmaster.

MAX BLAU (1918-)—An International Master and many-time champion of Switzerland.

BENJAMIN M. BLUMENTHAL (1884-1947, Russia)—One of the leading chess theorists of his time, he achieved chess immortality with his "Blumenthal's Counter Gambit to the Queen's Pawn Opening."

JACOBO BOLBOCHAN (1906-)—An Argentine International Master.

JULIO BOLBOCHAN (1920-)—An International Master and several-time Champion of Argentina.

ISAAC BOLESLAVSKY (1919-)—A prominent Soviet International Grandmaster.

MIKHAIL M. BOTVINNIK (1911-)—Three-time World Champion and one of the leading players of the 20th century, he is an International Grandmaster and was Soviet Champion on six occasions. He holds the Order of Lenin.

VLADIMIR BRON (1909-)—One of the leading Soviet endgame composers.

DAVID BRONSTEIN (1924- , Kiev)—A Soviet International Grandmaster and former Soviet Champion.

RUDOLF CHAROUSEK (1873-1900, Prague)—One of the great young players of the late 19th century, his career was cut short by tuberculosis.

ABRAM CHASSIN (1923-)—A Soviet International Master.

MOSHE CZERNIAK (1910- , Poland)—An Israeli International Master.

ARNOLD DENKER (1914-)—A leading American International Master, he was U.S. Champion, 1944–1946.

DOLFI DRIMER (1934-)—A Rumanian International Master.

ARTHUR DUNKELBLUM (1906- , Cracow)—One of the leading players in Belgium, he was Champion of that country and an International Master.

BERTHOLD ENGLISCH (1851-1897)—One of the most outstanding players of the 19th century.

LARRY EVANS (1932- , New York City)—An International Grandmaster and many-time American Champion.

STEFAN FAZEKAS (1898-1967, Satoraljaujhely, Hungary)—An International Master, he was Champion of Great Britain in 1957.

REUBEN FINE (1914-)—A psychoanalyst, he is an International Grandmaster and five-time U.S. Open Champion. He was one of the leading American players of the 1930s.

ROBERT FISCHER (1943-)—The famous World Champion, International Grandmaster, and American Champion, he joined a small Christian sect. A child prodigy, he achieved International Grandmaster rank at the age of 15.

SALO FLOHR (1908- , Horodenka, Russia)—An International Grandmaster, he left Czechoslovakia for the Soviet Union.

PAULINO FRYDMAN (1905- , Poland)—An International Master, he became an Argentine citizen in the 1930s.

SEMION FURMAN (1920-)—A Soviet International Grandmaster, he is considered one of the best chess coaches in that country.

YEFIM GELLER (1925-)—An International Grandmaster and former Soviet Champion.

HARRY GOLEMBEK (1911-)—An International Master and three-time British Champion, he is one of the best-known writers on the game in the world.

GISELA GRESSER (1910- , Detroit)—Born Kahn. American Woman Champion on many occasions and is an International Woman's Master.

ERNST GRUNFELD (1893-1962)—An Austrian, he was an International Grandmaster. Grunfeld's Defense carries his name.

EDUARD Y. GUFELD (1936-)—A Soviet International Grandmaster.

ISIDOR GUNSBERG (1854-1930, Budapest)—One of the foremost players of the late-19th century.

YUZEFA GURFINKEL (1919-)—A Soviet International Woman's Master.

VITALY HALBERSTADT (1903-1967, Odessa, Russia)—One of the most famous endgame theoreticians in chess.

DANIEL HARRWITZ (1823-1884, Breslau, Germany)—One of the first great German competitors.

WILLIAM R. HARTSTON (1947- , London)—British Champion in 1973 and an International Master.

ISRAEL A. HOROWITZ (1907-)—An American International Master, he is Editor of the *Chess Review.*

BERNARD HORWITZ (1807-1885, Mecklenburg-Streilitz, Germany)—One of the famous "Berlin Pleiades" and a major figure in chess in the 19th century.

DAVID M. JANOWSKI (1868-1927, Volkovysk, Poland)—One of the truly great players of his time, he drank himself to death.

SHIMON KAGAN (1942-)—An Israeli International Master.

ILYA KAN (1909-)—A Soviet International Master.

JULIO KAPLAN (1950- , Buenos Aires)—Raised in Puerto Rico, he is an International Master and was World Junior Champion in 1967.

MONA KARFF (1914-)—A leading U.S. player, she held the U.S. Woman's Championship on numerous occasions. She is an International Woman's Master.

ISAAC KASHDAN (1905- , New York City)—An International Grandmaster and former U.S. Open Champion.

GYULA KLUGER (1914-)—An International Master from Hungary.

HANS KMOCH (1894- , Austria)—A noted International Master.

IGNATZ KOLISCH (1837-1889, Pressbourg, Hungary)—An outstanding 19th-century player.

GEORGE KOLTANOWSKI (1903-, Antwerp, Belgium)—An International Master and a leading exponent of blindfold chess, he was a noted TV chess analyst in the U.S.

IMRE KONIG (1899- , Kula, Hungary)—An International Master who lived in the U.S. and Great Britain after leaving his homeland.

VICTOR KORCHNOI (1931- , Leningrad)—The International Grandmaster who lost an attempt at the World Championship in 1978 after defecting from the Soviet Union. He was the Soviet Champion three times. He is part Jewish.

GREGORY KOSHNITSKY (1907- , Russia)—Champion of Australia twice during the 1930s and '40s.

YAIR KRAIDMAN (1932- , Haifa)—An Israeli International Master.

ALLA KUSHNIR (1941-)—One of the leading International Woman's Masters, she lost several attempts at the World Championship. She is a Soviet citizen.

EDWARD LASKER (b. 1885, Berlin)—An International Master, he won the U.S. Open Championship five times.

EMANNUEL LASKER (1868-1941, Berlinchen, Germany)—One of the titanic figures in the chess world, he was World Champion, 1894–1921. His father was a cantor.

ANATOLY LEIN (1931-)—An International Grandmaster from the Soviet Union, he emigrated to the U.S. and shared the Championship of the 1976 U.S. Open.

GRIGORI LEVENFISH (1889-1961)—A Soviet International Grandmaster.

IRINA LEVITINA (1954-)—Soviet Champion in 1971 and an International Woman's Master.

DAVID LEVY (1945-)—A British International Master.

VLADIMIR LIBERSON—A Soviet International Grandmaster.

ANDREA LILIENTHAL (1911- , Moscow)—An International Grandmaster who shared the 1940 Soviet Championship, he lived in Hungary but later returned to the U.S.S.R.

JOHANN LOWENTHAL (1810-1876, Budapest)—One of the leading players of the 19th century and an important personality in British chess circles.

HENRIQUE MECKING (1952-)—An International Grandmaster and Brazilian Champion at least three times.

JACQUES MIESES (1865-1954, Leipzig, Germany)—An International Grandmaster.

MIGUEL NAJDORF (1910- , Warsaw)—The frequent Champion of Argentina and International Grandmaster. He was in Argentina when Hitler invaded Poland, so he stayed there.

ARON NIMZOWITSCH (1886-1935, Riga, Latvia)—Of international grandmaster stature, he was one of the most influential theoreticians in modern chess history.

LEV POLUGAEVSKY (1934-)—A Soviet International Grandmaster.

YOSEF PORAT (1909- , Germany)—Born Heinz Foerder. An Israeli International Master.

SAMUEL RESHEVSKY (1911-)—One of the most famous child chess prodigies, he is an International Grandmaster and was U.S. Champion five times. Although he was the leading American player for several decades, the world title always eluded him.

RICHARD RETI (1889-1929, Pezinok, Czechoslovakia)—A leading player of his era and an important theorist.

AKIBA RUBINSTEIN (1882-1961, Stawiski, Poland)—A brilliant International Grandmaster who went insane.

CARL SCHLECHTER (1874-1918)—The famous "Drawing Master," he was an outstanding player. He starved to death during World War I.

SAMUEL SCHWEBER (1936-)—An Argentine International Master.

LEONID SHAMKOVITCH (1923-)—A Soviet International Grandmaster who emigrated to the U.S., he shared the 1976 U.S. Open title.

VASILY SMYSLOV (1921- , Moscow)—A Soviet International Grandmaster, he was World Champion, 1957–1958, as well as Soviet Champion in 1949. He is part Jewish.

BORIS SPASSKY (1937- , Leningrad)—World Champion, 1968–1972, and an International Grandmaster, he was also Soviet Champion twice and World Junior Champion.

RUDOLF SPIELMANN (1883-1942, Vienna)—Was of international grandmaster caliber.

LEONID STEIN (1934-1973, Kamenetz-Podolsk, U.S.S.R.)—An International Grandmaster, he was Soviet Champion three times in the 1960s.

HERMAN STEINER (1905-1955, Dunaiskoi Stredi, Hungary)—An International Master, he was U.S. Champion in 1948.

LAJOS STEINER (1903- , Hungary)—An International Master, he was Australian Champion three times after World War II.

WILHELM STEINITZ (1836-1900)—The great World Champion and the leading player in the world during the last quarter of the 19th century.

MARK TAIMANOV (1926-)—A Soviet International Grandmaster, he was once Soviet Champion.

MIKHAIL TAL (1936-   )—The famous World Champion from 1960 to 1961. An International Grandmaster, he was Soviet Champion three times.

SIEGBERT TARRASCH (1862-1934)—One of the great players of his time, clearly of international grandmaster caliber.

SAVIELLY TARTAKOVER (1887-1956, Rostov-on-Don, Russia)—An International Grandmaster and a major theorist.

VLADIMIR VUKOVIC (b. 1898)—A Yugoslav International Master.

RAYMOND WEINSTEIN (1941-   )—An American International Master, he was also U.S. Junior Champion.

SIMON WINAWER (1838-1919, Warsaw)—One of the strongest players of the 19th century.

DANIEL YANOFSKY (1925-   , Brody, Poland)—An International Grandmaster and seven-time Champion of Canada, he was also British Champion.

MIKHAIL YUDOVICH (1911-   )—A Soviet International Master.

BERNARD ZUCKERMAN (1943-   )—An International Master, he was American Junior Champion in 1961.

JOHANNES ZUCKERTORT (1842-1888, Riga, Latvia)—One of the premier competitors of the 19th century.

FENCING

See also Olympic Medalists.

DANIEL BUKANTZ (1917-   , New York City)—U.S. Foil Champion in 1949, 1952, 1953, and 1957.

ABRAM COHEN (1924-   , Brooklyn)—U.S. Epée Champion in 1955 and 1956 and Silver Medal winner in Team Epée at the 1955 Pan-American Games.

HERBERT COHEN (1940-   , New York City)—U.S. Foil Champion in 1964 and a Gold Medal winner in Team Foil at the 1963 Pan-American Games.

RALPH COOPERMAN—Won Gold Medals in Team Foil and Team Sabre at the 1954 and 1958 British Empire Games, Gold Medals in Individual and Team Sabre and Team Foil at the 1962 Games, Silver Medals in Individual Sabre at the 1954 and 1958 Games, and a Bronze Medal in Individual Foil at the 1962 Games.

MARTIN J. DAVIS (1937-   , St. Louis)—Won a Gold Medal in Team Foil at the 1963 Pan-American Games.

LENNIE DERVBINSKY—A recent immigrant from the Soviet Union, he was the 1977 National AAU Epée Champion, the youngest man ever to win the title.

GILBERT EISNER (1940-   , New York City)—U.S. Epée Champion in 1962, NCAA Foil Champion (from NYU) in 1960, and winner of a Gold Medal in Team Epee at the 1963 Pan-American Games.

WALTER V. FARBER—Won Gold Medals in Team Sabre at the 1959 and 1963 Pan-American Games and Silver Medals in Individual Sabre those same years.

MAXWELL R. GARRET (1917-   , New York City)—Born Max Goldstein. A President of the National Fencing Coaches of America, he was a very successful coach at the U. of Illinois.

ERNEST GITTERMAN—Canadian National Foil, Epée, and Sabre Champion in 1936.

EUGENE GLAZER (1939-   , New York City)—NCAA Foil Champion from NYU in 1960 and winner of a Gold Medal in Team Foil at the 1959 Pan-American Games.

HAROLD GOLDSMITH (1930-   , Germany)—Won Gold Medals in Foil at the 1955 Pan-American Games and in Individual and Team Foil at the 1959 Games. He also won Silver Medals in Team Epée and Team Foil at the 1955 Games. He was NCAA Foil Champion from CCNY in 1952.

BYRON KRIEGER (1920-   , Detroit)—NCAA Foil Champion in 1942 and winner of Gold Medals in Team Foil and Team Sabre at the 1951 Pan-American Games.

STANLEY LEKATCH—National AAU Sabre Champion in 1978.

PAUL LEVY—Won a Gold Medal in Team Epée at the 1959 Pan-American Games.

NORMAN LEWIS—U.S. Champion in Foil in 1939 and U.S. Epée Champion in 1948, 1949, and 1950.

NATHANIEL LUBELL (1916-   , New York City)—Foil Champion in 1948 and won Gold Medals in Team Foil and Team Sabre at the 1951 Pan-American Games.

BROOKE MAKLER—National AAU Epée Champion in 1978.

PAUL T. MAKLER—Won a Silver Medal in Team Foil at the 1955 Pan-American Games.

JAMES MARGOLIS (1936-   , New York City)—NCAA Epée Champion from Columbia U. in 1957 and winner of a Gold Medal Team Epée at the 1963 Pan-American Games.

JAMES MELCHER—Won a Gold Medal in Team Epée and a Bronze Medal in Individual Epée at the 1971 Pan-American Games.

ARLEEN MELNICK—From Paterson College, she was Intercollegiate Champion in 1965.

DAVID MICAHNIK (1938-   , Hazelton, Pa.)—U.S. Epée Champion in 1960.

STEVE NETBURN—National AAU Epée Champion in 1969.

YURI RABINOVICH—An immigrant from the Soviet Union, he was the 1975 NCAA Sabre Champion, representing Wayne State.

JAMES STRAUCH—U.S. Epée Champion in 1947.

ALBERT WOLFF— U.S. Epée Champion in 1946 and won a Gold Medal in Team Foil at the 1951 Pan-American Games.

THE FIRST . . .

lefty to win a world boxing title—**AL McCOY** (*see* Boxing)

woman to teach law at Harvard—**SOIA MENTSCHIKOFF** (*see* Legal Scholars)

physician to take out a ruptured appendix—**SIMON BARUCH** (*see* Doctors)

woman to become a major criminal judge—**ROSE HEILBRON** (*see* Judges)

professional baseball player—**LIPMAN PIKE** (*see* Baseball)

Jew to travel in space—**BORIS VOLYNOV** (*see* Aviators, Astronauts, and Others)

Pulitzer Prize winner—**HERBERT BAYARD SWOPE** (*see* Journalists)

woman senator of the Republic of Ireland—**ELLEN BISCHOFF-SHEIM** (*see* Political Figures: Irish)

airline passenger to cross the Atlantic—**CHARLES A. LEVINE** (*see* Aviators, Astronauts, and Others)

woman to win the Iron Cross—**LOUISE MANUEL GRAFEMUS** (*see* Military Figures: Germans)

FOOTBALL

GEORGE ABRAMSON (1903- , Eveleth, Minn.)—All-America Honorable Mention guard from the U. of Minnesota in 1922 and 1923, and a Second Team All-America in 1924. He was also Second Team All-Pro with the Green Bay Packers in 1925.

JOSEPH A. ALEXANDER (b. 1898, Syracuse, N.Y.)—A lineman from Syracuse U., he was First Team All-America in 1918 and 1919 at guard and First Team All-America at center in 1920. He played pro football 1921–1927 and was All-NFL in 1925 with the New York Giants. He is in the College Football Hall of Fame.

LYLE ALZADO (1949- , Brooklyn)—From tiny Yankton (S. Dak.) College, he was a great All-Pro defensive end for the Denver Broncos in the 1970s.

RAY BAER (1905- , Louisville, Ky.)—An All-America Honorable Mention lineman in 1925 and 1926 and a Second Team All-America in 1927. He was selected for the All-Time Michigan Team.

JOHN BARSHA (1900- , Russia)—Also a fine basketball player, he was an All-America Honorable Mention halfback for Syracuse in 1918. *See also* Basketball.

ARTHUR BLUETHENTHAL (1891–1918, Wilmington, N.C.)—A First Team All-America center for Princeton in 1911 and a Third Team All-America pick in 1912. He was killed in action in World War I.

MORRIS BODENGER (1909- , New Orleans)—An All-America Honorable Mention guard from Tulane U. in 1929 and 1930. He played with the Detroit Lions and other pro teams in the 1930s.

NORMAN CAHN (1892–1965, Denver)—One of the most famous NFL referees for 23 years (1922–1945).

AL DAVIS (1929- , Brockton, Mass.)—Formerly a coach with the Los Angeles Chargers, he became Head Coach and General Manager of the Oakland Raiders in 1963. Still running the Raiders from the front office, he is one of the sharpest football men in the U.S.

ABRAHAM ELIOWITZ (1910- , New York City)—A halfback from Michigan State, he was an All-America Honorable Mention in 1931 and 1932.

FRANK FERST (b. 1899, Savannah, Ga.)—An All-America Honorable Mention back from Georgia Tech in 1921.

HERBERT FLEISHHACKER, JR. (1907- , San Francisco)—An All-America Honorable Mention quarterback from Stanford in 1928–1929 and a member of the All-Time Stanford Team.

SAM FOX (1924- , Washington, D.C.)—An end from Ohio State, he was an All-America Honorable Mention in 1941. He played pro ball with the New York Giants and was All-Rookie in 1945. He later coached with the Ottawa Rough Riders and was Head Coach at Catholic U., Washington, D.C.

LEONARD FRANK (1889–1911, Chicago)—A First Team All-America tackle from the U. of Minnesota in 1911.

VICTOR H. FRANK (1900- , Philadelphia)—A Second Team All-America guard from the U. of Pennsylvania in 1918.

BENNY FRIEDMAN (1905- , Cleveland)—A First Team All-America back from the U. of Michigan in 1925 and 1926. A great pro quarterback with many teams, including the New York Giants, he was All-Pro quarterback 1927–1931.

SIDNEY GILLMAN (1911- , Minneapolis)—An All-America Honorable Mention end from Ohio State in 1932 and 1933. He later became one of the leading pro coaches, Head Coach of the Los Angeles Rams, the San Diego Chargers, and, later, the Houston Oilers.

FRANK GLICK (b. 1893, Pittsburgh)—An All-America Honorable Mention halfback from Princeton in 1915 and First Team All-East the same year.

MARSHALL GOLDBERG (1918-   , Elkins, W.Va.)—One of the all-time great college running backs, he was an All-America Honorable Mention from the U. of Pittsburgh in 1936 and First Team All-America in 1937 and 1938. He won the Walter Camp Award in 1937. He also had a successful career with the Chicago Cardinals before and after World War II.

CHARLES R. "BUCKETS" GOLDENBERG (1911-   , Odessa, Russia)—An All-America Honorable Mention running back from the U. of Wisconsin in 1930 and an even bigger star as a pro. He played for the Green Bay Packers, 1933–1945, and was an All-Pro pick in 1939, 1940, and 1942.

LOUIS J. GORDON (1908-   , Chicago)—A First Team All-America tackle from the U. of Illinois in 1929. He played pro football 1930–1938 for the Packers, Cardinals, Dodgers, and Bears. He was a member of the All-Time Illinois Team.

JEROME GREEN (1936-   , Atlanta)—An end from Georgia Tech, he was with the Boston Patriots at that position in 1960.

TERRY GROSSMAN—The star tight end of the Pittsburgh Steelers in the 1970s.

PHILIP J. HANDLER (1908-   , Fort Worth, Tex.)—An All-America Honorable Mention guard from Texas Christian U. in 1929. He was an All-Pro lineman with the Chicago Cardinals in 1931, 1932, and 1933, and later coached with the Cardinals and Bears for more than 20 years.

SIG HARRIS (1883-1964, Dubuque, Iowa)—A Quarterback from the U. of Minnesota, he was a First Team All-America in 1903.

ARNOLD HORWEEN (b. 1898, Chicago)—A First Team All-America from Harvard in 1920, he played for the Chicago Cardinals in the 1920s.

RALPH HORWEEN (b. 1896, Chicago)—An All-America Honorable Mention fullback from Harvard in 1916, and a tough running back with the Chicago Cardinals, 1921–1923.

MAX KADESKY (1901-   , Winstead, Conn.)—A Third Team All-America end from the U. of Iowa in 1922 and All-Western Conference in 1921.

EDWIN B. "KING KONG" KAHN (1911-1945, New York City)—A tough guard for the U. of North Carolina who later played pro ball with the Boston and Washington Redskins. He was killed in World War II.

AARON H. KALLET (1887-1965, Warsaw)—A First Team All-America end from the U. of Syracuse in 1911. He was selected to the All-Time Syracuse Team.

MIKE KATZ—A guard for the New York Jets in the 1960s, he was Junior Mr. America and Mr. East Coast in bodybuilding.

PHIL KING (1872-1938, Washington, D.C.)—A running back and quarterback from Princeton, he was a First Team All-America in 1891, 1892, and 1893. He was elected to the College Football Hall of Fame. He became a Christian.

IRVING KUPCINET (1912-   , Chicago)—The well-known talk show host and newspaperman was a star back at the U. of North Dakota and played with the Philadelphia Eagles.

MOSES LAITERMAN—A placekicker with the Charlotte Hornets in the World Football League in the mid-1970s.

BERNARD LEMONICK—A guard/linebacker from the U. of Pennsylvania, he was a First Team All-America defensive player in 1949.

ISAREL LEVENE (1885-1930)—An end from the U. of Pennsylvania, he was a First Team All-America in 1905 and 1906.

MARVIN D. LEVY (1926-   )—Head Coach of the Kansas City Chiefs, he formerly coached at New Mexico, William and Mary, and elsewhere. He is a Phi Beta Kappa.

LUCIUS N. LITTAUER (1859-1944, Gloversville, N.Y.)—Coach of the first football team at Harvard (1881).

FRED LOWENTHAL (1879-1931, Chicago)—A lineman from the U. of Illinois, he was First Team All-Western and All-America Honorable Mention in 1901.

SIDNEY LUCKMAN (1916- , Brooklyn)—One of the greatest players in football history, he was a halfback from Columbia U., a Third Team All-America in 1937, and a First Team All-America in 1938. As a pro quarterback with the Chicago Bears, he was All-Pro in 1941, 1942, 1943 (he was MVP that year), 1944, and 1947. He was elected to both the College Football Hall of Fame and the Pro Football Hall of Fame.

JOSEPH MAGIDSOHN (b. 1888, Tukum, Russia)—A Second Team All-America halfback from the U. of Michigan in 1909 and a First Team All-America in 1910.

FRANKLIN R. MEADOW (1912- , New Haven, Conn.)—An end from Brown, he was a Third Team All-America in 1932.

RONALD J. MIX (1938-)—An end from Southern Cal, he was an All-America Honorable Mention in 1959. He developed into one of the greatest offensive tackles in the history of the NFL, with the San Diego Chargers, and was All-Pro several times.

ARTHUR B. MODELL (1925- , Brooklyn)—Owner of the Cleveland Browns since 1961.

LEROY MONSKY (1916- , Montgomery, Ala.)—A guard from the U. of Alabama, he was a First Team All-America in 1937 and was selected to the All-Time Alabama starting team.

PETER P. NEFT (1934- , Pittsburgh)—Second Team All-East quarterback with the U. of Pittsburgh in 1955, he later played with the British Columbia Lions.

ED NEWMAN—From Duke, he was a starting guard for the Miami Dolphins in 1978.

HARRY NEWMAN (1909- , Detroit)—A quarterback from the U. of Michigan, he was an All-America Honorable Mention in 1930 and First Team All-America in 1932, the year he was chosen as the Player of the Year by Helms Athletic Foundation. He played three years with the New York Giants in the 1930s.

RED PEARLMAN (b. 1898, Pittsburgh)—Played pro ball, 1919-1925, for several teams, including the famous Steubenville pro outfit.

MERVIN PREGULMAN (1922- , Lansing, Mich.)—A lineman from the U. of Michigan, he was an All-America Honorable Mention guard in 1941, an All-America Honorable Mention center in 1942, and a First Team All-America guard in 1943. He played with the Packers, Lions, and Bulldogs, 1946-1949.

DONALD ROGERS (1936- , South Orange, N.J.)—A center from the U. of South Carolina, he played for the Chargers in the 1960s.

AARON ROSENBERG (1912- , Brooklyn)—A star guard from the U. of Southern California who was a First Team All-America in 1932 and 1933. He is the same Aaron Rosenberg who produces films and TV shows.

CARROLL ROSENBLOOM (1908-1978)—The famous owner of the Baltimore Colts and later of the Los Angeles Rams.

A. SIDNEY ROTH (1916- , Brooklyn)—A guard from Cornell, he was a First Team All-America in 1938.

JACK SACK (1902- , Pittsburgh)—An All-America Honorable Mention guard from the U. of Pittsburgh in 1922 and selected for the All-Time Pittsburgh U. Team. He also played pro ball.

HERMAN "BIFF" SCHNEIDMAN (1913- , Rock Island, Ill.)—A star halfback at Iowa who played for the Green Bay Packers and Chicago Cardinals, 1935-1940.

ALEX SCHOENBAUM (1915- , Richmond, Va.)—A tackle from Ohio State, he was an All-America Honorable Mention in 1937 and 1938.

HARRY L. SCHWARTZ (1906- , Charlotte, N.C.)—An All-America Honorable Mention center from the U. of North Carolina in 1927 and Second Team All-Southern in 1928.

MARCHY SCHWARTZ (1909- , New Orleans)—A First Team All-America halfback from Notre Dame in 1930 and 1931. He was later Stanford's Head Coach. His father was Jewish.

HENRY SEMANSKY (1900-1951, New Bedford, Mass.)—A member of the U. of Vermont's All-Time Team, he was an All-America Honorable Mention end in 1923.

ALLIE SHERMAN (1923- , Brooklyn)—A quarterback from Brooklyn College, he played for the Philadelphia Eagles, 1943-1947. He later became one of the outstanding coaches in pro football, leading the New York Giants to championships in the 1960s.

DAVID SMUKLER (1914- , Newark)—A big fullback from Temple, he was a Third Team All-America in 1934. He played with the Eagles, Lions, and Boston Yankees, 1936-1940.

MORT STAROBIN (1902-1942)—A tackle from the U. of Syracuse, he was an All-America Honorable Mention in 1926.

WILLIAM STEIN (1924- , Elizabeth, N.J.)—A quarterback from Georgia Tech, he was a Third Team All-America in 1943. He became an NFL referee.

PAUL "TWISTER" STEINBERG (1880-?, New York City)—One of the great early professional running backs. He played with the football Philadelphia Athletics, the Syracuse All-Stars, Franklin, and the Canton Ohio Bulldogs in the early 1900s.

CHARLES A. TAUSSIG (1881-1949, Annapolis, Md.)—From Cornell, he was an All-America Honorable Mention end in 1901.

JOSEPH K. TAUSSIG (b. 1877, Dresden, Germany)—Starting quarterback for Navy in 1897 and 1898.

ABRAHAM B. WATNER (1891-1961)—President of the Baltimore Colts in the early 1960s.

SAMUEL A. WEISS (1902- , Warsaw)—A quarterback from Duquesne, he was elected to its All-Time Team and later became a leading referee in the NFL. *See also* Congressmen and Congresswomen.

SIDNEY YOUNGELMAN—A tackle from the U. of Alabama, he played for the 49ers, Eagles, Browns, Titans, and Bills, 1955–1963, and was selected as a Second Team All-Pro Defensive Tackle in 1960.

GOLF

AMY ALCOTT—One of the leading players on the pro tour, she was Professional Rookie of the Year in 1975–1976.

HERMAN BARRON (b. 1909, Port Chester, N.Y.)—One of the top golfers in the U.S. for a generation, he won the Western Open (1946) and many other tournaments. He was a member of the 1947 Ryder Cup Team and was World Senior pro champion in 1963.

SIDNEY BREWS (b. 1899, Blackheath, England)—One of the leading golfers in South Africa, he won the South African Open six times, the Belgian Open, the Dutch Open, and the French Open in the 1920s and 1930s. He converted to Judaism.

ANDREA COHN (1940- , Waterloo, Iowa)—A pro on the tour in the 1960s and 1970s.

MARTIN FLECKMAN—On the Pro Tour, he was the first golfer to win the first tournament he entered, the Cajun Classic in 1967.

BRUCE FLEISCHER—From Hialeah, Florida, he was the 1968 U.S. National Amateur Champion and is now on the pro circuit.

FRED GUTMAN (1917-)—Amateur Champion of Austria in 1936 and Amateur Champion of Germany in 1937, just before he fled Hitler.

ROBERT JACOBSON (1918-   )—Won the 1934 U.S. Amateur Championship.

ELAINE ROSENTHAL (b. 1896)—One of the leading women golfers in the U.S., she won many tournaments, including the 1917 North-South Tournament, and was the winner of the Women's Western Tournament three times.

JANE W. SELZ—Amateur Champion of Mexico in 1960, she also won the Western Open in 1932.

DICK SIDEROWF—One of the leading amateurs in the U.S., he won the British Amateur in 1973 and 1976.

GYMNASTICS

See also Olympic Medalists

MARSHALL AVENER—National AAU All-Around Champion and the NCAA All-Around Co-Champion in the early 1970s.

MICHAEL AUFRECHT—NCAA Champion from the U. of Illinois in side horse in 1962.

RONALD BARAK—National AAU Champion in horizontal bars in 1964 and NCAA Champion from Southern Cal in horizontal bars, parallel bars, and all-around in 1964.

STEVE COHEN—From Penn State, he was National AAU Side Horse Champion in 1966 and Rings Champion in 1968.

DONALD FABER—National AAU Champion in free calisthenics in 1954 and NCAA Champion from UCLA in free exercise in 1955.

JOSEPH GOLDENBERG—National AAU Champion in the flying rings in 1936, 1939, and 1941.

ABRAHAM I. GROSSFELD (1934-   , New York City)—One of the greatest gymnasts ever in the U.S., he won six Gold, three Silver, and five Bronze Medals at Pan-American Games in 1959 and 1963, and was National AAU Champion in horizontal bars in 1955, 1956, and 1957. He was also NCAA Champion from the U. of Illinois in 1957 (horizontal bars) and 1958 (all-around, free exercise, horizontal bars). He is now a leading coach.

LEONARD HARRIS—National AAU Champion in still rings in 1954.

JENIFER LIEBENBERG—From South Africa, she was a Women's Pair Champion at the 1970 World Trampoline Championships.

EDWARD LINDENBAUM—National AAU Champion in the rope climb in 1913 and 1914.

NORMAN MARKS—NCAA Champion from Los Angeles State in free exercise in 1957.

DANIEL J. MILLMAN (1946-   , Culver City, Calif.)—World Trampoline Champion in 1964 and U.S. Trampoline Champion in 1963.

JOSEPH SALZMAN—Coached the U.S. Women's Olympic Team in 1948.

COURTNEY SHANKEN—NCAA Champion from the U. of Chicago in the rope climb and in all-around in 1941.

EARL SHANKEN—NCAA Champion from the U. of Chicago in the long horse in 1940, 1941, and 1942.

ARTHUR SHURLOCK—National AAU Champion in the side horse in 1957 and 1958 and National AAU Champion in horizontal bars in 1959. He was also NCAA Champion from the U. of California in the side horse in 1959.

STANLEY TARSHIS—NCAA Champion from Michigan State in horizontal bars in 1959 and 1960.

FRED TUROFF—Number one ranked American gymnast in 1970.

HANDBALL

MORTON ALEXANDER—AAU One-Wall Champion in 1940.

SEYMOUR ALEXANDER—AAU One-Wall Champion in 1931.

KEN DAVIDOFF—AAU One-Wall Champion in 1963.

JOEL DAVIDSON—AAU One-Wall Champion in 1973.

JOSEPH GARBER—AAU One-Wall Champion in 1938 and 1942.

MAX GOLD—AAU Four-Wall Champion in 1920.

HARRY GOLDSTEIN—AAU One-Wall Champion in 1934 and 1937.

HYMAN GOLDSTEIN—Elected to the Helms Handball Hall of Fame, he was Commissioner of the U.S. Handball Association.

PAUL HABER—One of the best-known players, he was USHA Singles Champion at least five times.

VICTOR HERSHKOWITZ (1919- , New York City)—Certainly one of the greatest handball players in history, with more than 30 national championships in singles and doubles, including wins at one, three, and four walls and the U.S. Handball Association Championship and AAU crown several times.

JIMMY JACOBS (1931-)—U.S., AAU, and World Champion, he is considered to be the greatest four-wall player of all time.

IRVING JACOBS—AAU One-Wall Champion in 1933.

FRED LEWIS—USHA Singles Champion in 1972 and 1974.

JACK LONDIN—AAU One-Wall Champion in 1935.

DAVID MARGOLIS—AAU One-Wall Champion in 1936.

SHEILA MAROSHICK—USHA Women's Champion, she was the top female handball player in the world in the 1960s.

GEORGE NELSON—AAU Four-Wall Champion in 1927.

STEVE SANDLER—AAU One-Wall Champion seven times, and Four-Wall Champion in 1973.

MICHAEL SCHMOOKLER—AAU One-Wall Champion in 1929.

KEN SCHNEIDER—AAU Four-Wall Champion in 1950.

STUFFY SINGER—USHA Singles Champion in 1968.

ARTHUR WOLFE—AAU One-Wall Champion in 1941.

HOCKEY

See also Olympic Medalists

ROSS BROOKS (1938- , Toronto)—The excellent goalie of the Boston Bruins.

HY BULLER—A defenseman for the Detroit Red Wings and the New York Rangers, 1943-1945 and 1951-1954. He was Second Team All-Star in 1951-1952.

CECIL HART (1883-1940, Bedford, Quebec)—The famous manager of the Montreal Canadiens.

GIZZY HART—A pro player with the Victoria Cougars and Canadiens, 1924-1928 and 1932-1933.

MAX KAMINSKY—A pro player with Ottawa and the Boston Bruins, 1933-1936.

MAX LABOVICH—Played for the Rangers in 1943-1944.

ALEXANDER H. LEVINSKY (1912- , Syracuse)—Played for Toronto, the Rangers, and the Chicago Black Hawks, 1930-1939.

MOE ROBERTS (1905-)—Played for the Black Hawks in 1951-52.

MICHAEL VEISOR—A goalie with the Chicago Black Hawks in the 1970s.

LAWRENCE ZEIDEL (1929- , Montreal)—After playing with the Red Wings and the Black Hawks, 1951-1954, he returned to the NHL in the 1960s. He was a defenseman.

ICE SKATING

See also Olympic Medalists

ARTHUR J. APFEL (1923-)—South African Champion in 1939, British Figure Skating Champion in 1946, and British Empire Figure Skating Champion in 1947. He finished third in the World Championships that year.

BENJAMIN BAGDADE (1902- , Montreal)—President of the U.S. Amateur Skating Union, 1947-1951.

LAWRENCE DEMMY (1933-)—European Dancing Champion, 1954-1955, and World Dance Skating Champion, 1951-1955.

OTTO GOLD—A well-known Austrian skater, he took second in the European Figure Skating Championships in 1930.

LILLY KRONBERGER—A Hungarian, she was Women's Figure Skating Champion of the World, 1908-1911.

ERICH MULLER—Figure Skating and Dance Skating Champion of South Africa, 1950 and 1951.

GISELA REICHMANN—An Austrian and one of the most beautiful skaters of her era. Her best competitive performance was second in the World Championships of 1923.

LOUIS RUBENSTEIN (1861-1931, Montreal)—The greatest North American skater of the 19th century, he was Canadian, U.S., and North American Champion in the 1880s. He later served as Vice-President of the International Skating Union and as President of the International Skating Union of America.

JUDO

See also Olympic Medalists

IRWIN COHEN—National AAU Judo Champion at 176 pounds in 1971 and at 189 pounds in 1977, and one of the premier competitors in the U.S. in the 1970s.

STEVE COHEN—National AAU Judo Champion at 172 pounds in 1977.

JORGE GLESER—From Columbia U., he was National Collegiate Under-205-pound Champion in 1971.

LIONEL JEDEIKEN—National Judo Champion of Rhodesia in 1978.

SHOOTING

See also Olympic Medalists

DOV BEN-DOV (1927- , Palestine)—An outstanding shooter, he received a Bronze Medal for Israel at the Asian Games in 1954.

MILTON FRIEND (1935- , Malden, Mass.)—An NCAA All-America, he won the National Gallery Rifle Championship in 1959 and has been a member of many teams that have won National Championships.

SUSAN S. HARDY (1934- , Highland Park, Ill.)—Grand American Women's

Handicap Champion in 1959 and a member of the 1962 Women's All-America Shooting Team.

PHILO JACOBY (1837-1922, Lauenburg, Prussia)—One of the great early competitive shooters in the U.S., he won the Berlin Shooting Championship in 1868 and led the U.S. team to victory at the 1876 World Shooting Championships.

ROBIN LAVINE—South African Small Bore Rifle Champion in 1956.

DEREK PARTRIDGE—Appropriately named for a shooter, he was Trap-Shooting Champion of the 1973 Nordic Games. He is British.

MORTON SOLOMON (1903- , New York City)—National Rifle Association Indoor Champion (Metallic Sights) in 1928 and 1931. Among his other notable victories were the National Military Rifle Championship in 1930 and 1931 and National Rifle Association Indoor Kneeling Championship in 1928.

WILLIAM WARSHAL—National Picket Revolver Champion of the U.S. in 1935.

LAWRENCE E. WILLNER—NCAA All-America in Revolver in 1953 and 1954, representing the U.S. Military Academy.

SWIMMING AND DIVING

See also Olympic Medalists

EUGENE ADLER—National AAU Long-Distance Champion in 1953.

JEFFREY ALLEN—100 and 200 Freestyle Champion of Ireland in 1963.

JULIO ARANGO—From Colombia, South America, and Cal State, Los Angeles, he was an NCAA All-America in the 1,650 and 800 relay in 1970. He won Gold Medals in 200 backstroke and the 1,500 freestyle at the South American Games in 1970.

WALTER ARNOLD—Diving Champion of Austria in 1924 and 1925.

WILLIAM BACHRACH (1879-1959)—One of the leading coaches in the U.S., he was the long-time coach at the Illinois Athletic Club and produced many outstanding swimmers, including Johnny Weissmuller.

JULIUS BALASZ—Czech National Diving Champion on many occasions.

ISAAC BARKEN—One of the leading swimming coaches in the Soviet Union and coach of its Olympic team.

CHARLES BATTERMAN—AAU National One- and Three-Meter Diving Champion in 1944, and One- and Three-Meter NCAA Champion from Columbia U. that year.

EVA BEIN—National AAU Long-Distance Champion in 1931.

GUSTAVE BERMAN—Intercollegiate Fancy Diving Champion in 1911.

JOHN BLUM—National AAU Relay Champion in 1950, NCAA 220 Freestyle Champion and All-America from Yale in 1950.

ROMAN BRENNER—From the Soviet Union, he was 1954 European Springboard and Highboard Champion, and Soviet Champion frequently.

BARBARA CHESNEAU—A member of the National AAU Champion 400 Relay Team in 1961.

DESMOND V. COHEN—200 Breaststroke Champion of South Africa in 1946.

NORMAN CROWN—100 Freestyle Champion of South Africa in 1946.

JUDITH DEUTSCH-HASPEL—100 Freestyle Champion of Austria in 1934, 1935, and 1936.

PETER ELLIOTT—Springboard Diving Champion of Great Britain in 1948 and High-Diving Champion in 1953.

ALLEN ENGELBERG—From Harvard, he was on the NCAA Champion 400 Freestyle Team in 1961 and All-America that year.

BERNARD EPSTEIN—From CCNY, he was All-America in breaststroke in 1924 and 1925.

CHARLOTTE EPSTEIN (1885-1938, New York City)—Founder of the National Women's Life-Saving League (later known as the New York Women's Swimming Association), she was an important pioneer force in the development of women's swimming in the U.S.

MEYER FELDBERG—200 Butterfly Champion of South Africa in 1958 and 1959.

LORRAINE FISCHER—A great relay performer, she was National AAU Champion at various distances in 1939, 1940, 1941, and 1945.

PETER I. FOGARASY—National AAU 200-meter Breaststroke Champion in 1960, All-America from North Carolina State in 1961.

MARIA FRANK—Hungarian National Champion in the 100 freestyle in 1958 and 1959 and 400 Champion in 1958.

PAUL FRIESEL (1911- , New York City)—Developed and popularized the butterfly stroke and held a number of early world records.

JANOS GERGELY—A noted Hungarian Olympic coach.

CARMEL GOODMAN—South African National 200 Breaststroke Champion in 1973.

R. J. GREENBERG—National AAU Relay Champion in 1927.

ALFRED GUTH—1,500 Freestyle Champion of Austria in 1925 and 1927.

FRANZ GUTTREUR—200 Freestyle Champion of Czechoslovakia in 1920.

PAUL HABER—100 Breaststroke Champion of Austria in 1964.

EUGENE HEILPERN—From Ohio State, he was All-America in breaststroke in 1936.

BASIL HOTZ—100 and 200 Breaststroke Champion of South Africa in 1964.

FRANK M. JELENKO—From Rutgers, he was on the 1929 NCAA Champion 200 Freestyle Relay Team.

BERNARD KAHN—From the U. of Michigan, he was All-America in backstroke and relay in 1951.

HARRY I. KALLMAN—From Ohio State, he was All-America in diving in 1936.

LESTER KAPLAN—From CCNY, he was All-America in breaststroke in 1934.

JERRY KATZ—From the U. of Texas, he was All-America in freestyle in 1960.

PAUL KATZ—From Yale, he was All-America in the freestyle relay in 1970.

LES KLENERMAN—100 Freestyle Champion of South Africa in 1947.

IDY M. KOHN—100 Backstroke Champion of Austria in 1930.

NORMAN M. KRAMER—From Rutgers, he was on the 1931 and 1933 NCAA Champion 400 Freestyle Relay Team, and on the Champion 300 Medley Relay Team in 1931.

WALTER KRISSEL—From Columbia U. He was NCAA One-Meter Diving Champion in 1925 and All-America in 1924 and 1925.

AARON KURTZMAN—From Seton Hall, he was All-America in backstroke in 1951.

RUTH LANGER—Born in Austria, she was Long-Distance Champion of England in 1939.

DEBORAH LEE—On the National AAU Champion 400 Freestyle Team in 1960 and was an All-America Women's Waterpolo selection.

JERRY LEVIN—From Rutgers, he was All-America in relay in 1942.

DEBBIE LIPMAN—Was U.S. National Indoor 10-meter Diving Champion in 1973 and ranked Number Five diver in the world in the early 1970s.

FRITZI LOWY—Austrian 100 Freestyle Champion, 1925-1931, 200 Champion in 1925, and 400 Champion, 1925-1931.

LEOPOLD MAYER—100 Freestyle Champion of Austria in 1903.

WILLY MEISL—100 Backstroke Champion of Austria in 1917.

ROBERT MILLER—From Illinois U., he was All-America in relay in 1955.

CHARLEY MINDER—From Southern Methodist U., he was All-America in the butterfly in 1970.

RICHARD G. MORSE—From the U. of Indiana, he was All-America in diving in 1964.

EVA PAJOR—100 Backstroke Champion of Hungary in 1955, and 1956.

CAROL PENCE—National AAU 100 Breaststroke Champion in 1949, Relay Champion in 1950 and 1951, AAU Indoor 100 Breaststroke Champion in 1948 and 1951, and AAU 250-yard Breaststroke Champ in 1950 and 1951.

YOAR RAANAN (1924-   , Egypt)—Winner of a Gold Medal and a Silver Medal for Israel in diving at the Asian Games in 1954. He was British Diving Champion in 1956.

ROY ROMAIN—From Great Britain, he was 1947 European 200-meter Breaststroke Champion and 1950 British Empire Champion.

AL RUBENSTEIN—From the U. of Illinois, he was All-America in relay in 1956.

EDWIN SABOL—National AAU Relay Champion in 1938 and All-America freestyler from Ohio State the same year.

IMRE SAROZI—Coached the 1956, 1960, and 1964 Hungarian Olympic teams.

SEYMOUR SCHLANGER—From Ohio State, he was NCAA 440 Freestyle and 1,500 Freestyle Champion and All-America in 1945.

MORLEY SHAPIRO—From Ohio State, he was NCAA Three-Meter Diving Champion in 1954 and All-America in 1954 and 1955.

DONALD SHEFF—National AAU and NCAA Relay Champion several times, he was All-America from Yale in 1951.

GEORGE SHEINBERG—From CCNY, he was All-America in freestyle in 1934.

DORIS SHIMAN—National AAU 100 Breaststroke Champion in 1934.

NORMAN SIEGAL—National AAU Relay Champion in 1943 and All-America from Rutgers in 1942.

ABRAHAM SIEGEL—National AAU Relay Champion in 1918.

STEVE SKILKEN—NCAA All-America in diving in 1972.

MARTIN SMITH—From Yale, he was All-America in freestyle in 1954.

DAVE SOLOMON—From Ohio U., he was All-America in the butterfly in 1970.

NANCY SPITZ— All-America in 1971 and an outstanding freestyle swimmer.

PAUL STEINER—The greatest swimmer in Czechoslovakia in the 1920s and '30s, he held almost 40 national records in his long career.

DAVID STELLER—From Cornell, he was All-America in backstroke in 1958.

ROBERTO STRAUSS—A freestyler from Mexico, he won six Medals at the Central American Games (including one Gold) in 1970.

JORGE TELCH—From Mexico, he won a Bronze Medal in springboard diving at the Central American and Caribbean games in 1970.

ODON TOLDI—A Hungarian, he set a world record in the 200-yard breaststroke in 1911.

ROBERT WEINBERG—From the U. of Michigan, he was National AAU Champion on the 880 freestyle relay in 1947 and National AAU Champion on the 300-yard Medley Relay in 1948. He was also an NCAA Champion and All-America, 1947-1949.

BARBIE WEINSTEIN—National Junior Olympic Diving Champion in 1969 and 1970.

EMANUEL WERNAU—An Austrian, he was European Diving Champion in 1889.

HEIDI BIENENFELD WERTHEIMER—200 Breaststroke Champion of Austria, 1925–1931.

HAL WHITE—From Rutgers, he was All-America in breaststroke in 1934.

JOSEPH WOHL—Held the world record in the 500-yard and 880 backstroke in 1931. He was All-America from Syracuse U. in 1929.

JABEZ WOLFFE (1877–1943)—An Englishman, he is considered one of the greatest distance swimmers in history.

MICHAEL WOLK—From Colgate, he was All-America in freestyle and butterfly in 1958.

TABLE TENNIS

VICTOR BARNA (1911–1972, Budapest)—Considered the greatest player in the world until the rise of the Oriental stars (against whom he never had the opportunity to play). He won an unbelievable 22 World Championships.

LASZLO BELLAK—A Hungarian, he was World Mixed Doubles Champion in 1938.

DORA BEREGI—An Englishwoman, she was World Doubles Champion in 1950.

RICHARD BERGMANN (1919-   )—An Austrian and a defensive genius, he held seven World Championships.

ABRAHAM BERENBAUM—U.S. Singles Champion in 1935.

BERNARD BUKIET—U.S. Singles Champion in 1957, 1963, and 1966.

GLENN COWAN—On the team that toured mainland China in the famous "Ping-Pong diplomacy" games of 1971.

SANDOR GLANCZ—A Hungarian, he was World Doubles Champion with Victor Barna in 1933.

SVETLANA GRINBERG—From the Soviet Union, she was World Doubles Champion in 1970.

R. GUSIKOFF—U.S. Singles Champion in 1959.

SIDNEY HEITNER—U.S. Singles Co-champion in 1933.

JACK HOWARD—A leading American player, he was on the U.S. team that toured mainland China in 1971.

ROLAND JACOBI—A Hungarian, he was World Table Tennis Champion in 1927.

JAMES M. JACOBSON—U.S. Singles Co-champion in 1933.

SUZY JAVOR (1933-   , Hungary)—National Champion of Australia on many occasions.

ISTVAN KELEN—A Hungarian, he was World Mixed Doubles Champion with A. Sipos in 1929 and, with another partner, in 1933.

ERWIN KLEIN—An American, he was World Mixed Doubles Champion in 1956 and U.S. Singles Champion in 1961, 1964, and 1965.

G. KLEINOVA—A Czech, she was World Mixed Doubles Champion in 1936.

ALFRED LIEBSTER—An Austrian, he was World Doubles Champion in 1928.

ZOLTAN MECHLOVITS—A Hungarian, he was World Table Tennis Champion in 1928.

RICHARD MILES—An American, he was World Mixed Doubles Champion in 1948 and U.S. Singles Champion, 1945–1955 and 1962.

REBA K. MONNESS—U.S. Singles Champion in 1950.

LEAH THALL NEUBERGER—An American, she was World Mixed Doubles Champion in 1948 and 1962 and U.S. Singles Champion in 1947, 1949, 1951–1953, 1955–1957, and 1961.

MARTIN REISMAN—U.S. Singles Champion in 1958 and 1960.

ANGELICA ROSEANU (1921– , Bucharest, Rumania)—The greatest woman player in history, she was World Singles Champion, 1950–1955, and held a total of 17 World Championships. She emigrated to Israel.

SOL SCHIFF—An American, he was World Doubles Champion in 1938 and U.S. Singles Champion in 1934.

MARCUS SCHUSSHEIM—U.S. Singles Champion in 1931 and 1932.

DORLY SHIPP (1924– , Austria)—Australian National Champion in 1948, 1953, 1954, and 1956.

A. SIPOS—A Hungarian, she was World Table Tennis Champion in 1932 and 1933.

MIKLOS SZABADOS—A Hungarian, he was World Table Tennis Champion in 1931. He was also a many-time World Doubles and Mixed Doubles Champion.

ELLA ZELLER—A Rumanian, she was World Doubles Champion with Angelica Roseanu in 1955 and 1956.

TENNIS

See also Olympic Medalists

MICHAEL BELKIN—U.S. National Junior Outdoor Champion in 1962, Number One Canadian player in the 1960s and 1970s, and Number Seven in the U.S. in 1965.

HELEN I. BERNHARD (1921– , New York City)—Number Four ranked singles player in the U.S. in 1942.

BARBARA BREIT (1937–)—Number Eight ranked woman player in the world in 1955 and Number Six singles player in the U.S. in 1954. In addition, she was ranked Third in U.S. doubles in 1955.

ANGELA BUXTON (1934–)—A leading player in Great Britain, she was number Two there and Number Five in the World in 1956.

PIERRE DARMON (1933– , Tunisia)—Number One ranked player in France from the mid-1950s to the mid-1960s, and was Number Eight in the World in 1963.

EVA D. DE JONG—Number One ranked woman in Holland in 1962.

IRVING DORFMAN—Number Three in doubles in the U.S. in 1948.

PABLO EISENBERG—Number Nine doubles player in the U.S. in 1954.

LYNN EPSTEIN—U.S. National Woman's Junior Champion in 1976.

EDWARD W. FEIBLEMAN (b. 1899)—Number Seven U.S. doubles player in 1931.

JOSEPH FISHBACH—U.S. Junior National Indoor Champion in 1937 and 1938.

HERBERT FLAM (1928– , New York City)—Number Four in the World in 1957 and Number Two in the U.S. in 1956 and 1957.

ALLEN FOX (1939– , Los Angeles)—Number Four in the U.S. in 1962.

RAYNI FOX (1956–)—U.S. National Woman's Junior Champion in 1974.

MYRON J. FRANKS (1936–)—Bronze Medal winner for the U.S. in the Pan-American Games in 1959, he was ranked Number Seven in the U.S. in 1959 and Number Three in doubles in 1956, 1957, and 1959.

ILSE FRIEDLEBEN (b. 1893, Germany)—Number One ranked woman player in Germany, 1922–1926, and one of the leading players in Europe.

GRANT GOLDEN—Number Ten in the U.S. in 1953, 1956, and 1957, and Number Two in doubles in 1953.

BENJAMIN GORCHAKOFF—Number Eight U.S. doubles player in 1929.

BRIAN GOTTFRIED—One of the leading players in the U.S., he was Number Six in 1975, Professional Rookie of the Year in 1973, and Wimbledon Doubles Champion in 1976.

LARRY GOTTFRIED—U.S. National Junior Champion in 1976 after winning the 16-and-under title in 1975.

SEYMOUR GREENBERG (1920- , Chicago)—Number Five in the U.S. rankings in 1943.

KATHY HARTER—Number Five player in the U.S. in 1968.

LADISLAV HECHT (1910- , Zilina, Czechoslovakia)—Number One player in Czechoslovakia in the mid-1930s, he emigrated to the U.S. and was ranked Number Ten in 1942. He was the Number Eight ranked doubles player in the world in 1934.

MARCO HECHT—U.S. Junior National Indoor Champion in 1930, 1931, and 1932. One of the great young players, he never realized his potential.

GLADYS M. HELDMAN (1922-)—One of the people who put together women's professional tennis, she is Publisher and Editor of *World Tennis*, the leading magazine in the game.

JULIE M. HELDMAN (1945- , Berkeley, Calif.)—Number Two in the U.S. in 1968 and 1969 and U.S. Girls' Champion in 1963.

CAROLYN SWARTZ HIRSCH—U.S. Girls' National Hard Court Champion in 1922.

EDWARD JACOBS (1909-)—Number Nine U.S. doubles player in 1931 and 1934.

WILLIAM JACOBS—U.S. Junior National Indoor Champion in 1929.

ANITA KANTER—Number Ten in the world and Number Six in the U.S. in 1952.

RUTH KAUFMANN—Number One ranked woman player in Switzerland, 1954-1956 and 1958-1960.

ILANA KLOSS—Number One ranked South African woman, and 1972 Junior Singles Champion at Wimbledon, and the 1976 USTA Doubles Champion.

BOB KREISS—With his brother, Mike, Number Nine U.S. doubles player in 1971.

MIKE KREISS—With his brother, Bob, Number Nine U.S. doubles player in 1971.

MILLICENT HIRSCH LANG—U.S. Girls' National Indoor Champion in 1933.

MAUD ROSENBAUM LEVI—Italian Champion in 1927, 1928, and 1929, Number Two in Italy in 1931, and Number Five in the U.S. in 1934.

DOROTHY W. LEVINE—U.S. National Indoor Champion and Doubles Champion, both 1954-1957.

EDMUND L. LEVY—Number Seven U.S. doubles player in 1921.

HARRY E. LIKAS, JR. (1924- , San Francisco)—Number Six in doubles in the U.S. in 1946 and Number Ten in singles in 1948 and 1952.

ROD MANDELSTAM—A South African who attended the U. of Miami, he was Number Nine U.S. doubles player in 1964.

ERNA MARCUS—U.S. National Indoor Doubles Champion in 1909.

SAMUEL MATCH (1933- , Los Angeles)—Number Four U.S. doubles player in 1948 and the Number Eight singles player in 1949.

BONNIE MENCHER—U.S. Girls' National Indoor Champion in 1958.

GERALD MOSS—Number Three U.S. doubles player in 1955.

LAWRENCE NAGLER—Number Five U.S. doubles player in 1962.

TOM OKKER—From the Netherlands, he is a top professional who has won many major tournaments and was ranked in the top ten frequently. He was Number Four in the world in 1969.

DANIEL PRENN (1905- , Poland)—Number One ranked player in Germany, 1928-1932, and Number Six in the world in 1932 and Number Seven in doubles in 1934. He went to England after the rise of Hitler.

HENRY J. PRUSOFF (1912- , Seattle)—Number Three doubles player in the U.S. in 1940 and the Number Eight singles player that same year.

PAM RICHMOND—From Arizona State, she was National Collegiate Singles and Doubles Champion in 1971.

ALAN ROBERTS—U.S. National Junior Outdoor Champion in 1957.

RICHARD SAVITT (1927- , Bayonne, N.J.)—One of America's top players, he was ranked Number Three in the world in 1951 and Number Two in the U.S. that year in both singles and doubles. He won the 1951 Wimbledon Tournament.

LEN SCHLOSS—Number Ten doubles player in the U.S. in 1967.

HOWARD SCHOENFIELD—U.S. National Junior Tennis Champion in 1975.

SIDNEY SCHWARTZ—Number Four U.S. doubles player in 1950.

ABRAHAM A. SEGAL (1931- , Johannesburg)—Number Eight in the world in 1958 and Number One in South Africa in 1962 and 1963.

JULIUS SELIGSON (1909- , New York City)—Number Nine player in the U.S. in 1929.

LINDA SIEGELMAN—U.S. National 16-and-under Champion in 1977.

LEONARD L. STEINER—U.S. Junior National Indoor Champion in 1946.

GRACE SURBER—U.S. National Indoor Doubles Champion in 1939.

DOROTHEA SWARTZ—U.S. Girls' National Hard Court Champion in 1925 and 1926.

ROGER WERKSMAN—U.S. Junior National Hard Court Champion in 1956.

VAN WINITSKY—U.S. National Junior Champion in 1977.

CAROLE WRIGHT—U.S. National Indoor Champion in 1960 and 1962.

TRACK AND FIELD

See also Olympic Medalists.

ROSE AUERBACH—National AAU Champion in the javelin throw in 1937 and 1938.

MARGARET BERGMANN—National AAU Champion in the high jump in 1937 and 1938 and shotput champion in 1937 (a very rare combination).

FREYDA BERMAN—Won a Bronze Medal in the 440 relay for Canada at the 1958 British Commonwealth Games.

SARA MAE BERMAN—Broke the world record for the woman's marathon in 1971 and was one of the leading distance runners in the world in the early 1970s.

MAX BEUTEL—National AAU Champion in the 3,000-meter walk in 1937.

SAM BLEIFER—National AAU Champion in the 3,000-meter walk in 1945.

HENRY CIEMAN—A Canadian, he broke the world record for the one-mile run and the world indoor record for the 1,500-meter walk the same year, both in 1936.

HORACE J. COHEN—From Great Britain, he won a Silver Medal in the 440 relay at the British Empire Games in 1930.

SYBIL KOFF COOPER—National AAU Champion in the 80-meter hurdles in 1940.

MORRIS DAVIS—National AAU Champion in the 15-kilometer walk in 1935.

ELIOTT DENMAN—National AAU Champion in the 3,000-meter walk in 1959.

INGEBORD MELLO DE PREISS—From Argentina, she won Gold Medals in the shot and discus at the 1951 Pan-American Games.

BORIS DJERASSI—Number One hammer thrower in the U.S. in 1975.

MARTIN ENGEL (1932- , New York City)—Broke the American record for the hammer throw in 1953, and was the Number Seven ranked man in the world in that event. He was the Number Three man in the world in the 35-pound weight throw in 1954.

MORRIS FLEISCHER—National AAU Champion in the 20-kilometer walk in 1948 and in the 30-kilometer walk in 1937, 1945, and 1946.

VICTOR FRANK, JR. (1925- , Philadelphia)—Number Three in the discus in 1949 and Number Four in the shot in 1951, one of the relatively few men to be ranked in both events.

ALVIN FRIEDEN—From the U. of Texas, he was on the team that broke the world record in the 400 relay in 1954 and 1955.

SOLOMON FURTH (1907- , Brooklyn)—Broke the world record for the indoor 70-yard low hurdles in 1931, and was also an outstanding triple jumper.

IGOR FYELD—From the Soviet Union, he was the Number Ten pole vaulter in the world in 1967.

IOSIF GAMSKIY—From the Soviet Union, he was the Number Five hammer thrower in the world in 1971.

JACK GOLDBERG—A hurdler from Tufts U., he was Number Eight in the world (indoor) in 1953.

SAM GOLDBERG—Number Seven decathlon man in the U.S. in 1967.

GERDA GOTTLIEB (1916- , Austria)—Broke the women's world record in the high jump in 1934.

JOE GOULD—Number Nine javelin thrower in the U.S. in 1977.

CHARLEY GROHSBERGER—National AAU Champion in the 1,600 relay in 1943.

GARY GUBNER (1942- , New York City)—One of the great American weightmen, he broke the world record (indoor) for the shot in 1962. He was the Number One indoor shotputter in the world and Number Two outdoors in 1962. He repeated as Number One indoors in 1963.

MICHAEL HERMAN (1937- , Brooklyn)—U.S. National Indoor Longjump Champion and the Number Ten world decathlon performer in 1959. He was the Number Three indoor long jumper in the world in 1958.

ABIGAIL HOFFMAN (1947-)—A Canadian, she broke the world indoor record for the 440 in 1963 and the world record for the 880 in 1964. She was National Champion of Canada in both events in 1964 and was Pan-American Games, winner at 800 meters in 1971.

HARRY HOFFMAN—National AAU Champion in the 1,600 relay in 1935.

IRV HOROWITZ—National AAU Champion in the 15-kilometer walk in 1936.

CLAIRE ISICSON (1921- , Brooklyn)—Tied the world 50-meter record in 1938.

MARIA T. ITKINA (1932- , Smolensk)—Broke the world record in the 400 meters in 1955, the world record for 220 yards in 1956, and the world record for 440 yards in 1959. She was also the European 400-meter Champion in 1958 and 1962 and was one of four women who broke the world record in the 800-meter relay in 1963.

NATHAN JAEGER—National AAU Indoor Champion in the mile walk in 1937 and 1941.

HARRY KANE (1933- , London)—Broke the British record for the 440 hurdles and was the Number Seven man in the world in that event, both in 1954.

IRA KAPLAN (1928- , Brooklyn)—Number Seven man in the world in the indoor sprints in 1948.

FRANK C. KAUFMAN (1891-1943)—From the U. of Pennsylvania, he was on the team that broke the world record in the mile relay in 1915.

IRVING KINTISCH (1923-)—From NYU, he was Number Six in the world in the indoor shot in 1948.

SEMYON KOCHER—From the Soviet Union, he was Silver Medalist in the 1973 World University Games in the 400-meter dash.

MARTIN KORIK—From the U. of Tennessee, he was the Number Eight man in the world in the pole vault (indoors) in 1951.

GAVRAIL KOROBKOV—The leading track coach in the Soviet Union after World War II.

SVYETLANA KRACHEVSKAYA—From the Soviet Union, she was the Number Five shotputter in the world in 1977.

AHUVA KRAUS (1932- , Palestine)—Won a Gold Medal for Israel in the high jump at the Asian Games in 1954.

ABRAM KRIVOSHEYEV (1933- , Vitebsk, U.S.S.R.)—Soviet National Champion in the 800 meters in the 1960s.

SAM KRONMAN—National AAU Indoor Champion in the standing long jump in 1918.

VICTOR KUDINSKIY—From the Soviet Union, he is considered one of the all-time great steeplechasers. He was Number One in the world in 1966.

SHAUL LADANY—From Israel, he won the National AAU 100-kilometer Walking Championship in 1974 and holds the world record in the 50-mile walk.

HAROLD LAMB—National AAU Champion in the 1,600 relay in 1935.

STANLEY LAMBERT (1928- , Brooklyn)—From NYU, he was Number Two shotputter in the world in 1949 and 1950 as well as Number Two indoors in 1950.

JOEL LANDAU (1937- , Englewood, N.J.)—From Harvard, he was Number Nine in the world in the 120 hurdles in 1959.

HENRY H. LASKAU (1916- , Berlin)—One of the greatest walkers in American history, he won over 40 U.S. National Championships and broke the world record for the indoor mile in 1950.

STANLEY LEVENSON—A Canadian, he was U.S. National AAU Champion in the 440 relay in 1956.

PHIL LEVY—National AAU Outdoor Champion in the discus in 1937. He was later known as Phil Fox.

BERNARD LICHTMAN—National AAU Pentathlon Champion in 1919.

JERRY LIEBENBERG—From Western Michigan, he was Number Five steeplechaser in the U.S. in 1970 and 1971.

SAMUEL LIEBGOLD (1869-1943)—A leading American walker, he broke the American record for the mile outdoors in 1894 and for the mile indoors in 1896. He was the American champion in walking events on many occasions.

WILLIAM LUBIN—National AAU Champion in the 1,600 relay in 1944.

ROBERT J. MACK (1942- , Newark)—From Yale, he was Number Ten in the world in the three- and six-mile runs in 1962.

STEVE MARCUS—From UCLA, he was the Number Eight shotputter in the U.S. in 1967.

ISAAC MATZA—From NYU, he was Number Eight in the world in both the half-mile and the 1,000 in 1957, and Number Ten in the world in the indoor mile in 1956.

BERNARD MAYER (1923- , New York City)—One of America's top shotputters in the early 1950s, he was Number Four in the world in 1948 and Number Two indoors, 1951-1954.

JACK MEKLER (1932- , South Africa)—One of the leading distance runners in South Africa, he won a Silver Medal in the marathon at the 1954 British Commonwealth Games.

IRVING MONDSCHEIN (1925- , Brooklyn)—Number Three in the world in the high jump in 1947 and 1949 and Number Six in the world in the decathlon in 1949. He was U.S. National Decathlon Champion in 1944, 1946, and 1947.

JERROLD MONKOFSKY (1937- , New York City)—From NYU, he was Number Ten shotputter indoors in the world in 1959.

LAWRENCE E. MYERS (1858-1899, Richmond, Va.)—One of the truly great track stars in American and world history, he was U.S. National Champion 15 times as well as British Champion. He held numerous world records, but the most remarkable thing about him was his range—he was a champion and a record-holder at practically every distance from the shortest sprints to the mile run.

LAZAR NARODITSKIY (1937- , Kiev, U.S.S.R.)—One of the leading steeple-chasers at his peak, he was the Number Three man in the world in 1968.

HAL ALEC NATAN (1906- , Berlin)—Member of a German relay team that tied the world 400-meter record in 1929.

DOROTHY NUSSBAUM—National AAU Champion in the 50-yard dash in 1932.

SYDNEY D. PIERCE (1901- , Montreal)—From McGill U., he was the leading hurdler in Canada and National Champion in 1923 and 1924.

DAVID POLITZER—National AAU Outdoor Champion in the long jump in 1918.

CHARLES PORES (1897-1951)—An American, he held the U.S. record for one hour (the run, not the length of time he held the record), the 5-mile run, and the 15-mile run.

DAVID REISBORD—From Occidental College (Los Angeles), he was on a relay team that broke the world record in the two-mile and on another team that broke the U.S. four-mile record in 1957.

MORT REZNICK—National AAU Indoor Champion in the 35-pound weight throw in 1933.

SAMUEL ROSEN—National AAU Indoor Champion in the 300-yard run in 1925.

BOB ROSENCRANTZ—Number Five 50-kilometer walker in the U.S. in 1977.

EDIT SAMUEL—From Hungary, she was the Number 14 high jumper in the world in 1977.

MILTON SANDLER—National AAU Indoor Champion in the 600 in 1933, 1934, and 1935.

MARC SAVAGE (1945- , Los Angeles)—From UCLA, he was Number Six pole vaulter in the world in 1966 and Number Four in the U.S.

FRED SHARAGA—National AAU Champion in the 3,000 meter walk in 1944 and Champion at the 15-kilometer in 1943 and 1944.

CARL SHINE (1937- , Newton, Mass.)—From the U. of Pennsylvania, he was the Number Eight indoor shotputter in the world in 1958.

BILL SILVERBERG—From the U. of Kansas, he was the Number Nine steeplechaser in the U.S. in 1965.

IRA SINGER—National AAU Indoor Champion in the 60-yard dash in 1931.

RONALD SOBLE—A long jumper from the U. of Michigan, he was Number Eight in the world in 1951.

ANATOLIY SOLOMIN—From the Soviet Union, he was Number Eight man in the world in the 20-kilometer walk in 1977.

MILT SONSKY—Number Three javelin thrower in the U.S. in 1972.

JONAS SPIEGEL (1939- , Brooklyn)—A sprinter from the U. of Maryland, he was Number Ten in the world indoors in 1959.

MICHAEL SPRING—A member of two U.S. Olympic teams, he was an outstanding distance runner and won the Boston Marathon in 1904.

WILLIAM STEINER—National AAU Outdoor Champion in the 20-mile run in 1932.

DANIEL STERN (1849-1923)—A leading American walker of the 19th century, he was U.S. National Champion in both the one- and three-mile walks.

LEWIS STIEGLITZ (1935- , Hartford, Conn.)—From the U. of Connecticut, he was Number Five in the world at six miles in 1959 and broke the American record in the 10,000 meters in 1960.

SAMUEL STOLLER (1915- , Cincinnati)—From the U. of Michigan, he tied the American record in the 60-yard dash in 1936 and was a member of the U.S. Olympic Team that year.

ALLAN TOLMICH (1917- , Detroit)—From Wayne State, he was one of the top hurdlers in the U.S. in the 1930s, when he broke and rebroke many U.S. and collegiate records, and broke the world record for the 200-meter hurdles in 1939.

LEN WALTERS—A quarter-miler from Great Britain, he won a Gold Medal in the 1,600 relay at the British Commonwealth Games in 1970.

NORMAN WASSER—Number Two in the indoor shot in 1948 and Number Five in the world outdoors in 1947.

RON WAYNE—Number Six marathon runner in the U.S. in 1977. He won the 1974 NCAA Marathon.

MACK WEISS—National AAU Champion in the 50-kilometer walk in 1929.

WILLIAM WERNER—National AAU Indoor Champion in the standing long jump in 1929, 1930, and 1931.

JAMES WILSON—National AAU Champion in the 3,000-meter walk in 1943, the 10-kilometer walk in 1942, 1944, and 1945, and the 30-kilometer walk in 1942.

T. C. YOHANNAN—From India, he was the Number Seven longjumper in the world in 1974. He holds the Asian record in the event.

EUGENE ZUBRINSKY (1941-)—From San Jose State, he was Number Nine in the U.S. in the high jump in 1964.

VOLLEYBALL

HARLAN COHEN—Now a noted coach, he won a Silver Medal as a player at the 1963 Pan-American Games.

PETER COLBERT—Won a Silver Medal at the 1963 Pan-American Games.

MILTON FRIEDMAN, JR.—Won a Silver Medal at the 1963 Pan-American Games.

EUGENE SELZNICK (1930-)—Considered the greatest volleyball player in American history. He won two Gold Medals at the Pan-American Games in 1955 and 1959 and was the first U.S. athlete named to an All-World Team (1956).

WATER POLO

See also Olympic Medalists

BELA KOMJADI (1892-1933)—Built Hungary into one of the foremost water polo powers.

ALEX KOSEGI (1917- , Hungary)—The leading waterpolo coach in Australia.

ISAAC MANSOOR—One of the leading players in India, he led their 1948 Olympic Team.

PART VIII

WEIGHTLIFTING

See also Olympic Medalists.

A. ABRAHAMS—From Germany, he was the European 165-pound Champion in 1909 and 1914.

J. BARUCH—From Germany, he was the European 181-pound Champion in 1924.

ISSY BLOOMBERG—From South Africa, he won the Silver Medal at the 1950 British Commonwealth Games and was National Champion of South Africa several times.

RICHARD GILLER—National AAU Champion at 165 pounds in 1955.

PAUL S. GOLDBERG—An American, he was Pan-American Games Lightweight Silver Medalist in 1959 and National AAU Champion at 148 pounds in 1959 and 1961.

RICHARD E. GRENNAWALT—An American, he was Pan-American Games Featherweight Silver Medalist in 1951 and National AAU Champion at 132 pounds in 1950.

GARY GUBNER—The great American shotputter was also a leading weightlifter who broke four junior world records in 1962, broke the U.S. record in the press in 1965, and at one time was ranked fourth on the all-time list for total lifts in the three standard categories. He was National AAU Heavyweight Champion in 1966.

BENJAMIN HELFGOTT (1929- , Lodz, Poland)—One of the leading lifters in Great Britain, he won several British Lightweight Championships. He won the Bronze Medal at the 1958 British Commonwealth Games.

FRANK KAY— National AAU Champion at 181 pounds in 1941, 1942, and 1946.

EDWARD L. LEVY (1851-1932, London)—One of the greatest lifters in history, he broke or held 14 world records in the 1800s and was the first official World Champion in 1891.

DAVID MAYOR—National AAU Heavyweight Champion in 1937.

ISRAEL MEKHANIK—From the Soviet Union, he broke many world records in the lightweight class and was European Lightweight Champion in 1947, when he was well past his peak.

LARRY MINTZ—National AAU Lightweight Champion in 1966.

TERRY PURDUE—Representing Wales, he won a Silver Medal in Heavyweight Weightlifting at the British Commonwealth Games in 1970. He held the British and British Commonwealth record in his class.

DAVID ROTHMAN—National AAU Champion at 112 pounds in 1935.

M. RUDMAN—From the Soviet Union, he was European 181-pound Champion in 1957.

N. SHATOV—From the Soviet Union, he was European 165-pound Champion in 1947.

V. VIKHOVSKY—From the .Soviet Union, he was European 123-pound Champion in 1957.

WRESTLING

See also Olympic Medalists.

LOUIS BAISE—From South Africa, he was British Commonwealth Games Flyweight Champion in 1954.

ALFRED BRULL (1876-1944)—A Hungarian, he served as President of the World Wrestling League in the 1920s.

ANDREW FITCH—An American, he was Pan-American Games Flyweight Champion (freestyle) in 1963 and was NCAA 115-pound Champion from Yale in 1959.

SAMUEL FLEISCHER—National AAU 135-pound Champion in 1909.

STEPHEN FRIEDMAN—National AAU 165-pound Champion in 1961.

MAX GANS—National AAU Champion at 114 pounds *and* at 125 pounds in 1919.

LEON GENUTH—From Argentina, he was the Pan-American Games Middleweight Champion (freestyle) in 1951 and 1955.

SYDNEY GREENSPAN—From South Africa, he won a Silver Medal as a Light-Heavyweight at the 1938 British Empire Games.

RON GRINSTEAD—Was Light-Heavyweight Wrestling Champion of Great Britain in 1972 and competed in the Olympic Games that year.

ELI HELIKMAN—National AAU 135-pound Champion in 1912.

MAX HIMMELHOCH— National AAU 125-pound Champion in 1910.

RUDY LEIBOVITCH—From Canada, he was a Lightweight Silver Medalist at the 1954 British Commonwealth Games.

LEONARD LEVY—National AAU Heavyweight Champion in 1942 and NCAA Heavyweight Champion in 1941.

FRED J. MEYER—One of the greatest American wrestlers of his era, he was National AAU 174-pound Champion *and* Heavyweight Champion in 1921, and 191-pound *and* Heavyweight Champion in 1922.

FRED OBERLANDER (1911- , Vienna)—One of the great heavyweight wrestlers, he won the French Championship eight times and the British Championships eight times, and was Champion in Austria before leaving that country. His greatest single accomplishment was winning the European Heavyweight Championship in 1935.

PHILIP OBERLANDER—From Canada, he was a Welterweight Silver Medalist at the British Commonwealth Games in 1962.

SAMUEL PAMMOW—National AAU 114-pound Champion in 1920.

DAVID PRUZANSKY—One of the most remarkable athletes in the U.S., he won *both* the National AAU 139-pound Judo Championship and the 136-pound National AAU Wrestling (freestyle) Championship in the early 1970s.

BENJAMIN REUBIN—National AAU 158-pound Champion in 1914 and 1915.

GORDON ROSENBERG—National AAU Champion at 112 pounds in 1928.

RUDOLF SCHWARTZ (b.1887, New York City)— National AAU Champion at 105 pounds in 1908.

SAMUEL SCHWARTZ—National AAU Heavyweight Champion in 1916.

DAVID SHAPIRO—From the U. of Illinois, he was NCAA 165-pound Champion in 1946.

BENJAMIN SHERMAN—National AAU 165-pound Champion in 1929.

RALPH S. SILVERSTEIN—From the U. of Illinois, he was NCAA 175-pound Champion in 1935.

HERBERT SINGERMAN—From Canada, he won a Bronze Medal in Bantamweight Wrestling at the British Commonwealth Games in 1970.

RICHARD SOFMAN—National AAU 125-pound Champion in 1966, 1968, and 1974.

HOWARD STUPP—A Canadian, he was a Greco-Roman Gold Medalist at the 1975 Pan-American Games.

DAN VERNIK—From Argentina, he won a Bronze Medal in Heavyweight Wrestling at the 1971 Pan-American Games.

Part IX
Prize Winners

238

NOBEL PRIZE WINNERS

PEACE

TOBIAS M. C. ASSER (1838-1913)—From Holland, he won the 1911 Nobel Prize for his work in international law and his service on the Hague Arbitration Court.

MENACHEM BEGIN (1913- , Brest-Litovsk, Poland)—The Prime Minister of Israel won the 1978 Nobel Prize for his efforts toward peace in the Middle East.

RÉNE S. CASSIN (1887-1976, Bavonne, France)—Won the 1968 Nobel Prize for his activities in the area of human rights, including his role in the development of the Universal Declaration on Human Rights. He was President of the Commission of Human Rights of the UN. He taught at the U. of Paris for many years.

ALFRED H. FRIED (1864-1921, Vienna)—Won the 1911 Nobel Prize for his role as a peace propagandist. He founded the German Peace Society.

HENRY A. KISSINGER (1923- , Fürth, Germany)—Won the 1973 Nobel Prize for his contributions to the Paris Peace talks that "ended" the Vietnam war. He became U.S. Secretary of State years after fleeing Nazi Germany, and was also Director of the National Security Agency for a time in the Nixon administration.

LITERATURE

S. Y. AGNON (1888-1970, Buczacz, Galicia)—Born Samuel Joseph Czaczkes. Won the 1966 Nobel Prize for his contributions to Hebrew literature. He was an Israeli.

SAUL BELLOW (1915- , Lachine, Quebec)—Won the 1976 Nobel Prize for his contributions to English Literature. See Writers: Americans and Canadians.

HENRI BERGSON (1859-1941, Paris)—The great French philosopher won the 1927 Nobel Prize. He was considered to be one of the greatest intellects of his time.

PAUL HEYSE (1830-1914, Berlin)—Won the 1910 Nobel Prize for his contributions to German Literature. His mother was Jewish.

NELLY SACHS (1891-1970, Berlin)—Won the 1966 Nobel Prize for her beautiful and moving poetry.

ISAAC BASHEVIS SINGER (1904- , Radzymin, Poland)—The great American Yiddish novelist and writer won the 1978 Nobel Prize. See Writers: Americans and Canadians.

MEDICINE AND PHYSIOLOGY

JULIUS AXELROD (1912-)—An American, he won the 1970 Nobel Prize for his work on noradrenalin formation and behavior.

DAVID BALTIMORE (1938-)—An American, he won the 1975 Nobel Prize for his work on the relationship between viruses and cancer.

ROBERT BARANY (1876-1936)—An Austrian, he won the 1914 Nobel Prize for his work on diseases of the ear. He was one of the leading otologists of his time.

KONRAD BLOCH (1912- , Neisse, Germany)—An American, he won the 1964 Nobel Prize for his work on acid metabolism and cholesterol. He taught at Harvard.

BARUCH S. BLUMBERG (1925- , New York City)—An American, he won the 1976 Nobel Prize for his work on the origin of infectious diseases.

SIR ERNEST B. CHAIN (1906- , Berlin)—An Englishman, he won the 1945 Nobel Prize for his contributions to the discovery and development of penicillin.

GERALD M. EDELMAN (1929- , New York City)—Won the 1972 Nobel Prize for his work on the structure of gamma globulin and antibody molecules. A member of the National Academy of Sciences, he is a foremost figure in immunology.

PAUL EHRLICH (1854-1915, Strehlen, Germany)—Won the 1908 Nobel Prize for his pioneering work on immunization. His discovery of Salvarson was a major step toward the control of syphilis.

JOSEPH ERLANGER (1874-1965, San Fransisco)—Won the 1944 Nobel Prize (with Gasser) for his research on nerve differentiation and kidney secretion.

HERBERT S. GASSER (1888-1963, Platteville, Wis.)—Won the 1944 Nobel Prize with Erlanger and was one of the leading neurophysiologists in the world.

FRANCOIS JACOB (1920- , Nancy, France)—Won the 1965 Nobel Prize for his research on genetic function. A military hero of World War II, he became one of the leading biologists in the world.

SIR BERNARD KATZ (1911- , Leipzig, Germany)—A British citizen, he won the 1970 Nobel Prize for his work on nerve impulses. He served as Vice-President of the British Royal Society.

ARTHUR KORNBERG (1918- , Brooklyn)—Won the 1959 Nobel Prize for his synthesis of DNA.

SIR HANS A. KREBS (1900- , Hildesheim, Germany)—Won the 1953 Nobel Prize for his work on the citric acid cycle. He taught at Oxford and was a member of the British Royal Society.

KARL LANDSTEINER (1868-1943, Vienna)—Won the 1930 Nobel Prize for his work on the classification of blood groups and his discovery of the Rh factor. He became a Catholic.

JOSHUA LEDERBERG (1925- , Montclair, N.J.)—Won the 1958 Nobel Prize for his work on genetic organization. He was one of the very few Nobel winners (perhaps the only one) to have a syndicated newspaper column. He taught at Stanford U.

FRITZ A. LIPMANN (b. 1899, Königsberg, Germany)—An American, he won the 1953 Nobel Prize for his work on metabolism. He was the discoverer of coenzyme A.

OTTO LOEWI (1873-1961, Frankfurt)—Won the 1936 Nobel Prize for his work on nerve impulses.

SALVADOR E. LURIA (1912- , Turin, Italy)—An American, he won the 1969 Nobel Prize for his work on microbial genetics, which formed the basis for modern molecular biology.

ANDRE M. LWOFF (1902- , Allier, France)—Won the 1965 Nobel Prize for his contributions to the study of viruses. He was one of the leading biologists in France.

ELIE METCHNIKOFF (1845-1916, Ivanovka, Russia)—Won the 1908 Nobel Prize for his pioneering work in embryology. His mother was Jewish.

OTTO MEYERHOFF (1888-1951, Hanover, Germany)—Won the 1923 Nobel Prize for his work on oxygen consumption and lactic acid metabolism. He was one of the world's leading biochemists.

HERMAN J. MULLER (1890-1967, New York City)—Won the 1946 Nobel Prize for his discoveries in the field of mutations. He did important early research in animal genetics.

DANIEL NATHANS (1928- , Wilmington, Del.)—Won the 1978 Nobel Prize for his cancer research. He is one of the world's leading microbiologists.

MARSHALL W. NIRENBERG (1927- , New York City)—Won the 1968 Nobel Prize for his study of the genetic code. One of the leading biochemists in the world, he belongs to the National Academy of Sciences.

TADEUS REICHSTEIN (b. 1897, Wloclawek, Poland)—A Swiss, he won the 1950 Nobel Prize for his work on adrenal cortex hormones. He achieved a vitamin synthesis in 1933, an accomplishment that should have won him the Nobel Prize that year.

HOWARD M. TEMIN (1934- , Philadelphia)—An American, he won the 1975 Nobel Prize for his research on genetics. He teaches at the U. of Wisconsin.

SELMAN WAKSMAN (b. 1888, Priluki, Russia)—An American, he won the 1952 Nobel Prize for his work on antibiotics (the term was first used by him). He was a member of the National Academy of Sciences, and will always be remembered for his gift to humanity of streptomycin.

GEORGE WALD (1906- , New York City)—Won the 1967 Nobel Prize for his work on eye pigments and the role of vitamin A in sight. He taught at Harvard for many years and was an outspoken critic of American involvement in Vietnam.

OTTO WARBURG (1883-1970, Freiburg, Germany)—Won the 1931 Nobel Prize for his research and discoveries concerning the respiratory enzyme. The Germans allowed him to continue his work during the Hitler regime.

ROSALYN S. YALOW (1921- , Bronx)—Won the 1977 Nobel Prize for her work on radioimmunoassay, becoming the second woman to win the Prize in Medicine.

CHEMISTRY

ADOLF VON BAEYER (1835-1917, Berlin)—Won the 1905 Nobel Prize for his work on hydroaromatic compounds and organic dyes. One of his major contributions was discoveries that led to synthetic indigo. The holder of the British Royal Society's Davy Medal, he was the son of a Jewish mother.

MELVIN CALVIN (1912- , St, Paul, Minn.)—Won the 1961 Nobel Prize for his work on photosynthesis using radioactive tracers. He worked and taught at the U. of California.

FRITZ HABER (1868-1934, Breslau)—Won the 1918 Nobel Prize for his work in synthesizing ammonia. He served as Director of the Kaiser Wilhelm Research Institute and built it into a major chemistry research center, and also served as President of the German Chemical Society.

GEORG C. DE HEVESY (1885-1966, Budapest)—Won the 1943 Nobel Prize for his pioneering work with isotopes. He was codiscoverer of the Element 72 (Hafnium) and he won the 1959 Atoms for Peace Award.

HENRI MOISSAN (1852-1907, Paris)—Won the 1906 Nobel Prize for his development of the Moissan Electric Furnace and his work on fluorine. His mother was Jewish.

MAX. F. PERUTZ (1914- , Vienna)—A British subject, he won the 1962 Nobel Prize for his work on globular protein structure.

WILLIAM H. STEIN (1911- , New York City)—Won the 1972 Nobel Prize for his work on amino acids and peptides. He is a member of the National Academy of Sciences.

OTTO WALLACH (1847-1931, Königsberg, Germany)—Won the 1910 Nobel Prize for his research on alicyclic compounds. He was one of the leading figures in German chemistry and served as President of the German Chemical Society.

RICHARD M. WILLSTATTER (1872-1942, Karlsruhe, Germany)—Won the 1915 Nobel Prize for his work on chlorophyll. He did important research on gas masks for the Germans in World War I and was Director of the German State Chemical Laboratory.

PHYSICS

HANS A. BETHE (1906- , Strasbourg, France)—Won the 1967 Nobel Prize for his work on the energy produced by star systems. An American, he was Director of the Theoretical Physics Division at Los Alamos and also served on President Eisenhower's Science Advisory Committee. His mother was Jewish.

FELIX BLOCH (1905- , Zurich, Switzerland)—An American, he won the 1952 Nobel Prize for his work on neutron magnetism.

HAGE BOHR (1922-)—A Dane, he won the 1975 Nobel Prize for his work on the mysteries of atomic structure. He is part Jewish.

NIELS BOHR (1885-1962, Copenhagen, Denmark)—Won the 1922 Nobel Prize (at the age of 37 at a time when the award always went to older researchers) for his pioneering work on the atom's structure. The complementarity principle in physics owes much to his work. He was smuggled out of Denmark to England, where he worked on the development of the atomic bomb. He won the Atoms for Peace Award in 1956. His mother was Jewish.

MAX BORN (1882-1970, Breslau, Germany)—Won the 1954 Nobel Prize for his research on quantum mechanics. He was one of the most important theoretical physicists of his time.

ALBERT EINSTEIN (1879-1955, Ulm, Germany)—Won the 1921 Nobel Prize for his relativity theory. He was one of the most influential men in history, and his name has become synonymous with genius.

RICHARD P. FEYNMAN (1918- , New York City)—Won the 1965 Nobel Prize for his major contributions to quantum electrodynamic theory. Feynman Integrals and Feynman Graphs are familiar to physics students and researchers all over the world.

JAMES FRANCK (1882-1964, Hamburg)—Won the 1925 Nobel Prize for his work on the electron's effect on the atom.

DENNIS GABOR (b. 1900, Hungary)—A British citizen, he won the 1971 Nobel Prize for his role in developing holography. He is a member of the British Royal Society.

MURRAY GELL-MANN (1929- , New York City)—Won the 1969 Nobel Prize for his work on subatomic particles. One of the leading physicists in the world, Gell-Mann coined the term *quark*.

DONALD A. GLASER (1926- , Cleveland)—Won the 1960 Nobel Prize for his development of the research bubble chamber.

GUSTAV HERTZ (1887-1950, Hamburg)—Won the 1925 Nobel Prize for his work on the electron-atom relationship. The son of a Jewish father, he became a Christian and taught in East Germany after World War II.

ROBERT HOFSTADTER (1915- , New York City)—Won the 1961 Nobel Prize for his research on subatomic particles. He taught at Stanford.

BRIAN D. JOSEPHSON (1940- , Cardiff, England)—Won the 1973 Nobel Prize for his contributions to the development of the transistor.

LEV D. LANDAU (1908-1968, Baku, Russia)—Won the 1962 Nobel Prize for his work on the theory of condensed matter. The leading physicist in the Soviet Union (he held three Stalin Prizes), he was kept alive after a car accident through an incredible series of operations.

GABRIEL LIPPMANN (1845-1921, Luxembourg)—A Frenchman, he won the 1908 Nobel Prize for his work on interference phenomenon. The world's leading authority on the electron, he served as President of the French Academy of Science.

ALBERT A. MICHELSON (1852-1931, Strelno, Prussia)—The first American to win the prize in a science category, the 1907 Nobel Prize for his work on the velocity of light. His work is considered crucial to Einstein's theory of relativity.

BENJAMIN R. MOTTELSON (1926-)—A Dane (although born in the U.S.), he won the 1975 Nobel Prize for his work on atomic structure.

ARNO A. PENZIAS (1933- , Munich)—An American, he won the 1978 Nobel Prize in Physics for his work on the "big bang" theory of creation.

ISIDOR I. RABI (1898- , Rymanow, Austria-Hungary)—Won the 1944 Nobel

Prize for his work on molecular beams. A Professor at Columbia, he was a major advisor to the U.S. Atomic Energy Commission.

BURTON RICHTER (1931- , New York City)—Won the 1976 Nobel Prize for his discovery of subatomic particles.

JULIAN S. SCHWINGER (1918- , New York City)—Won the 1965 Nobel Prize for his pioneering work in quantum electrodynamics. He is a Professor at Harvard.

EMILIO SEGRE (1905- , Tivoli, Italy)—Won the 1959 Nobel Prize for his work on the antiproton.

OTTO STERN (1888-1969)—Won the 1943 Nobel Prize for his work on the use of the molecular beam.

ECONOMICS

KENNETH J. ARROW (1921- , New York City)—Won the 1972 Nobel Prize. He served on the President's Council of Economic Advisors and is a member of the American Academy of Arts and Sciences.

MILTON FRIEDMAN (1912- , Rahway, N.J.)—The most famous economist in the U.S., he won the 1976 Nobel Prize for his work as the leading anti-Keynesian economist. He served as an economic advisor in the Nixon administration and teaches at the U. of Chicago.

LEONID KANTOROVICH (1912-)—One of the leading economists in the Soviet Union, he won the 1975 Nobel Prize for his work on quantitative economics. He holds the Stalin Prize and the Lenin Prize.

SIMON KUZNETS (1901- , Russia)—Won the 1971 Nobel Prize for his work on economic growth. He is an American.

PAUL SAMUELSON (1915- , Gary, Ind.)—Won the 1970 Nobel Prize for his contributions to economic theory. A Professor at M.I.T., he is the author of the most widely used introductory economics textbook in the world.

HERBERT A. SIMON (1916- , Milwaukee)—Won the 1978 Nobel Prize for his work on organizational theory.

PULITZER PRIZE WINNERS

REPORTING

MEYER BERGER, *New York Times,* 1950.
ROBERT CAHN, *Christian Science Monitor,* 1967.
ALVIN H. GOLDSTEIN, *Chicago Daily News,* 1925.
MONROE KARMIN, *Wall Street Journal,* 1967.
WILLIAM LAURENCE, *New York Times,* 1937.
ANTHONY LEWIS, *New York Times,* 1955, 1963.
J. ANTHONY LUKAS, *New York Times,* 1968.
MIRRIAM OTTENBERG, *Washington Evening Star,* 1960.
HERBERT BAYARD SWOPE, *New York World,* 1917.

INTERNATIONAL REPORTING

MAX FRANKEL, *New York Times,* 1973.
ALFRED FRIENDLY, *Washington Post,* 1968.
DAVID HALBERSTAM, *New York Times,* 1964.
SEYMOUR HERSH, *Dispatch News Service,* 1970.

HENRY KAMM, *New York Times*, 1978.
WALTER LIPPMANN, *New York Herald Tribune* Syndicate, 1962.
A. M. ROSENTHAL, *New York Times*, 1960.
SYDNEY H. SCHANBERG, *New York Times*, 1976.
LOUIS STARK, *New York Times*, 1942.
IRA WOLFERT, North American Newspaper Alliance.

EDITORIAL WRITING

PAUL GREENBERG, *Pine Bluff* (Ark.) *Commercial*, 1969.
LOUIS ISAAC JAFFEE, *Norfolk Virginian-Pilot*, 1929.

COMMENTARY

DAVID S. BRODER, *Washington Press*, 1973.
WILLIAM SAFIRE, *New York Times*, 1978.

CORRESPONDENCE

ARTHUR KROCK, *New York Times*, 1935, 1938.

EDITORIAL CARTOONING

HERBERT BLOCK, Newspaper Enterprise Assn., 1942; *Washington Post and Times Herald*, 1954.
RUBE GOLDBERG, *New York Sun*, 1948.

HISTORY

BERNARD BAILYN, *The Ideological Origins of the American Revolution*, 1968.
DANIEL J. BOORSTIN, *The Americans*, 1974.
HERBERT FEIS, *Between War and Peace*, 1961.
OSCAR HANDLIN, *The Uprooted*, 1952.
RICHARD HOFSTADTER, *The Age of Reform*, 1956.
MICHAEL KAMMEN, *People of Paradox*, 1973.
LEONARD LEVY, *The Origin of the Fifth Amendment*, 1969.
IRWIN UNGER, *The Greenback Era*, 1965.

BIOGRAPHY

ROBERT A. CARO, *The Power Broker*, 1975.
LEON EDEL, *Henry James*, 1963.
JUSTIN KAPLAN, *Mr. Clemens and Mark Twain*, 1967.
JOSEPH LASH, *Eleanor and Franklin*, 1972.
ERNEST SAMUELS, *Henry Adams* (3 volumes), 1965.
LOUIS SHEAFFER, *O'Neill, Son and Artist*, 1974.

GENERAL NONFICTION

ERIK A. ERICKSON, *Gandhi's Truth*, 1971.
RICHARD HOFSTADTER, *Anti-Intellectualism in American Life*, 1964.
NORMAN MAILER, *The Armies of the Night*, 1969.
CARL SAGAN, *The Dragons of Eden*, 1978.
BARBARA TUCHMAN, *The Guns of August*, 1963; *Stilwell and the American Experience in China 1911–1945*, 1972.
THEODORE H. WHITE, *The Making of the President*, 1960, 1962.

FICTION

SAUL BELLOW, *Humboldt's Gift*, 1976.
EDNA FERBER, *So Big*, 1925.
MACKINLAY KANTOR, *Andersonville*, 1956.
BERNARD MALAMUD, *The Fixer*, 1967.
HERMAN WOUK, *The Caine Mutiny*, 1952.

POETRY

ANTHONY HECHT, *The Hard Hours*, 1968.
MAXINE KUMIN, *Up Country*, 1973.
STANLEY KUNITZ, *Selected Poems, 1926–1958*, 1959.
HOWARD NEMEROV, *Collected Poems*, 1978.
GEORGE OPPEN, *Of Being Numerous*, 1969.
KARL SHAPIRO, *V-Letter and Other Poems*, 1945.

DRAMA

MARVIN HAMLISCH (and others), *A Chorus Line*, 1976.
MOSS HART and GEORGE S. KAUFMAN, *You Can't Take It with You*, 1937.
GEORGE S. KAUFMAN, MORRIE RYSKIND, and IRA GERSHWIN, *Of Thee I Sing*, 1932.
SIDNEY KINGSLEY, *Men in White*, 1934.
JOSEPH KRAMM, *The Shrike*, 1952.
FRANK LOESSER and ABE BURROWS, *How to Succeed in Business without Really Trying*, 1962.
ARTHUR MILLER, *Death of a Salesman*, 1949.
ELMER RICE, *Street Scene*, 1929.
RICHARD RODGERS and OSCAR HAMMERSTEIN II, *South Pacific*, 1950.
HOWARD SACKLER, *The Great White Hope*, 1969.
JEROME WEIDMAN, JERRY BOCK, and SHELDON HARNICK, *Fiorello!*, 1960.

MUSIC

AARON COPLAND, *Appalachian Spring*, 1945.
MARIO DAVDOVSKY, *Synchronisms No. 6 for Piano and Electronic Sound*, 1971.
JACOB DRUCKMAN, *Windows*, 1972.
LEON KIRCHNER, 1967, Quartet No. 3, 1967.
ERNEST TOCH, Symphony No. 3, 1956.
RICHARD WERNICK, *Visions of Terror and Wonder*, 1977.

SPECIAL CITATION

OSCAR HAMMERSTEIN II (and Richard Rodgers), *Oklahoma*, 1944.
MAX KASE, *New York Journal-American*, 1952.
ARTHUR KROCK, *New York Times*, 1951.
WALTER LIPPMANN, *New York Herald Tribune*, 1958.
LESTER MARKEL, *New York Times*, 1953.
C. L. SULZBERGER, *New York Times*, 1951.

CRITICISM

ALAN M. KRIEGSMAN, *Washington Post*, 1976.
HAROLD C. SCHONBERG, *New York Times*, 1971.

PHOTOGRAPHY

NATHANIEL FEIN, *New York Herald Tribune*, 1949.
STANLEY FORMAN, *Boston Herald American*, 1976, 1977.
NEAL ULEVICH, *Associated Press*, 1977.

ACADEMY AWARD WINNERS

1927

BENJAMIN GLAZER—Adaptation Writing for *Seventh Heaven*.
BEN HECHT—Original Writing for *Underworld*.
LEWIS MILESTONE—Best Comedy Director for *Two Arabian Knights*.

1929–1930

LEWIS MILESTONE—Best Director for *All Quiet on the Western Front*.
NORMA SHEARER—Best Actress for *The Divorcee*.

1934

HERBERT MAGIDSON—Best Song for "Continental" from *The Gay Divorcee*.
ROBERT RISKIN—Adaptation Writing for *It Happened One Night*.
LOUIS SILVERS—Best Score for *One Night of Love*.

1935

BEN HECHT—Original Writing for *The Scoundrel*.
NATHAN LEVINSON—Technical Award for sound recording.
MAX STEINER—Best Song for "The Informer" from *The Informer*.
HARRY WARREN and AL DUBIN—Best Song for "Lullaby of Broadway" from *Gold Diggers*.

1936

SEYMOUR FELIX—Best Dance Direction for "A Pretty Girl Is Like a Melody" from *The Great Ziegfeld*.
LEO FORBSTEIN—Best Score for *Anthony Adverse*.
JEROME KERN—Best Song for "The Way You Look Tonight" from *Swing Time*.
PAUL MUNI—Best Actor for *The Story of Louis Pasteur*.
LUISE RAINER—Best Actress for *The Great Ziegfeld*.

1937

KARL FREUND—Best Cinematography for *The Good Earth*.
LUISE RAINER—Best Actress for *The Good Earth*.
JOSEPH SCHILDKRAUT—Best Supporting Actor for *The Life of Emile Zola*.

1938

ERICH W. KORNGOLD—Best Original Score for *The Adventures of Robin Hood*.

CONVERTS TO JUDAISM

CARROLL BAKER—*See* Film Stars
SIDNEY BREWS—*See* Golf.
ROD CAREW—*See* Baseball.
SAMMY DAVIS, JR.—*See* Entertainers.
JACQUELINE DU PRE—*See* Cellists.
CAROLYN JONES—*See* Film Stars.
MARILYN MONROE—*See* Film Stars.
ELEANOR PARKER—*See* Film Stars.
ELIZABETH TAYLOR—*See* Film Stars.
ROY THINNES—*See* Television Performers.

1939

HAROLD ARLEN and E. Y. HARBURG—Best Song for "Over the Rainbow" from *The Wizard of Oz*.
LEO SHUKEN—Best Score for *Stagecoach*.

1940

BENJAMIN GLAZER—Best Original Story for *Arise, My Love*.
VINCENT KORDA—Best Interior Color Cecoration for *The Thief of Baghdad*.
NATHAN LEVINSON—Special Award for service to the U.S. Military.

1941

SIDNEY BUCHMAN—Best Screenplay Writing for *Here Comes Mr. Jordan*.
BERNARD HERRMANN—Best Score for *All That Money Can Buy*.
NATHAN JURAN—Best Black-and-White Interior Decoration for *How Green Was My Valley*.
JEROME KERN and OSCAR HAMMERSTEIN II—Best Song for "The Last Time I Saw Paris" from *Lady Be Good*.
HERMAN J. MANKIEWICZ—Best Original Screenplay for *Citizen Kane*.
HARRY SEGALL—Best Original Story for *Here Comes Mr. Jordan*.

1942

IRVING BERLIN—Best Song for "White Christmas" from *Holiday Inn*.
DANIEL J. BLOOMBERG—Technical Award for sound engineering.
MICHAEL KANIN—Best Original Screenplay for *Woman of the Year*.
NATHAN LEVINSON—Best Sound Recording for *Yankee Doodle Dandy*.
MAX STEINER—Best Score (Nonmusical) for *Now, Voyager*.
WILLIAM WYLER—Best Director for *Mrs. Miniver*.

1943

DANIEL J. BLOOMBERG—Technical Award for sound engineering.
MICHAEL CURTIZ—Best Director for *Casablanca*.
JULIUS J. EPSTEIN, PHILIP G. EPSTEIN, and HOWARD KOCH—Best Screenplay Writing for *Casablanca*.
NORMAN KRASNA—Best Original Screenplay for *Princess O'Rourke*.
HARRY WARREN and MACK GORDON—Best Song for "You'll Never Know" from *Hello, Frisco, Hello*.

1944

DANIEL J. BLOOMBERG—Technical Award for sound engineering.
MAX STEINER—Best Score (Nonmusical) for *Since You Went Away*.
MORRIS STOLOFF—Best Score for *Cover Girl*.

1945

DANIEL J. BLOOMBERG—Technical Award for sound engineering.
RICHARD RODGERS and OSCAR HAMMERSTEIN II—Best Song for "It Might As Well Be Spring" from *State Fair*.
WALTER WANGER —Special Award for service.
BILLY WILDER—Best Director for *The Lost Weekend*.
BILLY WILDER—Best Screenplay Writing for *The Lost Weekend*.

1946

SAMUEL GOLDWYN—Irving G. Thalberg Memorial Award.
ERNST LUBITSCH—Special Award for service to motion pictures.
DANIEL MANDELL—Best Film Editing for *The Best Years of Our Lives*.
MORRIS STOLOFF—Best Score (Musical) for *The Jolson Story*.
HARRY WARREN—Best Song for "On the Atchison, Topeka and the Santa Fe" from *The Harvey Girls*.
BILLY WILDER—Best Director for *The Best Years of Our Lives*.

1947

NATHAN LEVINSON—Technical Award for sound engineering.
WILLIAM N. SELIG—Special Award for contributions to motion pictures.
SIDNEY SHELDON—Best Original Screenplay for *The Bachelor and the Bobbysoxer*.
KURT SINGER—Technical Award.
ALLIE WRUBEL—Best Song for "Zip-a-Dee-Doo-Dah" from *Song of the South*.

1948

SID GRAUMAN—Special Award.
JAY LIVINGSTON—Best Song for "Buttons and Bows" from *Paleface*.
JERRY WALD—Irving G. Thalberg Memorial Award.
WALTER WANGER—Special Award.
DAVID WECHSLER—Best Story for *The Search*.
ADOLPH ZUKOR—Special Award.

1949

AARON COPLAND—Best Score (Nonmusical) for *The Heiress*.
FRANK LOESSER—Best Song for "Baby It's Cold Outside" from *Neptune's Daughter*.
JOSEPH L. MANKIEWICZ—Best Director for *A Letter to Three Wives*.
JOSEPH L. MANKIEWICZ—Best Screenplay Writing for *A Letter to Three Wives*.

1950

ADOLPH DEUTSCH—Best Score (Musical) for *Annie Get Your Gun*.
JUDY HOLLIDAY—Best Actress for *Born Yesterday*.

JAY LIVINGSTON—Best Song for "Mona Lisa" from *Captain Carey, USA*.
JOSEPH L. MANKIEWICZ—Best Director for *All About Eve*.
JOSEPH L. MANKIEWICZ—Best Screenplay Writing for *All About Eve*.
LOUIS B. MAYER—Special Award.
FRANZ WAXMAN—Best Score (Nonmusical) for *Sunset Boulevard*.
BILLY WILDER—Best Screenplay Story for *Sunset Boulevard*.

1951

ARTHUR FREED—Irving G. Thalberg Memorial Award.
ALAN JAY LERNER—Best Story and Screenplay for *An American in Paris*.
FRANZ WAXMAN—Best Score (Nonmusical) for *A Place in the Sun*.
FRED ZINNEMANN—Best Short Subject for *Benjy*.

1952

JOSEPH M. SCHENCK—Special Award.
CHARLES SCHNEE—Best Screenplay for *The Bad and the Beautiful*.
DIMITRI TIOMKIN—Best Score (Nonmusical) for *High Noon*.
DIMITRI TIOMKIN—Best Song for "High Noon."

1953

SAMMY FAIN—Best Song for "Secret Love" from *Calamity Jane*.
SOL HALPRIN—Technical Award for his role in developing CinemaScope.
FRED ZINNEMANN—Best Director for *From Here to Eternity*.

1954

ADOLPH DEUTSCH—Best Score (Musical) for *Seven Brides for Seven Brothers*.
KARL FREUND—Technical Award.
BORIS KAUFMAN—Best Black-and-White Cinematography for *On the Waterfront*.
DANNY KAYE—Special Award for service.
MILTON KRASNER—Best Color Cinematography for *Three Coins in the Fountain*.
BUDD SCHULBERG—Best Story snd Screenplay for *On the Waterfront*.
JULES STYNE and SAMMY CAHN—Best Song for "Three Coins in the Fountain."
DIMITRI TIOMKIN—Best Score (Nonmusical) for *The High and the Mighty*.

1955

JAY BLACKTON and ADOLPH DEUTSCH—Best Score (Musical) for *Oaklahoma!*
PADDY CHAYEFSKY—Best Screenplay for *Marty*.
SAMMY FAIN—Best Song for "Love Is a Many-Splendored Thing" from the film of the same name.
DANIEL FUCHS—Best Story for *Love Me or Leave Me*.
SONYA LEVIEN—Best Story and Screenplay for *Love Me or Leave Me*.
DELBERT MANN—Best Director for *Marty*.

1956

BUDDY ADLER—Irving G. Thalberg Memorial Award.
DANIEL J. BLOOMBERG—Technical Award.

EDDIE CANTOR—Special Award for service.
TED HIRSCH—Technical Award.
JAY LIVINGSTON—Best Song for "Whatever Will Be, Will Be" from *The Man Who Knew Too Much*.
S. J. PERELMAN—Best Adapted Screenplay for *Around the World in 80 Days*.

1957

RED BUTTONS—Best Supporting Actor for *Sayonara*.
SAMMY CAHN—Best Song for "All The Way" from *The Joker Is Wild*.
SAMUEL GOLDWYN—Jean Hersholt Humanitarian Award.
B. B. KAHANE—Special Award for service.

1958

SAM LEAVITT—Best Black-and-White Cinematography for *The Defiant Ones*.
ALAN JAY LERNER—Best Adapted Screenplay for *Gigi*.
FREDERICK LOEWE and ALAN JAY LERNER—Best Song for "Gigi".
ANDRE PREVIN—Best Score (Musical) for *Gigi*.
DIMITRI TIOMKIN—Best Score (Nonmusical) for *The Old Man and the Sea*.
JACK L. WARNER—Irving G. Thalberg Memorial Award.

1959

SAMMY CAHN—Best Song for "High Hopes" from *A Hole in the Head*.
ROBERT P. GUTTERMAN—Technical Award.
ANDRE PREVIN—Best Score (Musical) for *Porgy and Bess*.
STUART A. REISS—Best Black-and-White Set Direction for *The Diary of Anne Frank*.
STANLEY SHAPIRO and MAURICE RICHLIN—Best Original Screenplay for *Pillow Talk*.
SIMONE SIGNORET—Best Actress for *Room at the Top*.
SHELLEY WINTERS—Best Supporting Actress for *The Diary of Anne Frank*.
WILLIAM WYLER—Best Director for *Ben-Hur*.

1960

RICHARD BROOKS—Best Adapted Screenplay for *Elmer Gantry*.
ERNEST GOLD—Best Score (Nonmusical) for *Exodus*.
STANLEY KRAMER—Irving G. Thalberg Memorial Award.
SOL LESSER—Jean Hersholt Humanitarian Award.

1961

BORIS LEVEN—Best Art or Set Direction (Color) for *West Side Story*.
DANIEL MANDELL—Best Film Editing for *The Apartment*.
ABBY MANN—Best Adapted Screenplay for *Judgment at Nuremberg*.
SID RAMIN and IRWIN KOSTAL—Best Score (Musical) for *West Side Story*.
JEROME ROBBINS—Special Award for service.
EUGEN SHUFTAN—Best Black-and-White Cinematography for *The Hustler*.
MORRIS STOLOFF and HARRY SUKMAN—Best Score for *Song Without End*.
ELIZABETH TAYLOR—Best Actress for *Butterfield 8*.
BILLY WILDER—Best Director for *The Apartment*.

BILLY WILDER and I. A. L. DIAMOND—Best Original Screenplay for *The Apartment*.

ROBERT WISE and JEROME ROBBINS—Best Director for *West Side Story*.

1962

STEVE BROIDY—Jean Hersholt Humanitarian Award.

ALEXANDER GOLITZEN—Best Art Direction (Black-and-White) for *To Kill a Mockingbird*.

NORMAN KOCH—Best Costume Design (Black-and-White) for *What Ever Happened to Baby Jane?*

1963

HERMAN BLUMENTHAL—Best Art Direction (Color) for *Cleopatra*.

SAMMY CAHN—Best Song for "Call Me Irresponsible" from *Papa's Delicate Condition*.

MELVYN DOUGLAS—Best Supporting Actor for *Hud*.

ANDRE PREVIN—Best Adapted Musical Score for *Irma La Douce*.

SAM SPIEGEL—Irving G. Thalberg Memorial Award.

1964

GEORGE CUKOR—Best Director for *My Fair Lady*.

MILTON FORMAN, RICHARD B. GLICKMAN, and DANIEL J. PEARLMAN—Technical Award for lighting engineering.

ANDRE PREVIN—Best Adapted Score for *My Fair Lady*.

RICHARD M. SHERMAN and ROBERT B. SHERMAN—Best Score for *Mary Poppins*.

RICHARD M. SHERMAN and ROBERT B. SHERMAN—Best Song for "Chim-Chim Cher-ee" from *Mary Poppins*.

LEONARD L. SOKOLOW—Technical Award.

SIDNEY P. SOLOW—Technical Award.

FRANK TARLOFF—Best Original Screenplay for *Father Goose*.

1965

MARTIN BALSAM—Best Supporting Actor for *A Thousand Clowns*.

IRWIN KOSTAL—Best Adapted Score for *The Sound of Music*.

JOHNNY MANDEL—Best Song for "The Shadow of Your Smile" from *The Sandpiper*.

FREDERICK RAPHAEL—Best Original Screenplay for *Darling*.

SHELLEY WINTERS—Best Supporting Actress for *A Patch of Blue*.

ROBERT WISE—Best Director for *The Sound of Music*.

WILLIAM WYLER—Irving G. Thalberg Memorial Award.

1966

HENRY BERMAN and STEWART LINDER—Best Film Editing for *Grand Prix*.

CLAUSE LELOUCH—Best Original Story and Screenplay for *A Man and A Woman*.

WALTER MATTHAU—Best Supporting Actor for *The Fortune Cookie*.

ELIZABETH TAYLOR—Best Actress for *Who's Afraid of Virginia Woolf?*

HASKELL WEXLER—Best Black-and-White Cinematography for *Who's Afraid of Virginia Woolf?*

ROBERT WISE—Irving G. Thalberg Memorial Award.
FRED ZINNEMANN—Best Director for *A Man for All Seasons*.

1967

ELMER BERNSTEIN—Best Original Score for *Thoroughly Modern Millie*.
ARTHUR FREED—Special Award for service.
MIKE NICHOLS—Best Director for *The Graduate*.
ROD STEIGER—Best Actor for *In the Heat of the Night*.

1968

JACK ALBERTSON—Best Supporting Actor for *The Subject Was Roses*.
SAUL BASS—Best Short Subject for *Why Man Creates*.
ALAN and MARILYN BERGMAN—Best Song for "The Windmills of Your Mind" from *The Thomas Crown Affair*.
MEL BROOKS—Best Original Story and Screenplay for *The Producers*.
JAMES GOLDMAN—Best Adapted Screenplay for *The Lion in Winter*.
STANLEY KUBRICK—Best Special Effects for *2001: A Space Odyssey*.

1969

BURT BACHARACH—Best Score (Nonmusical) for *Butch Cassidy and the Sundance Kid*.
BURT BACHARACH and HAL DAVID—Best Song for "Raindrops Keep Fallin' on My Head" from *Butch Cassidy and the Sundance Kid*.
HERMAN BLUMENTHA ,—Best Art Direction for *Hello, Dolly!*
WILLIAM GOLDMAN—Best Adapted Screenplay for *Butch Cassidy and the Sundance Kid*.
GOLDIE HAWN—Best Supporting Actress for *Cactus Flower*.
GEORGE JESSEL—Jean Hersholt Humanitarian Award.
JOHN SCHLESINGER—Best Director for *Midnight Cowboy*.
JACK SOLOMON and MURRAY SPIVACK—Best Sound for *Hello, Dolly!*

1970

FRANKLIN J. SCHAFFNER—Best Director for *Patton*.
LEONARD SOKOLOW—Technical Award.

1971

PADDY CHAYEFSKY—Best Original Story and Screenplay for *The Hospital*.
WILLIAM FRIEDKIN—Best Director for *The French Connection*.
JERRY GREENBERG—Best Film Editing for *The French Connection*.
DAVID WOLPER—Best Feature Documentary for *The Hellstrom Chronicle*.

1972

CHARLES BOREN—Special Award for labor relations.
JOEL GREY—Best Supporting Actor for *Cabaret*.
AL KASHA and JOEL HIRSCHHORN—Best Song for "The Morning After" from *The Poseidon Adventure*.
JEREMY LARNER—Best Original Story and Screenplay for *The Candidate*.
HOWARD T. LAZARE—Technical Award.
MANFRED MICHELSON—Technical Award.
EDWARD G. ROBINSON—Special Award.

1973

    MARVIN HAMLISCH—Best Adapted Scoring for *The Sting*.
    MARVIN HAMLISCH—Best Dramatic Score for *The Way We Were*.
    MARVIN HAMLISCH, ALAN BERGMAN, and MARILYN BERGMAN—Best Song for "The Way We Were."
    JOHN HOUSEMAN—Best Supporting Actor for *The Paper Chase*.
    GLORIA KATZ—Best Original Screenplay and Story for *American Graffiti*.
    GROUCHO MARX—Special Award.
    LAWRENCE WEINGARTEN—Irving G. Thalberg Memorial Award.
    LEW WASSERMAN—Jean Hersholt Humanitarian Award.

1974

    AL KASHA and JOEL HIRSCHHORN—Best Song for "We May Never Love Like This Again" from *The Towering Inferno*.
    ARTHUR KRIM—Jean Hersholt Humanitarian Award.

1975

    GEORGE BURNS—Best Supporting Actor for *The Sunshine Boys*.
    MILOS FORMAN—Best Director for *One Flew over the Cuckoo's Nest*.
    BO GOLDMAN—Best Adapted Screenplay for *One Flew over the Cuckoo's Nest*.
    LEE GRANT—Best Supporting Actress for *Shampoo*.
    MERVYN LEROY—Irving G. Thalberg Memorial Award.
    LEONARD ROSENMAN—Best Song Score for *Barry Lyndon*.
    JULES STEIN—Jean Hersholt Humanitarian Award.

1976

    PANDRO S. BERMAN—Irving G. Thalberg Memorial Award.
    PADDY CHAYEFSKY—Best Original Screenplay for *Network*.
    WILLIAM GOLDMAN—Best Screenplay Adaptation for *All the President's Men*.
    JERRY GOLDSMITH—Best Original Score for *The Omen*.
    LEONARD ROSENMAN—Best Original Song for *Bound for Glory*.
    BARBRA STREISAND—Best Song for "Evergreen" from *A Star Is Born*.
    HASKELL WEXLER—Best Cinematography for *Bound for Glory*.

1977

    WOODY ALLEN—Best Director for *Annie Hall*.
    WOODY ALLEN and MARSHALL BRICKMAN—Best Original Screenplay for *Annie Hall*.
    RICHARD DREYFUSS—Best Actor for *The Goodbye Girl*.
    PAUL HIRSCH—Best Editing for *Star Wars*.
    WALTER MIRISCH—Irving Thalberg Memorial Award.
    JONATHAN TUNICK—Best Adapted Score for *A Little Night Music*.

OLYMPIC MEDALISTS

BASKETBALL

SAMUEL BALTER (1909- , Detroit)—Won a Gold Medal in 1936 as a member of the U.S. Team. A great AAU player, he is in the Helms AAU Hall of Fame. He played collegiately at UCLA.

MOSES BLASS—From Brazil, he won a Gold Medal at the 1960 Games.

LAWRENCE H. BROWN (1940- , Brooklyn)—From the U. of North Carolina, he won a Gold Medal at the 1964 Games. He later was a fine player and coach in the ABA and NBA. He became head coach at UCLA in 1978.

ERNEST GRUNFELD (1955- , Rumania)—Won a Gold Medal with the U.S. Team at the 1976 Games. An All-America at the U. of Tennessee in 1976 and 1977, he plays with the Milwaukee Bucks of the NBA.

NANCY LEIBERMAN—Won a Silver Medal with the U.S. Team at the 1976 Games. She was considered the top woman basketball player in the college ranks at the beginning of the 1978–1979 season.

OSCAR MOGLIA—From Uruguay, he won a Bronze Medal at the 1956 Games.

BOXING

SAMUEL BERGER (1884-1925, Chicago)—Won the Gold Medal in the heavyweight division for the U.S. at the 1904 Games.

NATHAN BOR—From the U.S., he won a Bronze Medal as a lightweight at the 1932 Games.

HARRY DEVINE—Won the Bronze Medal in the featherweight division for the U.S. at the 1928 Games.

JACKIE FIELDS—Won a Gold Medal for the U.S. in the featherweight division in 1924, and was welterweight champion of the world 1929–30, and 1932–33.

MONTGOMERY HERSCOVITZ—A Canadian, he won the Gold Medal in the middleweight division at the 1920 Games.

HARRY ISAACS—From South Africa, he won the Bronze Medal in the bantamweight division at the 1928 Games.

SAMUEL MOSBERG (b. 1896, New York City)—Won the Gold Medal in the lightweight division at the 1920 Games.

CANOEING

LASZLO FABIAN (1936-)—A Hungarian, he won the Gold Medal in the 10,000-meter Kayak Doubles at the 1956 Games. He won the World Championship in 1958.

IMRE FARKAS—A Hungarian, he won the Bronze Medal in the 10,000-meter Canadian Doubles at the 1956 Games and the Bronze Medal in the 10,000-meter Canadian Tandem at the 1960 Games.

KLARA FRIED—A Hungarian, she won the Bronze Medal in the 500-meter Kayak Tandem at the 1960 Games.

NAUM PROKUPETS—Won a Bronze Medal in Canoeing for the Soviet Union at the 1968 Games.

ALEXANDER ROGOV—From the Soviet Union, he won the Gold Medal in the 500-meter Kayak at the 1978 Games.

LEON ROTTMAN (1934-   )—A Rumanian, he won Gold Medals in the 1,000-meter Canadian Singles and the 10,000-meter Canadian Singles at the 1956 Games, and the Bronze Medal in the 1,000-meter Canadian Singles at the 1960 Games.

CYCLING

FELIX SCHMAL—An Austrian, he won a Gold Medal and two Bronze Medals in Cycling at the 1896 Games.

EQUESTRIAN

EDITH MASTER—From the U.S., she won a Bronze Medal in Dressage as a member of the U.S. Equestrian Team at the 1978 Games.

NEAL SHAPIRO—A premier U.S. rider, he won the Bronze Medal in Individual Jumping and the Silver Medal in Team Jumping at the 1972 Games, and was Horseman of the Year in the U.S. in 1972.

FENCING

HENRY ANSPACH—A Belgian, he won the Bronze Medal in Team Epeé at the 1912 Games.

PAUL ANSPACH (b. 1882)—A Belgian, he won the Bronze Medal in Team Epée in 1908, Gold Medals for Individual Epée and Team Epée in 1912, the Silver Medal in Team Epée in 1920, and the Silver Medal for Team Epée in 1924. He was also President of the International Fencing Association.

NORMAN C. ARMITAGE (1907-   , Albany, N.Y.)—Born Cohn. Won the Bronze Medal in Team Sabre at the 1948 Games. He was U.S. National Sabre Champion in 1930, 1934–1936, 1939–1943, and 1945.

ALBERT AXELROD (1921-   , New York City)—Won the Bronze Medal in Individual Foil at the 1960 Games. He also won Gold Medals in Team Foil at the Pan-American Games in 1959 and 1963 and Silver Medals in Individual Foil at the 1955 and 1959 Pan-Am Games, and a Silver Medal in Team Foil at the 1955 Games. He was U.S. Foil Champion in 1955, 1958, and 1960, and was NCAA Foil Champion from CCNY in 1948.

YVES DREYFUS—From France, he won the Bronze Medal in Team Epée in 1956 and the Bronze Medal in Team Epée in 1964.

JENO FUCHS (1882-1954)—A Hungarian, he won Gold Medals in Individual Sabre and in Team Sabre at the 1908 and 1912 Games.

TAMAS GABOR (1889-1954)—A Hungarian who was World Sabre Champion in 1925, he won the Gold Medal in Team Sabre in 1928 and the Silver Medal in Individual and Bronze Medal in Team Sabre in 1924.

OSZKAR GERDE—A Hungarian, he won Gold Medals in Team Sabre in 1908 and in 1912.

SANDOR GOMBOS (b. 1895)—A Hungarian, he was World Sabre Champion in 1926 and 1927 and won a Gold Medal in Team Sabre at the 1928 Games.

OTTO HERSCHMANN—An Austrian, he won the Silver Medal in Team Sabre at the 1912 Games. In a rare combination, he also won medals in swimming (*see* Olympic Medalists: Swimming).

ALLAN L. N. JAY (1931-   , London)—World Foil Champion in 1959, he won Silver Medals in Individual and Team Epée at the 1960 Games. He also won Gold Medals at the British Commonwealth Games in 1950 (Australia, Team Epée), 1954 (Great Britain, which he represented at the 1960 Olympics, Team Epée and Team Foil), 1958 (Great Britain, Team Foil and Team Epée), and 1962 (Great Britain, Team Foil).

ENDRE KABOS (1906–1944)—A Hungarian and World Sabre Champion in 1933 and 1934, he won Gold Medals in Team Sabre in 1932 and 1936, the Gold Medal in Individual Sabre at the 1936 Games, and the Bronze Medal in Individual Sabre at the 1932 Games.

GRIGORY KRISS—From the Soviet Union, he won two Team Silver Medals at the 1968 Games. He had won a Gold Medal at the 1964 Games and was World Epée Champion in 1971.

ALEXANDRE LIPPMANN—From France, he won Gold Medals in Team Epée at the 1908 and 1924 Games, Silver Medals in Individual Epée in the 1908 and 1920 Games, and the Bronze Medal in Team Epée at the 1920 Games.

HELENE MAYER (1911–1953, Offenberg, Germany)—One of the greatest women fencers of all time, she was the 1929, 1931, and 1937 World Foil Champion and won the Gold Medal in Individual Foil at the 1928 Games and the Silver Medal in Individual Foil at the 1936 Games. She was so good that the Germans let her compete in 1936 despite the facts that her father was Jewish and that she was studying in the U.S. from 1932. She was U.S. Foil Champion, 1934–1935, 1937–1939, 1941–1942, and 1946.

MARK MIDLER (1931- , Moscow)—From the Soviet Union, he won the Gold Medal in Team Foil in 1960 and 1964.

ANDRE MOUYAL—From France, he was World Epée Champion in 1957 and won the Bronze Medal in Team Epee at the 1956 Games.

CLAUDE NETTER—From France, he won the Gold Medal in Team Foil at the 1952 Games.

JACQUES OCHS—From Belgium, he won the Gold Medal in Team Epée at the 1912 Games.

IVAN OSIIER (b. 1888)—The long-time Champion of Denmark won the Silver Medal in Individual Epée at the 1912 Games.

ATTILA PETSCHAUER (1904–1944)—A Hungarian, he won Gold Medals in Team Sabre at the 1928 and 1932 Games and the Silver Medal in Individual Sabre at the 1928 Games.

MARK RAKITA—From the Soviet Union, he won a Team Gold Medal and a Silver Medal at the 1968 Games. He had previously won a Gold Medal at the 1964 Games. He was World Sabre Champion in 1967.

YAKOV RYLSKY (1928- , East Kazakhstan, U.S.S.R)—From the Soviet Union, he was World Sabre Champion in 1958, 1961, and 1963. He won the Gold Medal in Team Sabre in 1964 and the Bronze Medal in Team Sabre in 1956.

GASTON SALMON—A Belgian, he won the Gold Medal in Team Epée in 1912.

ILONA SCHACHERER-ELEK—A Hungarian, she was 1934, 1935, and 1951 World Foil Champion. She won Gold Medals in Individual Foil at the 1936 and 1948 Games and the Silver Medal in Individual Foil at the 1952 Games. Many feel that she was the outstanding fencer of her time.

ZOLTAN SCHENKER—A Hungarian, he won the Gold Medal in Team Sabre at the 1912 Games and the Silver Medal (Team Sabre) and Bronze Medal (Team Foil) in 1924.

EDGAR SELIGMAN—From Great Britain, he won Silver Medals in Team Epée at the 1906, 1908, and 1912 Games.

JEAN STERN—From France, he won the Gold Medal in Team Epeé in 1908.

DAVID TYSHLER—From the Soviet Union, he won the Bronze Medal in Team Sabre at the 1956 Games.

ILDIKO USLAKY-REJTO (1937- , Budapest)—A Hungarian, she was the 1963 World Foil Champion. A deaf mute, she won Gold Medals in Team and Individual Foil in 1964 and the Silver Medal in Team Foil in 1960. She also won a Silver Medal and a Bronze Medal at the 1968 Games.

EDUARD VINOKUROV—From the Soviet Union, he won a Team Gold Medal at the 1968 Games, and was on the World Championship Team in 1971.

JOSEF VITEBSKY—From the Soviet Union, he won a Team Silver Medal at the 1968 Games.

LAJOS WERKNER—A Hungarian, he won Gold Medals in Team Sabre at the 1908 and 1912 Games.

GYMNASTICS

PHILIP ERENBERG (1909- , Russia)—An American, he won the Silver Medal in Indian Clubs in 1932.

ALFRED FLATOW—From Germany, he won Gold Medals in Parallel Bars, Team Horizontal Bars, and Team Parallel Bars and the Silver Medal in Horizontal Bars at the 1896 Games.

FELIX FLATOW—From Germany, he won Gold Medals in Team Horizontal Bar and Team Horizontal Bars at the 1896 Games.

IMRE GELLERT—Won a Silver Medal at the 1912 Games in Team Apparatus.

GEORGE J. GULACK (1905- , Riga, Latvia)—An American, he won the Gold Medal in Rings at the 1932 Games. He was National AAU Champion in the Flying Rings in 1928 and 1935.

AGNES KELETI (1921- , Budapest)—Born Agnes Klein. A Hungarian, she was World Uneven Bars Champion in 1956. A tremendous competitor, she won Gold Medals in 1952 (Freestanding Exercise) and 1956 (Beam Exercises, Freestanding Exercise, Combined Exercise Team, and Parallel Bars); Silver Medals in 1948 (Team Combined Exercise), 1952 (Combined Team), and 1956 (Combined Exercise Team and Combined Exercise); and Bronze Medals in 1952 (Uneven Parallel Bars and Team Hand Apparatus). She later emigrated to Israel.

ALICE KERTESZ—A Hungarian, she won a Gold Medal in Combined Exercise Apparatus Team and a Silver Medal in Combined Exercise Team at the 1956 Games.

MIKHAIL PERELMAN—From the Soviet Union, he won a Gold Medal in Men's Team at the 1952 Games.

VLADIMIR PORTNOI—From the Soviet Union, he won a Gold Medal in Men's Team at the 1960 Games and the Bronze Medal in the Long Horse the same year.

ICE HOCKEY

RUDOLF BALL—From Germany, he won a Bronze Medal at the 1932 Games. He was one of two token Jews allowed to compete for Nazi Germany in 1936.

ICE SKATING

FRITZIE BURGER—Part Jewish and an Austrian, she was the runner-up at the 1932 World Figure Skating Championships. She won Silver Medals in Figure Skating at the 1928 and 1932 Games.

ALAIN CALMAT—From France, he won the Silver Medal in Figure Skating at the 1964 Winter Games.

RAFAEL GRACH—From the Soviet Union, he won the Silver Medal for the 500 meters in 1956 and the Bronze Medal at the same distance at the 1960 Games. He was one of the leading speed skaters in his country in the 1950s.

IRVING JAFFEE (1906- , New York City)—The greatest speed skater in American history, he won Gold Medals for 5,000 meters and for 10,000 meters at the 1932 Games.

RONALD JOSEPH—From the U.S., he won the Bronze Medal in Pairs at the 1964 Games.

VIVIAN JOSEPH—Ron Joseph's sister, won the Bronze Medal in Pairs at the 1964 Games.

JUDO

JAMES S. BREGMAN (1941- , Arlington, Va.)—Won the Middleweight Bronze Medal at the 1964 Games. One of the leading American Judo competitors of the 1960s, he was National AAU Champion (165 pounds) in 1964.

ROWING

SYDNEY W. JELINEK (b. 1899)—Won a Bronze Medal in Four-with-Coxswain (he was the stroke) at the 1924 Games.

SHOOTING

ALLAN ERDMAN—From the Soviet Union, he won the Silver Medal in Free Rifle at the 1956 Games.

LEV VAINSHTEIN—From the Soviet Union, he won the Bronze Medal in Free Rifle at the 1952 Games. He became one of the leading shooting coaches in the U.S.S.R.

SOCCER

HARALD BOHR—From Denmark, he won a Bronze Medal at the 1908 Games.

SANDOR GELLER—A Hungarian, he won the Gold Medal in 1952.

ARPAD ORBAN—From Hungary, he won the Gold Medal in 1964.

BORIS RAZINSKY—From the Soviet Union, he won the Gold Medal at the 1956 Games.

SWIMMING

MARGARETE ADLER—An Austrian, she won the Bronze Medal in 400-meter Relay at the 1912 Games.

SEMYON BELITS-GEIMAN—From the Soviet Union, he won a Silver Medal in the 400 Freestyle Relay and a Bronze Medal in the 800 Freestyle Relay at the 1968 Games, and held Soviet and European records.

GERARD BLITZ—A Belgian, he broke the world record for the 400 Backstroke in 1921. He won the Bronze Medal in the 100 Backstroke at the 1920 Games.

ANDREA GYARMATI—From Hungary, she won the Silver Medal in the 100 Backstroke and the Bronze Medal in the 100 Butterfly at the 1972 Games.

ALFRED HAJOS-GUTTMAN (1878-1955)—A Hungarian, he won Medals in the 1,200 Freestyle and the 100 Freestyle at the 1896 Games.

HENRIK HAJOS-GUTTMAN—A Hungarian, he won the Gold Medal in the 1,000 Relay at the 1906 Games.

OTTO HERSCHMANN—An Austrian, he won the Bronze Medal in the 100 Freestyle at the 1896 Games.

KLARA MILCH—An Austrian, she won the Bronze Medal in the 400 Freestyle Relay at the 1912 Games.

PAUL NEUMANN—An Austrian, he won the Gold Medal in the 500 Freestyle at the 1896 Games.

MARILYN RAMENOFSKY (1946- , Phoenix, Ariz.)—Set the world record in the 400 Freestyle on several occasions and was considered the Number One woman in the world in that event in 1964. She won the Silver Medal in her specialty at the 1964 Games. She was National AAU Outdoor Champion in 1964 as well.

OTTO SCHEFF—An Austrian, who won the Gold Medal in the 400 Freestyle at the 1906 Games, the Bronze Medal in the 400 at the 1908 Games, and the Bronze Medal in the 1,600 Freestyle at the 1906 Games. He became a Christian.

ALBERT SCHWARTZ (1907-   , Chicago)—Won the Bronze Medal in the 100 Freestyle at the 1932 Games. He was National AAU 100 and 220 Freestyle Champion in 1931 and NCAA Champion in the 100 in 1929 and in the 50, 100, and 220 in 1930.

MARK SPITZ—The greatest swimmer in world history, he won seven Gold Medals and set seven world records at the 1972 Olympic Games: He won the 100 and 200 Freestyle, and the 100 and 200 Butterfly, and was a member of the victorious U.S. 400 and 800 Freestyle and 400 Medley Relay Teams. He won Gold Medals in the 400 and 800 Freestyle Relays, the Silver Medal in the 100 Freestyle, and the Bronze Medal in the 100 Butterfly at the 1968 Games.

JOSEPHINE STICKER—An Austrian, she won the Bronze Medal in the 400 Relay at the 1912 Games.

EVA SZEKELY (1927-   )—A Hungarian, she held the world record in the 100 Breaststroke in 1951. She won the Gold Medal in record-breaking time in the 200 Breaststroke at the 1952 Games, and won a Silver Medal in the same event at the 1956 Games.

JUDIT TEMES—A Hungarian, she won the Gold Medal in the 400 Freestyle Relay (her team broke the world record) at the 1952 Games, and won the Bronze Medal in the 100 Freestyle that same year.

OTTO WAHLE (1880-1963)—An Austrian, he won Silver Medals in the 200 Obstacle Race and the 1,000 Freestyle in 1900 and the Bronze Medal in the 400 Freestyle at the 1904 Games.

WENDY WEINBERG—From the U.S., she won the Bronze Medal in the 800 Freestyle at the 1978 Games.

TENNIS

BARON HUBERT L. DE MORPURGO—From Italy, he won the Bronze Medal at the 1924 Games.

TRACK AND FIELD

HAROLD M. ABRAHAMS (b. 1899, Bedford, England)—Won Gold Medals at 100 meters and in the 400 Relay at the 1924 Games.

GERALD H. ASHWORTH (1942-   , Haverhill, Mass.)—Won a Gold Medal as a member of the world-record breaking U.S. 400 meter Relay Team at the 1964 Games. He was the Number Seven indoor sprinter in the world and the Number Eight outdoors that year. His best U.S. ranking was Number Four, also in 1964.

NIKOLAI AVILOV—From the Soviet Union, he was (along with Mark Spitz) the star of the 1972 Games, winning the Gold Medal in the Decathlon (and ranked Number One in the world that year). He won the Bronze Medal in the event at the 1976 Games.

ODON BODOR—The leading Hungarian middle-distance runner of the early 20th century, he won a Bronze Medal in the 1,600 Relay at the 1908 Games.

LOUIS A. CLARKE (1901-   , Statesville, N.C.)—The one-time 100 indoor world record holder, he won a Gold Medal on the world record–setting 400-meter Relay team at the 1924 Games. From Johns Hopkins, he was the NCAA 100 Dash Champion in 1923.

LILLIAN COPELAND (1904-1964, New York City)—One of the greatest woman throwers in American history, she won the Gold Medal in the Discus at the 1932 Games and the Silver Medal in the same event at the 1928 Games. She held the world record in the shot, discus, and javelin—an incredible accomplishment—and was National AAU Champion in the shot from 1925 to 1928 and in 1931, National AAU Champion in the discus in 1926 and 1927, and National AAU Champion in the javelin in 1926 and 1931.

IBOLYA K. CSAK—A Hungarian, she won the Gold Medal in the Highjump at the 1936 Games and was the 1938 European Highjump Champion.

DANIEL FRANK—From the U.S., he won the Silver Medal in the Longjump at the 1904 Games.

HUGO M. FRIEND (b. 1882, Prague)—From the U.S., he won the Bronze Medal in the Long Jump at the 1906 Games. He was the National AAU High Hurdles and Long Jump Champion in 1905.

JAMES E. FUCHS (1927- , Chicago)—The world record holder in the shot in 1949 and 1950, he won the Bronze Medal in the event at the 1948 and 1952 Games. He was the Number One shotputter in the world, 1949–1951, and Number One indoors, 1949–1952. From Yale, he was the NCAA Shotput Champion in 1949 and 1950. His mother was Jewish.

CLAIR JACOBS—The former world record holder indoors in the pole vault, he won the Bronze Medal in that event at the Games in 1908.

ELIAS KATZ (1901-1947, Abo, Finland)—Won a Gold Medal in the 3,000-meter Relay at the 1924 Games and the Silver Medal in the Steeplechase that year. He was killed by the Arabs during the fighting in Palestine in 1947.

ABEL R. KIVIAT (b. 1892, New York City)—The former world record holder in the 1,500 meters (1912), he won the Silver Medal in that event at the 1912 Games. He was the National AAU Champion in the Mile in 1911, 1912, and 1914, National AAU Cross Country Champion in 1913, National AAU 600 Champion in 1911 and 1913, and National AAU 1,000 Champion in 1911, 1913, and 1914.

MOR KOVACS—Born Mor Koczan. A Hungarian, he won the Bronze Medal in the Javelin at the 1912 Games. He was murdered by the Nazis.

VERA KREPKINA (1933- , Kirov, Soviet Union)—A former Soviet 100 and 200 dash Champion, she set a world record in winning the Gold Medal in the Long Jump at the 1960 Games. She is of Jewish origin.

ALVAH T. MEYER (b. 1888, New York City)—Held the world record in the 300- and the 60-yard Dash, and won the Silver Medal in the 100 at the 1912 Games. He was National AAU 220 Champion in 1912, 60-yard-Dash Champion in 1911, 75-yard Champion in 1911 and 1914, 150-yard Champion in 1911, and 300-yard Champion in 1914.

MYER PRINSTEIN (1880-1925)—One of the greatest performers in American track and field history, he held the world record in the long jump at the turn of the century. He won Gold Medals in the Triple Jump at the 1900 Games, in the Triple Jump and Long Jump at the 1904 Games, and in the Long Jump at the 1906 Games. He also won the Silver Medal in the Long Jump at the 1900 Games. He was National AAU Long Jump Champion in 1898, 1902, 1904, and 1906.

FANNY ROSENFELD (1905- , Katrinaslov, Russia)—The greatest woman track and field athlete in Canadian history, she won a Gold Medal in the 400 Relay and a Silver Medal in the 100 at the 1928 Games. She held the Canadian record in the long jump, discus, shot, javelin, and standing long jump.

DAVID H. SEGAL (1937- , London)—Won a Bronze Medal in the 400 Relay at the 1960 Games and the Gold Medal in the 100 at the British Commonwealth Games in 1960. Ranked Number Nine in the world in the 200 in 1958, he also held the British 200 and 60 dash records.

STEPHEN A. SEYMOUR (1920- , New York City)—Born Seymour Cohen.

Won the Silver Medal in the Javelin at the 1948 Games. He was the Number One ranked Javelin thrower in the world in 1947 and was the American record holder. He was also the National AAU Javelin Champion in 1947, 1948, and 1950.

SARA SIMEONI—From Italy, she is the world record holder (1978) in the women's high jump. She won the Silver Medal in the event at the 1976 Games.

ELLIS R. SMOUHA—From Great Britain, he won a Bronze Medal in the 400 Relay at the 1928 Games.

IRENA KIRSZENSTEIN SZEWINSKA (1946- , Leningrad)—From Poland, she is considered by many to be the greatest woman track star of all time. At the Olympic Games, she received the following: 1964—Gold Medal in 400 Relay (a world record), the Silver Medal in 200 and Long Jump; 1968—Gold Medal in 200 and Bronze Medal in 100; 1972—Bronze Medal in 200; 1976—Gold Medal in 400. At the age of 31 (1977) she was Number One in the world in the 200 and 400; Number 3 in the 400 hurdles; and Number 8 in the 100.

FAINA MELNIK VELEVA (1945-)—From the Soviet Union, she is considered to be the greatest woman discus thrower of all time. She won the Gold Medal in the event at the 1972 Games, holds the world record, and was the Number One woman in the world in 1977 (her seventh Number One ranking). She is also a world class shotputter (Number 11 in 1977).

JADWIGA WAJSOWNA—Born Pana Weiss. From Poland, she won the Silver Medal in the Discus at the 1936 Games and a Bronze Medal in the event at the 1932 Games, and was the world record holder during the first half of the 1930s.

WATERPOLO

PETER G. ASCH—From the U.S., he won a Bronze Medal in Waterpolo at the 1972 Games.

ISTVAN BARTA (1895-1948)—A Hungarian, he won a Gold Medal in 1932 and a Silver Medal in 1928.

GERARD BLITZ—A Belgian who also won Olympic medals in swimming, he won Silver Medals in 1920 and 1924, and a Bronze Medal at the 1936 Games.

MAURICE J. BLITZ (b. 1891, Paris)—A Belgian, he won Silver Medals at the 1920 and 1924 Games.

GYORGY BRODY (1908-)—A Hungarian, he won Gold Medals at the 1932 and 1936 Games.

BORIS GOIKHMAN—From the Soviet Union, he won a Silver Medal at the 1960 Games and a Bronze Medal at the 1956 Games.

DEZSO GYARMATI (1927- , Miskolc, Hungary)—Won Gold Medals at the 1952, 1956, and 1964 Games, the Silver Medal at the 1948 Games, and the Bronze Medal at the 1960 Games. He is widely considered to be the greatest player who ever lived.

GYORGY KARPATI (1935- , Budapest)—Won Gold Medals at the 1952, 1956, and 1964 Games and a Bronze Medal at the 1960 Games.

C. BARRY WEITZENBERG—From the U.S., he won a Bronze Medal at the 1972 Games.

WEIGHTLIFTING

ISAAC BERGER (1936- , Jerusalem)—One of the greatest weightlifters of all time, a world record holder, and a member of Weightlifting Hall of Fame. He won the Gold Medal in the Featherweight class at the 1956 Games and the Silver Medals at the 1960 and 1964 Games. He was also World Champion in 1958 and 1961 and U.S. Champion at 132 pounds, 1955–1961 and 1964. He won Gold Medals at the 1959 and 1963 Pan-American Games.

HANS HAAS—Part Jewish and Austrian, he won the Gold Medal in the Lightweight Division at the 1928 Games and the Silver Medal at the 1932 Games.

GRIGORI NOVAK (1920- , Chernobyl, U.S.S.R.)—Won the Silver Medal as a Middle-Heavyweight at the 1952 Games and set many world records in the event. He was World Champion at 181 pounds in 1946.

RUDOLF PLYUKFELDER (1928- , Donetsk Oblast, U.S.S.R.)—World Champion at 181 pounds in 1959 and 1961, he won the Gold Medal in the Light-Heavyweight division at the 1964 Games. Part Jewish, he was the Soviet Champion on many occasions.

DAVID RIGERT—From the Soviet Union and a World Champion and record holder, he won the Gold Medal in Middle Heavyweight Weightlifting at the 1976 Games.

FRANK SPELLMAN (1922- , Paoli, Pa.)—Won the Gold Medal as a Middle-weight at the 1948 Games. He was also U.S. National Champion at 165 pounds in 1946 and 1948.

WRESTLING

SAMUEL N. GERSON—From the U.S., he won the Silver Medal in Featherweight Freestyle at the 1920 Games.

BORIS GUREVICH—From the Soviet Union, he was the 114-pound World Greco-Roman Champion in 1953 and 1958 and won Gold Medals in Flyweight Greco-Roman at the 1952 Games and in Middleweight Freestyle at the 1968 Games. He is certainly one of the greatest wrestlers of all time.

NIKOLAUS HIRSCHL—From Austria, he won Bronze Medals in Heavy-weight Greco-Roman and Heavyweight Freestyle at the 1932 Games and was European Heavyweight Champion in 1929 and 1934.

KAROLY KARPATI—A Hungarian, he won the Gold Medal in Lightweight Freestyle in 1936 and the Silver Medal in the same event in 1932.

ABRAHAM KURLAND—From Denmark, he won the Silver Medal in Lightweight Greco-Roman at the 1932 Games.

FREDERICK J. MEYER (1900- , Chicago)—Won the Bronze Medal in Heavyweight Freestyle at the 1920 Games. He was National AAU Freestyle Champion at 174 pounds in 1921, at 191 pounds in 1922, and as a Heavyweight in 1921 and 1922.

S. RABIN—From Great Britain, he won the Bronze Medal in Middleweight Freestyle at the 1928 Games.

LANDISLAU SIMON—From Rumania, he won the Bronze Medal in the Freestyle Heavyweight class at the 1978 Games.

RICHARD WEISZ (1879-1945)—A Hungarian National Champion and winner of the Gold Medal in Heavyweight Greco-Roman at the 1908 Games.

HENRY WITTENBERG (1918- , Jersey City)—One of the greatest wrestlers in American history, he won the Gold Medal in Light-Heavyweight Freestyle in 1948 and the Silver Medal in the same event at the 1952 Games. He was National AAU 174-pound Champion in 1940 and 1941 and 191-pound Champion, 1943–1944, 1946–1948, and 1952.

MISCELLANEOUS AWARDS

MARTIN AGRONSKY—Alfred I. Dupont–Columbia University Award for journalistic broadcasting, 1961.

FREDA ADLER—Herbert Bloch Award of the American Society of Criminology, 1972.

RICHARD ADLER and JERRY ROSS—Tony Award of the League of New York Theaters and Producers for composition and lyrics for *Damn Yankees*, 1956.

AMY ALCOTT—Named Pro Golf's Rookie of the Year by *Golf Digest*, 1975.

HANNAH ARENDT—Emerson-Thoreau Medal of the American Academy of Arts and Sciences, 1969.

ISAAC ASIMOV—Science fiction's Hugo Award for *The Gods Themselves*, 1973.

LAUREN BACALL—Woman of the Year Award of the Hasty Pudding Theatricals of Harvard U., 1967.

JENNIE LOITMAN BARRON—National Mother Award of the American Mothers Committee, 1959.

STANLEY F. BERGSTEIN—Horseman Award, 1970.

MARTIN BERMAN—Robert F. Kennedy Journalism Award (television), 1974.

ELMER BERNSTEIN—Western Heritage Award of the National Cowboy Hall of Fame and Western Heritage Center (music) for "Hallelujah Trail," 1966.

JEREMY BERNSTEIN—Science Writing Award in Physics and Astronomy of the American Institute of Physics and the U.S. Steel Foundation, 1976.

HANS BLUMENFELD—Distinguished Service Award of the American Institute of Planners, 1969.

W. MICHAEL BLUMENTHAL—As the head of the Bendix Corporation, he was Executive of the Year of the National Management Association, 1974.

MARCEL BREUER—Gold Medal of the American Institute of Architects, 1968.

SAMUEL BRODY—Arnold W. Brunner Memorial Prize in Architecture of the National Institute of Arts and Letters, 1975.

PAUL J. COHEN—From Stanford U., he won a National Medal of Science (U.S.), 1967.

SEYMOUR S. COHEN—Passano Award (for medical research), 1974.

VICTOR COHN—Sigma Delta Chi Award for Distinguished Service in Journalism, 1951.

VICTOR COHN—James T. Grady Award for Interpreting Chemistry for the Public, awarded by the American Chemical Society, 1971.

SIMON DINITZ—From Ohio State U., he won the Edwin Sutherland Award of the American Society of Criminology, 1974.

CARL DJERASSI—Award for Creative Invention of the American Chemical Society, 1973.

DAVID DUBINSKY—The noted labor leader was awarded the Presidential Medal of Freedom, 1969.

LEO EDEL—The famous biographer won the Gold Medal of The American Academy of Arts and Letters and the National Institute of Arts and Letters, 1976.

HARLAN ELLISON—Nebula Award (Best Novella) of the Science Fiction Writers of America for "A Boy and His Dog," 1969.

NORMAN FABEROW—Louis I. Dubin Award of the American Society of Suicidology, 1973.

PETER FALK—Emmy Award for his role as Columbo, 1971–72.

ARTHUR FIEDLER—Gold Baton Award of the American Symphony Orchestra League, 1976.

HERBERT FRIEDMAN—Superintendent of the Naval Research Laboratory of the Atmosphere and Astrophysics Division (Dept. of the Navy), he won the President's Award for Distinguished Federal Civilian Service (U.S. Civil Service Commission), 1964.

SANFORD D. GARELIK—Of the N.Y. Police Dept., he won the Award for

Outstanding Law Enforcement Achievement of the Society of Professional Investigators, 1967.

STAN GETZ—National Music Award from the American Music Conference, 1976.

EDWARD L. GLASER—Computer Sciences Man of the Year (Data Processing Management Association), 1974.

MILTON GLASER—Medallist Award of the American Institute of Graphic Arts, 1972.

HARRY GOLDBLATT—Francis Amory Prize (for reproductive system research) of the American Academy of Arts and Sciences, 1961.

HETTY GOLDMAN—From the Institute for Advanced Study at Princeton, she won the Gold Medal for Distinguished Archaeological Achievement of the Archaeological Institute of America, 1966.

MICHAEL GOLDMAN—A Professor at Princeton, he won the George Jean Nathan Award for Dramatic Criticism for the 1975–76 season.

EVERETT GREENBAUM—Laurel Award for TV Writing (Writers Guild of America, West), 1977.

ERNEST GRUENING—Margaret Sanger Award of Planned Parenthood–World Population, 1968.

JACK HALPERN—Award in Organic Chemistry of the American Chemical Society, 1968.

LAWRENCE HALPRIN—Allied Professions Medal of the American Institute of Architects, 1964.

DUSTIN HOFFMAN—Man of the Year Award of the Hasty Pudding Theatricals of Harvard U., 1972.

RED HOLZMAN—Of the New York Knicks, he was Coach of the Year in the NBA for the 1969–70 season.

JOSEPH KAPLAN—Haley Space Flight Award of the American Institute of Aeronautics and Astronautics, 1956.

MORRIS A. KATZ—Frank A. Chambers Award of the Air Pollution Control Association, 1965.

DANNY KAYE—Splendid American Award of the Thomas A. Dooley Foundation, 1966.

LINCOLN KIRSTEIN—Award for Distinguished Service to the Arts of the American Academy of Arts and Letters and the National Institute of Arts and Letters, 1958.

SANDY KOUFAX—The great Dodger pitcher won the Cy Young Award, 1966.

MURRAY KRAMER—Kramer Award (named after him) for outstanding sports journalism, in 1967, given by Boston U.

ARTHUR KROCK—The famous columnist of the *New York Times* won the John Peter Zenger Award of the U. of Arizona, 1966.

JOSEPH KRUMGOLD—Newbery Medal for Children's Literature for *Onion John,* 1960.

RUBEN LEVIN—Eugene V. Debs Award (labor), 1975.

H. A. LIEBHAFSKY—Award in Analytical Chemistry of the American Chemical Society, 1962.

BENNIE LOM—Player of the Game in the 1929 Rose Bowl Game.

JACK MENDELSOHN, LARRY SIEGEL, and ARNIE ROSEN—Television-Radio Award of the Writers Guild of America, West, for an episode of *The Carol Burnett Show,* 1971.

HERMAN F. MONDSCHEIN—Chief Hydrologist of the U.S. Weather Bureau's River Forecast Center, he won the NOAA (National Oceanic and Atmospheric Administration) Award, 1976.

JOHN OAKES—Of the *New York Times,* he won the Audubon Medal of the National Audubon Society, 1976.

IRVING M. POLLACK—Then Director of the Division of Trading of Markets of the Securities and Exchange Commission, he won the Rockefeller Public Service Award, 1968.

SYLVIA PORTER—Woman of the Year Award given by the *Ladies Home Journal,* 1975.

SELWYN RAAB—A reporter on the *New York Times,* he won the Heywood Broun Award of the Newspaper Guild, 1974.

SAMSON RAPHAELSON—Laurel Award for Screen Writing Achievement of the Writers Guild of America, West, 1977.

HERBERT RIBNER—Aero-Acoustics Award of the American Institute of Aeronautics and Astronautics, 1976.

AL "FLIP" ROSEN—The Cleveland Indian third baseman won the American League's Most Valuable Player Award, 1953.

GEORGE ROSEN—Goddard Astronautics Award of the American Institute of Aeronautics and Astronautics, 1975.

HAROLD A. ROSEN—Aerospace Communication Award of the American Institute of Aeronautics and Astronautics, 1968.

LOUIS C. ROSENBERG—Fine Arts Medal of the American Institute of Architects, for etchings, 1949.

LEONARD ROSENBLUTH—From the U. of North Carolina, he was College Basketball's Player of the Year, 1957.

THEODORE ROSENGARTEN—National Book Award for *All God's Dangers: The Life of Nate Shaw,* 1975.

NETTIE ROSENSTEIN and JACK HORWITZ—The "Winnie," the Coty American Fashion Critics' Award, 1947.

A. M. ROSENTHAL—On the staff of the *New York Times,* he won the Carr Van Anda Award of Ohio U., 1976.

PEARL RUBENSTEIN—Tastemaker Award of the R. T. French Company for her book *Feasts for Two,* 1973.

ALBERT B. SABIN—Murray-Green Award for Community Service of the AFL-CIO, 1967.

JONAS E. SALK—Distinguished Service Medal of the American Legion, 1955.

MEYER SCHAPIRO—A professor at Columbia U. for a half-decade, he won the National Book Critics Circle Award in 1978 for *Modern Art: 19th and 20th Centuries.*

LALO SCHIFRIN—Grammy (best original jazz composition) for "The Cat," 1964.

JAMES R. SCHLESINGER—Then Secretary of Defense, he won the H. H. Arnold Award of the Air Force Association, 1975.

DELMORE SCHWARTZ—Bollingen Prize in Poetry of the Yale U. Library, 1959.

LOIS SHERR—A landscape architect, she won one of the Mademoiselle Awards given by that magazine, 1964.

URI SHULEVITZ—Caldecott Medal of the American Library Association for his illustrations in *The Fool of the World and the Flying Ship,* 1969.

JULIUS SHULMAN—Architectural Photography Medal of the American Institute of Architects, 1969.

ABE SILVERSTEIN—Reed Aeronautics Award of the American Institute of Aeronautics and Astronautics, 1964.

JEROME SKOLNICK—From the U. of California, he won the August Vollmer Award of the American Society of Criminology, 1922.

ANNA SOKOLOW—Dance Magazine Award in 1961.

ROBERT M. SOLOW—John Bates Clark Award of the American Economic Association, 1961.

RAPHAEL SOYER—Award of Merit Medal of the American Academy of Arts and Letters and the National Institute of Arts and Letters, 1957.

PAULA SPERBER—Bowling's Woman of the Year, 1971.

LEONARD SPIGELGASS—Valentine Davies Award of the Writers Guild of America, West, 1966.

MARK SPITZ—Sullivan Award (A.A.U.) as the finest amateur athlete in the U.S., 1971.

ARTHUR C. STERN—Richard Beatty Mellon Award of the Air Pollution Control Association, 1970.

RICHARD G. STERN—Arts and Letters Award of the National Institute of Arts and Letters, 1968.

ELLEN SULZBERGER STRAUS—Women of Conscience Award of the National Council of Women of the U.S., 1970.

JACOB VINER—Francis A. Walker Medal of the American Economic Association, 1962.

ROMAN VISHNIAC—ASMP Award of the American Society of Magazine Photographers, 1956.

GEORGE WALD—Rumford Medal (for radiant energy research) of the American Academy of Arts and Sciences, 1959.

ABRAHAM WALKOWITZ—Marjorie Peabody Waite Award of the National Institute of Arts and Letters, 1962.

ELI WALLACH—Delia Austrain Award of the Drama League of New York for his performance in *Major Barbara*, 1957.

SIDNEY J. WEINBERG—Public Service Award of the Advertising Council, 1957.

BILLY WILDER—New York Film Critics Circle Award (best direction) for *The Lost Weekend*, 1945.

SAUL WINSTEIN—James Flack Norris Award in Physical Organic Chemistry of the American Chemical Society, 1967.

SAMUEL YELLIN—Craftsmanship Medal of the American Institute of Architects, for his work in iron, 1922.

INDEX OF BIRTHPLACES

Glaser, Julius A.; see I Government Officials (Austrians)
Gold, Ernest; see VII Composers of Film Scores
Goldscheid, Rudolf; see I Political Figures (Austrians)
Goldzier, Julius; see I U.S. Congressmen and Congresswomen
Gottlieb, Gerda; see VIII Track and Field
Graf, Herbert; see VI Other Figures in Classical Music
Gregor, Arthur; see VI Poets (Americans)
Gruen, Victor D.; see II Architects
Harris, Jed; see VI Theatrical Producers
Hartmann, Heinz; see IV Psychologists
Hartmann, Moritz; see I Revolutionaries
Hazai, Samu; see I Military Figures (Austrians, Hungarians, and Austro-Hungarians)
Hellerm, Hermann; see IV Political Scientists
Hertz, Emanuel; see IV Historians
Herz, Henri; see VI Composers
Herzog, Reginald O.; see V Chemists
Hilferding, Rudolf; see I Men and Women of the Left (Germans)
Hitschmann, Edward; see IV Psychologists
Hoff, Hans; see IV Psychologists
Hoffer, Willi; see IV Psychologists
Hoffman, Stanley; see IV Political Scientists
Homolka, Oscar; see VII Film Stars
Horovitz, Leopold; see VI Artists
Hoselitz, Bert F.; see IV Economists
Husserl, Edmund G.; see IV Philosophers
Jerusalem, Wilhelm; see IV Psychologists
Juran, Nathan; see VII Art Directors and Designers
Kahan, Louis; see VI Artists
Kanner, Leo; see IV Psychologists
Kaufman, Felix; see IV Philosophers
Kelman, Herbert C.; see IV Psychologists
Kitsee, Isador; see V Inventors, Industrial Designers, and Engineers
Klein, Edmund; see II Doctors and Medical Researchers
Klein, Melanie R.; see IV Psychologists
Klemperer, Paul; see II Doctors and Medical Researchers
Kmoch, Hans; see VIII Chess
Kolisch, Rudolf; see VI Violinists
Kortner, Fritz; see VI Stars of the Theater
Kreisky, Bruno; see I Government Officials (Austrians)
Krips, Josef; see VI Conductors
Kronfeld, Robert; see V Aviators, Astronauts, and Others
Kunz, Josef L.; see IV Legal Scholars
Landsteiner, Karl; see IX Nobel Prize Winners (Medicine and Physiology)
Lang, Fritz; see VII Film Directors
Lazarsfeld, Paul; see IV Sociologists
Leinsdorf, Erich; see VI Conductors
Lieben, Adolph; see V Chemists
Lieben, Robert von; see V Inventors, Industrial Designers, and Engineers
Lippmann, Edmund O. von; see V Chemists
List, Emanuel; see VI Classical and Opera Singers
Loewe, Frederick; see VI Popular Music Composers and Lyricists
Lowie, Robert H.; see IV Anthropologists
Lucca, Pauline; see VI Classical and Opera Singers

Machlup, Fritz; see IV Economists
Mahler, Gustav; see VI Composers
Massary, Fritzi; see VI Musical Comedy Figures
Meisel, John; see IV Political Scientists
Meitner, Lise; see V Pioneers of Atomic Energy
Mises, Ludwig E. von; see IV Economists
Mottl, Felix J.; see VI Conductors
Nadel, Siegfred F.; see IV Anthropologists
Neutra, Richard J.; see II Architects
Oberlander, Fred; see VIII Wrestling
Ohrbach, Nathan M.; see III Business Leaders
Padover, Saul; see IV Political Scientists
Pallenberg, Max; see VI Stars of the Theater
Paneth, Friedrich A.; see V Chemists
Perutz, Max F.; see IX Nobel Prize Winners (Chemistry)
Petschek, Ignaz; see III Business Leaders
Pleskow, Eric; see VII Film Executives
Polanyi, Karl; see IV Economists
Polgar, Alfred; see VI Literary and Drama Critics and Agents
Popper, Sir Karl R.; see IV Philosophers
Preminger, Otto L.; see VII Film Directors
Pryce-Jones, David; see IV Social Critics
Rabi, Isidor I.; see IX Nobel Prize Winners (Physics)
Rainer, Luise; see VII Film Stars
Rank, Otto; see IV Psychologists
Rappaport, Henry; see II Doctors and Medical Researchers
Redl, Fritz; see IV Psychologists
Reich, Wilhelm; see IV Psychologists
Reik, Theodor; see IV Psychologists
Reinhardt, Max; see VI Theatrical Directors and Teachers
Roth, Henry; see VI Writers (Americans and Canadians)
Rudel, Julius; see VI Other Figures in Classical Music
Rumpler, Eduard; see V Aviators, Astronauts, and Others
Sachs, Hans; see IV Psychologists
Sakel, Manfred; see IV Psychologists
Schanzer, Carlo; see I Government Officials (Italians)
Schoenberg, Arnold; see VI Composers
Schoene, Lotte; see VI Classical and Opera Singers
Schon, Sir Frank; see I Government Officials (British)
Schwarz, Rudolf; see VI Conductors
Shipp, Dorly; see VIII Table Tennis
Singer, Joseph; see I Military Figures (Austrians, Hungarians, and Austro-Hungarians)
Sommer, Emil von; see I Military Figures (Austrians, Hungarians, and Austro-Hungarians)
Spiegel, Sam; see VII Film Producers
Spielmann, Rudolf; see VIII Chess
Spitz, René; see IV Psychologists
Starer, Robert; see VI Composers
Steinbach, Emil; see I Government Officials (Austrians)
Steiner, Max; see VII Composers of Film Scores
Stekel, Wilhelm; see IV Psychologists
Stengel, Erwin; see IV Psychologists
Sternberg, Josef von; see VII Film Directors
Stoessinger, John G.; see IV Political Scientists
Strasberg, Lee; see VI Theatrical Directors and Teachers

Straus, Oscar; see VI Composers
Streusand, Ira; see VIII Basketball
Stroheim, Erich von; see VII Film Directors
Tannenbaum, Frank; see IV Historians
Tauber, Richard; see VI Classical and Opera Singers
Tausk, Viktor; see IV Psychologists
Thorn, Sir Jules; see III Business Leaders
Toch, Ernest; see VI Composers
Ulmer, Edgar G.; see VII Film Directors
Vogel, Simon; see I Military Figures (Austrians, Hungarians, and Austro-Hungarians)
Walbrook, Anton; see VII Film Stars
Weininger, Otto; see IV Philosophers
Weisskopf, Victor F.; see V Pioneers of Atomic Energy
Werner, Heinz; see IV Psychologists
Wiesner, Julius von; see V Botanists
Wilder, Billy; see VII Film Directors
Wittgenstein, Paul; see VI Pianists
Wolf, Eric R.; see IV Anthropologists
Zinnemann, Fred; see VII Film Directors
Zweig, Stefan; see VI Writers (Germans and Austrians)
See also Czechoslovakia; Hungary; Poland; Yugoslavia (for other birthplaces in Austro-Hungarian Empire)

Bavaria, see Germany

Belgium

Bernheim, Louis; see I Military Figures (Others)
Errera, Paul J.; see IV Legal Scholars
Goldsmith, Raymond W.; see IV Economists
Hymans, Paul; see I Government Officials (Others)
Koltanowski, George; see VIII Chess
Levi-Strauss, Claude; see IV Anthropologists
Levy, Lazare; see VI Pianists
Wiener, Ernest E.; see I Military Figures (Others)

Bessarabia, see Rumania

Brazil

Burle-Marx, Roberto; see II Architects
Lafer, Horacio; see I Government Officials (Others)
Marx, Walter Burle; see VI Conductors
Steinbruch, Aarao; see I Political Figures (Others)
Wald, Arnold; see II Lawyers

Bukovina, see Rumania and/or Russia

Bulgaria

Aftalion, Albert; see IV Economists
Arie, Rafael; see VI Classical and Opera Singers
Canetti, Elias; see VI Writers (Others)
Pascin, Jules; see VI Artists
Weissenberg, Alexis; see VI Pianists

Canada

Abel, Elie; see II Journalists; VII Television Newscasters
Asper, I. H.; see I Political Figures (Canadians)
Bagdade, Benjamin; see VIII Ice Skating
Bellow, Saul; see IX Nobel Prize Winners (Literature); VI Writers (Americans and Canadians)
Berne, Eric; see IV Psychologists
Blankstein, Cecil N.; see II Architects

Branden, Nathaniel; see IV Philosophers
Brant, Henry D.; see VI Composers
Bronfman, Samuel; see III Business Leaders
Brooks, Ross; see VIII Hockey
Caplan, Rupert; see VII Television Executives Producers, Directors, and Writers
Chercover, Murray; see VII Television Executives Producers, Directors, and Writers
Cohen, Leonard; see VI Rock, Pop, and Folk Artists (and Others)
Cornblatt, Isadore C.; see I Military Figures (Canadians)
Firestone, Shulamith; see I Feminists
Fishman, William H.; see II Doctors and Medical Researchers
Gelber, Marvin; see I Government Officials (Canadians)
Givens, Philip S.; see I Mayors
Goffman, Erving; see IV Sociologists
Gold, H.L.; see VI Science Fiction Writers and Editors
Goldenberg, H. Carl; see I Government Officials (Canadians)
Gotier, Allan; see I Government Officials (Canadians)
Gray, Herbert; see I Government Officials (Canadians)
Green, Lorne; see VII Television Performers
Greenspoon, Henry; see II Architects
Hall, Monty; see VII Television Performers
Hart, Cecil; see VIII Hockey
Hayden, Melissa; see VI Dancers
Jacobi, Lou; see VI Comedians
Keyfitz, Nathan; see IV Sociologists
Klein, Abraham M.; see VI Poets (Canadians)
Koffman, Moe; see VI Jazz Performers
Kruschen, Jack; see VI Comedians
Laskin, Bora; see I Judges
Levy, Leonard W.; see IV Historians
Lipton, Maurice; see I Military Figures (Canadians)
London, George; see VI Classical and Opera Singers
Morris, Lionel; see I Government Officials (Canadians)
Phillips, Nathan; see I Mayors
Pierce, Sydney D.; see VIII Track and Field
Rakoff, Alvin; see VII Television Executives Producers, Directors, and Writers
Rasminsky, Louis; see I Government Officials (Canadians)
Richler, Mordecai; see VI Writers (Americans and Canadians)
Rosen, George; see VIII Baseball
Rosenthal, A. M.; see II Journalists
Rubenstein, Louis; see VIII Ice Skating
Safer, Morley; see VII Television Newscasters
Sahl, Mort; see VI Comedians
Saltzman, Harry; see VII Film Producers
Senensky, Bernie; see VI Jazz Performers
Shapiro, Lionel; see VI Writers (Americans and Canadians)
Shatner, William; see VII Television Performers
Shuster, Joe; see VI Cartoonists and Caricaturists
Steinberg, David; see VI Comedians
Steirman, Hy; see II Magazine Publishers and Journalists
Strand, Mark; see VI Poets (Canadians)

Michel-Levy, Auguste; see V Inventors, Industrial Designers, and Engineers
Milhaud, Darius; see VI Composers
Moch, Jules S.; see I Government Officials (French)
Moissan, Henri; see IX Nobel Prize Winners (Chemistry)
Monteux, Pierre; see VI Conductors
Morhange, Pierre; see VI Poets (French Language)
Paraf, Pierre; see VII Television Executives, Producers, Directors, and Writers
Pissarro, Camille; see VI Artists
Pontremili, Emmanuel; see II Architects
Proust, Marcel; see VI Writers (French)
Raynal, David; see I Government Officials (French)
Roland-Manuel; see VI Composers
Rosenthal, Manuel; see VI Conductors
Rueff, Jacques; see IV Economists
Schrameck, Abraham; see I Political Figures (French)
Schumann, Maurice; see I Political Figures (French)
Schwarz-Bart, André; see VI Writers (French)
See, Edmond; see VI Playwrights
See, Leopold; see I Military Figures (French)
Steiner, George; see VI Literary and Drama Critics and Agents
Stern, Jacques; see I Government Officials (French)
Supino, Paolo; see I Military Figures (Italians)
Tarn, Nathaniel; see VI Poets (British)
Vercors; see VI Writers (French)
Villon, Pierre; see I Political Figures (French)
Wahl, Jean; see IV Philosophers
Waldteufel, Emil; see VI Composers
Weil, Adrienne; see I Military Figures (French)
Weil, André; see V Mathematicians
Weil, Simone; see IV Philosophers
Wolff, Albert L.; see VI Conductors
Wormser, Oliver B.; see I Government Officials (French)
Wyler, William; see VII Film Directors
Zay, Jean; see I Government Officials (French)

Galicia, see Poland

Germany

Abraham, Karl; see IV Psychologists
Abraham, Max; see V Physicists
Adler, Dankmar; see II Architects
Adorno, Theodor W.; see IV Sociologists
Albu, Sir George; see III Business Leaders
Albu, Isidor; see II Doctors and Medical Researchers
Alexander, Moses; see I Governors of American States
Arendt, Hannah; see IV Philosophers
Arendt, Otto; see IV Economists
Arnstein, Walter L.; see IV Historians
Arons, Leo; see V Physicists
Aschaffenburg, Gustav; see I Cops and Robbers (including Criminologists)
Ascherson, Paul; see V Botanists
Askenasy, Paul; see V Chemists
Baeyer, Adolf von; see IX Nobel Prize Winners (Chemistry)
Ballin, Albert; see III Business Leaders

Bamberger, Ludwig; see I Government Officials (Germans)
Bamberger, Simon; see I Governors of American States
Barnert, Nathan; see I Mayors
Baruch, Simon; see II Doctors and Medical Researchers
Baum, Werner; see IV Educators
Bedacht, Max; see I Men and Women of the Left (Americans)
Beit, Sir Alfred; see III Business Leaders
Belmont, Auguste; see I Political Figures (Americans)
Bendix, Reinhard, see IV Sociologists
Benjamin, Walter; see VI Literary and Drama Critics and Agents
Berger, Ludwig; see VII Film Directors
Bergmann, Ernst D.; see V Chemists
Berlinger, Emile; see V Inventors, Industrial Designers, and Engineers
Bernstein, Julius; see II Doctors and Medical Researchers
Blech, Leo; see VI Conductors
Bloch, Konrad; see IX Nobel Prize Winners (Medicine and Physiology)
Bloch, René; see I Military Figures (French)
Blumenger, Leopold; see I Military Figures (Americans)
Blumenfeld, Walter; see IV Psychologists
Blumenthal, Jacob; see I Pianists
Blumenthal, W. Michael; see I Government Officials (Americans)
Boas, Franz; see IV Anthropologists
Bondy, Curt; see IV Psychologists
Born, Max; see IX Nobel Prize Winners (Physics)
Boschwitz, Rudy; see I U.S. Senators
Braude, Ernest A.; see V Chemists
Bucky, Gustav; see II Doctors and Medical Researchers
Buhler, Charlotte; see IV Psychologists
Burghardt, Hermann; see V Explorers
Cahnman, Werner J.; see IV Sociologists
Caro, Heinrich; see V Chemists
Caro, Nikodem; see V Chemists
Cassel, Sir Ernest J.; see III Business Leaders
Chain, Sir Ernest B.; see IX Nobel Prize Winners (Medicine and Physiology)
Citroen, Paul; see VI Artists
Cohn, Ferdinand J.; see II Doctors and Medical Researchers
Cohn, Fritz; see V Astronomers
Cohn, Lassar; see V Chemists
Cohnheim, Julius; see II Doctors and Medical Researchers
Coser, Lewis A.; see IV Sociologists
Damrosch, Walter J.; see VI Conductors
David, Ferdinand; see VI Violinists
Dawison, Bogumil; see VI Stars of the Theater
Dreifuss, Arthur; see VII Film Directors
Dreyfuss, Barney; see VIII Baseball
Edinger, Ludwig; see II Doctors and Medical Researchers
Ehrenberg, Victor L.; see IV Historians
Ehrlich, Paul; see IX Nobel Prize Winners (Medicine and Physiology)
Einstein, Albert; see IX Nobel Prize Winners (Physics)
Eisenstaedt, Alfred; see VI Photographers
Eisler, Hanns; see VI Composers

Rava, Maurizio; see I Government Officials (Italians)
Segre, Emilio; see IX Nobel Prize Winners (Physics)
Sonnino, Sidney; see I Government Officials (Italians)
Valabrega, Cesare; see VI Pianists
Ventura, Rubino; see I Military Figures (Italians)
Vivante, Cesare; see IV Legal Scholars
Wollemborg, Leone; see I Government Officials (Italians)
Zevi, Bruno; see II Architects

Jamaica
Ashenheim, Sir Neville N.; see I Government Officials (Jamaicans)
Cordova, Jacob de; see II Newspaper and Magazine Publishers
Matalon, Eli; see I Government Officials (Jamaicans)

Japan
Schaffner, Franklin; see VII Film Directors

Jerusalem, see Israel

Latvia
Abramowitz, Raphael; see I Men and Women of the Left (Russians)
Aronson, Naum L.; see VI Sculptors
Berlin, Sir Isaiah; see IV Political Scientists
Davidoff, Leo M.; see II Doctors and Medical Researchers
Davydov, Karl; see VI Cellists
Fitelberg, Grzegorz; see VI Conductors
German, Yuri P.; see VI Writers (Russians)
Gulack, George J.; see IX Olympic Medalists (Gymnastics)
Halsman, Philippe; see VI Photographers
Hillquit, Morris; see I Men and Women of the Left (Americans)
Hirschfeld, Isador; see II Doctors and Medical Researchers
Hirshhorn, Joseph H.; see III Business Leaders
Krook, Dorothea; see VI Literary and Drama Critics and Agents
Mintz, Paul; see I Government Officials (Russians and Close Relatives)
Nimzowitsch, Aron; see VIII Chess
Tynyanov, Yuri; see VI Literary and Drama Critics and Agents
Zuckertort, Johannes; see VIII Chess

Lebanon
Moyal, Esther; see II Journalists

Lithuania
Abrams, Charles; see IV Sociologists
Antokolski, Mark; see VI Sculptors
Berenson, Bernard; see VI Other Figures in Art
Bernstein, Herman; see I Government Officials (Americans)
Bernstein-Sinaieff, Leopold; see VI Sculptors
Bobtelsky, Max; see V Chemists
Davis, Abel; see I Military Figures (Americans)
Dickstein, Samuel; see I U.S. Congressmen and Congresswomen
Gary, Romain; see VI Writers (French)
Godowsky, Leopold; see VI Pianists
Goldberg, Alexander; see V Inventors, Industrial Designers, and Engineers
Goldman, Emma; see I Revolutionaries

Gruenstein, Nathan; see V Chemists
Guenzburg, Ilya Y.; see VI Sculptors
Guss, Benjamin; see I Political Figures (Canadians)
Harvey, Laurence; see VII Film Stars
Heifetz, Jascha; see VI Violinists
Hillman, Sidney; see I Labor Leaders
Himmelstein, Lena; see III Business Leaders
Izis; see VI Photographers
Jochelson, Vladimir; see IV Anthropologists
Kentridge, Morris; see I Political Figures (South Africans and Rhodesians)
Klabin, Mauricio; see III Business Leaders
Laurence, William L.; see II Journalists
Levinas, Emmanuel; see IV Philosophers
Levitan, Isaac I.; see VI Artists
Lipchitz, Jacques; see VI Sculptors
Lovestone, Jay; see I Men and Women of the Left (Americans)
Maller, Julius B.; see IV Sociologists
Mears, Otto; see III Business Leaders
Millin, Sarah Gertrude; see VI Writers (South Africans)
Minkowski, Hermann; see V Mathematicians
Rappoport, Charles; see I Men and Women of the Left (French)
Schwarz, Solomon; see I Political Figures (Russians)
Shahn, Ben; see VI Artists
Shmushekevich, Yaacov; see I Military Figures (Russians)
Soutine, Chaim; see VI Artists
Stern, Lina; see II Doctors and Medical Researchers
Sure, Barnett; see V Chemists
Volpe, Arnold; see VI Conductors
Wainhouse, David W.; see I Government Officials (Americans)
Zundelevitch, Aaron; see I Revolutionaries

Luxembourg
Lippman, Gabriel; see IX Nobel Prize Winners (Physics)
Mayer, Arno J.; see IV Historians

Manchuria
Utkin, Joseph P.; see VI Poets (Russians)

Mexico
Brenner, Anita; see II Journalists

Netherlands
Bakker-Nort, Betsy; see I Feminists
Blake, George; see I Spies and Counterspies
Cohen, Ernest J.; see V Chemists
Da Costa, Joseph M.; see VI Sculptors
De Klerk, Michael; see II Architects
Dresden, Sem; see VI Composers
Heijermans, Herman; see VI Playwrights
Honden, Jacob van der; see II Doctors
Israels, Jozef; see VI Artists
Kann, Jacobus H.; see III Business Leaders
Kolthoff, Izaak M.; see V Chemists
Mulisch, Harry; see VI Writers (Others)
Polak, Carel H. F.; see I Political Figures (Dutch)
Polak, Willem; see I Government Officials (Dutch)
Stein, Louis B.; see VIII Bowling
Troostwijk, Mauris; see I Mayors
Van Den Bergh, Sidney J.; see I Military Figures (Others)

Van Derhoeden, Jacob; see II Doctors and
Medical Researchers
Van Raalte, Eduard E.; see I Government Officials
(Dutch)
Visser, Lodewijk E.; see I Judges
Wijnkoop, David; see I Left (Others)

Netherlands Antilles

De Leon, Daniel; see I Men and Women of the Left
(Americans)

New Zealand

Barnett, Sir Louis; see II Doctors and Medical
Researchers
Fisher, Sir Woolf; see III Business Leaders
Myers, Sir Michael; see I Judges

Norway

Abrahamsen, David; see I Cops and Robbers
(including Criminologists)
Levin, Robert; see VI Other Figures in Classical
Music
Philipson, Charles; see I Government Officials
(Others)

Palestine, see Israel

Panama

Delvalle, Max; see I Government Officials
(Others)

Persia

Nathan, Mulla I.; see I Spies and Counterspies
See also Iran

Poland

Agnon, S. Y.; see IX Nobel Prize Winners
(Literature)
Allen, Irving; see VII Film Producers
Antin, Mary; see VI Writers (Americans and
Canadians)
Ardon, Mordecai; see VI Artists
Arnon, Daniel I.; see V Botanists
Avineri, Shlomo; see IV Political Scientists
Baginsky, Adolf A.; see II Doctors and Medical
Researchers
Begin, Menachem; see IX Nobel Prize Winners
(Peace)
Berenblum, Isaac; see II Doctors and Medical
Researchers
Berenson, Leon; see II Lawyers
Berman, Jacob; see I Men and Women of the Left
(Poles)
Berson, Arthur J. S.; see V Meteorologists
Bloch, Ivan; see IV Social Critics
Brandys, Kazimierz; see VI Writers (Poles)
Bregman, Sidney; see II Architects
Bronowski, Jacob; see IV Philosophers
Chwistek, Leon; see IV Philosophy
Cohen, Myron; see VI Comedians
Courant, Richard; see V Mathematicians
Czerniak, Moshe; see VIII Chess
Damrosch, Leopold; see VI Conductors
Deutsch, Helene; see IV Psychologists
Deutscher, Isaac; see VI Writers (Americans and
Canadians)
Dickstein, Szymon; see I Men and Women of the
Left (Poles)
Drabowsky, Myron W. "Moe"; see VIII Baseball

Drobner, Boleslaw; see I Men and Women of the
Left (Poles)
Dubinsky, David; see I Labor Leaders
Dunkelbaum, Arthur; see VIII Chess
Edelstein, Morris M.; see I U.S. Congressmen and
Congresswomen
Eisenstadt, S. N.: see IV Sociologists
Emin (Pasha); see I Government Officials
(Austrians)
Epstein, Jean; see VII Film Directors
Epstein, Paul S.; see V Physicists
Factor, Max; see III Business Leaders
Fajans, Kasimir; see V Chemists
Farbstein, David Z.; see I Political Figures
(Others)
Feinstone, Morris; see I Labor Leaders
Feuermann, Emanuel; see VI Cellists
Fisz, Benjamin; see VII Film Producers
Ford, Alexander; see VII Film Producers
Freudenthal, Alfred M.; see V Inventors, Industrial
Designers, and Engineers
Frydman, Paulino; see VIII Chess
Funk, Casimir; see II Doctors and Medical
Researchers
Gelbard, José Ber; see I Government Officials
(Argentines)
Gerson, Louis L.; see IV Political Scientists
Getzels, Jacob W.; see IV Psychologists
Glicenstein, Enrico; see VI Artists
Glueck, Sheldon; see I Cops and Robbers
(including Criminologists)
Goldman, Bernard; see I Revolutionaries
Goldstein, Kurt; see IV Psychologists
Goldwyn, Samuel; see VII Film Executives
Gruenberg, Louis; see VI Composers
Gumplowicz, Ludwig; see IV Sociologists
Haendel, Ida; see VI Violinists
Halberstaedter, Ludwig; see II Doctors and
Medical Researchers
Halpern, Lipman; see II Doctors and Medical
Researchers
Heilperin, Michael A.; see IV Economists
Helfgott, Benjamin; see VIII Weightlifting
Herman, Josef; see VI Artists
Hirshberg, Yehudah; see V Chemists
Hirszfeld, Ludwik; see II Doctors and Medical
Researchers
Horowitz, Louis J.; see III Business Leaders
Huberman, Bronislaw; see VI Violinists
Infeld, Leopold; see V Physicists
Iskowitz, Gershon; see VI Artists
Janowski, David M.; see VIII Chess
Jasienski, Bruno; see VI Writers (Poles)
Joselewicz, Berek; see I Military Figures (Poles)
Kalecki, Michal; see IV Economists
Kallen, Horace M.; see IV Philosophers
Kallet, Aaron H.; see VIII Football
Karlin, Samuel; see V Mathematicians
Katch, Kurt; see VII Film Stars
Katzir, Aharon; see V Chemists
Katz-Suchy, Juliusz; see I Government Officials
(Poles)
Kaufman, Boris; see VII Cinematographers
Kentner, Louis; see VI Pianists
Kibel, Wolf; see VI Artists
Kisling, Moise; see VI Artists
Kober, Arthur; see VI Playwrights
Kon, Feliks; see I Men and Women of the Left
(Poles)

Kronecker, Hugo; see II Doctors and Medical Researchers
Kronecker, Leopold; see V Mathematicians
Landau, Leopold; see II Doctors and Medical Researchers
Landowska, Wanda; see VI Pianists
Lasker, Eduard; see I Political Figures (Germans)
Lauterpacht, Sir Hersch; see I Judges
Lazerowitz, Morris; see IV Philosophers
Lebensold, Fred; see II Architects
Lemian, Boleslaw; see VI Poets (Poles)
Le Witt, Jan; see VI Artists
Lieberman, Herman; see I Men and Women of the Left (Poles)
Lipski, Abraham; see V Inventors, Industrial Designers, and Engineers
Litvinov, Maxim M.; see I Government Officials (Russians and Close Relatives)
Loewenstein, Rudolph M.; see IV Psychologists
Lubell, Samuel; see I Political Figures (Americans)
Luxemburg, Rosa; see I Men and Women of the Left (Germans)
Mandelstam, Osip E.; see VI Poets (Russians)
Marckwald, Willy; see V Chemists
Marcoussis, Louis; see VI Artists
Marmorek, Alexander; see II Doctors and Medical Researchers
Martin, Ross; see VII Television Performers
Masserman, Jules H.; see IV Psychologists
Matz, Israel; see III Business Leaders
Meyerson, Emile; see IV Philosophers
Minc, Hilary; see I Government Officials (Poles)
Mond, Bernhard S.; see I Military Figures (Poles)
Muni, Paul; see VII Film Stars
Muter, Mela; see VI Artists
Myer, Sidney; see III Business Leaders
Nadelman, Elie; see VI Sculptors
Najdorf, Miguel; see VIII Chess
Namier, Sir Lewis; see IV Historians
Natanson, Marc; see I Men and Women of the Left (Russians)
Natanson, Mark; see I Revolutionaries
Neiman, Yehudah; see VI Artists
Ostrogorski, Moses; see IV Philosophers
Ostrolenk, Bernhard; see IV Economists
Palmer, Lilli; see VII Film Stars
Peiper, Tadeusz; see VI Writers (Poles)
Perelman, Chaim; see IV Philosophers
Perlman, Jacob; see IV Economists
Perlman, Nathan D.; see I U.S. Congressmen and Congresswomen
Perlman, Selig; see I Labor Leaders
Pipes, Richad E.; see IV Historians
Prenn, Daniel; see VIII Tennis
Radin, Max; see IV Legal Scholars
Radin, Paul; see IV Anthropologists
Radzinowicz, Sir Leon; see I Cops and Robbers (including Criminologists)
Rambert, Dame Marie; see VI Dancers
Reichert, Israel; see V Botanists
Reichstein, Tadeus; see IX Nobel Prize Winners (Medicine and Physiology)
Rose, Alex; see I Political Figures (Americans)
Rose, Ernestine; see I Feminists
Rosenstock, Joseph; see VI Conductors
Rosten, Leo; see VI Writers (Americans and Canadians)
Rubinstein, Akiba; see VIII Chess

Rubinstein Artur; see VI Pianists
Rubinstein, Helena; see III Business Leaders
Sabin, Albert B.; see II Doctors
Schaff, Adam; see I Men and Women of the Left (Poles)
Schneiderman, Rose; see I Labor Leaders
Seymour, David; see VI Photographers
Singer, Isaac Bashevis; see IX Nobel Prize Winners (Literature); VI Writers (Americans and Canadians)
Stachel, Jacob; see I Men and Women of the Left (Americans)
Stern, Anatol; see VI Poets (Poles)
Stokes, Rose Pastor; see I Men and Women of the Left (Americans)
Strasburger, Eduard; see V Botanists
Stryjkowski, Juljan; see VI Writers (Poles)
Szerying, Henryk; see VI Violinists
Szulc, Tad; see II Journalists
Szwarc, Michael; see V Chemists
Szyr, Eugenius; see I Government Officials (Poles)
Talmon, Jacob L.; see IV Historians
Tansman, Alexander; see VI Composers
Tarski, Alfred; see IV Philosophers
Tausig, Karl; see VI Pianists
Traube, Moritz; see V Chemists
Trepper, Leopold; see I Spies and Counterspies
Tuwim, Julian; see VI Poets (Poles)
Ulam, Adam; see IV Political Scientists
Ulam, S. M.; see V Mathematicians
Veinberg, Moissey S.; see VI Composers
Warner, Harry; see VII Film Executives
Warski-Warszawski, Adolf; see I Men and Women of the Left (Poles)
Weber, Max; see VI Artists
Weiss, Samuel A.; see I U.S. Congressmen and Congresswomen; VIII Football
Wieniawski, Henri; see VI Violinists
Winawer, Simon; see VIII Chess
Wohl, Henryk; see I Men and Women of the Left (Poles)
Yanofsky, Daniel; see VIII Chess
Zamenhof, Ludwik; see VI Writers (Poles)

Portugal

Amzalak, Moses B.; see IV Economists

Prussia, see Germany

Quebec, see Canada

Rhodesia

Harris, Ralph S.; see I Mayors

Rumania

Aderca, Felix; see VI Writers (Others)
Banus, Maria; see VI Poets (Rumanians)
Bertini, Gary; see VI Conductors
Blank, Maurice; see III Business Leaders
Chagrin, Francis; see VI Composers
Cohn, Benedict; see V Aviators, Astronauts, and Others
David, Jean; see VI Artists
Diamond, I. A. L.; see VII Screenwriters
Feller, Shneyur; see IV Legal Scholars
Finer, Herman; see IV Political Scientists
Fondane, Benjamin; see VI Poets (French Language)
Fried, Miriam; see VI Violinists

Gaston-Marin, Gheorghe; see I Government Officials (Rumanians)

Gelerter, Ludwig L.; see I Men and Women of the Left (Rumanians)

Gluck, Alma; see VI Classical and Opera Singers

Gold, Benjamin; see I Men and Women of the Left (Americans)

Gruenberg, Karl; see IV Historians

Grunfeld, Ernest; see IX Olympic Medalists (Basketball)

Haskil, Clara; see VI Pianists

Heller, Stephen; see VI Pianists

Hellman, Marcel; see VII Film Producers

Houseman, John; see VI Theatrical Producers; VII Film Stars

Ionesco, Eugene; see VI Playwrights

Kandel, Isaac L.; see IV Educators

Katz, Mindru; see VI Pianists

Klapper, Paul; see IV Educators

Layton, Irving; see VI Poets (Canadians)

Leibowitz, Samuel S.; see I Civil Rights Leaders

Luttwak, Edward N.; see I Military Figures (Americans)

Moreno, Jacob L.; see IV Psychologists

Natra, Sergiu; see VI Composers

Pauker, Ana; see I Government Officials (Rumanians)

Peltz, Isaac; see VI Writers (Others)

Porumbacu, Veronica; see VI Poets (Rumanians)

Postan, Michael M.; see IV Historians

Robinson, Edward G.; see VII Film Stars

Roseanu, Angelica; see VIII Table Tennis

Schmidt, Joseph; see VI Classical and Opera Singers

Schwarzbard, Shalom; see I Men and Women of the Left (Others)

Steinberg, Saul; see VI Artists

Tzara, Tristan; see VI Poets (French Language)

Wechsler, David; see IV Psychologists

Wechsler, Israel; see II Doctors and Medical Researchers

Wiesel, Elie; see VI Writers (Americans and Canadians)

Russia

Abelmann, Ilya S.; see V Astronomers

Adler, Saul A.; see II Doctors and Medical Researchers

Aldanov, Mark; see VI Writers (Russians)

Aliger, Margarita Y.; see VI Poets (Russians)

Angoff, Charles; see VI Literary and Drama Critics and Agents

Askenasy, Eugen; see V Botanists

Axelrod, Pavel; see I Revolutionaries

Azeff, Eugene; see I Spies and Counterspies

Babel, Isaac; see VI Writers (Russians)

Babin, Victor; see VI Pianists

Bagrit, Sir Leon; see III Business Leaders

Bagritski, Eduard; see VI Poets (Russians)

Baizerman, Saul; see VI Sculptors

Bakst, Leon; see VI Artists

Baron, Bernhard; see III Business Leaders

Barsha, John; see VIII Football

Bass, Benny; see VIII Boxing (World Champions)

Bely, Victor A.; see VI Composers

Berkman, Alexander; see I Men and Women of the Left (Americans)

Berlin, Irving; see VI Popular Music Composers and Lyricists

Bernstein, Ossip; see VIII Chess

Bidney, David; see IV Anthropologists

Bill-Belotserkovski, Vladimir; see VI Playwrights

Bittelman, Alexander; see I Men and Women of the Left (Americans)

Black, Max; see IV Philosophers

Black, Sir Misha; see V Inventors, Industrial Designers and Engineers

Blanter, Matvey I.; see VI Composers

Blaustein, Louis; see III Business Leaders

Bloch, Max; see IV Philosophers

Blom, Adolph; see VI Dancers

Blume, Peter; see VI Artists

Blumenthal, Benjamin M.; see VIII Chess

Bodansky, Oscar; see V Chemists

Brailowsky, Alexander; see VI Pianists

Brik, Osip N.; see VI Literary and Drama Critics and Agents

Brodetsky, Selig; see V Aviators, Astronauts, and Others

Brodski, Alexander; see V Chemists

Brodski, Israel; see III Business Leaders

Brodsky, Adolf; see VI Violinists

Brodsky, Isaac; see VI Artists

Brown, Lew; see VI Popular Music Composers and Lyricists

Brown, Newsboy; see VIII Boxing (Other Boxers)

Carter, Victor M.; see VII Film Executives

Cherkassky, Shura; see VI Pianists

Chernyakhovski, Ivan D.; see I Military Figures (Russians)

Cohen, Morris Raphael; see IV Philosophers

Croll, David A.; see I Mayors

Dan, Fyodor I.; see I Men and Women of the Left (Russians)

De Grunwald, Anatole; see VII Film Producers

Delfont, Bernard; see VI Theater Managers and Owners

Dorfman, Joseph; see IV Economists

Drootin, Benjamin; see VI Jazz Performers

Dujovne, Leon; see IV Philosophers

Dunayevski, Isaac; see VI Composers

Dushman, Saul; see V Physicists

Duvdevani, Shmuel; see V Botanists

Dymshyts, Veniamin E.; see IV Economists

Ehrenburg, Ilya G.; see VI Writers (Russians)

Eitingon, Max; see IV Psychologists

Ellison, Daniel; see I U.S. Congressmen and Congresswomen

Elman, Mischa; see VI Violinists

Epstein, Abraham; see IV Economists

Erenberg, Philip; see IX Olympic Medalists (Gymnastics)

Erlich, Ludwik; see II Lawyers

Feinberg, Samuel Y.; see VI Composers

Finkelman, Jacob; see IV Legal Scholars

Fishberg, Maurice; see II Doctors and Medical Researchers

Flohr, Salo; see VIII Chess

Fondiller, William; see V Inventors, Industrial Designers, and Engineers

Frank, Semyon; see IV Philosophers

Freedman, Samuel; see IV Educators

Frisch, Efraim; see VI Writers (Germans and Austrians)

Gabrielovitch, Osip S.; see VI Pianists

Gaskell, Sonja; see VI Dancers

Gerchunoff, Alberto; see VI Writers (Others)

Gerschenkron, Alexander; see IV Economists

Oistrakh, David F.; see VI Violinists

Orloff, Chana; see VI Sculptors

Pasternak, Boris L.; see VI Writers (Russians)

Piatigorsky, Gregor; see VI Cellists

Podoloff, Maurice; see VIII (Basketball)

Potofsky, Jacob S.; see I Labor Leaders

Rabinowitch, Eugene; see V Pioneers of Atomic Energy

Radek, Karl; see I Men and Women of the Left (Russians)

Rand, Ayn; see IV Philosophers

Rappoport, Anatol; see V Mathematicians

Razran, Gregory; see IV Psychologists

Rickover, Hyman; see I Military Figures (Americans)

Rifkind, Simon H.; see II Lawyers

Roback, Abraham A.; see IV Psychologists

Rosen, Phil; see VII Film Directors

Rosenblum, Sigmund G.; see I Spies and Counterspies

Rosenfeld, Fanny; see IX Olympic Medalists (Track and Field)

Rosenthal, Moriz; see VI Pianists

Rothko, Mark; see VI Artists

Rubenstein, Ida; see VI Dancers

Rubin, Samuel; see III Business Leaders

Rubinstein, Anton; see VI Pianists

Rubinstein, Sergey; see IV Psychologists

Ruttenberg,Joseph; see VII Cinematographers

Samoilovich, Rudolf; see V Explorers

Sarnoff, David; see VII Television Executives, Producers, Directors, and Writers

Schneider, Alan; see VI Theatrical Directors and Teachers

Seldin, Harry M.; see II Doctors and Medical Researchers

Sevitzky, Fabien; see VI Conductors

Sharfman, Isaiah; see IV Economists

Shiplacoff, Abraham; see I Men and Women of the Left (Americans)

Shulman, Harry; see IV Legal Scholars

Singerman, Berta; see VI Poets (Others)

Spivakovsky, Tossy; see VI Conductors

Steinberg, Isaac N.; see I Men and Women of the Left (Russians)

Strunsky, Simeon; see II Journalists

Sverdlov, Yakov M.; see I Men and Women of the Left (Russians)

Swerling, Jo; see VII Screenwriters

Tartakover, Savielly; see VIII Chess

Titiev, Mischa; see IV Anthropologists

Tobenkin, Elias; see II Journalists

Toll, Herman; see I U.S. Congressmen and Congresswomen

Triolet, Elsa; see VI Writers (French)

Trotsky, Leon; see I Men and Women of the Left (Russians)

Tsfassman, Alexander; see VI Jazz Performers

Veksler, Vladimir; see V Physicists

Velikovsky, Immanuel; see V Astronomers

Vishniac, Roman; see VI Photographers

Voronoff, Serge; see II Doctors and Medical Researchers

Waksman, Selman; see IX Nobel Prize Winners (Medicine and Physiology)

Waten, Judah; see VI Literary and Drama Critics and Agents

Welsh, Al; see V Aviators, Astronauts, and Others

Wolberg, Lewis R.; see IV Psychologists

Wolfson, Harry A.; see IV Historians

Yarmolinsky, Avrahm; see VI Literary and Drama Critics and Agents

Yaroslavsky, Yemelyan; see I Men and Women of the Left (Russians)

Young Montreal; see VIII Boxing (Other Boxers)

Zak, Abram; see III Business Leaders

Zariski, Oscar; see V Mathematicians

Zaslavsky, David; see II Journalists

Zemurray, Samuel; see III Business Leaders

Zhitnitski, Mark; see VI Artists

Zilboorg, Gregory; see IV Psychologists

Zimbalist, Efrem; see VI Violinists

Zinoviev, Grigori; see I Men and Women of the Left (Russians)

Zucrow, Maurice J.; see V Aviators, Astronauts, and Others

See also Union of Soviet Socialist Republics (after 1917)

Scotland

Heilbron, Sir Ian M.; see V Chemists

Levy, Hyman; see V Mathematicians

Temianka, Henri; see VI Violinists

Serbia, see Yugoslavia
Slovakia, see Czechoslovakia
South Africa

Addleson, Norman C.; see I Judges

Bloch, Hyman M.; see I Judges

Broomberg, Elly; see I Political Figures (South Africans and Rhodesians)

Bryer, Monte; see II Architects

Colman, George; see I Judges

Cranko, John; see VI Dancers

Fortes, Meyer; see IV Anthropologists

Frankel, Sally; see IV Economists

Friedman, Joseph J.; see I Judges

Galgut, Oscar; see I Judges

Gluckman, Max; see IV Anthropologists

Goldin, Bennie; see I Judges

Gordimer, Nadine; see VI Writers (South Africans)

Hermer, Manfred; sée II Architects

Hirschhorn, Clive; see VI Literary and Drama Critics and Agents

Jacobson, Dan; see VI Writers (South Africans)

Jacobson, Sydney; see II Journalists

Kantorowich, Roy; see II Architects

Kuper, Leo; see IV Sociologists

Leon, Raymond N.; see I Judges

Le Roith, Harold H.; see II Architects

Mekler, Jack; see VIII Track and Field

Moss, Samuel; see I Mayors

Pincus, Joel; see I Political Figures (South Africans and Rhodesians)

Sachs, Albert L.; see I Civil Rights Leaders

Scheckter, Jody; see VIII Auto Racing

Schrire, Velva; see II Doctors and Medical Researchers

Segal, Abraham A.; see VIII Tennis

Segal, Ronald; see VI Writers (British)

Suzman, Helen; see I Political Figures (South Africans and Rhodesians)

Tobias, Phillip; see IV Anthropologists

Widman, Alfred B.; see I Mayors

Zuckerman, Lord Solly; see I Government Officials (British)

Sweden

Heckscher, Elifilip; *see* IV Historians

Josephson, Jacob A.; *see* VI Conductors

Lamm, Martin; *see* VI Literary and Drama Critics and Agents

Levertin, Oscar I.; *see* VI Literary and Drama Critics and Agents

Rubenson, Robert; *see* V Meteorologists

Switzerland

Bloch, Ernest; *see* VI Composers

Bloch, Felix; *see* IX Nobel Prize Winners (Physics)

Botstein, Leon; *see* IV Educators

Breval, Lucienne; *see* IV Classical and Opera Singers

Dreyfus, Camille; *see* V Chemists

Dreyfus, Henry; *see* V Chemists

Elegenheimer, Julien; *see* II Architects

Gold, Harry; *see* I Spies and Counterspies

Goldschmidt, Victor M.; *see* V Chemists

Grock, Charles A. W.; *see* VI Entertainers

Guggenheim, Meyer (and Family); *see* III Business Leaders

Guggenheim, Paul; *see* I Judges

Liebermann, Wolf; *see* VI Composers

Pap, Arthur; *see* III Business Leaders

Rachel; *see* VI Stars of the Theater

Starobinski, Jean; *see* VI Literary and Drama Critics and Agents

Thalberg, Sigismund; *see* VI Pianists

Weininger, Otto; *see* IV Philosophers

Tangier, International Zone of

De Toledano, Ralph; *see* II Magazine Publishers and Journalists

Transylvania, *see* Rumania

Trieste, *see* Italy

Tunisia

Darmon, Pierre; *see* VIII Tennis

Memmi, Albert; *see* VI Writers (French)

Perez, Victor; *see* VIII Boxing (World Champions)

Turkey

Benaroya, Avram; *see* V Inventors, Industrial Designers, and Engineers

Gerez, Josef H.; *see* VI Poets (Others)

Martov, Julius; *see* I Men and Women of the Left (Russians)

Riklis, Meshulam; *see* III Business Leaders

Schildkraut, Rudolf; *see* VI Stars of the Theater

Union of Soviet Socialist Republics (U.S.S.R.)

Ashkenazy, Vladimir D.; *see* VI Pianists

Asimov, Isaac; *see* VI Science Fiction Writers and Editors

Belinkov, Arkadii V.; *see* VI Literary and Drama Critics and Agents

Brodsky, Yosif; *see* VI Poets (Russians)

Bronstein, David; *see* VIII Chess

Dameshek, William; *see* II Doctors and Medical Researchers

Dostrovsky, Israel; *see* V Physicists

Drootin, Benjamin; *see* VI Jazz Performers

Granin, Daniel A.; *see* VI Writers (Russians)

Itkina, Maria T.; *see* VIII Track and Field

Kogan, Leonid B.; *see* VI Violinists

Korchnoi, Victor; *see* VIII Chess

Krepkina, Vera; *see* IX Olympic Medalists (Track and Field)

Krivosheyev, Abram; *see* VIII Track and Field

Kunsman, Roman; *see* VI Jazz Performers

Naroditskiy, Lazar; *see* VIII Track and Field

Novak, Grigori; *see* IX Olympic Medalists (Weightlifting)

Plisetskaya, Maya; *see* VI Dancers

Plyukfelder, Rudolf; *see* IX Olympic Medalists (Weightlifting)

Runitsch, Ossip; *see* VII Film Stars

Rylsky, Yakov; *see* IX Olympic Medalists (Fencing)

Smyslov, Vasily; *see* VIII Chess

Spassky, Boris; *see* VIII Chess

Stein, Leonid; *see* VIII Chess

Stern, Isaac; *see* VI Violinists

Szewinska, Irena Kirszenstein; *see* IX Olympic Medalists (Track and Field)

Talmi, Igal; *see* V Physicists

Werth, Alexander; *see* II Journalists

See also Russia (before 1917)

Venezuela

Benazar, Rafael Serfaty; *see* I Political Figures (Others)

Desola, René; *see* I Government Officials (Others)

Hahn, Reynaldo; *see* VI Other Figures in Classical Music

Wales

Abse, Dannie; *see* VI Poets (British)

Janner, Lord Barnett; *see* I Political Figures (British)

Yugoslavia

Davico, Oscar; *see* VI Writers (Others)

Gerskovic, Leon; *see* I Government Officials (Yugoslavians)

Hajek, Markus; *see* II Doctors and Medical Researchers

Pijade, Moses; *see* I Government Officials (Yugoslavians)

Reti, Rudolf; *see* VI Composers

Rodzinsky, Artur; *see* VI Conductors

UNITED STATES

ALABAMA

Birmingham

Allen, Mel; *see* VII Television Newscasters

Friedman, David F.; *see* VII Film Executives

Gadsden

Lowi, Theodore J.; *see* IV Political Scientists

Mobile

Berkin, Carol R.; *see* IV Historians

Proskauer, Joseph M.; *see* I Political Figures (Americans)

Montgomery

Jonas, Nathan S.; *see* III Business Leaders

Monsky, Leroy; *see* VIII Football

Selma

Lehman, William; *see* I U.S. Congressmen and Congresswomen

Korman, Harvey; *see* VII Television Performers
Kupcinet, Irving; *see* VIII Football
Laven, Arnold; *see* VII Film Directors
Lester, Jerry; *see* VI Comedians
Levi, Edward H.; *see* I Government Officials (Americans)
Levin, Meyer; *see* VI Writers (Americans and Canadians)
Levin, Theodore; *see* I Judges
Levy, Lillian; *see* II Journalists
Levy, Lou; *see* VI Jazz Performers
Loeb, Marshall; *see* II Magazine Publishers and Journalists
Lowenthal, Fred; *see* VIII Football
Maling, Arthur; *see* VI Writers (Americans and Canadians)
Mandel, Loring; *see* VII Television Executives, Producers, Directors, and Writers
Mandelbaum, David G.; *see* IV Anthropologists
Meyer, Frederick J.; *see* IX Olympic Medalists (Wrestling)
Meyer, Lawrence R.; *see* II Journalists
Mezzrow, Mezz; *see* VI Jazz Performers
Morris, Ira N.; *see* I Government Officials (Americans)
Nemer, Jerry; *see* VIII Basketball
Oppenheim, Morrie; *see* VIII Bowling
Paley, William S.; *see* VII Television Executives, Producers, Directors, and Writers
Pam, Hugo; *see* I Cops and Robbers (including Criminologists)
Perlstein, Meyer A.; *see* II Doctors and Medical Researchers
Pflaum, Irving P.; *see* II Journalists
Pollack, Ben; *see* VI Jazz Performers
Raphael, Frederic; *see* VI Writers (British)
Reuben, David; *see* II Doctors and Medical Researchers
Rieff, Philip; *see* IV Sociologists
Rose, Arnold; *see* IV Sociologists
Rosenwald, Lessing J.; *see* III Business Leaders
Rudolf, Lloyd I.; *see* IV Political Scientists
Rukeyser, Merryle S.; *see* II Journalists
Sachs, Leonard; *see* VIII Basketball
Schottland, Charles I.; *see* I Government Officials (Americans)
Schreiber, Avery; *see* VII Television Performers
Schwartz, Albert; *see* IX Olympic Medalists (Swimming)
Sheldon, Sidney; *see* VI Writers (Americans and Canadians)
Siegel, Don; *see* VII Film Directors
Silverman, Leslie; *see* V Inventors, Industrial Designers, and Engineers
Stern, Gerald; *see* VI Poets (Americans)
Thinnes, Roy; *see* VII Television Performers
Tureck, Rosalyn; *see* VI Pianists
Wallace, Irving; *see* VI Writers (Americans and Canadians)
Wallenstein, Alfred; *see* VI Conductors
Weingarten, Lawrence; *see* VII Film Producers
Weintraub, Mickey; *see* VIII Baseball
Wine-Volner, Jill; *see* I Government Officials (Americans)
Yates, Sidney R.; *see* I U.S. Congressmen and Congresswomen
Zeitlin, Denny; *see* VI Jazz Performers
Ziegfeld, Florenz; *see* VI Theatrical Producers

Highland Park
Hardy, Susan S.; *see* VIII Shooting

Kankakee
Shapiro, Samuel H.; *see* I Governors of American States

Macomb
Birenbaum, William; *see* IV Educators

Morton
Lilienthal, David E.; *see* I Government Officials (Americans)

Pekin
Bloom, Sol; *see* I U.S. Congressmen and Congresswomen

Peoria
Frank, Nathan; *see* I U.S. Congressmen and Congresswomen
Friedan, Betty; *see* I Feminists
Lawton, Samuel T.; *see* I Military Figures (Americans)

Rock Island
Almond, Gabriel A.; *see* IV Political Scientists
Schneidman, Herman "Biff"; *see* VIII Football

Springfield
Rosenwald, Julius; *see* III Business Leaders

Waukegan
Benny, Jack; *see* VI Comedians

Wilmington
Abt, Isaac A.; *see* II Doctors and Medical Researchers

INDIANA

Fort Wayne
Heilbroner, Louis W.; *see* VIII Baseball
Nathan, George J.; *see* IV Social Critics

Gary
Samuelson, Paul; *see* IX Nobel Prize Winners (Economics)

Indianapolis
Kwitny, Jonathan; *see* II Journalists

Kokomo
Kraus, Milton; *see* I U.S. Congressmen and Congresswomen

Muncie
Cohen, Benjamin V.; *see* I Political Figures (Americans)

Noblesville
Levinson, Salmon O.; *see* IV Legal Scholars

South Bend
Pollack, Sydney; *see* VII Film Directors

Terre Haute
Silberstein, Abraham; *see* V Aviators, Astronauts, and Others

Winchester
Wise, Robert; *see* VII Film Directors

IOWA

Des Moines
Silberman, Charles E; *see* II Magazine Publishers and Journalists

Levenson, Joseph R.; *see* IV Historians
Levine, Jack; *see* VI Artists
Levine, Joseph E.; *see* VII Film Producers
Malkiel, Burton G.; *see* VI Economists
Manuel, Frank E.; *see* IV Historians
Meiselman, David I.; *see* VI Economists
Melnick, Joseph; *see* II Doctors and Medical Researchers
Newman, Barry; *see* VII Television Performers
Nimoy, Leonard; *see* VII Television Performers
Rabb, Maxwell M.; *see* I Political Figures (Americans)
Ratshesky, Abraham; *see* I Government Officials (Americans)
Revson, Charles H.; *see* III Business Leaders
Shapiro, Harry L.; *see* IV Anthropologists
Slepian, Joseph; *see* V Inventors, Industrial Designers, and Engineers
Walters, Barbara; *see* VII Television Newscasters
Wein, George T.; *see* VI Jazz Performers
White, Harry D.; *see* IV Economists
White, Robert M.; *see* V Meteorologists
Wyzanski, Charles E., Jr.; *see* I Judges

Brockton
Davis, Al; *see* VIII Football
Kaminsky, Max; *see* VI Jazz Performers

Brookline
Wallace, Mike; *see* VII Television Newscasters

Cambridge
Epstein, Jason; *see* II Magazine Publishers and Journalists
Greenblatt, Stephen J.; *see* VI Literary and Drama Critics and Agents

Chelsea
Cohen, Morris; *see* V Chemists
Kramer, Benjamin; *see* VIII Basketball
Marget, Arthur W.; *see* IV Economists
Stang, Arnold; *see* VII Television Performers
Swartz, Harvie; *see* VI Jazz Performers

Clinton
Schanberg, Sydney H.; *see* II Journalists

Fall River
Kanovitz, Howard; *see* VI Artists
Nannes, Caspar H.; *see* II Journalists
Wexler, Harry; *see* V Meteorologists

Haverhill
Ashworth, Gerald H.; *see* IX Olympic Medalists (Track and Field)

Holyoke
Swados, Harvey; *see* VI Writers (Americans and Canadians)

Lawrence
Bernstein, Leonard; *see* VI Conductors

Lynn
Silverman, Al; *see* II Magazine Publishers and Journalists

Malden
Albertson, Jack; *see* VII Television Performers
Friend, Milton; *see* VIII Shooting

Mattapan
Richmond, Frederick W.; *see* I U.S. Congressmen and Congresswomen

New Bedford
Semansky, Henry; *see* VIII Football

Newton
Shine, Carl; *see* VIII Track and Field

Peabody
Rosenfelt, Frank E.; *see* VII Film Executives

Quincy
Dana, Bill; *see* VI Comedians

Salem
Michaelson, Julius C.; *see* I Political Figures (Americans)

Somerville
Goodman, Nelson; *see* IV Philosophers

Taunton
Abels, Jules; *see* IV Economists

Wakefield
Horovitz, Israel; *see* VI Playwrights

Worcester
Behrman, S. N.; *see* VI Playwrights
Chafetz, Morris E.; *see* I Government Officials (Americans)
Gibbs, Georgia; *see* VI Rock, Pop, and Folk Artists (and Others)
Kunitz, Stanley J.; *see* VI Poets (Americans)

MICHIGAN
Ann Arbor
Mintz, Morton A.; *see* II Journalists

Detroit
Balter, Samuel; *see* IX Olympic Medalists (Basketball)
Cohen, Herman; *see* VII Film Producers
Gresser, Gisela; *see* VIII Chess
Krieger, Byron; *see* VIII Fencing
Levine, Philip; *see* VI Poets (Americans)
Mandel, Harvey; *see* VI Jazz Performers
Newman, Harry; *see* VIII Football
Pressman, David; *see* V Chemists
Reulbach, Edward M.; *see* VIII Baseball
Stein, Herbert; *see* I Government Officials (Americans)
Tolmich, Allan; *see* VIII Track and Field
Wiesner, Jerome B.; *see* I Government Officials (Americans)
Zeitlin, Maurice; *see* IV Sociologists
Zweig, Barry K.; *see* VI Jazz Performers

Grand Rapids
Seidman, L. William; *see* I Government Officials (Americans)

Kalamazoo
Ferber, Edna; *see* VI Writers (Americans and Canadians)
Israel, Edward; *see* V Explorers

Lansing
Pregulmam, Mervin; *see* VIII Football

MINNESOTA
Duluth
Dylan, Bob; *see* VI Rock, Pop, and Folk Artists (and Others)

Eveleth
Abramson, George; *see* VIII Football

Minneapolis
Elazar, Daniel J.; *see* IV Political Scientists
Gillman, Sidney; *see* VIII Football
Shapiro, Irving S.; *see* III Business Leaders
Sher, Jack; *see* VII Screenwriters
Todd, Mike; *see* VII Film Producers

St. Paul
Aberle, David F.; *see* IV Anthropologists
Calvin, Melvin; *see* IX Nobel Prize Winners (Chemistry)
Decter, Midge; *see* IV Social Critics
Lee, Pinky; *see* VI Comedians
Perlman, Alfred E.; *see* III Business Leaders
Saxon, David S.; *see* IV Educators

MISSISSIPPI
Bodenheim, Maxwell; *see* VI Writers (Americans and Canadians)

Columbus
Schwab, Joseph J.; *see* IV Educators

Ellisville
Myers, Charles S. "Buddy"; *see* VIII Baseball

Natchez
Meyer, Adolph; *see* I U.S. Congressmen and Congresswomen

Utica
Borah, Woodrow Wilson; *see* IV Historians

MISSOURI
Columbia
Wiener, Norbert; *see* V Mathematicians

Farmington
Pelty, Barney; *see* VIII Baseball

Kahoka
Smelser, Neil J.; *see* IV Sociologists

Kansas City
Asner, Edward; *see* VII Television Performers
Bacharach, Burt; *see* VI Rock, Pop, and Folk Artists (and Others)
Kling, Johnny; *see* VIII Baseball

St. Joseph
Cherniss, Harold; *see* IV Philosophers

St. Louis
Carnovsky, Morris; *see* VI Stars of the Theater
Davis, Martin J.; *see* VIII Fencing
Fishbein, Morris; *see* II Doctors and Medical Researchers
Freund, Paul A.; *see* IV Legal Scholars
Hirschfeld, Albert; *see* VI Cartoonists and Caricaturists
Holtzman, Ken; *see* VIII Baseball
Kranzberg, Melvin; *see* IV Historians
Roos, Lawrence; *see* I Mayors
Rosenfeld, Alvin; *see* VII Television Newscasters
Swope, Gerald; *see* III Business Leaders
Taussig, Frank W.; *see* IV Economists
Winters, Shelley; *see* VII Film Stars

Springfield
Lipman, David; *see* II Journalists

MONTANA
Butte
Bender, Lauretta; *see* IV Psychologists

NEBRASKA
Lincoln
Sorensen, Theodore C.; *see* I Political Figures (Americans)

Lost Nation
Stone, "Silent George"; *see* VIII Baseball

Omaha
Baer, Max; *see* VIII Boxing (World Champions)
Katleman, Harris L.; *see* VII Television Executives, Producers, Directors, and Writers
Zorinsky, Edward; *see* I U.S. Senators

NEVADA
Virginia City
Michelson, Charles; *see* I Political Figures (Americans)

NEW HAMPSHIRE
Derry
Cohen, Nathan E.; *see* IV Sociologists

NEW JERSEY
Chafetz, Janet Saltzman; *see* IV Sociologists
Ginsberg, Allen; *see* VI Poets (Americans)
Gitlow, Benjamin; *see* I Men and Women of the Left (Americans)
Handler, Philip; *see* V Chemists
Pollak, Walter H.; *see* I Civil Rights Leaders
Stewart, Elaine; *see* VII Film Stars

Alliance
Golder, Benjamin M.; *see* I U.S. Congressmen and Congresswomen

Atlantic City
Bacharach, Harry; *see* I Mayors
Zugsmith, Albert; *see* VII Film Directors

Bayonne
Levin, Marc L.; *see* VI Jazz Performers
Savitt, Richard; *see* VIII Tennis

Camden
Dash, Samuel; *see* I Political Figures (Americans)

Elizabeth
Cohen, Jerome A.; *see* IV Legal Scholars
Solotaroff, Theodore H.; *see* VI Literary and Drama Critics and Agents
Stein, William; *see* VIII Football

Englewood
Landau, Joel; *see* VIII Track and Field

Hoboken
Stieglitz, Alfred; *see* VI Photographers

Jersey City
Goldfarb, Ronald C.; *see* IV Legal Scholars
Gunsberg, Sheldon; *see* VII Film Executives
Newman, Phyllis; *see* VII Television Performers
Okun, Arthur M.; *see* IV Economists
Wilde, Larry; *see* VI Comedians
Wittenberg, Henry; *see* IX Olympic Medalists (Wrestling)

Long Branch
Abrams, M. H.; *see* VI Literary and Drama Critics and Agents
Frank, Waldo D.; *see* IV Social Critics
Kamm, Herbert; *see* II Journalists

Mailer, Norman; *see* VI Writers (Americans and Canadians)

Montclair

Lederberg, Joshua; *see* IX Nobel Prize Winners (Medicine and Physiology)

Morristown

Forman, Allen S.; *see* VIII Baseball

Newark

Aronson, Louis V; *see* III Business Leaders

Fiedler, Leslie; *see* VI Literary and Drama Critics and Agents

Garfunkel, Art; *see* VI Rock, Pop, and Folk Artists (and Others)

Kurtz, Paul; *see* IV Philosophers

Lewis, Jerry; *see* VII Film Stars

Lindsey, Mort; *see* VIII Bowling

Lowenstein, Allard K.; *see* I U.S. Congressmen and Congresswomen

Mack, Robert J.; *see* VIII Track and Field

Riesenberg, Saul; *see* IV Anthropologists

Ritz, Al; *see* VI Comedians

Ritz, Harry; *see* VI Comedians

Ritz, Jim; *see* VI Comedians

Ritz Brothers; *see* VI Comedians

Roth, Philip; *see* VI Writers (Americans and Canadians)

Schary, Dore; *see* VII Film Producers

Schulman, Ira; *see* VI Jazz Performers

Smukler, David; *see* VIII Football

Tumin, Melvin; *see* IV Sociologists

Wald, Jerry; *see* VI Jazz Performers

Weiss, Nathan; *see* IV Educators

New Brunswick

Baskin, Leonard; *see* VI Sculptors

Douglas, Michael; *see* VII Television Performers

Paterson

Janowitz, Henry D.; *see* II Doctors and Medical Researchers

Joelson, Charles S.; *see* I U.S. Congressmen and Congresswomen

Kahn, Alfred E.; *see* I Government Officials (Americans)

Midler, Bette; *see* VI Rock, Pop, and Folk Artists (and Others)

Shane, Maxwell; *see* VII Screenwriters

Rahway

Friedman, Milton; *see* IX Nobel Prize Winners (Economics)

Rosenhayn

McCoy, Al; *see* VIII Boxing (World Champions)

South Orange

Kraft, Joseph; *see* II Journalists

Rogers, Donald; *see* VIII Football

Teaneck

Snow, Phoebe; *see* VI Jazz Performers

Trenton

Antheil, George; *see* VI Composers

Katz, Daniel; *see* IV Psychologists

Linowitz, Sol M.; *see* III Business Leaders

Union Hill

Cousins, Norman; *see* II Magazine Publishers and Journalists

NEW MEXICO

Seligman Arthur; *see* I Governors of American States

NEW YORK

Berman, Ronald; *see* I Government Officials (Americans)

Brown, Harold; *see* I Government Officials (Americans)

Feldman, Herman; *see* I Military Figures (Americans)

Forman, Philip; *see* I Judges

Gilbert, Jacob H.; *see* I U.S. Congressmen and Congresswomen

Goodman, Paul; *see* IV Social Critics

Rodgers, Richard; *see* VI Popular Music Composers and Lyricists

Albany

Armitage, Norman C.; *see* IX Olympic Medalists (Fencing)

Freedman, Alfred M.; *see* IV Psychologists

Alden

Brown, Murray; *see* IV Economists

Amsterdam

Douglas, Kirk; *see* VII Film Stars

Babylon

Dangerfield, Rodney; *see* VI Comedians

Bronx, see New York City

Brooklyn

Allen, Woody; *see* VII Film Stars

Alpern, David; *see* II Magazine Publishers and Journalists

Alzado, Lyle; *see* VIII Football

Angrist, Alfred A.; *see* II Doctors and Medical Researchers

Auerbach, Red; *see* VIII Basketball

Baxt, George; *see* VI Writers (Americans and Canadians)

Berg, David; *see* VI Cartoonists and Caricaturists

Berlinger, Warren; *see* VII Television Performers

Brown, Lawrence H.; *see* IX Olympic Medalists (Basketball)

Celler, Emanuel; *see* I U.S. Congressmen and Congresswomen

Cohen, Abram; *see* VIII Fencing

Cohen, William W.; *see* I U.S. Congressmen and Congresswomen

Cohn, Alvin G.; *see* VI Jazz Performers

Comden, Betty ; *see* VI Musical Comedy Figures

Cooperman, Alvin; *see* VII Television Executives, Producers, Directors, and Writers

Copland, Aaron; *see* VI Composers

Cornfeld, Bernie; *see* III Business Leaders

Diamond, Neil; *see* VI Rock, Pop, and Folk Artists (and Others)

Dreyfuss, Richard; *see* VII Film Stars

Edelman, Herb; *see* VII Television Performers

Eisenstadt, Harry; *see* VIII Baseball

Fabricant, Solomon; *see* IV Economists

Ferkauf, Eugene; *see* III Business Leaders

Fleischer, Richard; *see* VII Film Directors

Frye, David; *see* VI Comedians

Furth, Solomon; *see* VIII Track and Field

Garment, Leonard; *see* I Government Officials (Americans)

Tanenbaum, Sidney H.; *see* VIII Basketball
Udoff, Yale M.; *see* VI Playwrights
Volk, Lester D.; *see* I U.S. Congressmen and Congresswomen
Wald, Jerry; *see* VII Film Producers
Walk, Neal; *see* VIII Basketball
Wallach, Eli; *see* VII Film Stars
Wolf, Emanuel L.; *see* VII Film Executives
Wolpert, Stanley A.; *see* IV Historians
Yaged, Sol; *see* VI Jazz Performers
Zaslofsky, Max; *see* VIII Basketball
Ziring, Lawrence; *see* IV Political Scientists
Zukofsky, Paul; *see* VI Violinists

Buffalo

Bunshaft, Gordon; *see* II Architects
Farber, Marvin; *see* IV Philosophers
Hofstadter, Richard; *see* IV Historians
Janis, Irving L.; *see* IV Psychologists
Lewis, Mel; *see* VI Jazz Performers
Opler, Marvin K.; *see* IV Psychologists
Opler, Morris E.; *see* IV Anthropologists
Shawn, Dick; *see* VI Comedians

Corning

Ansorge, Martin C.; *see* I U.S. Congressmen and Congresswomen

Cortland

Silverman, Sime; *see* II Magazine Publishers and Journalists

Delhi

Mendel, L. Benedict; *see* V Chemists

Ellenville

Resnick, Joseph Y.; *see* I U.S. Congressmen and Congresswomen

Far Rockaway

Cohen, I. Bernard; *see* IV Historians

Forest Hills, *see* New York City

Gloversville

Littauer, Lucius, N.; *see* I U.S. Congressmen and Congresswomen; VIII Football
Pinkel, Benjamin; *see* V Aviators, Astronauts, and Others

Great Neck

Goddard, Paulette; *see* VII Film Stars

Harleyville

Kamen, Milt; *see* VI Comedians

Lawrence

Lipton, Peggy; *see* VII Television Performers

Liberty

Passow, Aaron H.; *see* IV Educators

Lindenhurst

Barry, Jack; *see* VII Television Performers

Mineola

Weil, Gordon L.; *see* II Magazine Publishers and Journalists

Mount Vernon

Buchwald, Art; *see* II Journalists
Jackson, Gabriel; *see* IV Historians

New Rochelle

Bielenson, Anthony C.; *see* I U.S. Congressmen and Congresswomen

Josephtal, Louis M.; *see* I Military Figures (Americans)
Oppen, George; *see* VI Poets (Americans)

New York City

Abrahams, Mort; *see* VII Television Executives, Producers, Directors, and Writers
Abramovitz, Moses; *see* IV Economists
Abzug, Bella; *see* I U.S. Congressmen and Congresswomen
Adams, Don; *see* VI Comedians
Adams, Joey; *see* VI Entertainers
Adelson, Howard L.; *see* IV Historians
Adler, Luther; *see* VII Film Stars
Adler, Mortimer J.; *see* IV Philosophers
Albert, Mimi; *see* VI Writers (Americans and Canadians)
Aldan, Daisy; *see* VI Poets (Americans)
Alexander, Shana; *see* II Magazine Publishers and Journalists
Allen, Irwin; *see* VII Film Producers
Altman, Benjamin; *see* III Business Leaders
Altman, Oscar L.; *see* IV Economists
Altschul, Barry; *see* VI Jazz Performers
Anthony, Edward; *see* II Magazine Publishers and Journalists
Appley, Mortimer H.; *see* IV Educators
Arkin, David; *see* VI Popular Music Composers and Lyricists
Arnold, Danny; *see* VII Television Executives, Producers, Directors, and Writers
Arrow, Kenneth J.; *see* IX Nobel Prize Winners (Economics)
Arthur, Beatrice; *see* VII Television Performers
Astrachan, Samuel; *see* VI Writers (Americans and Canadians)
Atlas, David; *see* V Meteorologists
Axelrod, Albert; *see* IX Olympic Medalists (Fencing)
Axelrod, George; *see* VII Screenwriters
Bacall, Lauren; *see* VII Film Stars
Bache, Jules S.; *see* III Business Leaders
Backer, George; *see* II Newspaper and Magazine Publishers
Baker, Mac; *see* VIII Basketball
Balsam, Martin; *see* VII Film Stars
Barrett, Laurence I.; *see* II Journalists
Barry, Gene; *see* VII Television Performers
Bass, Saul; *see* VII Art Directors and Designers
Becker, Abraham S.; *see* IV Economists
Beer, George L.; *see* IV Historians
Behrman, Martin; *see* I Mayors
Belinsky, Robert "Bo"; *see* VIII Baseball
Bell, Marvin; *see* VI Poets (Americans)
Bender, Jules; *see* VIII Basketball
Bender, Lulu; *see* VIII Basketball
Bendick, Robert L.; *see* VII Television Executives, Producers, Directors, and Writers
Benjamin, Richard; *see* VII Film Stars
Bennett, Jay; *see* VI Writers (Americans and Canadians)
Benstock, Bernard; *see* VI Literary and Drama Critics and Agents
Benswanger, William E.; *see* VIII Baseball
Benzer, Seymour; *see* II Doctors and Medical Researchers
Berg, Moe; *see* VIII Baseball
Berger, Arthur V.; *see* VI Composers
Berger, Meyer; *see* II Journalists

Yglesias, Helen; *see* VI Literary and Drama Critics and Agents
Young Otto; *see* VIII Boxing (Other Boxers)
Yurick, Sol; *see* VI Writers (Americans and Canadians)
Zeicher, Oscar; *see* IV Historians
Zelenko, Herbert; *see* I U.S. Congressmen and Congresswomen
Zellner, Arnold; *see* IV Economists
Zwerin, Michael; *see* VI Jazz Performers

Port Chester
Barron, Herman; *see* VIII Golf

Poughkeepsie
Gilman, Benjamin A.; *see* I U.S. Congressmen and Congresswomen

Queens, *see* New York City

Richmond Hill, *see* New York City

Rochester
Hays, Arthur Garfield; *see* I Civil Rights Leaders
Kammen, Michael G.; *see* IV Historians
Kanin, Garson; *see* VII Film Directors
Kanin, Michael; *see* VII Screenwriters
Kirstein, Lincoln; *see* VI Dancers
Miller, Mitch; *see* VI Rock, Pop, and Folk Artists (and Others); VII Television Performers
Rabin, Benjamin J.; *see* I U.S. Congressmen and Congresswomen
Rose, Peter I.; *see* IV Sociologists

Schenectady
Kramer, Barry; *see* VIII Basketball
Sagarin, Edward; *see* IV Sociologists

Staten Island *see* New York City

Syracuse
Alexander, Joseph A.; *see* VIII Football
Levinsky, Alexander H.; *see* VIII Hockey
Marshall, Louis; *see* II Lawyers
Rosen, Samuel; *see* II Doctors and Medical Researchers
Ross, Lillian; *see* II Magazine Publishers and Journalists
Shubert, Jacob J.; *see* VI Theater Managers and Owners
Shubert, Lee; *see* VI Theater Managers and Owners
Shubert, Sam; *see* VI Theater Managers and Owners
Shubert Family; *see* VI Theater Managers and Owners

Westhampton
Steiger, Rod; *see* VII Film Stars

White Plains
Slavitt, David; *see* VI Writers (Americans and Canadians)

Yonkers
Caesar, Sid; *see* VII Television Performers
Davidson, Avram; *see* VI Science Fiction Writers and Editors
Klein, Edward; *see* II Journalists

NORTH CAROLINA

Asheville
Schandler, Herbert Y.; *see* I Military Figures (Americans)

Charlotte
Schwartz, Harry L.; *see* VIII Football

Franklinton
Sales, Soupy; *see* VI Comedians

Statesville
Clarke, Louis A.; *see* IX Olympic Medalists (Track and Field)

Warrenton
Mordecai, Alfred; *see* I Military Figures (Americans)

Wilmington
Bluethenthal, Arthur; *see* VIII Football

Winston-Salem
Cosell, Howard; *see* VII Television Newscasters

OHIO

Grossman, Morton I.; *see* II Doctors and Medical Researchers

Akron
Resnik, Judith; *see* V Aviators, Astronauts, and Others

Bellefontaine
Herskovits, Melville J.; *see* IV Anthropologists

Cedarville
Parker, Eleanor; *see* VII Film Stars

Cincinnati
Bara, Theda; *see* VII Film Stars
Cohen, Alfred M.; *see* I Civil Rights Leaders
Einstein, Edwin; *see* I U.S. Congressmen and Congresswomen
Fleischmann, Julius; *see* I Mayors; VIII Baseball
Fleischmann, Max; *see* VIII Baseball
Frankel, Samuel; *see* I Spies and Counterspies
Gradison, Willis, Jr.; *see* I U.S. Congressmen and Congresswomen
Kramer, Louis C.; *see* VIII Baseball
Kronenberger, Louis; *see* VI Literary and Drama Critics and Agents
Kuhn, Thomas; *see* IV Historians
Levine, James; *see* VI Conductors
Rauh, Joseph L.; *see* I Labor Leaders
Stoller, Samuel; *see* VIII Track and Field

Cleveland
Beller, William S.; *see* I Military Figures (Americans)
Chaikin, William E.; *see* VII Film Executives
Da Silva, Howard; *see* VII Film Stars
Fish, Robert L.; *see* VI Writers (Americans and Canadians)
Friedman, Benny; *see* VIII Football
Glaser, Donald A.; *see* IX Nobel Prize Winners (Physics)
Glasser, William; *see* IV Educators
Gold, Herbert; *see* VI Writers (Americans and Canadians)
Greenfield, James L.; *see* II Journalists
Jaffe, Leonard; *see* V Aviators, Astronauts, and Others
Metzenbaum, Howard; *see* I U.S. Senators
Newman, Paul; *see* VII Film Stars
Peixotto, George D.; *see* VI Artists
Seltzer, Louis B.; *see* II Journalists

Shapp, Milton; see I Governors of American States

Shulman, Alix Kates; see VI Writers (Americans and Canadians)

Siegel, Jerry; see VI Cartoonists and Caricaturists

Spiro, Melford E.; see IV Anthropologists

Stone, Steve; see VIII Baseball

Weissman, Marvin; see I Government Officials (Americans)

Dayton
Rose, Mauri; see VIII Auto Racing

Hamilton
Hurst, Fannie; see VI Writers (Americans and Canadians)

Loudonville
Bacher, Robert F.; see V Pioneers of Atomic Energy

Middleport
Kauff, Benjamin M.; see VIII Baseball

Youngstown
Cohen, Kalman J.; see IV Economists

OREGON

Portland
Aiken, Henry D.; see IV Philosophers
Meier, Julius; see I Governors of American States
Neuberger, Richard L.; see I U.S. Senators
Simon, Norton; see III Business Leaders

PENNSYLVANIA
Miller, Hyman; see I Mayors

Allegheny
Stein, Gertrude; see VI Writers (Americans and Canadians)

Allegheny City
Gans, Bird; see IV Educators

Boiling Springs
Kaufman, David S.; see I U.S. Congressmen and Congresswomen

Braddock
Rosenbloom, Benjamin L.; see I U.S. Congressmen and Congresswomen

Bryn Mawr
Silvert, Kalman H.; see IV Political Scientists

Chester
Hayes, Isaac I.; see V Explorers

Doylestown
Hammerstein, Oscar, II; see VI Popular Music Composers and Lyricists

Elkins Park
Oakes, John B.; see II Journalists

Farrell
Marks, Marc L.; see I U.S. Congressmen and Congresswomen

Harrisburg
Kantor, Jacob R.; see IV Psychologists

Hazelton
Micahnik, David; see VIII Fencing

Johnstown
Baker, Carroll; see VII Film Stars
Freed, Alan; see VI Rock, Pop, and Folk Artists (and Others)

Nanticoke
Edelman, Murray; see IV Political Scientists

Paoli
Spellman, Frank; see IX Olympic Medalists (Weightlifting)

Philadelphia
Abrams, Cal; see VIII Baseball
Adler, Freda; see I Cops and Robbers (including Criminologists)
Adler, Harry C.; see II Newspaper and Magazine Publishers
Auslander, Joseph; see VI Poets (Americans)
Bacharach, Isaac; see I U.S. Congressmen and Congresswomen
Blitzstein, Marc; see VI Composers
Bohm, David; see V Physicists
Brenner, David; see VI Comedians
Brooks, Richard; see VII Film Directors
Chomsky, Noam A.; see IV Social Critics
Chudoff, Earl; see I U.S. Congressmen and Congresswomen
Eilberg, Joshua; see I U.S. Congressmen and Congresswomen
Fischer, Louis; see VI Writers (Americans and Canadians)
Fisher, Eddie; see VI Rock, Pop, and Folk Artists (and Others)
Fishman, Joshua; see IV Psychologists
Frank, Victor, Jr.; see VIII Track and Field
Frank, Victor H.; see VIII Football
Frankel, Lee K.; see III Business Leaders
Gabel, Martin; see VI Stars of the Theater
Gamson, William A.; see IV Sociologists
Getz, Stan; see VI Jazz Performers
Gilbert, Milton; see IV Economists
Goldblatt, Emanuel; see VIII Basketball
Goldman, Peter L.; see II Magazine Publishers and Journalists
Gross, Bertram M.; see IV Political Scientists
Guggenheim, Simon; see I U.S. Senators
Hays, Isaac; see II Doctors and Medical Researchers
Hyneman, Edwin I.; see VIII Baseball
Kallen, Kitty; see VI Rock, Pop, and Folk Artists (and Others)
Kaplan, Morton A.; see IV Political Scientists
Kershner, Irvin; see VII Film Directors
Kline, Nathan S.; see II Doctors and Medical Researchers
Klugman, Jack; see VII Television Performers
Lester, Richard; see VII Film Directors
Levinsky, Battling; see VIII Boxing (World Champions)
Levinson, Richard L.; see VII Television Executives, Producers, Directors, and Writers
Levy, David; see VII Television Executives, Producers, Directors, and Writers
Levy, Jonas P.; see I Military Figures (Americans)
Levy, Uriah Phillips; see I Military Figures (Americans)
Lumet, Sidney; see VII Film Directors
Martin, Sylvia Wene; see VIII Bowling
May, Elaine; see VI Comedians

Merton, Robert K.; *see* IV Sociologists
Odets, Clifford; *see* VI Playwrights
Phillips, Henry M.; *see* I U.S. Congressmen and Congresswomen
Riesman, David; *see* IV Sociologists
Rodell, Fred M.; *see* IV Legal Scholars
Rubin, Morton J.; *see* V Meteorologists
Sacks, Leon; *see* I U.S. Congressmen and Congresswomen
Seltzer, Walter; *see* VII Film Producers
Siegel, Herbert J.; *see* III Business Leaders
Skolnikoff, Eugene B.; *see* IV Political Scientists
Stern,Julius D.; *see* II Newspaper and Magazine Publishers
Sterne, Simon; *see* II Lawyers
Stoloff, Morris; *see* VII Composers of Film Scores
Stone, I. F.; *see* II Magazine Publishers and Journalists
Susann, Jacqueline; *see* VI Writers (Americans and Canadians)
Sykes, Jay G.; *see* II Journalists
Temin, Howard M.; *see* IX Nobel Prize Winners (Medicine and Physiology)
Tendler, Lew; *see* VIII Boxing (Other Boxers)
Wolfman, Bernard; *see* IV Legal Scholars
Wynn, Ed; *see* VI Comedians
Zimmerman, Paul L.; *see* II Journalists

Pittsburgh

Berman, Pandro S.; *see* VII Film Producers
Bronfenbrenner, Martin; *see* IV Economists
Faberow, Norman L.; *see* IV Psychologists
Glick, Frank; *see* VIII Football
Jacobs, Newton P.; *see* VII Film Executives
Kaufman, George S.; *see* VI Playwrights
Levant, Oscar; *see* VII Television Performers
Levey, James J.; *see* VIII Baseball
Neft, Peter P.; *see* VIII Football
Pearlman, Red; *see* VIII Football
Sack, Jack; *see* VIII Football
Selznick, David O.; *see* VII Film Producers
Sherman, Harvey; *see* IV Political Scientists
Silverman, Alexander; *see* V Chemists
Strick, Joseph; *see* VII Film Directors

Pottsville

Becker, Gary S.; *see* IV Economists
Bondy, Leo J.; *see* VIII Baseball

Scottdale

Goldenberg, Leonard; *see* VII Television Executives, Producers, Directors, and Writers

Scranton

Katz, Norman B.; *see* VII Film Executives
Legman, G.; *see* VI Writers (Americans and Canadians)

Wilkes-Barre

Kline, Franz; *see* VI Artists
Mankiewicz, Joseph L.; *see* VII Screenwriters
Teicher, Louis; *see* VI Rock, Pop, and Folk Artists (and Others)
Ungar, Sanford J.; *see* II Journalists
Weinstein, Rose M.; *see* VIII Bowling

York

Silberman, Laurence H.; *see* I Government Officials (Americans)
Sirovich, William I.; *see* I U.S. Congressmen and Congresswomen

RHODE ISLAND

Newport

Israel, Dorman D.; *see* V Inventors, Industrial Designers, and Engineers

Pawtucket

Levine, Irving R.; *see* VII Television Newscasters

Providence

Licht, Frank; *see* I Governors of American States

SOUTH CAROLINA

Blackville

Blatt, Solomon; *see* I Political Figures (Americans)

Camden

Baruch, Bernard; *see* I Political Figures (Americans)
De Leon, David C.; *see* I Military Figures (Americans)

Charleston

Dittenhoefer, Abraham J.; *see* II Lawyers
Freed, Arthur; *see* VII Film Producers
Keyserling, Leon H.; *see* I Government Officials (Americans)
Levin, Lewis C.; *see* I U.S. Congressmen and Congresswomen
Phillips, Philip; *see* I U.S. Congressmen and Congresswomen

Spartanburg

Rosen, Al; *see* VIII Baseball

TENNESSEE

Chattanooga

Adler, Julius D.; *see* I Military Figures (Americans)

Memphis

Fortas, Abe; *see* I Judges
Hexter, Jack; *see* IV Historians
Siodmak, Robert; *see* VII Film Directors

Winchester

Shore, Dinah; *see* VII Television Performers

TEXAS

Amarillo

Jones, Carolyn; *see* VII Film Stars

Dallas

Benson, Robby; *see* VII Film Stars
Marcus, Stanley; *see* III Business Leaders

El Paso

Ochs, Phil; *see* VI Rock, Pop, and Folk Artists (and Others)

Fort Worth

Handler, Philip J.; *see* VIII Football

Galveston

Levy, Marion J.; *see* IV Political Scientists

Lockhart

Strauss, Robert S.; *see* I Government Officials (Americans)

San Antonio

Goodman, A. W.; *see* V Mathematicians
Lewenthal, Raymond; *see* VI Pianists

Rosenman, Samuel I.; *see* I Political Figures (Americans)

UTAH

Logan
Newman, Joseph M.; *see* VII Film Directors

Salt Lake City
Kahn, Florence Prag; *see* I U.S. Congressmen and Congresswomen
Watters, Leon L.; *see* II Doctors and Medical Researchers

VERMONT

Burlington
Stone, Marvin L.; *see* II Magazine Publishers and Journalists

VIRGINIA

Fels, Joseph: *see* III Business Leaders
Untermyer, Samuel; *see* IV Legal Scholars

Arlington
Bregman, James S.; *see* IX Olympic Medalists (Judo)

Norfolk
Lidman, David; *see* II Journalists

Petersburg
Stern, Arthur C.; *see* V Inventors, Industrial Designers, and Engineers

Richmond
Cohen, Edwin S.; *see* I Government Officials (Americans)
Ezekiel, Mordecai; *see* IV Economists
Mayer, Levy; *see* II Lawyers
Myers, Lawrence E.; *see* VIII Track and Field
Schoenbaum, Alex; *see* VIII Football

VIRGIN ISLANDS

Benjamin, Judah P.; *see* I Government Officials (Americans)
Yulee, David Levy; *see* I U.S. Senators

WASHINGTON

Seattle
Guthman, Ed; *see* II Journalists
Jaffe, Louis L.; *see* IV Legal Scholars
Prusoff, Henry J.; *see* VIII Tennis
Shain, Irving; *see* IV Educators

Spokane
Lesser, Sol; *see* VII Film Producers

Tacoma
Cannon, Dyan; *see* VII Film Stars

WASHINGTON, D.C.

Atz, Jacob H.; *see* VIII Baseball
Bernstein, Carl; *see* II Journalists
Fefferman, Charles L.; *see* V Mathematicians
Fox, Sam; *see* VIII Football

Friedel, Samuel N.; *see* I U.S. Congressmen and Congresswomen
Goldman, Eric F.; *see* IV Historians
Hawn, Goldie; *see* VII Film Stars
King, Phil; *see* VIII Football
Ottenberg, Miriam; *see* II Journalists
Polmar, Norman; *see* I Military Figures (Americans)
Rose, Leonard; *see* VI Cellists

WEST VIRGINIA

Charleston
Peyser, Theodore A.; *see* I U.S. Congressmen and Congresswomen
Strauss, Lewis L.; *see* I Government Officials (Americans)

Elkins
Goldberg, Marshall; *see* VIII Football

WISCONSIN

Blumenfeld, Ralph D.; *see* II Newspaper and Magazine Publishers

Kenosha
Gordon, Bert I.; *see* VII Film Producers

Milwaukee
Annenberg, Walter N.; *see* I Government Officials (Americans)
Anthony, Joseph; *see* VI Theatrical Directors and Teachers
Cohen, Wilbur J.; *see* I Government Officials (Americans)
Herschenson, Bruce; *see* I Political Figures (Americans)
Mikva, Abner J.; *see* I U.S. Congressmen and Congresswomen
Minow, Newton N.; *see* VII Television Executives, Producers, Directors, and Writers
Rosenblum, Morton; *see* II Journalists
Schmerling, Louis; *see* V Chemists
Simon, Herbert; *see* IV Political Scientists
Simon, Herbert A.; *see* IX Nobel Prize Winners (Economics)
Wachman, Marvin; *see* IV Educators
Wilder, Gene; *see* VII Film Stars

Platteville
Gasser, Herbert S.; *see* IX Nobel Prize Winners (Medicine and Physiology)

Racine
Alperovitz, Gar; *see* IV Historians

Rhinelander
Wasserman, Dale; *see* VI Musical Comedy Figures

Sheboygan
Mason, Jackie; *see* VI Comedians

Superior
Arnovich, Morrie; *see* VIII Baseball
Bazelon, David L.; *see* I Judges

INDEX OF NAMES

INDEX OF NAMES